THE OFFICIAL RED BOOK®

A GUIDE [BOOK OF]
LINCOLN [CENTS]

Fourth E[dition]

History · Rarity · Values · Grading · Varieties

Q. David Bowers

Foreword by

David W. Lange

Whitman Publishing, LLC
PUBLISHING SINCE 1934
Whitman.com

A GUIDE BOOK OF
LINCOLN CENTS
Fourth Edition

© 2023 Whitman Publishing, LLC
1974 Chandalar Drive, Suite D, Pelham, AL 35124

THE OFFICIAL RED BOOK is a trademark of Whitman Publishing, LLC.

All rights reserved, including duplication of any kind and storage in electronic or visual retrieval systems. Permission is granted for writers to use a reasonable number of brief excerpts and quotations in printed reviews and articles, provided credit is given to the title of the work and the author. Written permission from the publisher is required for other uses of text, illustrations, and other content, including in books and electronic or other media.

Correspondence concerning this book may be directed to
Whitman Publishing, Attn: Lincoln Cents, at the address above.

ISBN: 0794849970
Printed in China

Disclaimer: Expert opinion should be sought in any significant numismatic purchase. This book is presented as a guide only. No warranty or representation of any kind is made concerning the completeness of the information presented. The author, a professional numismatist, regularly buys, sells, and holds certain of the items discussed in this book.

Caveat: The values given are subject to variation and differences of opinion. Before making decisions to buy or sell, consult the latest information. For certain issues that are normally found with areas of light striking, well-struck coins with full detail may command significantly higher prices. The Mint color on a Lincoln cent can affect its value, but opinions can differ on the quality, originality, and other aspects of such color. Past performance of the rare coin market or any coin or series within that market is not necessarily an indication of future performance, as the future is unknown. Such factors as changing demand, popularity, grading interpretations, strength of the overall coin market, and economic conditions will continue to be influences. Also see introductory material in chapter nine.

About the cover: Victor D. Brenner's iconic portrait of Abraham Lincoln is surrounded by varieties and reverse designs of the Lincoln cent dating from 1909 to the present. (all shown enlarged)

Other books in the Bowers Series include: *A Guide Book of Morgan Silver Dollars; A Guide Book of Double Eagle Gold Coins; A Guide Book of United States Type Coins; A Guide Book of Modern United States Proof Coin Sets; A Guide Book of Shield and Liberty Head Nickels; A Guide Book of Flying Eagle and Indian Head Cents; A Guide Book of Washington Quarters; A Guide Book of Buffalo and Jefferson Nickels; A Guide Book of United States Commemorative Coins; A Guide Book of United States Tokens and Medals; A Guide Book of Gold Dollars; A Guide Book of Peace Dollars; A Guide Book of the Official Red Book of United States Coins; A Guide Book of Franklin and Kennedy Half Dollars; A Guide Book of Civil War Tokens; A Guide Book of Hard Times Tokens; A Guide Book of Mercury Dimes, Standing Liberty Quarters, and Liberty Walking Half Dollars; A Guide Book of Half Cents and Large Cents; A Guide Book of Barber Silver Coins; A Guide Book of Liberty Seated Silver Coins; A Guide Book of Modern United States Dollar Coins; A Guide Book of the United States Mint; A Guide Book of Gold Eagle Coins; A Guide Book of Continental Currency and Coins; and A Guide Book of Quarter Eagle Gold Coins.*

Whitman Publishing is a leader in the antiques and collectibles field.
For a complete catalog of numismatic reference books, supplies, and
storage products, visit Whitman Publishing online at www.Whitman.com.

If you enjoy Lincoln cents, join the American Numismatic Association.
Visit www.Money.org for membership information.

Whitman®

CONTENTS

FOREWORD

Like most numismatists of my generation, I discovered the hobby of collecting coins through the Lincoln cent series. My introduction occurred at a very tender age, around six or seven, and I have my older brother Doug to thank for that. In the early 1960s coin collecting was all the rage, and it seems that every boy (and a few girls) were eagerly trying to fill their Whitman folders with Lincoln cents from 1909 to 1940 (No. 9004) and from 1941 onward (No. 9030). These folders were perhaps the most familiar tools of the coin hobby at the time, and competition to be the first to complete either one was keen in every American neighborhood.

Most young hobbyists soon tired of the pursuit and moved on to other interests, and my brother was no exception. I was gifted his partially filled Whitman folders and his one-volume library, which consisted of the 1964 Whitman *Blue Book*. Since that day, I have never known a time when I was not either fully consumed with numismatics or, as during high school, at least keeping it in my peripheral vision.

As a child I eagerly pestered everyone I could find to examine their pocket change and their "penny jars" that each household seemed to keep. I managed to add several missing coins to the collection, but it became evident that the best years of cent hunting were already past. Soon I hit a wall, and only the newly released issues were being found. Additional folders were acquired for Buffalo and Jefferson nickels, Mercury and Roosevelt dimes, and even Washington quarters, though that series really cut into my candy and model-kit funds. Still yearning to add more Lincolns to my stalled collection, I made my very first numismatic purchase: a 1914 cent in Good condition for 75 cents—almost the same value it carries today in the *Red Book!* This exchange occurred at the coin and stamp counter in the local F.W. Woolworth store, and the very fact that old coins could be bought at general retail stores itself brings on a wave of nostalgia for a time long past.

When it seemed that this costly course would be my only hope of adding to my Lincoln collection, a miracle occurred. Our next-door neighbor Bob, who seemed to have every hobby under the sun, came over to our house bringing along daughter Robin and his home-built coin cabinet stuffed with plastic tubes full of coins. His job included emptying the parking meters along San Francisco's waterfront, and he very carefully bought anything old or interesting that people had stuffed into these machines. In his hobby box he had tubes of such exotic fare as Shield nickels, Liberty Seated dimes and three-cent pieces. But, most importantly, he had a tube for every date in the Lincoln cent series from 1909 through 1940. That evening he very thoughtfully filled most of the remaining openings in my Whitman folder, leaving only about half a dozen slots for the key dates. This magical occasion was captured on film by my brother, who had just received a camera for his birthday, and I cherish both that image and my memory of the experience. Included in this photo is my father standing behind me with a warm smile, the same one he had into his 90s.

It would be another 45 years before I finally finished that circulated collection of Lincoln cents with the purchase of the key 1909-S V.D.B. In the meantime, I'd already completed a second set in Mint State and About Uncirculated grades. Though beautiful, these coins meant less to me than the worn pieces which carried with them so many associations. I sold the high-grade set at auction, yet I still have my circulated collection, since upgraded from Whitman folders to Whitman albums.

Twenty-five years ago I wrote several titles in a series of "Complete Guide" books, and one of these focused on Lincoln cents. Though published in 1996, it has been reprinted several times, in each instance with a different cover design. Later it was my privilege to be a contributor to Q. David Bowers's first edition of the present book, which has succeeded my own as the current reference to the series. And now, it is my even greater privilege to write this foreword for my long-time correspondent, good friend, and fellow Rittenhouse Society member, Dave Bowers.

No one captures the appeal of collecting coins like QDB, while simultaneously telling us everything we need

June 1967: Young numismatist David W. Lange, his father (standing), and the neighbors who helped build his Lincoln cent collection.

to know about the subject at hand. To read *A Guide Book of Lincoln Cents* is to learn this series in depth and to fully appreciate the changing face of the Lincoln cent over more than a century. Included, too, are great anecdotes about the year in which each issue was coined. The only way to truly appreciate an old coin is to understand the role it played at the time, and by placing each entry in its historical context, Dave Bowers has brought it to life. Comparing his book's great photos of Mint State coins with the same issues worn nearly slick, as so often found, gives a sense of how many generations used these coins in everyday life.

Chapters on history, the various mints, grading and buying Lincoln cents, and even ways of collecting the series make Dave's book a treasure in its own right. So much of the information is applicable to any coin type that this reference is a must-have for any numismatic library.

David W. Lange
Lakewood Ranch, Florida

David W. Lange was Director of Research for Numismatic Guaranty Company in Sarasota, Florida, and the author of nine books on United States coinage and related subjects. For many years he has been an instructor at the American Numismatic Association's Summer Seminar on the subject of collecting United States type coins. Lange was the 2017 recipient of the ANA's Numismatist of the Year Award.

AUTHOR'S PREFACE

My love affair with Lincoln cents goes back a long way—to 1952, in fact, when at the age of 13 I was a junior high school student in Forty Fort, Pennsylvania. Like most kids of my age, I found the world around me swirled with exciting things to explore and collect, including rocks and minerals. I subscribed to several publications in the field, and at one time investigated ordering specimens by mail from Ward's Natural Science Establishment in Rochester, New York, only to discover that everything offered was beyond my reach. My earnings at the time amounted to 50¢ an hour for such things as mowing lawns and pulling weeds in the summer and shoveling snow in the winter, plus $5 per week allowance.

Seeking technical details of the quartz crystals and other minerals I had collected, I learned that the standard reference on the subject was by someone named Dana, and that the Osterhout Library in nearby Wilkes-Barre had a copy. Upon calling at the front desk I was informed that a kid my age could not look at books in the reference section.

Someone told me that Robert W. Rusbar, the town tax collector of Forty Fort, had a fine collection of minerals. I telephoned him and received a warm invitation to visit. Soon I stood fascinated as he opened drawers and showed me geodes, crystals, and other interesting things. An hour or so later, as I was set to leave, he asked me if I had any interest in old coins.

I told him that I had a well-worn Columbian half dollar that my grandfather had once owned, and that at a church fundraiser I had bid on a little latticework cast-iron bank filled with fascinating Indian head pennies, but that was about it. I was aware of Buffalo nickels, Standing Liberty quarters, and other things in pocket change, but I had never stopped to study them.

He showed me his two albums of Lincoln pennies, pointing out that *cents* was the proper term. Near the front was a coin he had bought in New York City, at the coin department in either Macy's or Gimbel's (I don't recall), for an amazing $10. The cent, lightly worn, looked quite ordinary to me, until he pointed out the 1909 date in combination with a tiny S mintmark under the numbers, and on the back, the tiny letters V.D.B.

I became excited as all get-out! Surely, later that afternoon I'd find one of these for myself! As I left he gave me as a gift two blue Whitman folders, one with spaces for cents from 1909 to 1940, and the other for dates 1941 onward. He showed me his copy of the *Red Book* and told me where I could buy one, which I did soon afterward, the 1952–1953 edition. The 1909-S V.D.B. was listed at retail prices of $9 Fine and $13.50 Uncirculated.

Imbued with energy and excitement, I looked through cents I had accumulated, after which I went to the Forty Fort State Bank. The tellers there found it interesting that I liked coins, and with a stake of $5 to $10 I kept getting rolls of coins, looking through them, and bringing them back to exchange for others. Before long I had all of the date and mintmark varieties up to 1952, except the elusive 1909-S V.D.B., 1914-D, and 1931-S. Many coins dating back to the late 1930s still had mint brilliance. The Philadelphia Mint cents of 1909 with V.D.B. were common, and after accumulating a pile of them, I put the extras back in a roll—so as not to impair my capital.

From collecting Lincoln cents my interest expanded. I soon set upon building a numismatic library, eagerly reading issues of *The Numismatist* and the *Numismatic Scrapbook Magazine*, gathering basic reference books, joining the Wilkes-Barre Coin Club, and becoming thoroughly immersed. I could not join the American Numismatic Association (ANA), as youngsters were not wanted. My father signed on, so I could get current issues of *The Numismatist*. Collecting grew into part-time dealing in 1953. Soon I was an advertiser in the national publications. In 1955 in Omaha I had my first ANA bourse table, although I was still too young to belong to the association. Lee F. Hewitt, founder of the *Numismatic Scrapbook*, and my Dad both vouched for me.

In the same year my coin-dealing friend Jim Ruddy, in Johnson City, New York, operated the Triple Cities Coin Exchange in a second-floor office on Main Street. There was some local commotion about peculiar bright, new "pennies" that were fuzzy when you looked at them—everything looked double. Intrigued, he made it known he was a buyer for these oddities at 25¢ a coin. After getting a couple dozen of what we now know as the 1955 Doubled Die, he became worried, as there were no customers who were interested in such things. Today a single gem would command on the long side of $10,000. Jim and I became partners in 1958, and for years afterward we made these curious cents a specialty.

As the years went on my numismatic horizons expanded, including the writing of catalogs. Coins remained just as interesting to me, in their way, as the Temple of Diana was to Richard Halliburton. I enjoyed describing coins, telling what I found to be interesting, and their history.

In 1964 I wrote my first book, *Coins and Collectors*, which had a section about the 1955 Doubled Die. Even having been fortunate enough to have spent my entire career in numismatics, and having handled the Eliasberg, Norweb, Bass, Garrett, and other landmark collections, and just about every rarity in the book, I still enjoy Lincoln cents. Each time I see a 1909-S V.D.B. I think back to that day in 1952 when Bob Rusbar showed me his wonderful $10 coin, and to a few years later when I always stocked a nice supply of this popular rarity, but rarely listed them in print—since orders would pour in for these, and I wanted to sell *other* things! In the 1950s there were two coins that were hot as firecrackers: the 1909-S V.D.B. cent and, in bank-wrapped rolls, the even more popular 1950-D Jefferson nickel.

In recent decades Lincoln cents have come of age. Several fine books have been published about them (see the selected bibliography), including studies of all sorts of curious double-punched dies and the like (now in the mainstream and with lots of buyers in sight!), and more. In the 1950s a 1909-S V.D.B. cent, if in as-new condition, was described simply as "brilliant Uncirculated." I sold dozens of them for $20 to $30 each—every one picked out by me as attractive—a quality that I myself would have liked to keep forever. Today in the marketplace, we have MS-63BN, MS-65RD, and the like—an improvement perhaps, but who knows? The coins were every bit as interesting and as compelling to own back then as they are now.

One thing is certain: Ever since I discovered the excitement of Lincoln cents in 1952, they have remained in the numismatic limelight in the coin collecting world. Today, with all of the sophistication in grading that some think the market has, and with price sheets and lists everywhere, arriving weekly in your mailbox and daily on the Internet, it would seem that there is little left to the imagination with regard to Lincoln cents or anything else. Actually, there is a lot.

I hope this book will make you a smart buyer—to be able to look at, for example, 20 or 30 Mint State 1918-D cents and pick out the *one* coin that, in addition to being *original* red, is sharply struck with Full Details and has excellent eye appeal. Your competitors in the marketplace will simply look at labels on holders and write checks. Lucky you—for finding a *rarity* among such coins and, likely, paying no more to buy it! You will also learn that while the 1918-D is nearly always found poorly struck, the 1916 is nearly always found sharply struck. You will realize that finding a sharp 1916 is not unusual, but a sharp 1918-D is a coin worth celebrating!

Second, as a collector of Lincoln cents you will have the advantage that you don't have competition from investors who are driving up prices, except perhaps, among certain high-grade MS-67RD coins with low numbers certified. *You* will be careful when considering these—realizing that an ultra-grade coin is well worth having, but that a MS-68RD coin with a population report of just ten coins now might have a population of 20 or 30 coins a decade hence. Investment-oriented buyers are blissfully unaware of this possibility.

Third, by being smart you will realize that for many Lincoln cents in high grades, an MS-65BN coin, pristine and undipped, will cost just a small fraction of the price of an MS-65RD, possibly dipped, coin. The MS-65BN might be a far more desirable coin!

If you read this book and absorb and agree with the facts and commentary, then I believe that you will be in the top one percent of numismatic experts in the Lincoln cent series. In fact, I guarantee you'll know more than any dealer who has been in the trade for 10, 20, or more years, but who hasn't studied the series beyond reading price lists.

With a wealth of Lincoln cent information on hand, I've tried to pick and choose the most important and interesting facts and figures. To the extent that you may enjoy reading and benefit from this book, I will be pleased.

We all stand on the shoulders of others. In the credits and acknowledgments section you will find the names of the many fine people who have helped, and in the selected biography a list of books that established a foundation of knowledge that benefits all of us.

Writing this book has been very enjoyable. It has reinforced my continuous belief that Lincoln cents are among the most fascinating coins in the entire American series. Believe it or not, they also offer some of the greatest challenges—a delightful numismatic game that invites your participation.

Prices: Estimated market prices are given in various grades, based on information from multiple sources. These are given as an opinion and guide at the time of compilation, in the fall of 2022. Certain actual transactions may take place at higher or lower figures.

Style Notes: Limited editing has been done to certain quoted material. Grades of coins, such as Very Fine, Mint State, etc., have been capitalized, as has Proof, a method of manufacture. In this age of the Internet, certain facts and points were checked on various websites. Many photographs taken of coins in certified holders do not show the full rims of the specimens, due to overlapping by the holder.

Q. David Bowers
Wolfeboro, New Hampshire

PUBLISHER'S PREFACE

In the United States today the Lincoln cent is the most popular "classic" collector coin. Uniquely, it holds that position while also being one of the most popular *modern* coins.

To call the Lincoln cent a classic American coin is to group it with Buffalo nickels, Mercury dimes, Standing Liberty quarters, and Liberty Walking half dollars—all well-loved series that were born in the "Renaissance" era of U.S. coinage at the beginning of the 1900s.

Many active hobbyists collect Lincoln cents. So do people who don't consider themselves numismatists but enjoy saving interesting coins. Among other currently circulating coinage only Washington quarters—specifically, the 1999 to 2008 State quarters—have matched their broad popularity.

Since I started working at Whitman Publishing in 2004, Lincoln cents have never been far from the front burner, measured by reader interest, ongoing numismatic research, and sales of folders, albums, and other hobby supplies.

December 2006. Which grades would we include in the price charts, knowing that there are Brown, Red-Brown, and Red color designations in the higher Mint State conditions? "I need to figure out how to make the price grid not look like a bingo board!" Dave Bowers told me. By the spring of 2007 we were gathering images and photographing coins as needed, with staff photographer Tom Mulvaney focusing on early dates and major die varieties. (Tom, at the time, was also photographing hundreds of pieces for the *Guide Book of Canadian Coins and Tokens*, and the *Guide Book of United States Tokens and Medals*.) That June I invited Lincoln cent specialist Charles Daughtrey to write the book's foreword. Dave Bowers was simultaneously working on the first edition of the *Guide Book of United States Commemorative Coins*. He's always enjoyed working on multiple projects "in parallel," as he calls it, likening his process to a chess master who used to visit his son's elementary-school chess club in Shrewsbury: "They had 35 chess boards, and he played 35 opponents all at the same time!" I touched base with the United States Mint in May, looking for photographs and any new information on Lincoln cents. David W. Lange granted permission to quote from his *Complete Guide to Lincoln Cents*, and J.T. Stanton offered to go through his notes and photographs of die varieties. Ken Potter, Bill Fivaz, Kenneth Bressett, Sam Lukes, Stewart Blay, Roger W. Burdette, Randy Campbell, John Dannreuther, Beth Deisher, Lee Gast, Paul Gilkes, Bob Shippee, David Sundman, Frank Van Valen, and other numismatists shared photographs, discussed die varieties, and advised on questions and ideas. This kind of collaboration is fundamental to Dave Bowers's success as a researcher and author.

In the midst of all this activity, in June 2007, Fred L. Reed pitched his manuscript for a new book on Abraham Lincoln in numismatics. It would develop into two volumes—*Abraham Lincoln: The Image of His Greatness*, and, later, a sequel, *Abraham Lincoln: Beyond the American Icon*. Interest was building toward the 2009 bicentennial of Lincoln's birth.

Dave's manuscript was done and submitted for final editing before the end of July 2007. Layout and proofing came next, and we sent the book to press in September. (By that time the Sage of Wolfeboro, never one to rest for long, was well into his work on the *Whitman Encyclopedia of Colonial and Early American Coins*.) In early November I alerted the numismatic press that the book was on its way, and in December 2007 it was in readers' hands.

Collectors bought tens of thousands of copies of the first edition. When it debuted I wrote: "One of the goals of Whitman's Bowers Series is to offer the human touch that connects coins to people and to history. *A Guide Book of Lincoln Cents* lives up to that goal. I believe it will greatly please the numismatists who already collect these coins, and encourage others to start a new collection."

In an informal poll of 130 hobbyists in the summer of 2018, I found that 33 percent consider themselves active or very active collectors of Lincoln cents (constantly upgrading their sets, collecting die varieties by Fivaz-Stanton number, and/or filling albums and folders); 32 percent consider themselves casual collectors (collecting the coins, but not as their primary interest); 18 percent own some but don't consider themselves collectors (with more of an accumulation than a collection); and only 17 percent don't collect or own them at all. Comments from those polled include:

- "I'm an active collector of Lincoln cents. They're the first coins I started collecting."
- "I've collected them since 1957."
- "I like getting them from circulation, and also collect the Uncirculated Mint sets and basic Proofs."
- "Collectors are slowly coming to realize that pleasant and originally toned Lincolns are an overlooked and exciting area to explore—the last untapped field for toners."
- "Still have the 1909-S V.D.B. hole in my Dansco album . . . the only one missing. I will get one again someday (I've had a couple in the past)."
- "I'm working on filling a Whitman album with my daughter, and actively collecting Deep Cameo Proofs for my Lincoln Memorial set."
- "I love the series. I managed to cherrypick three Matte Proofs out of dealer stock over the years."
- "I actively collect a registry set, plus an an almost-complete raw set. Part of me needed to complete the sets I started as a kid in the 1960s. Back then I could only afford what I found in change. When I finally could afford to buy coins at a shop, this was the first set I worked on."
- "Absolutely love them. Wheat cents started my joy for the hobby! I collect a wide range now. Currently I am on a repunched-mintmark mission. I keep toners, Mint errors, varieties. I roll-hunt often, and cherrypick to the best of my ability."
- "Not only do I collect Lincoln cents in albums, I collect albums for Lincoln cents."
- "Lincolns were my primary collection, and the only date run I ever collected. I was able to assemble a date-and-mintmark set from 1909 to 1933 in average grade of MS-65BN in both NGC and PCGS. It took several years to complete, mostly from 2003 to 2014."

Hearing this kind of feedback from collectors, studying Whitman's book and product sales, and keeping up with ongoing research tells me that Lincoln cents are greatly appreciated. They're a numismatic evergreen—perennially popular—and we're happy to bring Dave Bowers's *Guide Book of Lincoln Cents* to the hobby community. It joins a robust list of Lincoln-centric numismatic books that have been published over the past 20-plus years. Collectors will find much new information in this third edition . . . and they can rest assured it won't be the last.

Dennis Tucker
Publisher, Whitman Publishing

CHAPTER ONE

PRELUDE TO
THE LINCOLN CENT
THE ONE-CENT PIECE IN HISTORY

TRADITION OF THE "PENNY"

By the time the Lincoln cent made its debut in circulation on August 2, 1909, the penny, as most called it, had been part of the American scene for more than a century. The first United States cents were struck in February 1793. Ever since then they have been made every year, with the solitary exception of 1815.

By 1793 pennies were a firmly established part of everyday life. Copper coins about the size of a present-day quarter dollar had circulated widely in the states after the Revolution. Usually referred to as pennies, coppers made by Vermont, Connecticut, New York, New Jersey, and Massachusetts from 1785 to 1788 bore no denomination, except those of Massachusetts, which were inscribed HALF CENT or CENT, this being the first use of the *cent* term in American coinage.

Prior to the state coinage, untold quantities of British halfpennies, of the same size, were imported into the American colonies, where they saw intense use as the smallest denomination in commerce and also were referred to as pennies.

Down through the decades, cents have been ubiquitous—part of the American way of life. There are few homes today that don't have a few tucked away in drawers, piggy banks, and elsewhere. They are of value too low to buy anything on their own, but in recent times they have been coined by the billions. The reason is simple: the pricing of merchandise at odd figures such as 59¢, 99¢, $1.49, and the like, requires cents to be given in change when nickels, dimes, and quarters are tendered for payment (one hardly ever sees half dollars or dollars). As if that were not enough, sales taxes such as 6 percent, 8 percent, or whatever, add to the use of these coins.

It has been suggested many times that cents be abolished. In September 2006 I was one of four numismatists invited to appear before Congress to discuss this subject as well as certain other U.S. Mint programs (the other guests were Beth Deisher, Christopher Cipoletti, and Fred Weinberg). The evidence clearly demonstrated that it cost more than a cent to make a one-cent piece and more than a nickel to make a five-cent piece. Despite discussion in that forum and in the media, the cent seems to be here to stay. Should it be

Amerikanischer Postwagen

Stage coach stop on the road from New York to Philadelphia, circa 1790s. A handful of pennies would buy dinner and a mug of ale.

The 1787 copper cent of Massachusetts was the first American coin to be specifically denominated CENT. Half cents and cents of this design were made with the dates 1787 and 1788 in a state-owned mint supervised by Joshua Witherle. After an audit revealed that each coin cost twice face value to produce, the facility was closed.

withdrawn from circulation, I dare say the American love affair with the Lincoln cent would spur saving and collecting them with an unprecedented passion.

OLD CENTS IGNITE THE NUMISMATIC HOBBY

If in some distant year cents disappear or are changed in size, this event will have a counterpart in history. The disappearance of cents of the large, heavy copper style by provisions of the Act of February 21, 1857, caused a great rush by citizens to find as many dates as they could, giving birth to coin collecting as a popular hobby. Some suggested *numismatologist* would be a good name for such an enthusiast, but ultimately *numismatist* prevailed, although to some devotees it was a tongue-twister. The collector's challenge in 1857 was

In January 1857 the last of the large copper cents were minted. Many were probably melted, since soon afterward the Treasury began redeeming the older cents. News of this created a wave of nostalgia across the country.

to find one of every date going back to 1793. There were no books or guides listing which dates were scarce or rare, and hardly anyone knew that no cents were minted in the year 1815. City newspapers such as the Boston *Evening Transcript* and the *New-York Dispatch*, as well as the just-launched *Historical Magazine*, contained news and comments plus inquiries from readers. It was a time of discovery and excitement.

While hardly anyone was able to assemble a complete run of cents from 1793 onward, because the 1799 was a rarity and the 1793 and 1804 were hard to find, many probably filled in sets from 1816 onward, except perhaps for the scarce 1823.

Then on May 25, 1857, the new, smaller cents of the Flying Eagle design made their debut. Excitement prevailed at the Philadelphia Mint as hundreds of men, women, and children stood in line to exchange old copper cents for new, or to buy the new cents using worn Spanish-American coins then in circulation as legal tender. A local newspaper told the story:

> Just as the State House bell had finished striking 9 o'clock the doors of the Mint were thrown open, and in rushed the eager crowd—paper parcels, well-filled handkerchiefs, carpet bags, baskets and all. But those who thought there was to be a grand scramble, and that the boldest pusher would be first served, reckoned without their host. The invading throng was arranged into lines which lead to the respective windows; those who bore silver had the post of honor assigned them and went to the right, while those who bore nothing but vulgar copper [old half cents and large cents] were constrained to take the left. . . .
>
> We estimated that at one time there could not have been fewer than 1,000 persons in the zigzag lines, weighed down with small change, and waiting patiently for their turn. Those who were served rushed into the street with their moneybags, and many of them were immediately surrounded by an outside crowd, who were willing to buy out in small lots and in advance on first cost. We saw quite a number of persons on the steps of the Mint dealing out the new favorites in advance of from 30 percent to 100 percent, and some of the outside purchasers even huckstered out the coin again in smaller lots at a still heavier advance.

Just to think of it—a thousand people lined up to get new cents. It would be déjà vu in 1909, when Lincoln cents were introduced. But, that is getting ahead of the story. The point is that "pennies" excite the public imagination and have been a foundation of numismatics ever since 1857.

ONWARD AND UPWARD

With that as a foundation, in 1858 coin collecting became a national hobby. The American Numismatic Society (ANS) was formed in New York City, several auctions were held, and excitement prevailed. In 1859 the *American Numismatical Manual* was the first large-format book to be published on the subject in the United States—complete with color illustrations, no less! The author, Dr. Montroville W. Dickeson, noted that 1793 cents could be found in circulation, or at least until recently.

After that—everything. The hobby was launched, and big time! As the years passed, the passion for collecting increased. The *American Journal of Numismatics* launched in 1866, *The Numismatist* launched in 1888, and the ANA formed in 1891. The 1880s saw an average of one coin auction *per week* for part of the decade. A *numismatist* was the thing to be, if you could pronounce the word—otherwise, *coin collector* served well.

And on down to the twentieth century, and now to the twenty-first. Lincoln cents, still being made after a more than 100-year run, are the latest chapter in the chronology of the basic denomination that catalyzed and in many ways still defines our hobby as we know it.

Now, a sketch of the federal one-cent pieces from 1793 onward: the predecessors to the Lincoln cent.

LARGE COPPER CENTS, 1793–1857

Authorized by the Mint Act of April 2, 1792, the first copper cents were struck at the Philadelphia Mint in February 1793. The engraver of the dies, fearful that the name of the nation would not fit with proper spacing, abbreviated it to AMERI. on the first die, then later rearranged the style to accommodate the full AMERICA. The initial design featured the head of Miss Liberty on the obverse, facing right, while on the reverse was a chain of 15 links, one for each state in the Union. These are known as 1793 Chain cents today: the Chain AMERI. for the earliest die, the Chain AMERICA for the later ones.

The *Argus*, published in Boston on March 26, 1793, quoting an account from New Jersey, gave this review of young America's first coin from the new Philadelphia Mint:

> The American *cents* (says a letter from Newark) do not answer our expectations. The chain on the reverse is but a bad omen for liberty, and liberty herself appears to be in a fright. May she not justly cry out in the words of the apostle, *"Alexander the coppersmith has done me much harm; the Lord reward him according to his works!"* [It will be remembered that Alexander Hamilton was at that time secretary of the Treasury.]

Perhaps in view of such criticism, the motif was discarded, and soon a new copper cent of 1793 made its appearance with Miss Liberty restyled and, on the reverse, a wreath. These are known as Wreath cents today. As it turned out, the Wreath cents were ephemeral as well, and in the late summer the Liberty Cap style made its debut, the chef d'oeuvre of talented artist Joseph Wright, the recently hired engraver at the Mint. His tenure was all too brief, cut short by his death (of yellow fever) on September 12 or 13 of the same year. Had this not occurred, a type set of coinage of the first decade of the Mint might be much different in appearance from the designs with which we are familiar today.

Liberty Cap cents continued to be made in 1794, 1795, and early 1796, from hand-engraved dies with many interesting characteristics. One variety of 1794 has ninety-four tiny, five-pointed stars around the reverse border, and another has the fraction bar on the 1/100 value omitted.

Partway through 1796 the Draped Bust design replaced the Liberty Cap style, the work of Robert Scot, the new engraver at the Mint. Scot is known to have engraved flat plates for printing maps and the like, and he may have produced plates for bank notes. Information is sketchy today, and no significant study of his life and career has ever been done. We do know that a few years later, at the turn of the nineteenth century, John Reich was hired to do several special projects and that in 1807, then on the Mint staff, Reich created what is known today as the Capped Bust design, first used on half dollars and $5 gold coins of that year and later expanded to other series. In 1808 he engraved the Classic Head motif for the copper cent. In 1817 Reich left the Mint to pursue his career elsewhere. It has been stated that Scot had severely impaired eyesight by that time, although he remained as the chief engraver until 1824, when he was succeeded by William Kneass, an engraver of bank note and other plates.

As time went on, engraving techniques improved and various mechanical processes were introduced. The wide variations seen in the hand-cut dies of 1793 cents were replaced by subtler differences in 1816, when the Matron Head design (probably the work of Reich) made its appearance. Although now and again there would be distinctively curious variet-ies—such as the 1817 with 15 instead of the regular 13 stars—most Matron Head and later cents looked the same at a quick glance. Only under a magnifying glass could differences be discerned, such as in the placement of stars and letters or in changes to the date, such as altering an unused 1822 die to read 1823 by punching a 3 over the last digit.

In 1835 Christian Gobrecht, a highly accomplished engraver of medal dies and plates for printing illustrations and bank notes, was hired at the Mint and later appointed chief engraver. Gobrecht experimented with several different portraits of Miss Liberty for use on the cent, finally settling on what we know today as the Braided Hair style. Introduced in 1839, it was the standard through 1857.

Throughout the early nineteenth century the copper cent was the most popular, the most ubiquitous, of American coins. A handful of pennies could buy a dinner, an over-night stay in a hotel, or passage on a coach drawn by a span of horses. As the passport to many delights, the cent endeared itself to everyone, resulting in the passion for them when they began disappearing in 1857.

TRANSITION OF THE COPPER CENT

In the meantime, by 1850, the cost of producing the large, heavy copper cents had risen, sharply reducing the profit their coinage made for the Mint. At the time copper cents (and also half cents, made in much smaller numbers) were produced for the Mint's own account. Copper would be bought in the marketplace, or blanks (planchets) ready for coining would be acquired from a supplier. Finished cents would be placed into circulation for face value, with the Mint account recording the profit made after metal and production costs were deducted. In contrast, silver and gold coins were made only at the request of depositors of these precious metals (who requested specific denominations, such as dollars or half eagles). The Mint charged a very small fee for refining and coinage, yielding little profit.

The very first copper cent made at the Philadelphia Mint, the Chain AMERI., was released in March 1793. Miss Liberty "appears to be in a fright," a press notice complained. This motif was soon replaced by that of the Wreath cent.

The Wreath cent of 1793 was successor to the Chain motif. The border is a circle of beads or dots. Miss Liberty is cut more deeply into the die, and the wreath is introduced on the reverse.

The Liberty Cap cent, designed by Joseph Wright in the summer of 1793, was produced through early 1796. Serrations or *dentils* are around the border.

Next came the Draped Bust cents made from 1796 to 1807, illustrated here by a variety of 1803.

The Classic Head, by engraver John Reich, was made from 1808 to 1814, as featured on this example of 1810. No cents were made in 1815.

Matron Head cents were made from 1816 through the mid-1830s, after which several intermediate motifs were used. An 1827 variety is shown here.

An 1839 cent of the style collectors call the *Booby Head*, from dies by Christian Gobrecht, who created several versions of Miss Liberty this year.

The Braided Hair design of 1839 to 1857 underwent several modifications. This 1853, gem Mint State coin with original red-orange color, with some surface flecks, is from a small hoard of the date.

As might be expected under such an arrangement, copper cents were produced continuously (except for 1815), while mintages of gold and silver coins were very erratic. As examples, quarter dollars were minted in 1796, then not again until 1804, then continuously for several years to 1807, then not again until 1815. Quarter eagles ($2.50 gold) were made from 1796 to 1798, then 1802 to 1808, then not again until 1821.

In the 1850s many experiments (smaller diameters, different alloys, etc.) were made to sustain the profits from cent coinage. Patterns were made through 1856, when a new alloy and size were decided upon. The format was codified the next year by the earlier-mentioned Act of February 21, 1857, which abolished the old, large cents and provided for the production of new cents, weighing 72 grains and made of copper-nickel (88 percent copper, 12 percent nickel). Although not specified by law, the diameter was ultimately set at three quarters of an inch. (Incidentally, laying four coins end to end is a handy way to measure three inches—a convenience if a ruler is not available.[1] This can be done with Lincoln cents today.)

FLYING EAGLE CENTS, 1856–1858

Chief engraver James B. Longacre created a new motif for the copper-nickel cent by taking Gobrecht's flying eagle design from the reverse of the 1836 silver dollar and combining it with the "agricultural" wreath Longacre himself had devised in 1854 for the Type II gold dollar and the new $3 denomination. In 1856 and early 1857 nearly 1,000 patterns, or test coins, of what became

The new Flying Eagle cent was first distributed on May 25, 1857.

known as the Flying Eagle cent were struck at the Mint and distributed to congressmen, newspaper editors, and others of influence. Such a design change, once announced to the public, was anticipated to be dramatic, and the Treasury Department wanted the transition to go smoothly. It did—and the release of the new cents on May 25, 1857, was a sensation, with a thousand or more people waiting in lines at the Mint.

As the hobby of coin collecting became popular, and as the new 1857 Flying Eagle cents were admired, it became known that patterns dated 1856 had been made. These were not to be found easily. Soon the Mint began restriking them for collectors, adding perhaps 1,500 or more to the original coinage of 1,000 pieces. To make them more attractive to numismatists, the restrikes were produced in Proof format, instead of the circulation-strike or satiny or prooflike surfaces of nearly all of the originals.

In 1857 some 17,450,000 Flying Eagle cents were struck with that date, followed by 24,800,000 more with the date 1858. By that time problems had developed in striking the designs to show the correct detail. The head and tail of the eagle on the obverse were opposite the heavy wreath on the reverse. During the coining process, the copper-nickel metal, a very hard alloy, flowed with difficulty, and often the head and tail of the eagle were weakly struck. In 1858 several different new designs were prepared, including a small, "skinny" eagle centered on the obverse, an Indian Head, and variations of the reverse wreath. By this time the Mint was very active in the "coin business," making and selling restrikes and the like, sometimes openly and other times under the table. Sets of 12 pattern cents of 1858 were made for collectors, with various combinations of the regular 1858 coinage dies and the new pattern dies.

INDIAN HEAD CENTS, 1859–1909

In 1859 a new design was adopted, incorporating on the obverse a Liberty Head in the form of Miss Liberty dressed in an Indian war bonnet, with UNITED STATES OF AMERICA surrounding, and the date below. The design was by Chief Engraver Longacre. The reverse displayed a laurel or olive (in Mint correspondence, both words are used) wreath enclosing ONE / CENT in two lines. These were made in quantity—36,400,000 for circulation and perhaps a thousand or so Proofs for collectors. For reasons seemingly not recorded, the reverse die was deemed unsatisfactory.

Toward the end of the year a new reverse with an oak wreath (and other species) and shield was used to produce patterns, or perhaps they were made for circulation—for the finish was circulation-strike format, not Proof. It is not known how many were made, but 500 to 1,000 might be a good guess. The late John J. Ford Jr. and the late Walter Breen considered that they might have been made as regular issues and listed them as such in the 18th (and final) edition of the *Standard Catalogue of United States*

The Indian Head cent of 1859, with Laurel Wreath reverse, was replaced in 1860 with the Oak Wreath and Shield reverse.

Coins. This was a useful reference that had been launched by Wayte Raymond in 1934, but that after 1946 lost its market share to the new *Guide Book of United States Coins*, which was more widely distributed, less expensive, and more popular with numismatists.

Cents with the Indian Head obverse and the new Oak Wreath and Shield reverse were produced continuously through early 1909. In the spring of 1864 the copper-nickel alloy was discontinued, and bronze, consisting of 95 percent copper and 5 percent tin and zinc, was substituted. This alloy remained in use into the twentieth century and in 1909 was the standard for the new Lincoln cent. With some gaps, this was the alloy employed until early 1982.

A minor change was made in autumn 1864 with the addition of the tiny initial L, for Longacre, to the ribbon on Miss Liberty's bonnet. For numismatists, Flying Eagle and Indian Head cents were numismatic favorites, both in Proof format and as circulation strikes. In the late nineteenth century dealers with walk-in trade had large stocks of these.

Along the way the 1877 cent was recognized as *the* rarity in the series. Mint records state that just 852,000 were made for circulation—the only figure to dip below several million in the series up to that point. It is possible that some of the cents struck in 1877 were from earlier-dated dies, for they turned out to be even harder to find in circulation than the low mintage might suggest.

In 1908 the San Francisco Mint struck cents for the first time, in the amount of 1,115,000 pieces. Unlike the situation for the 1877 cent, the 1908-S was recognized by collectors at the time, and modest quantities of Mint State coins were saved—making them scarce, but not rare, today. In 1909 at San Francisco, 309,000 1909-S Indian Head cents were made, and these too were saved at the time. Both the 1908-S and 1909-S cents were made of a bronze alloy that, when run through a metal-strip-rolling machine, stretched out certain incompletely blended components of the alloy (Bill Fivaz uses the term *improper metal mix*), imparting a "wood-grain" or streaky effect to the finished coins. The effect became more noticeable later on, as the coins acquired natural light toning. Also, the alloy was slightly lighter and of a distinctive yellow-brass hue, quite unlike that used at Philadelphia at the time. Accordingly, it is possible to differentiate these cents by looking at the obverse only, without checking for a mintmark—a little secret recognized by specialists, but not widely known. These same alloy characteristics are true for most of the Lincoln cents made in San Francisco in 1909, continuing into the early 1920s. Coins that have been dipped have lost these distinctions. Now *you* can tell the difference.

Lincoln portrait plaque in bronze by Victor David Brenner, 1907.

The first Lincoln cent. (enlarged 1.5x)

CHAPTER TWO

HISTORY OF THE WHEAT EARS REVERSE CENT, 1909–1958
EVOLUTION AND DISTRIBUTION

BACKGROUND OF THE NEW CENT
TIME FOR A CHANGE

Abraham Lincoln, the son of Thomas and Nancy Hanks Lincoln who became the 16th president upon his inauguration on March 6, 1861, was born on February 12, 1809, in Hodgenville, Kentucky. The year 1909 marked the 100th anniversary of his birth. In anticipation, in 1908 President Theodore Roosevelt thought it a good idea to honor him on a coin. Or, at least that is what certain newspaper accounts said. No surviving Mint or presidential correspondence supports this.[2]

Several years earlier, in 1905, Roosevelt had commissioned sculptor Augustus Saint-Gaudens to redesign the entire American coinage from the cent to the double eagle. The president had viewed coins of ancient Greece on display at the Smithsonian Institution. Admiring their sculptured relief and artistry, he felt that current U.S. coins were insipid in comparison. Saint-Gaudens, in failing health, died on August 3, 1907, having completed basic designs and models for the $10 and $20 gold coins only, although sketches and plaster models had been created for the cent. Another sculptor, Bela Lyon

Ancient Greek silver decadrachm of Syracuse, circa 400–390 B.C., signed by sculptor Euainetos. Scholars consider the chariot side to be the obverse and the portrait side to be the reverse. Numismatic art of this high caliber influenced Roosevelt to commission a complete redesigning of American coinage.

Theodore Roosevelt, who served as vice president from 1897 to 1901 and president from the latter date to 1909, is the only American president who ever took a deep interest in coinage designs. In 1908 he selected Victor D. Brenner to design a new one-cent piece to observe the 1909 centennial of Abraham Lincoln's birth.

Double eagle dated MCMVII (1907) by Augustus Saint-Gaudens, with High Relief features. This artistic triumph resulted from close collaboration between the sculptor and the president.

Pratt, was tapped to redesign the $2.50 and $5 gold coins. Redoing the other coins from the cent upward was not pursued.

Pratt's gold coins of 1908 were unappreciated, and many criticisms of the Indian Head designs he created appeared in *The Numismatist* and elsewhere. Apparently, Pratt was not considered as a designer for the new Lincoln coin.

A BIOGRAPHICAL SKETCH OF LINCOLN

Since hundreds of books have been written about Lincoln, and since the Internet provides more information about him than can be imagined, needed, or wanted, I give only a brief sketch here:

Young Abraham grew up in the semi-wilderness of the frontier, where his family had to work hard, and many daily duties were a struggle. When he was eight, he moved with his family to Indiana. When he was ten, his mother died, and in time he gained a stepmother,

The 1860 ABRA-HAM LIN-COLN, THE HANNIBAL OF AMERICA token is believed to be the earliest issued in connection with Lincoln's 1860 presidential campaign. This punny 19 mm token was the brainchild of William Leggett Bramhall, who gave semi-cryptographically the name of Lincoln's running mate, Hannibal Hamlin. The center of the reverse die at first read THE HANNIBAL OF AMERICA. Perhaps comparing Lincoln to the famous ancient military leader ruffled some feathers; for whatever reason, the inscription was blanked out by the heavy engraving of WIDEAWAKES over it. The Wideawakes were mostly young men who in 1860 supported Lincoln. The movement staged torchlight parades, including a memorable one in New York City. The original token and the token with altered reverse are both shown.

Beardless portrait of Abraham Lincoln, circa 1860, after a photograph by Hesler, engraved by T. Johnson. (*Century Magazine,* November 1886)

Statue of Lincoln standing, by Augustus Saint-Gaudens. Work on this was begun in 1884 and finished in 1887. (Library of Congress)

Seated Lincoln statue by Saint-Gaudens, created at his Cornish studio from 1897 to 1906, for Grant Park in Chicago. (Small-scale version at the Saint-Gaudens National Historic Site, Cornish, New Hampshire)

Sarah Bush Johnston Lincoln. With ambition and perseverance young Abe earned an education, largely learning to read, write, and do mathematics on his own. He worked hard on a farm, split rails to make fences, and kept a store in New Salem, Illinois, his adopted state.

As a young adult Lincoln was a captain in the Black Hawk War, after which he practiced law, riding the circuit of courts in his district. Elected in 1834, for eight years he served in the Illinois State Legislature. In 1847 and 1849 he was a representative to Congress. In 1858 he opposed Stephen A. Douglas in the race for the national Senate, and lost. His debates in that contest gained national attention and brought him the fame that secured the Republican nomination for president in 1860. With four candidates in the running and with the Democrats divided into North-South factions, Lincoln won the November election.

His stance against slavery was intolerable to the South, and on December 20 the state of South Carolina, followed by six others which soon formed the Confederate States of America, seceded from the Union. When Lincoln was inaugurated in March 1861, the federal government, referred to as the Union, was in disarray. Precipitated by the Confederate shelling and subsequent occupation of federal Fort Sumter in the Charleston, South Carolina, harbor on April 11, the Union's war against the South commenced on April 15. The engagement was expected to be of short duration, because Lincoln and others felt the Confederacy was ill prepared, with few resources. The president called for three-month enlistments from volunteer soldiers. After a calamitous loss to the rebels at the Battle of Bull Run in July, reality proved to be vastly different, and the Civil War lasted until early April 1865.

Lincoln was faced with reorganizing many departments in the government, supervising the Army and Navy, financing the war, and dealing with disarray in the monetary system. (The diverse array of coins, tokens, scrip, paper money, encased postage stamps, and other money of the Civil War—official and otherwise—would take a large book to describe in detail.) On January 1, 1863, he issued the Emancipation Proclamation, freeing slaves in the Confederacy, which had little practical effect until the war was over. In 1864 Lincoln won reelection against his opponent, General George B. McClellan, whom he had relieved of his Army command due to perceived poor performance: a case of "the slows," when action was needed.

Less than a week after the war ended on April 9, 1865, President Lincoln was shot while attending a performance at Ford's Theatre in Washington (the production being *Our American Cousin*, starring Laura Keene). He was rushed to a nearby boarding house and died in the early hours of April 15. During his tenure the country had known fewer than six weeks of peace. He was succeeded in the White House by his vice president, Andrew Johnson.

The president was survived by his widow, Mary Todd Lincoln, and two sons, Robert Todd and Thomas "Tad." Two other boys had died in their youth. After his passing, the president was remembered as a hero by the North and a scoundrel by the South. To freed slaves he was "the Great Emancipator."[3] When Lincoln cents became a reality years later in 1909, they were praised by Northerners and Black Southerners, but many White Southerners ignored them.

During his lifetime Lincoln's portrait appeared on federal paper money, since there was no law at the time to prevent the depiction of living persons. Indian peace and other medals, campaign tokens, and Civil War tokens bore his visage. After his death the

American Numismatic and Archaeological Society honored him with a large medal, from dies engraved by Emil Sigel. In 1866 the Philadelphia Mint created a pattern five-cent piece with his portrait, but the design never reached circulation.

The study "Lincoln in Numismatics," by Robert P. King, in *The Numismatist*, February 1924, remains the standard reference today. Following a casual introduction and discussion, King devoted over 100 pages to listing 887 tokens, medals, and related pieces. The same issue included a related study, "Obsolete Paper Money With Portrait of Lincoln," by D.C. Wismer, and a listing of federal paper money bearing the portrait of Lincoln, by George H. Blake. Then followed several other articles relating to Lincoln.

Designing the Lincoln Cent
Roosevelt and Brenner

In the autumn of 1908 a well-known sculptor, Victor David Brenner, was selected by Roosevelt to model his portrait for use on the obverse of a medal to honor workers on the Panama Canal, a project still in progress. The artist's name seems to have come to the fore in this October 1, 1908, letter from Mint Director Frank A. Leach to Philadelphia Mint Superintendent John H. Landis, who had not been aware of the artist or the medal, well in progress:

> When I was in Philadelphia a few weeks ago Mr. Barber told me that he had heard that the Panama Canal Commission intended to issue some medals—quite a large number. Yesterday a gentleman from their office called upon me to see about getting them struck off at your Mint, and in conversation I learned that when the idea of issuing the medals was first proposed, a draughtsman in the employ of the Commission submitted a design for the medals, which was subsequently given to Mr. [Frank] Millet to make the models, [and] upon his recommendation [Victor] Brenner of New York was employed to make the dies. The dies are about completed. The Commission desires the medals to be struck from bronze recovered on the isthmus from old French material that was used in the original canal enterprise.

Samples of the Panama Canal medal were ready by April 14, 1909, and afterward the Mint produced a run of 5,000.

During Roosevelt's sitting for Brenner in the summer of 1908, it seems that the two discussed American coinage designs and the work left unfinished by the death of Saint-Gaudens. The president admired Brenner's plaque with the portrait of Lincoln, created in 1907 (see page 8).

Later in the year, when the idea of a Lincoln coin came to the forefront of Roosevelt's mind, Brenner was contacted by Mint Director Leach. The artist accepted the commission, with a stipend of $1,000. Already into the project by January 4, 1909, he commented, "I was thinking of embodying the portrait of Mr. Lincoln on the cent piece, and find that it will compose very well." Brenner simply took his plaque portrait and adapted it for use on a coin.

The idea of this artist creating the new cent design met with Roosevelt's approval. By that time the Indian Head cent had been in circulation since 1859, and it was ripe for a change. Within two weeks preliminary models of the new cent were prepared by Brenner.

VICTOR DAVID BRENNER

By 1909 Brenner, born Viktoras Barnauskas (variant spellings occur) in Shavli, Lithuania, on June 12, 1871, was the most *numismatic* of American sculptors. Studying under his sculptor-and-engraver father, Viktoras developed his own skills, and by the time he was 13 he joined his father in the trade, which included engraving seals and dies. In 1890 he emigrated to America, where he was known as Victor David Brenner. In New York City he gained employment as an engraver of jewelry.

Sculpture and medals remained his primary interest. On November 19, 1894, he joined the American Numismatic and Archaeological Society, the leading organization in the hobby at the time. The next year he entered a competition to replace the design of the "Morgan" silver dollar, a project sponsored by the numismatic group and the National Sculpture Society. The Treasury Department and the Mint did not recognize the effort, and no change was made in the coinage. From 1898 to 1901 Brenner studied art in Paris, under Auguste Rodin and others, and immersed himself in the stimulating surroundings. He exhibited his work at the Paris International Exposition in 1900.

Back in America, in 1902 he joined the ANA as member 434, while in the same year serving as an instructor in the unfortunately short-lived American Numismatic and Archaeological Society's School for Die-Cutting in New York City. In the same city the Dietsch brothers, makers of jewelry, buckles, and ornaments, had a Janvier portrait reduction lathe, a device that was more sophisticated than any operated at the Philadelphia Mint. Brenner operated it for the Dietsch brothers and others, to create hubs to make dies for striking art medals. In 1904 he returned to Paris, where he stayed more than a year.

Returning to New York City, in 1906 he rejoined the ANA, now as member 841, having let his dues payments lapse. In 1907 much of his work was displayed in New York City and featured in the *Catalogue of Medals and Plaques by Victor D. Brenner, exhibited at the Grolier Club, March 7 to March 23, 1907*, for which Brenner wrote the introduction. His plaque of Lincoln (see page 8) was made and sold this year and was widely admired. By that time he was well known in American art circles. In 1909 he attended the New York Coin Club's meetings, lively events sometimes held in conjunction with an auction by Thomas L. Elder. In the same year a medal for the Lincoln centennial was produced

Victor D. Brenner at work on a model for a medal. His art was widely admired at the time. (*The Numismatist*, March 1909)

Brenner in his studio with a model of a Lincoln statue. (*Mehl's Numismatic Monthly*, March 1917)

by the Gorham Manufacturing Company from Brenner's models, featuring the same portrait used on his 1907 plaque. His 1910 booklet, "The Art of the Medal," was published by the ANS (which had dropped "and Archaeological" from its name in 1908).

Brenner hoped to design coins besides the cent. On April 18, 1910, he wrote to Mint Director Piatt Andrew to offer an "ideal head of Liberty" to be used on any coin. On April 3, 1913, he tried again, in a letter to Director George Roberts: "I have given considerable thought to designs suitable for the silver coinage, and I am sure we could arrive at fine results." Perhaps in response to expressed interest (although no supporting correspondence has been located), Brenner wrote to Roberts on February 7, 1914: "I take the liberty of sending to you three sets of sketches in the rough, and upon your advice I will be glad to restudy and make models of them for you to approve." Nothing came of these efforts, and in 1916 the silver coinage was redesigned by other artists—Adolph A. Weinman and Hermon A. MacNeil.

In addition to his single fling with circulating coinage, Brenner was very successful with his medallic art and enjoyed recognition and prosperity. He completed only one large-scale sculpture, *Song to Nature (Zeus and Persephone)*, a fountain in Schenley Park in Pittsburgh, Pennsylvania. Ill health forced him to slow down in 1921. In November of that year he was one of eight prominent artists invited to submit a design for the new Peace silver dollar. He was in good company with Hermon MacNeil, Chester Beach, Henry Hering, Robert Aitken, Adolph A. Weinman, John Flanagan, and Anthony de Francisci, the last named being the winner.

On April 4, 1924, the designer of the Lincoln cent died in New York City, survived by his wife of 11 years, the former Anna Reeb.

Over a long period of years Brenner's work has formed the focus of displays and articles by numismatists, most notably Glenn Smedley, who wrote several articles about him for *The Numismatist* in the early 1980s.

The artist's Lincoln Centennial medal as reviewed by Frank C. Higgins in *The Numismatist*, February 1909.

Bust of Lincoln created by Brenner and displayed in his studio for the balance of his lifetime. Measures 10.25 inches (26.6 cm) high. Cast by the Roman Bronze Works, Inc. N.Y. (Brenner estate to Medallic Art Co.; auction at Sotheby Parke Bernet, The Medallic Art Collection of American Bronzes, September 29, 1977, Lot 10; to D. Wayne Johnson, the present owner)

Detail of artist's signature on the back of the neck.

PROGRESS OF THE CENT DESIGN

Victor D. Brenner's design for the Lincoln cent evolved from a series of different designs, not only for the cent but for other denominations the artist hoped to modify. A letter dated February 1, 1909, from Brenner to Mint Director Frank A. Leach, describes the work in progress and advances the artist's new thought that perhaps a one-cent coin would not be ideal after all:

> I have expressed to you four plaster casts today; one is a new Lincoln head just finished resembling the one you have only in the mask.
>
> The model of this eagle is improved by the engraving you gave me, and if my last Lincoln head is adopted, the eagle could well be made for the other side. I think that a half dollar would be more suitable for the Lincoln coin than a penny. In a day or so I shall send on to you a helmeted head of Liberty for one side of the cent or nickel, so that with the head I am to send, I think the molds for the three coins would be accomplished, except the changing of the denominations and final finishing of detail on face and otherwise. I would also finish the hubs so as to get all I want in the ultimate size.
>
> I should consider it a privilege to have the cent and nickel adopted during the president's administration whose time expires but too soon.
>
> If the Lincoln half dollar could be adopted I might be able to get photographs ready by the 12th. The head naturally would have to be reduced in relief so as to bring it up with pressure.

By implication, Brenner envisioned himself as the heir to the unfinished work of Saint-Gaudens. No commissions for other coins were given to the artist, however, and Brenner settled down to working on the cent alone.

Leach replied to Brenner on February 2, 1909:

> Your letter of the first instant just received. It is useless at this time to make any attempt to change the designs of the subsidiary coins, as no changes in these coins can be made for seven years without permission of Congress. We have only two coins on which we can make a change now, the penny and the nickel. For one of these coins I had already requested Mr. Barber to submit a design, and therefore I can only use your design, if it is accepted, on the penny or the nickel. . . . All engravings must be done by the engravers at the Philadelphia Mint. I think we all prefer the second model of Lincoln which you sent.

Leach wrote to Secretary of the Treasury Franklin MacVeagh on February 9, 1909:

> In the matter of furnishing the designs for the proposed new one cent coinage, Mr. Victor Brenner is insistent upon introducing another design for the reverse coinage side in place of the one first offered. It is necessary that we should have some other design than the one first submitted by him, for I have discovered that it is an exact copy of the design used by the government of France on its two franc piece, the only difference being in the inscriptions.
>
> We should also refuse to adopt the second design offered, embracing a female figure, first, for the reason that there is a question as to its legality. This figure is supposed to symbolize Liberty, and to use it, it seems to me, would destroy our license to use the Lincoln head, so much desired, on the obverse side. The law does not

provide for two impressions or figures emblematic of Liberty. Then, as this is the simplest coin we have, it seems to me it should call for the plainest and most distinct design.

Another objection, which is not so serious, being only a mechanical one, is that a figure on the reverse side of the coin, unless of the lowest possible relief, would interfere with securing the best results in producing the Lincoln portrait on the obverse side.

Leach wrote to Brenner on February 9, 1909:

The subject of the design for the reverse of the penny has been discussed by the President and the Secretary and myself, and it was decided that owing to the law permitting of only one figure emblematic of Liberty to be on the coin, and the desire that the coin should be plain and simple, your suggestion of the female figure, left with me yesterday, is rejected; and you are requested to submit another design which shall be in compliance with the memorandum furnished you yesterday.

Brenner sent this to Leach on February 10, 1909:

I beg also to acknowledge receipt of your letter dated Feb. 9th, fixing the designs for the cent piece for the obverse to have the portrait of Mr. Lincoln with the word Liberty and the date of the coinage, for the reverse to have United States of America, One Cent and E Pluribus Unum. I shall submit my arrangement of the design to you shortly.

Chief Engraver Charles E. Barber wrote to Brenner in the same month:

Your letter of the 10th inst, received and the contents have been discussed with the Director who I understand has given you certain instructions regarding the design. Mr. Leach tells me that he has explained to you that he desired the field of the coin to be finished with a fixed radius or curve, therefore the model must be made with a fixed radius.

I find in your Lincoln medal that the field in front of the face is one plane while the field at the back of the head is an entirely different plane. This you will see will never do as we have to finish the field of the dies mechanically in order to comply with the wish of the Director, namely to have the field finished smooth and one radius. In making your design you must avoid as much as possible one bold part of your design coming opposite another on the other side of the coin, as that would be fatal to the coining of the piece.

In regard to what relief you had better adopt, I am sorry to say that I cannot give you any fixed instructions as so much depends upon the design of both sides and the particular metal the design is for, also the area of the coin.

You can look at the [Indian Head] cent, judge from that, and that is the extent of the relief that can be successfully used for the one cent coin, and you will also see that for the point of utility, that the design is good, as it is so arranged that no one point comes in opposition to another, and as these coins are struck by tons every year, not thousands, but millions and if the usual average per pair of dies was not produced, the Coiner would condemn the dies at once.

In designing for a coin you must give due weight to the mechanical requirements of coinage and remember that great quantities of coin are demanded against time, and therefore, everything that can be done to simplify both the making of the dies and the production of the coin, must be considered.

You also know that the coins drop from the press at the rate of 120 per minute and that unlike a medal there is no bronzing or finishing of any description, no chance to bring out the design by coloring. It comes from the press one color and that is the color of the metal whatever that may be.

Brenner wrote to Leach on February 26, 1909:

I have the honor to inform you that I have today expressed to you the completed models of the Lincoln penny also the molds of the same. I trust you will find them satisfactory. I will appreciate the permission of examining the hubs before they are hardened, and should any retouching be necessary, to do so under the supervision of Mr. Barber.

Leach wrote to Superintendent Landis of the Philadelphia Mint on February 27, 1909:

I send you by express today the models adopted by the President of the design for the proposed new issue of the one cent piece. I notice that Mr. Brenner insists upon putting his name in full on the obverse side. I am sorry to have to disappoint him in this matter, but after consultation with the Secretary of the Treasury upon the subject it was decided that only his initials could be permitted, and that in an unobtrusive way.

Mr. Brenner writes me that he desires to see the hub in time to have touched up any imperfections that he might notice. I wish you would advise me whether or not his request is practicable. As soon as the dies are ready and proof [pattern or sample] pieces struck I shall be pleased to be advised of the fact.

Brenner, stating to Leach on March 4, was cooperative regarding his name:

I fully agree with you that my name on the obverse looks obtrusive, and thanks for calling my attention to it. I shall take it out, and put it in small letters on the reverse near the rim.

Further correspondence dealt with slight revisions and retouchings requested by the artist. Chief Engraver Barber conceded that he would not resist these, because he had been humiliated by accusations by numismatists (Henry Chapman in particular) and others that he had interfered with the art of Saint-Gaudens and Pratt, and wanted to be spared this indignity in the future.

Significantly, the motto "In God We Trust" was not being considered as the new cent was being developed, possibly because President Roosevelt felt that the name of the Deity on coinage was a sacrilege. In any event, the inscription did not appear on the Indian Head cent currently in use. The inscription would be added after incoming President William H. Taft was inaugurated in March. The idea came from Director Leach and Chief Engraver Barber, as related in this letter Leach wrote to Brenner on May 22:

I have to inform you that I was not satisfied with the first proof of the Lincoln cent. I found that you had not dropped the Lincoln portrait down so that the head would come nearer the center of the coin, a matter I called your attention to when we were discussing the model. This is necessary to get the best result in bringing out the details of the features in striking the coin. Therefore, I had Mr. Barber make me a proof of this change, and as this left so much blank space over the top we concluded that it would be better to put on the motto "In God We Trust."

This change has made a marked improvement in the appearance of the coin. I cannot send a sample, but if you feel enough interest in the matter it would be better for you to go down to Philadelphia where Mr. Barber can explain and show you what has been done.

The Numismatist carried this in June:

Information from Washington indicates that the now long anticipated Lincoln cent will not be issued before August. When examples from the supposed completed dies were submitted to President Taft, it is said that he asked for the motto IN GOD WE TRUST to be placed on the coin. We are pleased to be able to give what we believe is the first description of the coin design as now decided upon.

The obverse will have the head of Lincoln (facing right) as modeled by sculptor Brenner, with IN GOD WE TRUST above, in the field, at left, will be the word LIBERTY, at right below center, 1909. The center of the reverse in five regular lines will bear the inscription E.P.U. [E PLURIBUS UNUM] / ONE / CENT / UNITED STATES / AMERICA, with two unjoined branches surrounding.

The Dies and Coinage

In New York City Henri Weil, using the Janvier portrait reduction lathe imported from France by the Dietsch brothers, created the final hub from a brass casting of the model. The Mint eventually used this hub to make *obverse* dies. This was done after Brenner asked the Mint for permission. The fee to Weil was $100. Brenner was at the shop as Weil did the work. Henri and Felix Weil, by that time, were in business as the Medallic Art Company.

At the time the Mint had a Janvier lathe, but no one was comfortable using it extensively. The machine stood mostly idle for many years, until it was employed by assistant engraver John Sinnock in reducing the models for the 1918 Illinois Centennial commemorative half dollar. In the meantime the Mint used its Hill portrait reduction lathe for most of its work, including, as implied by correspondence, some of Brenner's proposals in model form as well as the hub for the reverse die.

The work in New York was done prior to adding the motto IN GOD WE TRUST, which was done at the Mint after the change was directed by President Taft. Brenner suggested that it be placed near the top rim on the obverse.

In May 1909 Chief Engraver Barber supervised the making of 13 pattern strikings, all of which were certified as having been destroyed after they were inspected. Director Leach commanded that no samples be sent out, not even to Brenner.

Beginning on June 10 the Philadelphia Mint struck more than 25 million cents in anticipation of the release. A news item stated that the cents would be struck in an alloy of 95 percent copper, 3 percent tin, and 2 percent zinc, a more precise definition than the usual 95 percent copper and 5 percent tin and zinc. On July 1 the Mint closed for summer vacation, with a supply of the new coins on hand.

Minting in San Francisco began in July. On the West Coast cents were not popular in general circulation, and thus the demand was anticipated to be small. Only since the year before, and not in large quantities, had this denomination been minted in San Francisco.

After the fact, on July 14, Secretary of the Treasury Franklin MacVeagh officially approved the design. Standards remained the same as for the Indian Head cent: diameter: 0.75 inch (with a tolerance of plus or minus 0.0025 inch), weight 48 grains (with a tolerance of plus or minus 2 grains), bronze alloy of 95 percent copper, and now, specifically, a slight alloy change to 3 percent tin and 2 percent zinc. The administratively approved thickness of a finished coin was 0.062 inch.[4] In practice, it varied due to the height of the rim.

IN THE POPULAR PRESS

In June and July stories about the forthcoming new coins appeared in most newspapers, some carrying several features. As an example, the *Los Angeles Times* ran a detailed account of the history of the cent and of the minting process, a small part of which is quoted here.[5] The account inaccurately credited Chief Engraver Charles E. Barber with the design and did not mention Brenner at all!

> Mr. Barber, who is probably the most highly skilled expert in the business now living, in making his design for the Lincoln penny used for modeling purposes an extremely pure quality of beeswax, with which was mixed a small proportion of resinous gum, and a little of the finest vermillion.
>
> To begin with, he drew on a big slate a circle 12 inches in diameter—the coin model being made on a large scale for convenience—and then covered this circular space with a layer of the wax mixture three-quarters of an inch in thickness. On the surface he made the design in relief, with boxwood modeling tools—the method being much the same as that employed for modeling in clay. Where Mr. Lincoln's hair and beard were to be represented he used a brush of fine bristles.
>
> When the wax model is at length finished and approved an electrotype will be made from it, and from the latter will be produced the die for the coin by a simple mechanical process. For minting each piece, of course, two dies are used—one in the "stamp," or "hammer," and the other in the anvil beneath. Every time the hammer comes down upon the anvil a metal "blank" is transformed into authorized money of the United States. . . .
>
> It costs something to mint 1,000,000 cents . . . about $1,840. But for this sum the government gets material and stamps it with designs which give it a purchasing value of $10,000—a transaction which nets a clear profit of $8,160. Excellent business, to be sure.

THE RELEASE ON AUGUST 2, 1909
GET READY, GET SET

The new cents were scheduled to be released on August 2. Stocks had been supplied to banks that had ordered them, as well as to the Treasury and its Sub-Treasury branches (including Boston, Chicago, New York City, Chicago, and St. Louis), and all was set to go. Both mints had produced what they considered would be adequate quantities.

Interest had been high in the public press, with newspaper accounts about the new design, and collectors as well as ordinary citizens looked forward to getting the coins.

On the morning of August 2 long lines of eager buyers formed at the Treasury Building in Washington and in many other places. Although early applicants often obtained cents by the hundreds, soon the quantities were rationed. The Philadelphia Mint limited the payout to just two coins, while buyers at the Sub-Treasury in New York City could get 100 coins while they lasted.

In the meantime orders placed by mail were on hand at both mints, perhaps totaling several thousand coins. Commodore W.C. Eaton, an avid specialist in mintmarks, sent for 25 pieces of the San Francisco coins and received them in due course. In San Francisco the coins available to the public on August 2 were quickly gone. Among the lucky recipients was young Gobel Ziemer, who acquired a handful, then upon leaving the Mint saw dozens of people milling around, talking about the coins, and youngsters with a supply selling them for three cents each or two for five cents.[6] Outside the Philadelphia Mint, sales at a quarter each were reported before the price settled down to a few cents.

Newsboys, always on the lookout to make a dollar here and there, were early birds in many lines at banks across the country, getting cents by the hundreds before the demand was realized. They soon sold their prize coins at a profit, especially when the tellers ran out of coins—many before closing time on the first day. Banks telegraphed requests for additional coins to the two mints but were told that supplies were exhausted for the time being.

IN THE NEWSPAPERS

During the first two weeks of August 1909, newspapers across the country told of the distribution of the new Lincoln cent. Selected accounts reflect the excitement, some mentioning the artist's V.D.B. initials.

From the *Washington Post*, August 5, 1909:

New Cents Will Stay

Not to Be Called in Because of Designer's Initials

Precedent in Other Coins: All Except the Old Penny and the Nickel Give Credit to the Artist. Treasury Besieged by Mob Clamoring for Lincoln Penny, but It is Said There Will Be Enough for All.

The demand for the new Lincoln cent almost has reached the stages of a frenzy throughout the country. In Washington it has assumed moblike proportions, because of a false report that the issue was to be recalled. Persons of all races, sexes, and ages have become seized with a wild speculative mania. The United States Treasury sustained a three-hour "run" yesterday, unprecedented for tumult, and in all 80,000 of the ornate coins were given out—$800 worth.

From all the sub-treasuries of the country requests poured in on the Philadelphia Mint for new supplies of the coinage. The San Francisco Mint is making a small quantity, about $5,000 so far, for the Pacific slope, but the rest of the country is being supplied from Philadelphia. Two hundred and sixty thousand dollars of the pennies have been coined there, and the minting will continue. There is no prospect that there will be a shortage of supply.

According to the Treasury officials, the country gets excited over a new coin nowadays in a manner that must be described as nothing short of frenzy. In anticipation of the issue of the new pennies, orders have been flooding the Mint and Treasury offices. Banks have joined in the clamorous appeal, for to them it is becoming an important business advantage to be able to supply customers with shining new money.

About 3,000 persons, boys and old men predominating, were awarded allotments yesterday. They began coming in large numbers shortly before 11:00 and kept surging and clamoring until the gates were promptly closed at 2:00.

Doorkeeper Kept Busy

"In all my years on this post I never have seen the like," complained the veteran door-keeper when 2:00 finally came and he could "shoo" the newsboys away. "I have had to stand here for hours fighting people off. I wonder what's the matter with the people, anyway? They're getting crazy. I haven't had a chance to get a bite to eat, and I am completely worn out."

The mob about the corridor and steps was at times 600 strong, desperately struggling to get to the window where the coins were issued. At first all was tumult, for it had never been dreamed that police regulation would be necessary. It was soon seen, however, that system must be established, and a line of the penny applications was formed from the window, stretching, serpent-like, up and down the long corridor and out to the steps in front of the main entrance.

Boys at once set up a thriving business. The gatekeeper and Treasury officials had to accord them the same rights as any other citizen of the land, and as they could burrow through the crowd they got to the window first. Then they went out into the mob and began selling the coins to those who saw that it was impossible for them to reach the disbursing window in reasonable time. The rates fluctuated, from 3 cents to 5 cents each, the latter being the prevailing price. About 400 persons who were turned away when the doors were closed at 2:00 afforded a harvest for the youthful speculators.

Eager for Speculation

Aged men also were numerous in the throng. One of them came rushing up, perspiring and breathless, demanding to be shown where he might get the new coins. When the inquiry was made of him why he was so frantically eager for the pennies, he replied, "Don't you know, they are going to sell for a big premium? I want to get $25 worth." He was very much crestfallen when informed that not more than 25 pennies could be had, by one applicant.

From an office with a large working force came a young man. His fellow-employees had entrusted to him to get a supply of the new pennies. His role of purchasing agent did not work, however. He got 25 pennies for himself, but the rest of the office force must go to the Treasury in person.

It was explained yesterday that the Treasury has an abundant supply of the coins, or can easily provide itself from the Philadelphia Mint. The chief difficulty it has to contend with is the unpacking of the pennies from the kegs in which they come, and the sealing up in the little envelopes, the working force not being adequate for a penny-mad populace.

There is a strong demand for coins fresh from the mint, but the erroneous report that the new pennies would be withdrawn from circulation because the initials of the designer, Victor D. Brenner, appear on them, added greatly to the excitement in Washington. Such action would at once have sent them up to a high premium among coin collectors, and it was at once made apparent that a large part of Washington's population is keenly alert to pick up easy money. Unfortunately, the highly built hopes must be dashed to the ground, for the government is going to continue minting the pennies in abundant supply.

Designers Receive Credit

Almost all the coins in circulation bear the initials of the designers, the nickel and old penny being the only exceptions. Look at the handsome throat of the goddess, where it begins to taper off on the dime, and you will use the letter B. That is the initial of Barber, the designer. The 25-cent and 50-cent pieces bear the same stamp, showing the same authorship. On the dollar the letter M is to be found—Morgan being its designer. The $5 and $2.50 pieces carry the initials of Bigelow [sic; should be Bela Lyon] Pratt down to posterity, and the $10 and $20 coins are initialed by Saint-Gaudens.

The practice of giving designers credit for their work, just as painters affix their names, began in 1849, when the letter L first appeared on a double eagle, a man named Longacre then being the chief designer for the mint. Brenner is a native of Russia. . . .

The Mint authorities do not undertake to account for the remarkable interest that is taken throughout the country for new coins. In part, it is explained by the demand of fashionable women in the large cities to be supplied with clean, undefiled coin at the banks. Many bankers, therefore, are sending to the mints for new issues, even though forced to pay the expense of expressage. The sub-treasuries in the respective cities could furnish plenty of coin without this extra cost, but when milady imperiously throws back a money piece that has gathered a trifle of filth from circulation and makes the demand, "Oh, give me some new money," her desires must be gratified, just as it is always good policy to cater to the wishes of business customers.

Procured Clean Money

A New York bank ran out of clean, untainted money recently, and it found that it could obtain a supply of the shining, spick and span variety only at the New Orleans Mint. Though the cost of this long-distance expressage was considerable, the bank unhesitatingly sent on for the money, in order to satisfy the requirements of patrons.

Connecticut is said to be the only state from which no demand for freshly made coin has come, the explanation ventured being that up there the people are eager for any kind of coin, so long as it is coin of the realm.

The Treasury has a postal card prepared for answering inquiries in numismatics, and it is set forth that "no coins of the United States have been called in." The nearest thing to this was the suspension of the Saint-Gaudens double eagles, which was found necessary because they could not be stacked.

New Yorkers Seek Coins

New York, Aug. 4. Wall Street found diversion today in the sight of a line of applicants for the new Lincoln pennies, which stretched from the door of the United States Sub-Treasury. A report that the coins might be withdrawn from circulation because of the questioned legality of the issue with the initials of the designer upon the face [sic] of the coin, drew the coin collectors to the financial district in swarms.

Not more than a dollar's worth was given each applicant, and a premium was demanded by the possessors of the bright, new 1-cent pieces, in the belief that official action might result in making the coins comparatively rare.

Assistant Treasurer Terry said today that his attention had been directed to the matter, but that he had received no instructions from Washington to discontinue the distribution of the pennies.

The *New York Times* reported on August 6, 1909, that the new cent was particularly popular with New York's Black population as a result of Lincoln's connection to the emancipation of slaves. While this clipping has been received uncritically by some numismatists since that time, the 100-word article does call its own objectiveness into question by focusing on the *superstitiousness* of Black cent enthusiasts—a common racial stereotype levied against American Black communities at the time. The article closes, "Jewelers were kept busy making charms of the coins, which many colored people believe will bring good luck," but it is worth noting that Americans were purchasing such mementos across racial lines.

From the *Boston Daily Globe*, August 13, 1909:

Dollar for a Cent

South Egremont Farmer Gets 28 Lincoln Coins

Mr. Baldwin Liked Their Looks and Urged Boys to Collect Them

Great Barrington, Aug 12—In the little hamlet of South Egremont, the new cent brought record breaking prices for Berkshire County. Ephraim Baldwin, a well-to-do farmer, was just delighted with the Lincoln cents for they looked so much like gold and he told the youngsters that he would pay them one dollar for each one they could get for him.

The little village was searched, and every farmer who had been to town for some time was ordered to look through his collection of change to see if he had one of the new coins. There were 28 in all gathered and Mr. Baldwin paid the price of $28 for them.

The other extreme was reached in Pittsfield where a business house sold two Lincoln pennies for a cent as an advertising scheme.

THE V.D.B. CONTROVERSY
AUGUST 4, 1909

The excerpt below suggests that Secretary of the Treasury Franklin MacVeagh had not seen the cent prior to its release, and was surprised that the initials were there. His decision to remove them caused further demand for the coins on August 4, when news of the change circulated in the streets. The story, like the above account of the activity in Washington, tells of the great excitement in the city when the cents were released.

From the *New York Times* August 5, 1909:

New Dies Ordered for Lincoln Cents

WASHINGTON, Aug. 5. Secretary of the Treasury MacVeagh has decided to stop the minting of the new Lincoln cents. New dies will be prepared as soon as possible, substituting for the initials of the designer the single initial

Franklin MacVeagh, circa 1909.

"B" in an obscure part of the design. None of the cents issued so far will be called in, but the minting will be stopped because a sufficient supply is on hand. The initials V.D.B. are those of the designer, V.D. Brenner of New York, and the single initial will be, it is considered, a sufficient recognition of his work.

This decision created much surprise, as the Treasury Department announced yesterday that the new coins would be in circulation for the present at least, and that the use of the initials on them was in line with a custom that had prevailed for years. This prominence, however, awakened widespread criticism, and today's action followed further consideration of the matter.

Mr. MacVeagh said today that he did not know that the initials would appear in embossed form on the pennies, and that he was surprised when he saw them. It has been customary to allow designers to cut initials into the design somewhere, but they have usually been so small as to require a magnifying glass to discover them.

Sub-Treasury is Besieged

Reserves Called to Handle Crowds

With the Lincoln cent craze two days old, the Sub-Treasury yesterday was cleaned out of its supply and had to send hurried calls to Washington for reinforcements. All day long, from the time the office opened, a constant string of men and boys filed into the building where the shiny little "V.D.B." coins were being doled out in exchange for other currency.

So great did the crush become to Pine Street, from Nassau to William Street, that the police reserves had to be called out. They were obliged eventually to establish lines at either end of the street.

They Will Drop Two Initials and Show Only "B."

Designer Brenner Displeased.

While this "run on the Treasury" was going on, the news of Secretary MacVeagh's decision to stop the minting of any more coins with the initials of the artist, Victor D. Brenner, was received. Mr. Brenner was greatly cast down when he heard of it. At

Early birds, mostly newsboys and messengers, line up at the New York Sub-Treasury on August 4, 1909, awaiting their turn to buy Lincoln cents. (*Collier's Weekly*)

his studio, at 114 Twenty-Eighth Street, he declared that a serious injustice would be done him if the Secretary's order was carried out.

"If I find that this order has gone forth," said Mr. Brenner, "I shall write to Mr. MacVeagh about it. He should consult me before doing anything of the sort. It is a courtesy that is due me. . . .

"When my design was accepted by the Treasury, my full name was upon the coin. Secretary Cortelyou, with whom I had my dealings, assured me that my name should remain upon it. Mr. Leach of the Mint at Philadelphia understood this, too. When I received the first die of the coin, my name was there; just as I had engraved it. They sent me another die later, and on this my initials appeared instead of the whole name. I thought that was an exceedingly peculiar thing for them to do, but I decided to say nothing.

"Now that they are going to cut down the initials to one, I feel that I have a right to object. Why should they deny this courtesy to me? On all the coins with the exception of the cent with the Indian head the sculptor's initials have been allowed. You will find the initials of Saint-Gaudens upon the $20 and $10 gold pieces, and those of Bela Lyon Pratt upon the $5 and $2.50 pieces. Upon the silver dollars there is the initial 'M,' and on all other silver coins the initial 'B.'

"I am delighted," Mr. Brenner added, "that so much attention has been directed to the new cents. That pleases me, but the taking of my initials off takes half the satisfaction away."

Cents Sell Three for a Nickel, but They Are Not Worth It

Not in the history of the Sub-Treasury has there been a more feverish scramble to exchange money than has been witnessed since the Mint turned out these new cents. Wall Street, as it looked on yesterday, recalled the excitement about some of the institutions which suspended payment during the panic of two years ago.

While those who sought the brilliant little coins were impelled by the expectation that the cents, if mintage was stopped, would some day be worth infinitely more than their face value, numismatic experts coldly figured that the collectors were only fooling themselves. B.L. Belden, Director of the American Numismatic Society, calculated that, possibly in 25 years each of the coins might be worth 5 cents. The danger of a shortage in supply, however, has been minimized, he said, by the fact that 2,000,000 of them have been minted, and professional collectors have gathered up all they want of them.

The Sub-Treasury officials early in the day found themselves overwhelmed by the crowds. They soon found it necessary to close up two of the windows facing the corridor and place on them placards reading: "Positively no Lincoln pennies here."

Only at one window were the coins dished out, and most of those who received them stationed themselves at street corners to sell them. Three for 5 cents was the market price. "Here you are, three Lincoln cents for a nickel" was the call heard all over town.

Banks felt the demand upon them for the "V.D.B." issue, and the drain became so great by noon that the bank supply by the Sub-Treasury was limited to $10 lots. Even then just before closing hour the last cent had been passed over the counter. Exact figures were not obtainable, but it was stated that the Sub-Treasury on Wednesday received 300,000 cents and another allotment came in early yesterday morning.

A clerk in a Pine Street banking house was arrested by one of the police reserves while standing on the steps of his office. When he was told to move on he replied he had a right there. The lieutenant at the John Street Station, which heard the complaint, promptly ordered his release and lectured the policeman for having arrested him.

A cigar firm, which has a number of branches in the city, sent batches of the new cents to its stores yesterday morning, telling the clerks to give them to customers who asked for them in change. It was not long before the news got out, and the clerks were kept hard at it issuing "V.D.B." coins until the supply was exhausted. It did not take long.

Coinage was halted after August 4, and no more cents were struck until about August 12. In fact, Treasury Secretary Franklin MacVeagh *had* seen and approved of the V.D.B. initials earlier, as revealed by the memorandum from a meeting held with Barber in Washington on the afternoon of August 6, 1909 (sent by Assistant Secretary of the Treasury C.D. Norton to MacVeagh):

> Mr. Barber . . . of the Philadelphia Mint is here, and I should be glad to have you meet him before he returns to Philadelphia, if possible.
>
> The first issue of the Lincoln coin was exactly similar to the present issue except that the Lincoln head was placed near the top of the coin, and more of the bust was showing, and there was no motto "In God We Trust." In the second and final edition, the only change was that the head was brought nearer to the center of the coin, part of the shoulders were cut off, and the motto "In God We Trust" was set above. On the reverse side there has been no change. V.D.B.'s initials were in the samples which were showed to you and the president [Taft], Mr. Barber states.[7]

BEHIND THE SCENES

The *Times* story of "widespread criticism" about the use of the V.D.B. initials may have been something related in a communication from the Treasury Department, or there may have been another source. Of the dozens of newspaper accounts I have read, none published before August 5 revealed any such dissatisfaction. Later much folklore was invented. Some stated that using the artist's initials constituted advertising for a private individual, while others contended that when the Treasury Department "discovered" Brenner was Jewish, this

The inconsistency of it all. Cartoon in *The Numismatist*, combined issue of September and October 1909.

caused the change. None of this is reflected in any contemporary Treasury records or printed accounts.

It seems that Secretary of the Treasury Franklin MacVeagh had not seen a coin prior to its release, or if he did, he did not look at it carefully. Apparently clueless that the ASG monogram of Augustus Saint-Gaudens was currently appearing even more prominently on the obverse of $20 gold coins, he sought to find out why Brenner's initials had been allowed.

A letter from Philadelphia Mint Superintendent John H. Landis to Assistant Secretary of the Treasury C.D. Norton, August 4, 1909, stated:

As requested in your communication over the telephone this morning I have investigated the matter of the designer's initials on the Lincoln cent and find they were authorized by the Director of the Mint in his letter of February 27, 1909, copy of which I enclose. The design, as completed, was approved by the Honorable Secretary of the Treasury and the Director of the Mint July 15, 1909, copy of which is also enclosed.

I would say that it was proposed that the initial of Mr. Brenner's last name only be used, but as this was the same as that on the present subsidiary silver coins designed by Mr. Barber, it was not distinctive enough and the three initials had to be used.

All the United States coins, with the exception of the eagle and the five-cent nickel piece, have the initials or monogram of the designer upon them.

The information that all current coin designs, except two, had the engraver identified seems to have made no difference to MacVeagh. He still had a problem. On August 5 Assistant Secretary of the Treasury Norton wrote to his boss:

The letter B could be engraved in the mother die easily, but the V.D.B. cannot be erased from the mother die because it is intaglio. To make a new mother die with an inconspicuous B and without the V.D.B. would take at least fourteen days.

This delay can be avoided by simply erasing the V.D.B. from the hub and having no B whatever on the coin. From the amended hub the coinage dies can be rapidly and promptly struck off within three days and the mint can continue the coinage of the pennies for which there is a great demand (and in which there is a great profit to the government).

Mr. Barber favors cutting off the initials and leaving them off entirely. This is not unusual as there are no initials on the five-cent piece and formerly there were no initials on the eagle, half eagle or quarter eagle. On the other hand it is not unusual to have an initial show on a coin. St. Gaudens' initials appear on the gold pieces, Pratt's in the half eagle and quarter eagle, etc. I have before me a French five-franc piece coined in 1870 on which Barre's full name appears. On another piece coined in 1831, the name E.A. Oudine appears. An Italian 20 centime piece bears the full name of both the engraver and designer.

There are two reasons why Mr. Barber favors erasing the initials from the new penny; first, because it involves a delay of only three days in coining operations instead of a delay of about fourteen days. Second, because if the B is placed in an inconspicuous place, he fears that it may be confused with the B which now appears on the half-dollar which was engraved by himself. He is not willing to be held personally responsible for the Lincoln penny which he has always opposed and does not regard as a successful coin.

BRENNER'S REACTION

Brenner reacted unfavorably, as the August 5 *Times* article mentioned, but he reveals an alteration even more important to him. On August 5 he wrote to Piatt Andrew, Mint director designate, the successor to Landis:

Much has been said for and against my initials on the Lincoln cent, and as the designer of same, it was natural for me to express indignation to their being taken off. In reality there is a feature in the new cent which was brought in without my knowledge, and which concerns me most. Lincoln's bust in my design was to touch the edge of the coin. In the minted cents, the bust is separated from the border. This feature makes my coin lose much of its artistic beauty.

I beg you Sir, before more cents are minted, and before new dies are made, to kindly consider, and advise.

This reflects that he had not seen an example of the new cent prior to its official release. On August 7 MacVeagh directed that the V.D.B. initials be removed from the design, with no provision for the mention of Brenner in any other way.

August 12, 1909

Mint correspondence reveals that Chief Engraver Charles E. Barber had barely tolerated the "intrusion" of outside artist Brenner (following in the much-detested footsteps of Augustus Saint-Gaudens) into the Mint domain of designing coins. As noted earlier, Barber acquiesced, so as to avoid having more criticism heaped on his head. Barber was viewed as incompetent or worse by much of the community of medal sculptors, and by most numismatists.

To reiterate, Norton's August 5 letter to MacVeagh, given above, included this poignant comment about Barber: "He is not willing to be held personally responsible for the Lincoln penny which he has always opposed and does not regard as a successful coin."

This reveals that Barber's true view of the Lincoln cent must have been well known, not just at the Mint in Philadelphia, but within the Treasury Department in Washington. It must have been an especially bitter pill when numismatic catalogs and *The Numismatist* soon praised Brenner's new cent to the skies.

In August 1909 at their annual convention, members of the ANA passed a resolution protesting the removal of the V.D.B. initials. Over the next several months articles pointed out the inconsistency of MacVeagh's decision.

Brenner sent this letter on August 12 to *The Numismatist:*

> It is mighty hard for me to express my sentiments with reference to the initials on the cent. The name of the artist on a coin is essential for the student of history as it enables him to trace environments and conditions of the time said coin was produced. Much fume has been made about my initials as a means of advertisement; such is not the case. The very talk the initials has brought out has done more good for numismatics than it could do me personally. The cent not alone represents in part my art, but it represents the type of art of our period.
>
> The conventionalizing of the sheafs of wheat was done by me with much thought and I feel that with the prescribed wording no better design could be obtained. The cent will wear out two of the last ones in time, due entirely to the hollow surface.
>
> The original design had Brenner on it, and that was changed to the initials. Of course the issue rests with the numismatic bodies, and Europe will watch the outcome with interest.

On the same day Superintendent Landis sent 100 of the new V.D.B.-less cents to Director Leach, indicating that production of the revised version was underway by that time.

In Europe the October issue of *The Numismatic Circular,* published by Spink & Son, carried a request from Horatio R. Storer, M.D., of Newport, Rhode Island, that the matter be brought up for vote at the next meeting of the British Numismatic Society. Comments from Storer were quoted:

Probably through professional jealousy, the propriety of Mr. V.D. Brenner's initials appearing upon it was challenged. . . . My own opinion is that for an artist to attach his initials or signature on coins or medals has the same advantage as for a painter to place his name upon the canvas. In both instances, the historical interest is increased, the pecuniary worth enhanced, and the standards of the ideal conception and mechanical execution materially advanced.

THE CONTINUING STORY
CHANGES THROUGH THE 1920S

Protests and high hopes were to no avail, and for the remainder of Chief Engraver Barber's life, the cents showed no recognition of Brenner. By mid-August of 1909 the mints were again shipping Lincoln cents with no initials on the reverse.

The supply was still not equal to the demand, and shortages occurred, here and there, through the end of the year. Many coins, if not most, were saved as souvenirs in early August, and again when the unsigned coins became available a year or two later. When the novelty passed, these cents were spent.

In the meantime the Mint produced Matte Proof coins especially for collectors. Mintage of these special strikings continued through 1916, and then was halted.

In 1911 the Denver Mint struck Lincoln cents for the first time, initiating what would be a litany of Philadelphia-Denver-San Francisco, or, in numismatic jargon, PDS, output for many years to come, with only a few exceptions.

The June 1911 issue of *The Numismatist* mentioned this "collector" of Lincoln cents:

> Not a little surprise was occasioned the other day by a young woman who walked into a bank at Pittsburgh, Pennsylvania, and asked for 10,000 Lincoln cents. It was Eva Tanguay, who was playing in a local theatre, and who throws away 500 cents at every performance when she sings "Oh, You Money." She brought a supply from New York, but this was exhausted. The trust company supplied her with 1,000, and then wired to the Mint for a shipment of 10,000. While scattering the money, Miss Tanguay wears a coat of mail fashioned out of cents. There are 3,500 cents on the coat, which weighs about 35 pounds.

Eva Tanguay, in her day, was the most acclaimed of all female vaudeville artists and was popularly known as the "I Don't Care Girl," this referring to her usual sign-off number, "I Don't Care."

As the years went on, the sharpness of detail in the Lincoln cent hubs deteriorated, due to wear from making master dies. In 1916 the obverse was strengthened, after which, for a time, the cents were of exquisite sharpness.

The World War interfered with the normal production of coins. Although the United States did not formally enter the conflict, industries were mobilized to furnish military goods to England and other allies under attack by the Germans. The economy expanded, and there was a call for increased quantities of all coin denominations. Cent production reached a historic high in 1916, but the record would not stand. At the Denver and San Francisco mints in particular, but also at Philadelphia, the production of cents was made more efficient by spacing the dies slightly farther apart in the press. This reduced wear and die breakage but produced coins with weak details on the higher parts. Such practice continued through the end of the 1920s and had unfortunate effects for numismatists, as outlined in chapter 11 under the descriptions of various date and mintmark issues.

Chief Engraver Charles E. Barber died on February 18, 1917, at age 77, and was succeeded in the post by George T. Morgan, who had been an assistant engraver since 1876.

In autumn 1917 there was a nationwide shortage of cents. In the December issue of *The Numismatist*, editor Frank G. Duffield commented:

> The shortage of one-cent pieces, which has become so acute during the last few weeks is an economic problem, and has little or no direct relation to numismatics, unless substitutes for the humble coin are issued. But present-day collectors, few of whom were collectors during the Civil War, are thus given an object lesson of conditions at that time, when not only the cents, but all the small silver rapidly disappeared from circulation.
>
> The causes that led to it were somewhat different from those of the present time, but the same conditions prevailed, and were even intensified—there were not enough small coins in circulation for the needs of business. The striking of Civil War tokens by the merchants, the use of postage stamps and card money, and the issue by the government of fractional currency were the remedies. With the mints now working night and day and Sundays, the demand for cents still seems to be far in excess of the supply.

By this time most of the one-cent pieces in circulation were still of the Indian Head type, including about 20 percent dated prior to 1900.[8]

In 1918, with Barber in his grave and not on hand to protest, and with Franklin MacVeagh out of office as secretary of the Treasury (he had been replaced in 1913 by William G. McAdoo), the initials of the designer, V.D.B., were restored to the cent, this time in very tiny letters on the truncation of Lincoln's shoulder. McAdoo, assisted by Mint Director F.J.H. von Engelken, made the decision. There was scarcely any interest in or note of this, and most coin collectors and dealers were unaware of the modification.

In 1918 the initials of the designer, V.D.B., were added to the edge of the shoulder of Lincoln.

The November 1918 issue of *The Numismatist* included this:

> Associated Press correspondence from Honolulu states that the war has brought the heretofore despised cent to Hawaii. A year ago there were practically no cents in the island. Local banks now estimate that between 150,000 and 200,000 of the copper coins are in circulation there.

The imposition of a luxury tax required the payment of cents in change for many transactions, thus causing a shortage of these for a time. *The Numismatist*, June 1919, noted:

> It is reported that since May 1, when the new luxury tax went into effect, there has been an extraordinary demand for cents for the purpose of making change, although not so great as the demand several months ago. Notwithstanding the immense quantities of this coin that have been minted for months past, the supply does not seem to equal the demand.

A dispatch from Washington says that the U.S. mints and sub-treasuries have been flooded with orders for millions of one-cent pieces, and these coins have been shipped to banks by the bushels. To meet the continued demand the Philadelphia and Denver mints are working almost exclusively on one-cent pieces, and an extra shift of workers has been ordered for the Philadelphia Mint. Beginning May 7th, 2,000,000 one-cent pieces were expected to be turned out daily.

More from the same publication in August:

With a coinage of more than 370,000,000 bronze cents during the calendar year 1918, and with the continued coinage at the same rate during the first six months of 1919, there is still an insistent demand for more and more of these coins. How the Government will try to meet this demand is outlined in a dispatch from San Francisco to the Chicago *Herald-Examiner*, as follows:

Uncle Sam has placed his money factories on a 24-hour basis to make money enough for people to pay the war tax. All resources are to be used in turning out copper cents at the rate of 100,000,000 a month to meet the demand of the post-war revenue tax placed on small commodities. . . .

The demand is in excess of 150,000,000 cents a month, and with the new production San Francisco, for the first time, will be shipping pennies to fill the coin demand in Chicago and the Middle West. Heretofore the Philadelphia mint has coined all the copper. Since the introduction of coppers the mints have coined 3,300,000,000, most of which has passed into the small boys' banks.

Although the shortage of cents abated, production continued apace. Odd prices in stores, such as 99¢, $1.29, and the like, plus the federal war tax, required the use of these coins to make change. On its own a single cent had little buying power except in penny arcades and machines that vended candy or gum, or told your weight.

In 1922 the economy was in a recession, and there was little demand for new cents. In this year coinage was accomplished only at the Denver Mint. *The Numismatist* of August 1922 quoted Mint Director F.E. Scobey in "Coin Crop for 1922 a Failure":

"As for cents, only $70,000 have been coined at the Denver Mint, as against $492,000 the preceding year. . . . So what's the use of making more, when about the only things you can still buy with a penny nowadays are lollypops?"

The April 1927 issue of *The Numismatist* included this:

The cent, despite the high cost of most everything, still remains a medium of exchange not to be scoffed at. One company reports that in 1927 a total of 3,500,000,000 copper cents passed through its vending machines in payment for chewing gum, candy, and many other small parcels. The Treasury Department recently estimated that the current circulation of one-cent pieces is about 4,721,287,900.

THE 1930S

By 1933 the Lincoln cent had been in circulation for 25 years, making it eligible for a design change. With the economy at a low level and the cent remaining a favorite, there was no call to do so.

PENNY ARCADES

A line of children at a penny arcade in Schenectady, New York, in 1910.

Machines in a penny arcade at a state fair in Donaldson, Louisiana.

The Mills Novelty Company, supplier of coin-operated machines, suggested that "the penny arcade is more popular than the theatre," which it may well have been. A pocket full of pennies was sure to provide several hours of fun.

Autorama One Cent Vaudeville penny arcade at Savin Rock near Hartford, Connecticut.

One Cent Vaudeville at the junction of Canal and Royal streets in the heart of New Orleans.

The "Wheels of Industry" column in *Life* magazine (the old *Life* magazine of 1883 to 1936) on April 1, 1935, included this:

> *Pennies.* One of our researchers dropped a penny in a gum machine the other day. The machine buzzed, a piece of gum came out, and with it the idea of finding out how much gum was sold in vending machines all over New York. He was told that penny machines on the 8th Avenue subway lines sell about seven million sticks of chewing gum.

In 1936 the Philadelphia Mint resumed the production of Proofs for collectors. None had been made since 1916. The new Proofs were from dies polished to a mirror-like surface.

Wartime Changes
Experiments in 1942

Following the surprise attack on Pearl Harbor by Japanese aircraft on December 7, 1941, America went to war. For more than a year our country had been helping the beleaguered countries of Europe, most particularly England, resist Hitler's Nazi forces by supplying equipment, munitions, and other goods. In 1942 the United States went into high gear. Factories that had been making automobiles, refrigerators, radios, toys, hardware, and other consumer goods converted to the production of military equipment and supplies. Demand for coinage soared, as it always does in wartime. The Philadelphia Mint continued making Proof sets for collectors, then announced that production would cease in view of more important coinage matters.

The current alloy for Lincoln cents consisted of 95 percent copper and 5 percent tin and zinc. Tin was a particularly strategic metal for industry, and supplies from certain areas of the world, such as Southeast Asia, had been cut off by the Japanese. If copper and tin could be eliminated by using other materials for the cent, the nation would benefit.

Seven manufacturing companies were commissioned to experiment with metals other than these two, as well as other durable substances. Special dies were prepared for their use, because to send regular Lincoln cent dies outside of the Mint would have been a breach of security. John R. Sinnock, chief engraver of the Mint since 1926, prepared "nonsense" dies the size of a cent. These depicted on the obverse a female head as used on two-centavo coins of Colombia (which had been struck at the Mint under contract), with LIBERTY JUSTICE and 1942. The reverse illustrated a wreath first used on a popular nineteenth-century Washington medalet by Anthony C. Paquet (Baker No. 155), now with BORN / 1732 / DIED / 1799, replaced by UNITED / STATES in two lines.

The 1942 test pieces were made in many different substances, including plastic of several colors, fiber, zinc, white metal, and even tempered glass. At the Philadelphia Mint the same dies were used to strike a few in bronze and zinc-coated steel. Among the firms involved were the Hooker Chemical Co. and Durez Plastics and Chemicals, Inc., both of North Tonawanda, New York; the Colt Patent Firearms Co. in Hartford, Connecticut; and Tennessee Eastman Corporation.

Intrigued, in 1959 I obtained from Henry Berube, a brown plastic impression of these dies and published a photo of it on the front page of *Empire Topics* No. 8. Soon information was obtained from various people, including an executive of Hooker Chemical Co.

From Lester Merkin, the New York City dealer, I bought a gem Proof striking on a thin bronze planchet. Separately, a zinc-coated steel specimen came to hand. This publicity attracted the notice of the Treasury Department, and a Secret Service agent was dispatched to seize the items. Under protest, especially after learning that the Secret Service agent knew nothing about why he was confiscating the pieces, I gave them up, but secured a promise that after study they would be returned if they were found to be "legal." In any event, the agent told me that the reasons for the seizure would be explained soon in a letter from the Treasury Department. As of the fourth edition of this book I am still awaiting word!

NEW BRASS ALLOY FOR CENTS

Because copper was needed for military uses, production of cents was curtailed dramatically in July, and in December was discontinued entirely. Likely the majority of the cents of 1942 were made of a slightly different alloy, per this in the *Numismatic Scrapbook Magazine*, February 1942 (although it is likely that planchet stock on hand was used up before the new alloy was employed):

> The tin content of the one-cent piece has been reduced. The new cent consists of 95 percent copper and 5 percent zinc; instead of 95 percent copper, 4 percent zinc, and 1 percent tin. There is still some tin left in the new alloy but it is only a trace. Mrs. Ross, Director of the Mint, states that the change does not affect materially the quality or appearance of the coin. She also announced that the Bureau of the Mint expects to save 100,000 pounds of tin a year by the change. A stock of some 40,000 pounds of tin on hand at the Mints is being turned over to defense industries. Mint chemists are making experiments in an effort to cut the copper content of the cent.
>
> This new alloy is technically *brass*, no longer bronze, since no tin is present.

THE STEEL CENTS OF 1943

In 1942 Public Law 815 made the change of material a reality, to be implemented beginning in 1943 and continuing to December 31, 1946, by which time it was anticipated that the need for the alloys of bronze would have passed. The act provided for the production of one-cent and *three-cent* pieces of new materials, to be specified by the secretary of the Treasury.

1943-S zinc-coated steel cent.

The *Annual Report of the Director of the Mint* for fiscal year 1943 (July 1, 1942 to June 30, 1943) included this:

> Production of bronze 1 cent coins was sharply curtailed beginning in July 1942 and entirely discontinued in December 1942, due to the necessity of saving copper for our war industries. During the interim extensive experimentation was made with various substitute materials in an effort to determine a non-strategic material which would be satisfactory for coinage purposes and suitable for coin-operated devices.
>
> A zinc-coated steel coin was finally devised, production of which was commenced on February 23, 1943, pursuant to the act of December 18, 1942, Public Law No. 815, Seventy-seventh Congress. The standard weight of the new zinc-coated steel 1 cent is 42.5 grains, compared with 48 grains for the bronze 1 cent coin.

Metal Savings: Based upon the production of 5 cent and 1 cent coins during the fiscal year 1942, it is estimated that over 4,900 tons of copper and 300 tons of nickel will be freed annually for use in furtherance of the war efforts, as a result of the changes in minor coinage alloys.

Secretary of the Treasury Henry Morgenthau Jr., after consulting with the chairman of the War Production Board, announced the characteristics of the new cent on December 23, 1942:

1. It shall be composed of steel with the obverse and reverse sides covered with a coating of .00025 inches of zinc.
2. It shall weigh 41.5 grains.
3. It shall have a diameter of .750 inches.
4. It shall be in the shape of a disc.
5. It shall not vary in weight by more than 3 grains; it shall not vary in diameter by more than .002 inches; and the zinc coating shall not exceed .001 inches.
6. It shall contain the same design, devices, and legends as those used since 1909.

The plan was put in place and coins were made, beginning on Lincoln's birthday, February 12, 1943, in Philadelphia (or on February 26 or 27; accounts differ); and in Denver and San Francisco in March. The steel was low-carbon, and the zinc coating was added to prevent rust. On May 13, 1943, Acting Secretary of the Treasury D.W. Bell revised the weight and increased the tolerance:

1. It shall weigh 42.4 grains.
2. It shall not vary in weight by more than 3.5 grains.

By year's end well more than a billion zinc-coated steel cents had been made:

Philadelphia Mint: 684,628,670

Denver Mint: 217,660,000

San Francisco Mint: 191,550,000

The mints encountered great difficulties with the hardness of the steel planchets. Further, when released into circulation the cents quickly became spotted and stained—in a word, *ugly.*

Complaints poured into the Treasury Department. Moreover, many customers and merchants confused them with dimes. Certain coin-operated machines would not accept them.

It was suggested that the Mint punch a hole at the center of each, to differentiate them. Secretary of the Treasury Morgenthau stated that the cents would soon become dark, after which they would not be mistaken for dimes. In fact, Assistant Director of the Mint Leland Howard revealed that the coins would be artificially darkened "if a suitable process is found."[9]

On September 28, 1943, Senator C. Douglass Buck of Delaware introduced a bill to stop the coinage of steel cents and to withdraw those that remained in circulation. This measure did not pass.

Later Years
Back to Brass

The cents of 1943 were viewed as a failure, but no plans were made to make any changes until the next year.

On December 10, 1943, Acting Secretary of the Treasury D.W. Bell announced that as of January 1, 1944, the zinc-coated steel format would be abandoned and an alloy of 95 percent copper and 5 percent zinc (this defining *brass*) would be used, although that term was not used in his statement. The weight was to be 48 grains, the same as with the earlier bronze cents and the brass cents of 1942, not to vary by more than 2 grains. The diameter of .75 inch was not to vary by more than .002 inch.

The War Production Board made available quantities of copper, including scrap ammunition shells, which were refined and had zinc added to create the correct alloy. The use of shells was announced to give a patriotic aspect to the new cents, in hopes of deterring citizens from reminding the Treasury that a year earlier, copper needed to be used for war production. "The change was made as a result of the availability of fired brass cartridge cases, to which copper is added to produce the alloy."[10] No mention was made of public complaints, which were the real reason for the change. In December 1943 *The Numismatist* added these details:

CHANGES IN SHARPNESS OF DETAILS

1909 Matte Proof cent representing the portrait details as they appeared at the inauguration of the series. (All illustrations are enlarged 1.5x)

1915 Matte Proof cent showing a slight reduction of clarity, perhaps most noticeable at the top of the head, due to hub and master die wear.

1916 Circulation-strike cent with details strengthened in the hub and master die with tiny lines. From this point, the clarity of features declined through the ensuing decades.

1955-D cent with details as they appeared at that time. Lincoln's hair has become very indistinct. Full Details coins lack the clarity of earlier issues but should be good strikes considering the portrait wear; and all lettering should be sharp.

The Mint will use as a base for the new cents small arms cartridge cases recovered by military authorities from proving grounds, firing ranges and other training areas for troops. These cases consist of 70 percent copper and 30 percent zinc, and if melted down with enough virgin copper to bring the copper content up to 85% or 90%, the alloy is adaptable to coinage.

The former bronze coin consisted of 95% copper and 5% zinc and tin. The amount of copper needed will be about half that required for the all-virgin copper alloy. The Mint project will have an important place in the salvage of war-wasted materials.

After a scathing commentary about the poor quality of steel cents was published in the *Washington Post*, December 28, 1943, Director of the Mint Nellie Tayloe Ross replied:

The Post's statement implies that it was from choice rather than necessity that the Treasury changed the content of the coin. Far from it! The fact is that the Mint has been beset by harassing mechanical difficulties in the processing of this unsuitable material. We of the Mint heartily rejoice that the War Production Board now sees its way clear to allocate the necessary amount of copper to permit a return on January 1 to the coin with which the country is familiar.

I further state for your information, and that of Post readers, that the Mint, though operating 24 hours daily, finds its facilities sorely strained to meet the current demand of business for 1-cent pieces; a fact that points to the impracticability of calling in those of zinc-coated steel, already in circulation.

RETIRING THE STEEL CENTS

After the war the Treasury Department set in place a program to remove the steel cents from circulation, simply by retiring them through member banks of the Federal Reserve System. No announcements were made, lest the public think they would become rare and valuable. Notwithstanding this, many citizens kept each steel cent that came their way. By the mid-1950s the desire for such coins passed, and most of them, typically dark and spotted, were cashed in at banks.

In the *Numismatic Scrapbook Magazine*, December 1951, it was reported that over eight years an Albany, New York, salesman had accumulated 40,000 steel cents, storing them in five one-gallon jars. In July 1952 the same publication noted that the owner of a Detroit car wash had a contest offering prizes to children who found the most steel cents. The top ten winners each turned in more than 12,000, and the champion had 35,251.

THE PASSING YEARS

The *Annual Report of the Director of the Mint* for the fiscal year ended June 30, 1945, included this:

Mr. Joseph Steel, Superintendent of Coining at the San Francisco Mint and Mr. William P. Kruse, Machinist at the same institution invented a mechanical device for attaching, at very small cost, to regular coining presses, which makes possible the striking of two coins simultaneously. The result of the use of this device has been to increase the production of coinage presses equipped with it by 90 percent so that one press almost does the work of two.

This invention has been a large factor in the enormous amount of foreign and domestic coinage produced during this fiscal year; in fact, without it the volume of production would have been impossible, since presses had been added to the limit that the crowded conditions of the three coinage mint buildings would permit. This device can be used and is being used on all coinage, domestic and foreign of the sizes of quarters or less.

Coinage of cents one at a time, from a single pair of dies turning out 120 per minute, continued for many years, although multiple-die modern presses went into use later. Today some presses have four die pairs, but these are not currently used for Lincoln cents. In recent times cents have been coined from single pairs of dies, mounted horizontally in high-speed modern presses.[11]

In 1954 it was announced that the San Francisco Mint would close the next year. This spurred a scramble by collectors and the public to put away as many S-marked cents as possible. In 1955 the final Lincoln cents, together with dimes, were made there. In the same year, at a board of governors' meeting at the annual convention of the ANA held in Omaha, Nebraska, a discussion suggesting a new reverse design was held. There was no follow through after Leland Howard, a pompous minor Treasury official, dourly stated that no one in the government had any inclination to change any coin designs at the time. Howard liked to flaunt his authority, and to him coin collectors were a nuisance, and coin dealers were worse yet. At the time I and others had to apply to him for import licenses for gold coins, which were subject to certain restrictions. Those who bowed to his projected importance received speedier handling of their requests. As you might suppose, I was in the slow lane!

The discovery of the 1955, Doubled Die Obverse, cent attracted very little notice at the time, but by 1960 it was on the "must-have" list of many collectors. More than any other, this curious error catalyzed interest in unusual die varieties, not only in the Lincoln cent series but for other denominations as well.

The 1955-S cent was a great favorite with investors, and many millions were saved. The San Francisco Mint ended coinage operations that year, ostensibly forever. Its name was changed to the San Francisco Assay Office. Surprise! In the 1960s it reopened for production.

In 1958 the curtain came down on the Lincoln cent with wheat ears on the reverse, this marking the 50th year of coinage. It was time for a change, although few knew it was coming.

CHAPTER THREE

HISTORY OF THE MEMORIAL
REVERSE CENT, 1959–2008
EVOLUTION AND DISTRIBUTION

New Reverse Design
Surprise!

Through the pages of the monthly journals—*Numismatic News, Numismatic Scrapbook Magazine*, and *The Numismatist*—collectors were kept aware when Lincoln cents caused national attention or, at other times, excitement within the hobby. This time it was different. Apparently, no one in the Treasury Department thought to give advance notice of an announcement from James Hagerty, press secretary to President Dwight D. Eisenhower:

For Sunday Morning Release, December 21, 1958

President Eisenhower approved today the recommendation of the Secretary of the Treasury Robert B. Anderson for the minting of a new reverse side of the one cent Lincoln coin as a feature of the Lincoln Sesquicentennial observance. Production of the changed coin will begin January second.

In recommending the change on the Lincoln cent, the secretary of the Treasury and Department officials have been working with the Lincoln Sesquicentennial Commission, of which Senator John Sherman Cooper of Kentucky is chairman.

The portrait of Lincoln by Victor D. Brenner on the face of the cent will remain unchanged. The new reverse will portray the Lincoln Memorial, as viewed from the front of the entrance. Above the Memorial is the motto, "E Pluribus Unum," and above this, following the curve of the border, the words, "United States of America," below the Memorial, also following the curve, will appear the denomination "One Cent." These inscriptions are required by law to appear in United States coins.

The new permanent design was done by Frank Gasparro of the Philadelphia Mint, and selected by Secretary Anderson and the Director of the Mint William H. Brett.

Both Philadelphia and Denver Mints, which will begin production of the changed coin early in January, will have a supply for distribution on Lincoln's birthday, February twelfth.

More than 25 billion Lincoln cents of the present design have been minted since its adoption in 1909.

Apparently, discussions of designs, preparation of models, and other internal Mint activities relating to the design change had been taking place over a period of at least several months, while Mint and other governmental officials left the numismatic community in the dark.

The new reverse design of 1959. (enlarged 1.5x)

THE LINCOLN MEMORIAL

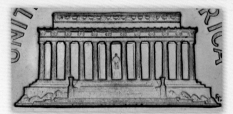

The Lincoln Memorial on the reverse of the cent of 1959. The initials of the designer, FG, are at the lower right.

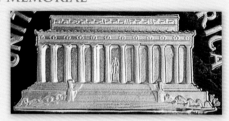

The Lincoln Memorial on the reverse of the cent of 1990. The initials of the designer, FG, are larger and certain details are sharper than on the 1959 version.

The Lincoln Memorial as shown on the back of a $5 note; design introduced in 1929.

Details of the Lincoln Memorial on the back of a $5 note. Daniel Chester French's statue of a seated Lincoln is heroic in size, but is set back sufficiently to become minor in the overall view of the building.

The Lincoln Memorial as photographed in 2014.

Detail of the upper left corner of the Lincoln Memorial showing state names on the architrave; 2004.

The Lincoln statue, by Daniel Chester French, within the Memorial.

THE NEW DESIGN

It was subsequently learned that four engravers at the Mint had been invited to submit designs appropriate to the 150th anniversary of Lincoln's birth. Suggestions were bandied about, including the favorite of the Lincoln Sesquicentennial Commission, a depiction of the president's birthplace cabin in Kentucky. Perhaps the recent (1946 to 1951) use of another cabin on the reverse of the unloved commemorative half dollars depicting Booker T. Washington turned the Mint staff away from that idea. In any event, Frank Gasparro's entry was chosen from 23 received. The selection was made by Secretary of the Treasury Robert B. Anderson and Director of the Mint William H. Brett. Models were made, as were hubs and other equipment. President Eisenhower gave his approval on December 20, and the announcement was made the next day.

At the time Gasparro was one of several assistants to Chief Engraver Gilroy Roberts, who had held the senior post since July 22, 1948. He selected the Lincoln Memorial in Washington, D.C., as his subject, although he had never personally viewed it. The motif was familiar of course, and, among other places, had appeared on the back of $5 bills since 1929. The engraver thought the combination of Lincoln's portrait with a colonnaded building on the reverse was a nice classical touch (similar in arrangement to certain ancient coins). This time there was no dispute about identifying the engraver. Gasparro's initials, FG, were placed in the field to the right of the building.

Faint artistic credit, or at least a footnote, should go to Daniel Chester French, who created the statue of Lincoln (discernible near the center of the building). The image of the same person on the obverse and reverse had few precedents in American coinage. Those were the 1900 Lafayette dollar, the 1921 Missouri commemorative half dollar (Daniel Boone on both sides), and the 1936 Elgin (Illinois) Centennial commemorative half dollar (the same pioneer on both sides).

FRANK GASPARRO

Frank Gasparro died from an injury sustained in a fall in his home on September 29, 2001, and was widely mourned. At the time he was retired as chief engraver at the Mint, having been appointed to that position on February 11, 1965, after Chief Engraver Gilroy Roberts, riding on his recent fame as the designer of the obverse of the incredibly popular 1964 Kennedy half dollar, decamped to take a lucrative position with the General Numismatics Corporation (the Franklin Mint).

More than any chief engraver up to that time, Gasparro was a warm, friendly, outgoing man who loved numismatics and enjoyed meeting members of the coin collecting community. He was ever ready to relate his experiences and to grant interviews. On several visits to the Philadelphia Mint during his tenure I received red carpet treatment—also from other Engraving Department staffers. Conversations with numismatists such as myself represented a chance for the artists to hear from the outside world of collectors, with which they were very familiar through weekly reading of *Coin World* and *Numismatic News*. Frank had his own office, adorned with various sketches and, usually, a few plaster or composition models of medals.

Self-portrait medal by the artist, 40.5 mm, silver. (Commissioned by Q. David Bowers and Raymond N. Merena in 1985)

He was born in Philadelphia on August 26, 1909, propitiously on the 100th anniversary of Lincoln's birth year. (The new Lincoln version without V.D.B. on the reverse had just reached circulation in a mad scramble a few weeks earlier, on August 2.) Frank became interested in art at an early age and studied the subject at the grade school level at the Fleisher Art Memorial. His father, a professional violinist, cautioned young Frank that except to a fortunate few, art offered little in the way of remuneration. Undaunted, Frank continued his studies with a renewed fervor. He maintained a connection with Fleisher for the rest of his life.

From 1924 through 1929 he studied under Giuseppe Donato, who had worked with Auguste Rodin, the famous French sculptor. This was one degree of separation from the experience of Lincoln cent artist Victor D. Brenner, who had actually worked under Rodin. Enrolling in the Pennsylvania Academy of Fine Arts in 1928, Gasparro studied there until 1931, later taking advantage of two European scholarships under which he studied in France, Italy, Germany, England, and Sweden. Returning to America, he became a professional sculptor. Private work was scarce during the Depression. He joined the Federal Arts Administration, one of the departments created by Franklin D. Roosevelt, as a sculptor in 1937.

In December 1942 he joined the Philadelphia Mint as an assistant engraver for $2,300 per year, where he went on to work on many projects, including medals, coins struck at the Mint for foreign nations, and more. In 1965 he was named chief engraver. Of all of his projects, his very favorite proposal was the 1977 pattern mini-dollar of the Liberty Cap design, inspired by a motif he had created for the ANA. He was very disappointed when Congress mandated that the obverse portray Susan B. Anthony. His favorite, among coins that were actually produced, was the Eisenhower dollar of 1971. He did not talk much about the Lincoln Memorial cent, except to comment that it might have been more artistic if it had been smaller, with wider margins to left and right.

He retired from the Mint on January 16, 1981, and in due course was succeeded by the highly talented Elizabeth Jones. Frank remained active in the private sector and maintained a studio in Haverford, Pennsylvania, accepting many commissions from clients. He visited the Mint frequently, and designed the reverse of the 1991 Mount Rushmore Anniversary commemorative silver dollar.

He was a fine gentleman who is fondly remembered by all who knew him.

IN THE ARTIST'S WORDS

An article by Maxwell Talleyrand, "Artists and the Lincoln Cent," in the *Numismatic Scrapbook Magazine*, quoted these comments from the artist:

> My first inspiration for the Lincoln Memorial reverse of the one-cent goes back to a number of Greek coins I observed, an ideal head on the obverse and a temple portal on the reverse with a deity in the portal. In fact, the Lincoln Memorial is Greek Classical in design, lending itself very well to a coin in linear design and detail.
>
> The conception of this design for the Lincoln reverse was an accumulation of thumbnail sketches and ideas of a Lincoln coin going back ten years while I have been associated with the Mint. I have always been a great admirer of Lincoln, having made various sculptures of him in the past.
>
> I remembered seeing several elevation plans for the Lincoln Memorial during its construction, at the Philadelphia Public Library, and I referred to these actual frontal

elevation plans for correct proportions. In these plans the figure of Lincoln is an integral part of the Memorial; on the coin you can see this seated figure in the center of the portal as it is in the building at Washington, D.C. With the aid of a strong glass full details of the figure can be seen.

I feel that the design of the Lincoln Memorial on the reverse of the one-cent is a fitting token of esteem to this great president as it shows a national shrine.

Unfortunately, during actual production of the new cent, "full details" of the Lincoln statue either were not transferred to the working dies or did not strike up properly, for even some *Proofs* do not show the features sharply.

With a nod to John R. Sinnock's design of the 1948 Franklin half dollar, on the Lincoln Memorial reverse the name of the country was given as UNITED STATES oF AMERICA, with a curious small "o," artistic license in both cases.

PRODUCTION AND DISTRIBUTION

Coinage proceeded apace at the Philadelphia and Denver mints on January 2, 1959, and on February 12, the 150th anniversary date, the cents were officially released through banks. Inevitably, as also happens with postage stamps before the authorized date, some escaped into the hands of delighted collectors.

In some areas of the country there was a rush to get the new cents, *The Numismatist* reported in March. In many other districts, however, there was less interest. The wild times of early August 1909 were not repeated. Within a short time there were more than enough coins to supply demand in most areas. In contrast, several years later in March 1964, when the first Kennedy half dollars were paid out by banks, they were rationed, and for months afterward they were very hard to obtain.

Many of the new coins were deliberately held back, which caused a shortage in some areas during the summer. On August 10, 1959, the Federal Reserve Bank of San Francisco sent a notice to bankers in its district, noting in part:

Immediately prior to February 12, 1959, a supply of the new coin was issued in observance of the Lincoln Sesquicentennial celebration. However, only a nominal supply of the new cent was issued at that time inasmuch as there was a sizeable backlog of 1958 mintage cents available for distribution. Subsequently, when the supply of 1958 cents was exhausted, the 1959 cent was issued in large quantities.

During the first half of this calendar year, the Philadelphia and Denver Mints produced over 560,000,000 pieces of the 1959 mintage as compared with 489,000,000 pieces of the 1958 mintage during the first half of the year 1958. These have been distributed in the usual manner through the Federal Reserve banks and branches to the commercial banks.

Contrary to some rumors there are no errors in the design [such as the small "o" in oF] or construction of the new 1959 Lincoln cent, and the change is a permanent one which by law must remain in effect for the next twenty-five years. No coins of the old design were manufactured after December 31, 1958.

One rumor, which was erroneous, has been prevailing to the effect that the new coin is being withdrawn from circulation, and another rumor that a limited mintage is expected is unfounded, as indicated by the high mintage in the first half of 1959.

Recently there has developed an unprecedented demand for cents which may be due in part to these distorted and erroneous statements. This large demand has over-taxed the wrapping facilities at some of our offices on occasion, making it necessary for such offices to ration the supply of wrapped cents available to the member banks. Additional supplies of cents are being received from Denver Mint at frequent intervals, but even so, the demand for cents has reduced the available supply of that coin at some offices to the point where we feel we should request our member banks to cooperate first, by not holding excessive stocks of cents in their vaults and, second, by not ordering from us in amounts beyond normal needs:

As has been the case in the past, shortages of any single denomination coin are quickly overcome, and it is expected that with the quieting of the rumors which have existed about the new cents, more than adequate stocks will be available at all our offices.

Indeed, the new cents were already plentiful in most areas of the United States, and soon they became common on the West Coast as well.

REVIEWING THE DESIGN

Reviews by numismatists were mixed. Don Taxay, in *U.S. Mint and Coinage*, 1966, suggested that the building looked like a "trolley car." One wag, picking up on a review of a building James Thurber once submitted to Harold Ross, editor of the *New Yorker*, offered the comment that the Memorial "was pretty ugly and a little big for its surroundings." The latter part of this view was, as noted, shared by Gasparro. Others liked it—as a fresh look on a design that had become timeworn.

In Philadelphia Harry J. Forman, a prominent dealer in bags and rolls of modern coins, told me that several customers had used the occasion to start "bag sets" of Lincoln cents, hoping to maintain them by date and mint as the years went on.

LATER YEARS

EXCITEMENT IN 1960

In May 1960 newspapers and television programs across America carried accounts of the fabulous, valuable, and rare 1960, Small Date, Lincoln cents. It was estimated that about two million of these were made in Philadelphia, and a much larger quantity in Denver. This electrified the numismatic community: Accounts were published of $50 face value bags (5,000 coins) selling for $12,000 or more.

The inauguration on April 21 of *Coin World* as the first weekly coin newspaper; the vast publicity and hoopla that developed in May for the 1960, Small Date, cent; and an expanded interest in coins in general served to ignite the market. Prices rose across the board, starting a boom that would last until 1964. Numismatics was a hot topic nationwide, and newcomers rushed to get in on the anticipated large profits in the offing.

Investigation revealed that the Small Date cents were made first. It was found at the Mint that the 0 in the date was too small and that the interior might break away on the die, causing the numeral to fill in (as it actually did on certain 1930-D cents). The date was made larger, but this was not announced. Soon Large Date cents replaced the Small Dates and were made in much larger quantities. At the Denver Mint the Small Date dies were used much longer before being replaced. After the varieties were publicized in May, Mint Director William H. Brett (apparently acting on general policy and without specific knowledge) stated that all were from the same master hub, and there was no difference.

Later the Mint admitted that, indeed, a change had been made. David W. Lange estimated the specific mintage of the Philadelphia Mint Small Date as 2,075,000 coins, and that all were coined in January before production was halted. No cents were struck in February, apparently as new dies were being prepared. Cents were the only denomination made at Philadelphia in March and April, these probably all being of the Large Date style, which was continued for the rest of the year.

In August Mint Director Brett, by now admitting that there were two different sizes, pooh-poohed the idea that 1960, Small Date, cents would have any lasting value, noting that by August 23 some 235,915,000 cents had been produced at the Philadelphia Mint (poignantly, without making any reference at all to the Small Date variety). Time and again, Mint officials embarrassed themselves, or at least looked naïve to outsiders, by making proclamations in defiance of what numismatic study and observance proved. That numismatists were *pests* who had to be tolerated, was the view of more than just a few at the Mint.

OTHER EVENTS

In 1962 the alloy for cents was changed from 95 percent copper, 5 percent tin and zinc (as it had been since 1947), to 95 percent copper, 5 percent zinc. Again, this can be referred to as *brass*, since *bronze* is defined as copper with tin and, sometimes, other metals added, while brass is copper and zinc. Brass had been used for most of 1942 and again in all of 1944 and 1945.

In the 1960s General Motors, working under a contract, devised what became known as the roller press. This was a huge mechanical contraption with multiple obverse and reverse dies mounted opposite each other. It was hoped that cents in particular and other coins could be made at lightning speed, which could be a godsend in the era of coin shortages. In use, many complications developed, however. After millions of dollars had been expended by both the Mint and General Motors, by mutual consent the project was abandoned as a practical failure in 1969.

In 1965 a nationwide coin shortage went into high gear with the hoarding of new Kennedy half dollars, released in March 1964 and hardly seen since, and the rising price of silver. Soon this spread to minor coins as well. Lincoln cents became scarce in circulation, and some department stores offered a premium to buy them in quantity.

Mint Director Eva Adams decided to discourage coin collectors by suspending the production of Proof sets and removing mintmarks from coins. The production of Lincoln cents for the next several years involved several atypical scenarios, including using the wrong dates, striking coins at San Francisco (where no coins had been minted since 1955), and setting up a facility in the West Point Bullion Depository. These events and their consequences for the Lincoln cent are detailed in chapter nine. In 1968 production returned to normal, mintmarks were again used at Denver and San Francisco, and the production of Proof sets resumed. For the first time the sets were made in San Francisco, and the coins each bore an S mintmark.

In 1969 the obverse of the Lincoln cent was modified, sharpening the features, which gradually had become less and less distinct since 1916, when the last enhancement was done. The hubs and master dies sustained wear as they were used to create other hubs and dies.

In 1970 Large and Small Date varieties were made, the first with the top of the 7 below the tops of 9 and 0, and the second with the tops of these numbers even with each other. This time notice was only taken among numismatists, not with national coverage in the media. The 1972 Doubled Die Obverse cent from the Philadelphia Mint created a stir with collectors and dealers. The reverse hub was modified slightly in 1973, including the enlargement of the FG initials (which were slightly reduced the following year, but still larger than before 1973) and the sharpening of some details.

In late 1973 the rising price of copper threatened to eliminate the profit the Mint made on cents. More than a million 1974-dated cents were struck in *aluminum*, in anticipation that these could be paid out, together with additional coinage in that metal, to alleviate a current shortage. Mint Director Mary Brooks passed out samples to Congressmen and others, without any request that they be returned. Excitement prevailed when numismatists learned of them, and Mrs. Brooks sought to have them returned. By that time most had disappeared. Details are given in chapter nine.

A rare 1974 aluminum Lincoln cent, one of about a dozen available to collectors. (enlarged 1.5x)

In 1975 Lincoln cents were struck at the San Francisco Mint, but without adding S mintmarks, a practice that continued for several years afterward—once again a punishment to numismatists who might have saved the coins in quantity.

A NEW COMPOSITION IN 1982

In 1982, with copper prices on the rise again, the cent composition was changed to copper-plated zinc. Released early in the year, the new coins contained 99.2 percent zinc and 0.8 percent copper as a coating. The newcomers weighed about 25 percent less than the bronze versions. All Proofs were struck in bronze this year. The copper-coated zinc blanks, supplied under contract by the Ball Corporation of Greenville, Tennessee, were soon found to be prone to blistering, flaking, and discoloration. This plagued circulation-strike cents in 1983 as well, after which the situation was mostly corrected.

David W. Lange commented:

> Coining of the zinc cents actually commenced on January 7, 1982 at the West Point Mint. (Little remembered today is that this facility produced nearly a billion cents from 1974 to 1985. As these bear no mintmarks, they are indistinguishable from those made at Philadelphia.) Soon thereafter, Philadelphia undertook this coinage, too. Denver continued to produce solely brass cents until October 21, 1982. That was conversion day—after coining brass cents in the morning, an hour's suspension was effected during which time all the remaining brass cents and planchets were cleared away, and the striking of zinc cents began. The first delivery of these from the Coining Division was made on the 27th . . . [In addition to making Proofs in brass, the] San Francisco did mint 1,587,245 zinc cents for general circulation in 1982. Like those made at West Point, however, these bear no mintmarks.[12]

THE CONTINUING STORY

In 1984 the relief of Lincoln's shoulder was reduced, solving the problem of weak striking in this area, which had been the case ever since 1909—never mind that upon inspection the shoulder now appeared *dented*.

In 1990 the S mintmark was added to the master die to make Proofs, that is, except for a few proofs. By mistake, a small number of 1990 Proof cents were made without any mintmark at all—creating a prime rarity that went on to be desired by collectors everywhere. Not many can be satisfied, since fewer than 100 examples are believed to have been identified. In 1985 the practice commenced of adding the mintmark to the master dies for Proof coins. In 1990 the method was extended to dies for circulating coins, this being applicable to products of the Denver Mint.

Other changes, some too subtle to notice except on close inspection, and tweaking of the design took place during this era. In 1997 strengthening was done to the portrait. Further "enhancements" to Lincoln's hair were made in 1999. By now the hair and beard details of Lincoln, if examined under low magnification, represented to many observers a lessening of the artistry of Brenner on the first cents of 1909.

The *2006 United States Mint Annual Report* revealed that the cost of making one-cent pieces had risen to 1.21¢ each, resulting in a loss being sustained on each one. In contrast, in fiscal year 2005 the cost had been 0.97¢ apiece. The media took notice, and in September hearings were held in Congress (see chapter one). Somehow, the lovable American "penny" survived, as we all hope it will continue to do in years to come.

CHAPTER FOUR

HISTORY OF THE BICENTENNIAL REVERSE CENT, 2009
EVOLUTION AND DISTRIBUTION

A NEW TRIBUTE TO LINCOLN ON THE CENT

Congress established the Lincoln Bicentennial Commission to plan events to honor the president on the 200th anniversary of his birth in 2009. These included a ceremony to rededicate the Lincoln Memorial in Washington, re-enactments of the Lincoln-Douglas debates, various programs, and even a ceremony to dedicate the obscure Lincoln Memorial Garden in Lincoln City, Indiana. Very few of these events attracted significant attention from the news media.

Title III of the Presidential $1 Coin Act of 2005 included this about the Lincoln cent:

SEC. 301. FINDINGS.

The Congress finds as follows:

The Bicentennial reverse designs. (enlarged 1.5x)

(1) Abraham Lincoln, the 16th president, was one of the Nation's greatest leaders, demonstrating true courage during the Civil War, one of the greatest crises in the nation's history.

(2) Born of humble roots in Hardin County (present-day LaRue County), Kentucky, on February 12, 1809, Abraham Lincoln rose to the Presidency through a combination of honesty, integrity, intelligence, and commitment to the United States.

(3) With the belief that all men are created equal, Abraham Lincoln led the effort to free all slaves in the United States.

(4) Abraham Lincoln had a generous heart, with malice toward none and with charity for all.

(5) Abraham Lincoln gave the ultimate sacrifice for the country he loved, dying from an assassin's bullet on April 15, 1865.

(6) All Americans could benefit from studying the life of Abraham Lincoln, for Lincoln's life is a model for accomplishing the "American dream" through honesty, integrity, loyalty, and a lifetime of education.

(7) The year 2009 will be the bicentennial anniversary of the birth of Abraham Lincoln.

(8) Abraham Lincoln was born in Kentucky, grew to adulthood in Indiana, achieved fame in Illinois, and led the nation in Washington, D.C.

(9) The so-called "Lincoln cent" was introduced in 1909 on the 100th anniversary of Lincoln's birth, making the obverse design the most enduring on the nation's coinage.

(10) President Theodore Roosevelt was so impressed by the talent of Victor David Brenner that the sculptor was chosen to design the likeness of President Lincoln for the coin, adapting a design from a plaque Brenner had prepared earlier.

(11) In the nearly 100 years of production of the "Lincoln cent", there have been only 2 designs on the reverse: the original, featuring 2 wheat-heads in memorial style enclosing mottoes, and the current representation of the Lincoln Memorial in Washington, D.C.

(12) On the occasion of the bicentennial of President Lincoln's birth and the 100th anniversary of the production of the Lincoln cent, it is entirely fitting to issue a series of 1-cent coins with designs on the reverse that are emblematic of the 4 major periods of President Lincoln's life.

SEC. 302. REDESIGN OF THE LINCOLN CENT FOR 2009.

(a) IN GENERAL—During the year 2009, the Secretary of the Treasury shall issue 1-cent coins in accordance with the following design specifications:

(1) OBVERSE.—The obverse of the 1-cent coin shall continue to bear the Victor David Brenner likeness of President Abraham Lincoln.

(2) REVERSE.—The reverse of the coins shall bear 4 different designs each representing a different aspect of the life of Abraham Lincoln, such as—

(A) his birth and early childhood in Kentucky;

(B) his formative years in Indiana;

(C) his professional life in Illinois; and

(D) his presidency, in Washington, D.C.

(b) ISSUANCE OF REDESIGNED LINCOLN CENTS IN 2009.—

(1) ORDER.—The 1-cent coins to which this section applies shall be issued with 1 of the 4 designs referred to in subsection (a)(2) beginning at the start of each calendar quarter of 2009.

(2) NUMBER.—The Secretary shall prescribe, on the basis of such factors as the Secretary determines to be appropriate, the number of 1-cent coins that shall be issued with each of the designs selected for each calendar quarter of 2009.

(c) DESIGN SELECTION.—The designs for the coins specified in this section shall be chosen by the Secretary—

(1) after consultation with the Abraham Lincoln Bicentennial Commission and the Commission of Fine Arts; and

(2) after review by the Citizens Coinage Advisory Committee.

SEC. 303. REDESIGN OF REVERSE OF 1-CENT COINS AFTER 2009.

The design on the reverse of the 1-cent coins issued after December 31, 2009, shall bear an image emblematic of President Lincoln's preservation of the United States of America as a single and united country.

SEC. 304. NUMISMATIC PENNIES WITH THE SAME METALLIC CONTENT AS THE 1909 PENNY.

The Secretary of the Treasury shall issue 1-cent coins in 2009 with the exact metallic content as the 1-cent coin contained in 1909 in such number as the Secretary determines to be appropriate for numismatic purposes.

SEC. 305. SENSE OF THE CONGRESS.

It is the sense of the Congress that the original Victor David Brenner design for the 1-cent coin was a dramatic departure from previous American coinage that should be reproduced, using the original form and relief of the likeness of Abraham Lincoln, on the 1-cent coins issued in 2009.

Members of the Mint's Artistic Infusion Program and staff sculptor-engravers were invited to submit designs, and 38 were received. Upon reviewing the results, several prominent numismatists expressed dissatisfaction, mainly suggesting that the somewhat complex scenes would have been better suited to coins of larger diameter. These ideas were adopted:

Birth and Early Childhood: The motif showed the log cabin in Kentucky in which Lincoln was born in 1809. It was designed by Richard Masters, an outside member of the Mint's Artistic Infusion Program, and modeled by Mint sculptor-engraver Jim Licaretz.

Formative Years: Designed and modeled by Mint sculptor-engraver Charles Vickers, this showed Lincoln, famous as a rail-splitter, setting his mallet aside to sit on a log and read a book.

Professional Life: This design shows lawyer and political debater Lincoln standing near the Illinois State Capitol in Springfield. It was designed by Joel Iskowitz of the Artistic Infusion Program and modeled by Mint sculptor-engraver Don Everhart.

Presidency: The motif is a view of the United States Capitol with the dome still under construction, as it appeared during the Civil War. Some critics have said that this had nothing in particular to do with Lincoln's life. It was designed by Artistic Infusion Program member Susan Gamble and modeled by Mint sculptor-engraver Joseph Menna.

There was, however, an unanticipated problem: The American economy was in recession in 2009, and the Treasury Department was already supplied with many cents. Accordingly, the need for new cents for circulation was much less than it had been earlier, and the mintage was much lower than collectors anticipated. Distribution of the 2009 coins was done by the Federal Reserve System, which placed the coins with banks specifically calling for them. Each of the four designs was launched in sequence, not at the same time. There was no nationwide program to promote collector interest, distribution was widely scattered, and the cents were not easily found in circulation the year of release. Anyone looking to build a set from circulating change was likely to be disappointed. In terms of coin programs, this became a non-event, and a great opportunity to popularize coin collecting was missed.

Circulation strikes were made in copper-plated zinc, the composition in use since 1982. The overall quality of sharpness and strike was excellent, with most coins grading well above MS-65. For the numismatic trade a bronze alloy of 95 percent copper and 5 percent tin and zinc was used—this being the alloy first used for cents with the Indian Head design in 1864 and continued through many of the early Lincoln cents. These had a special satin finish and were sold in sets.

CHAPTER FIVE

HISTORY OF THE SHIELD REVERSE CENT, 2010 TO DATE
EVOLUTION AND DISTRIBUTION

ANOTHER REVERSE

It was thought by many that the Lincoln Memorial reverse would be used again beginning in 2010. The Treasury Department decided differently and solicited new design ideas. The law authorizing the Bicentennial cents also stated the following:

> The design on the reverse of the 1-cent coins issued after December 31, 2009, shall bear an image emblematic of President Lincoln's preservation of the United States of America as a single and united country.

A shield motif designed by Lyndall Bass, a member of the Artistic Infusion Program, was selected as the new design. Modeling was done by Mint sculptor-engraver Joseph Menna. It was revealed November 12, 2009, during the launch ceremony for the 2009 Presidency reverse cent held at the United States Capitol.

Paul Gilkes reported on the launch of this design in *Coin World*, March 1, 2010:

> More than 1,000 collectors and members of the general public braved sub-freezing temperatures Feb. 11 in Springfield, Ill., for the opportunity to obtain rolls of 2010 Lincoln, Union Shield cents during official release ceremonies of the coin at the Abraham Lincoln Presidential Museum. It took less than three hours following the festivities for employees of U.S, Bank's Adam Street branch to distribute 1 million of the new coins wrapped in 50-coin rolls to attendees, who began waiting in line outside as much as five hours before the 9:30 a.m. program began inside the museum. U.S. Mint Director Edmund C. Moy was joined by Jan Grimes, acting executive director of the Abraham Lincoln Presidential Library and Museum, and ALPLM's curator, James Cornelius, in the coin launch ceremonies. . . .

The design, which was quite similar to various reverses used on privately-issued Civil War tokens in the early 1860s, elicited many complaints. However, after due consideration most numismatists came to like it as an improvement on the Lincoln Memorial style.

The features of the Lincoln portrait on the obverse were modified slightly to conform with the details in the original Brenner design of 1909.

MODERN TECHNOLOGY

By this time and for some years the mints had been using ultra–high speed Schuler presses for coining circulation strikes of various denominations. Arranged in banks of machines, the presses struck coins at a speed of more than a dozen a second, faster than the eye can see.

The new reverse design of 2010. (enlarged 1.5x)

The output of each was carried on a conveyor to a line containing many trays to receive the output of multiple presses, after which they were conveyed to storage in huge Kevlar bags for shipment to the Federal Reserve System. These images were taken at the Denver Mint in 2015 on a trip, following special arrangements made by Tom Jurkowsky of the U.S. Mint for the author of this book and some others.

A side view of one of a row of Schuler presses minting Lincoln cents.

The interior of the SP-61 (Schuler Press no. 61) coining press.

The back end of the Schuler press, where struck coins emerge. The small red container at the right is marked "Condemn," where misstruck and other unsatisfactory (except to numismatists) coins are tossed, to be destroyed.

Cents on a small conveyor emerging from the coining press.

Lincoln cents collecting in a small bin that was later emptied onto another conveyor.

2015-D cents hot (literally) off the press.

A conveyor system with bins containing thousands of 2015-D cents, the output from multiple presses.

CHAPTER SIX

MINTS AND THE
MINTING PROCESS
CIRCULATION STRIKES

MAKING OBVERSE AND REVERSE DIES
CREATING WORKING DIES

Lincoln cents are struck by a pair of dies fitted to one of three types of coining presses, discussed below. At the Mint presses are arranged in rows in a large room. Generally, at any given time multiple presses will be devoted to striking a single denomination, such as cents, then some days or weeks later changed to strike nickels or some other coin. By concentrating on one denomination at a time, the handling of planchets and the processing of coins after they are struck is simplified.

By the time the Lincoln cent was introduced in 1909, the dates on newly created coin series such as the gold coins of 1907 (designed by Augustus Saint-Gaudens) and 1908 (Bela Lyon Pratt) were added early in the process of die manufacturing, and the master die, complete with date, stamped it into the working die via working hubs. Accordingly, among Lincoln cents there are no differences in date placement or numeral size or spacing among a given year in this series, unless hubs and master dies were changed, as was the case in 1960 and again in 1970 when Large Date and Small Date varieties were created. Among cents dated 1944, as an example, hundreds of obverse dies, each with the date in precisely the same position, were used at the Philadelphia, Denver, and San Francisco mints.

THE DIE-MAKING PROCESS

For inclusion in the *Report of the Director of the Mint* for the fiscal year 1896, Chief Engraver Charles E. Barber contributed an overview of the die-making process in use at that time. During the era of Lincoln cents most of the steps remained about the same:

> Coinage and medal dies are prepared in the following manner: When a coin or a medal is required, the first thing to be obtained is the design. . . . After the design for the coin or medal is settled upon, the engraver prepares a model in wax, or any material he may prefer to use, of the design selected, or as much of it as he may think most desirable for the production of the medal or coin. The model is generally made three, four, or five times as large as the finished work is intended to be. When the model is finished an electrotype is made. This electrotype when sufficiently strong is prepared for the reducing lathe, and a reduced copy is made the size required for the coin or medal.
>
> The reducing lathe is a machine, working somewhat upon the principle of the pantograph, only in this case the one point traces or follows the form of the model, while another and much smaller point made in the form of a drill cuts away the material, and thus produces a reduction of the model. This process of reducing the design from the model is necessarily a very slow operation, as accuracy of the reduction depends entirely upon the slow motion of the machine and delicate handling of the operator. While it is not in the power of the operator or machine to improve the

model, it is quite an easy matter, if not properly managed, for the machine to distort or the operator to lose the delicacy of the model. The reducing machine can work either from a model in relief or intaglio, though the relief is more often used and is considered the better way.

In describing this process, I have said the engraver makes a model of the design he wishes to produce, or as much as he thinks desirable. To explain more fully, I would say some designs or parts of a design are not calculated for reducing by machine, and therefore the engraver only reduces so much of the design as he knows from experience will give the desired effect; the rest he cuts in . . . with gravers and chisels. When the reduction is made by the machine from the model it is then taken by the engraver and worked over and finished in all the detail and delicate parts, as the machine does not produce an entirely finished work. When finished by the engraver it is hardened and tempered. If the reduction has been made intaglio, when hardened it is completed and is called a die, and coins or medals can be struck from it; but if in relief, it is called a hub, and the process of making a die from it commences, which is done as follows:

The hub or relief being made hard, a piece of steel is prepared in the following manner to receive the impression of the hard hub: Take a block of steel sufficiently large to make your die, and carefully anneal it until it is quite soft. This is done by heating the steel to a bright red and allowing it to cool very gradually, being careful to exclude the air by packing the steel in carbon. The steel being soft, turn off the surface of the block of steel and smooth it before you commence the process called hubbing, which is as follows: Place the block of soft steel under the plunger of a strong screw press; then put the hard relief or hub on top of the soft steel, and bring down your plunger with a good sharp blow. This will give you an impression upon the soft steel. In order to make a proper impression, the process of annealing the steel and the one just described, called hubbing, must be repeated many times, until you have a perfect impression of the hub. This being obtained, you have a die which only requires being hardened and tempered to be ready for use. This process of making dies is followed for coinage and medal dies of the most artistic character.

To harden the steel dies, they are packed in cast-iron boxes filled with carbon to exclude the air, and when heated to a bright red are cooled suddenly with water. As this would leave them too hard, and liable to crack and break on the edges, the temper is what is technically called drawn, which is done by gently heating until you notice a color appearing upon the surface of the steel. A light straw color is a good color for cutting tools, but dies are generally brought to a deeper color, and in some cases to a blue.

As to the hardening of working dies, it was the practice for much of the twentieth century to ship dies unhardened from the Philadelphia Mint to the branches in Denver and San Francisco. This was to make them unsatisfactory for use, in the event that they were stolen. The branch mints used their own shops for the hardening and finishing of the dies, resulting in some differences in appearance among coins of a given year from the three mints.

A pair of dies used to strike 1999-D Lincoln cents. The face of each die was ground off before the Mint sold these as scrap.

CHANGES

Occasionally during the span of the Lincoln cent from 1909 to date, slight changes and adjustments have been made in the design and the relief (degree of elevation of the features). These include strengthening the obverse details in 1916 and making various adjustments to both the obverse and the reverse details in the later Memorial Reverse series (such modifications beginning in a significant way in 1969).

While obverse dies were always discarded soon after the end of a calendar year when their dates became obsolete, reverse dies were kept in service until they wore out. Records show that in some fiscal years obverses were more durable than reverses, and in other years the opposite was true. Mint records generally show the number of dies made, not the number specifically used. In modern times the die faces have been chromium plated to reduce wear and to extend life. In fiscal year 1920 the average die was used to strike 450,000 coins, or more than double the 183,751 obverse and 144,314 reverse impressions of 1909. In 1927 chrome-plating equipment was installed at the Philadelphia Mint. Dies so plated lasted much longer, sometimes striking in the range of a million coins. These are averages, and some dies broke after only a few tens of thousands of coins were made, while others lasted longer.

MINTMARKS

Mintmarks were first employed on cents in 1908 in San Francisco, at which time the Indian Head cent was the standard. S mintmarks were punched into the 1909 Indian Head cent reverse dies as well. When Lincoln cents made their debut in 1909, those made in San Francisco bore a small S mintmark on the obverse under the date. In 1911 the Denver Mint made its first cents, each with a D mintmark.

D (Denver Mint) and S (San Francisco Mint) mintmarks on Lincoln cents. Mintmarks were punched into working dies by hand from 1909 until 1990, after which they were included in master dies.

Although the date was included in the master die for these later series, mintmarks were separately punched by hand into each working die. The mintmarks thus varied slightly in their appearance. Variations include doubling of a mintmark if it was punched twice, slightly off register, or in a few instances, if the letter was first punched at a tilt and then corrected. Some were even punched horizontally by mistake, as with the 1909-S, S Over Horizontal S. Two overmintmarks, the 1944-D, D Over S, and the 1946-S, S Over D, represent dies originally destined for one mint that were overpunched with a letter signifying another. Actually, two different dies were made of the 1944-D, D Over S, with one showing the undermintmark more clearly.

Beginning in 1985, by which time *Proof* coins had been made in San Francisco since 1968 (in contrast to their being made in Philadelphia in most earlier years), the S mintmark was included in the master die. To err is human, it is said, and in 1990, sure enough, one Proof die had a mistake—omitting the mintmark! Apparently, a circulation-strike die was used and given a mirror finish. Beginning in 1990 the D mintmark was added this way for circulation-strike dies.

All Lincoln cent dies were made at the Philadelphia Mint, until recent years when a supplementary facility was set up in Denver (by which time mintmarks were in the master dies). During the coin shortage of 1965 to 1967 mintmarks were not placed on cents struck at branch mints. Beginning in 1975 circulation strikes (but not Proofs) made at San Francisco lacked a mintmark. These were acts of vengeance against the numismatic community, which was falsely blamed for creating nationwide coin shortages. Over a long period of time many Mint directors, who were political appointees and did not know an obverse from a

Details of a Proof 1968-S cent and a Proof 1990 cent lacking the S mintmark. On the 1990 coin the date is higher in the field and more widely separated from the border.

reverse before they took office, viewed coin collectors as a first-class nuisance to the normal "factory" operations of the Mint. In recent times certain (but not all) Mint directors have been very warm to numismatists, helping with research and inquiries, meeting and greeting collectors at coin shows, and the like.

As D and S mintmarks are now included in the master dies that are used to make multiple working dies, doubled, tilted, and other position variations of mintmarks within a given year no longer occur.

THE COINING PROCESS
PREPARING THE PLANCHET

Lincoln cents as well as other coins are struck on planchets—circular disks the approximate diameter of the finished coin.[14] For cents, blanks were cut out of long strips of bronze alloy, much as a cookie cutter would punch out pieces of dough. Sometimes this was done at the Mint, first by using ingots to create narrow strips and punching out one disk at a time, later by using gang punches making a tremendous noise and stamping out multiple blanks in one blow. At other times it was the practice for many years to simply order finished blanks from a supplier, such as the Scovill Manufacturing Company of Waterbury, Connecticut, removing the planchet cutting process from Mint supervision. Each blank for a bronze cent had to be of a specified diameter and with a weight of 48 grains, plus or minus a small tolerance.

The *Annual Report of the Director of the Mint*, 1913, told of making ingots and planchets at the Mint, beginning with a description of a strip-rolling mill:

Two large 16-inch rolls are breaking down and finishing bronze and nickel. The ingots used are 23 inches long, 4-1/8 inches wide, and three-fourths of an inch thick. A copper ingot will produce 2,200 blanks and the nickel ingots about 1,500 blanks. The two cutting presses, each running 170 revolutions per minute, are used in cutting bronze and nickel blanks. When

Punch presses for cutting blank planchets from metal strips at the Philadelphia Mint in the early twentieth century.

cutting these blanks six pieces of the former and five of the latter are punched at each stroke, making respectively 1,020 and 850 pieces per minute.

Up to date cleaning and annealing machinery consisting of rotary annealing furnaces, tumbling barrels, and centrifugal dryers prepare[s] the blanks for stamping. In addition to the rotary annealing furnaces two strip annealing furnaces have been added. Gas is used to operate these furnaces. The object of this plant is to keep the workings of the base metal isolated as much as possible from those of the precious metals and also to turn out the minor coin more rapidly and at less expense. Owing to the increasing demand for minor coin we will be compelled to enlarge this plant in the near future by installing two additional rolls and more cutting presses.

After the circular blank is ready it is put into a milling or upsetting machine and run at high speed between a roller and an edge, in an area in which the diameter decreases slightly, forcing the metal up on ridges on both sides of the coin. This process creates what is called a *planchet*. The resultant planchet is blank on both sides but has a raised rim.

Although procedures have varied over time, it was customary to anneal the planchets by heating followed by slow cooling, to soften the metal. If this process was not done correctly, a planchet would be too hard, and coins made from it would not strike up completely in the deeper recesses of the die. After annealing, planchets were cleaned in a soapy or acidic mixture (diluted sulfuric acid), rinsed, and then dried by tumbling in sawdust or by exposure to currents of air. At the end of this the dry planchets were ready for coining. Tumbling around in a cleaning machine imparted countless nicks and marks to both sides. It was hoped, at least by numismatists, that during the squeezing and compression of the planchet in the coining press, these would be obliterated. In practice at many times in the past, as discussed elsewhere in this book, the dies did not come completely together in the coining press, and the deepest areas of the dies, representing the highest areas on the finished coins, were not completely struck—resulting in marks from the original planchets still being visible. Bill Fivaz calls these *planchet abrasions*, which seems fitting enough. This same feature could be caused by planchets that were too hard, from improper annealing. On Lincoln cents made before the 1990s this is particularly noticeable on Lincoln's shoulder if a low-power magnifying glass is used.

Lincoln cents minted since 1982 are composed of 99.2 percent zinc and 0.8 percent copper, this constituting the core. The core is separately plated with copper, to create a copper-plated zinc coin. To create such planchets, the core metal is mixed in crucibles in a furnace, then poured into heavy ingots. These are run through a succession of rollers in a roller or strip mill, with the rollers being more closely spaced with each pass. Strips are produced, which become successively thinner and larger in area. As an intermediate process, strips, rolled into coils for convenience in handling, are heated in a furnace, then cooled slowly—the annealing process that softens the metal—after which they are further reduced by a roller mill.

Adjusted to the proper thickness, the strips are trimmed, then run through a blanking press—the same process described earlier for bronze cents. This consists of gang punches, very noisy in their operation, that punch round disks for coinage, the first step in creating *planchets*. The remaining perforated strip, called *scissel*, is melted and recycled. The disks are milled to give them raised rims. Then they are cleaned, after which they are immersed in a plating bath to give them a copper coating. The planchets for copper-coated zinc cents are not annealed. The above process for copper-plated zinc cents could be done at a mint, but it has been the practice in recent times to obtain finished planchets from outside contractors. Quality can vary, and in 1982 and 1983 there were severe problems from blistering and flaking of planchets, also discoloring.

A finished Lincoln cent measures 3/4 inch, or 19.1 mm, this being precisely the same diameter as found on the sparkling new Flying Eagle cents first released to the public on that long-ago day of May 25, 1857.

STRIKING THE CENTS

The working dies are fitted to a coining press powered by an electric motor. Although much new equipment was installed in the Philadelphia Mint when it relocated to new quarters in autumn 1901, some old-style presses remained in use for decades. Equipment at the Denver and San Francisco mints is a mixture of old and new. The typical old-style press is vertical with more or less an elliptical frame, with an area at the center to hold the dies. The hammer and anvil dies, top and bottom, can be removed at will when they became worn or damaged. The top or hammer die is fixed to a matrix that moves up and down as the flywheel on the press rotates and actuates a cam. This general type is called a "knuckle press." Such machines typically struck 120 cents per minute.

Bliss-brand presses were in wide use at the Philadelphia and Denver mints until the year 2000, when they were replaced with horizontal-stroke Schuler-brand presses, using single die pairs and a simplified gravity feed for planchets. The mechanisms are simpler than on vertical presses. The Schuler presses turn out about 720 coins per minute. Unlike earlier machines, the new ones have the dies and attendant mechanisms enclosed and not visible from the outside. Bliss presses, using up to four die pairs in vertical operation, were kept on hand to be used as backup when the Schuler presses were down, or for special projects. The San Francisco and West Point Mints used Bliss presses for specialty coinage where high-speed production was not as important.[15]

Modern Schuler presses are higher speed and sometimes have grouped gang dies, striking as many as four coins in a single blow, spewing out about 600 cents per minute. Both old and new presses are very noisy, necessitating the wearing of ear protection when operators spend extended time near them.

In the early days of the Lincoln cent planchets were fed by hand by an attendant into a tall tube mounted, not far from the dies, at the left front of the press. Each planchet would be grasped by mechanical fingers, taken to position and dropped into the collar mounted immediately above the anvil die. The fingers then retracted automatically, the hammer die came down and stamped the coin, which was then forced from the collar,

The Coining Room at the Philadelphia Mint in the era when Lincoln cents were first made.

after which mechanical fingers ejected the finished product. At that point each coin went down a slide at the back of the press, which fed into a little hopper or bin. More automated processes were developed later for the planchet-feeding and striking processes.

On presses using multiple die pairs, a dial feeder has openings containing planchets, which are struck as that part of the plate is between the dies. The same mechanism receives the finished coins and ejects them. This arrangement is different from the mechanical fingers and other mechanisms used on older machines. Currently, high-speed Schuler presses are used to coin Lincoln cents with single die pairs mounted horizontally, as described above. Technology continues to evolve: often new processes are interwoven with old, and no single description of the minting process fits all situations.

In recent times a "riddler" machine, essentially a sieve with openings slightly larger than a cent, has been used to check the finished coins. Oversized pieces will not fall through. Thus are caught many double-struck coins and certain other types of mint errors.

An operator feeds blank planchets into a hopper on the front of a knuckle-action press. A tub of blanks is on a pedestal in front. As coins are minted, they are ejected out of the back of the press and fall down into a container (not visible).

WHY SHARPLY STRUCK LINCOLN CENTS ARE SCARCE

It was and still is the intention of the mints to produce the largest number of one-cent pieces in the shortest amount of time and with the least amount of effort. In fact, in the era in which silver and gold coins were being struck, minor coins were held in generally low regard at the mints, and less attention was paid to them than to denominations struck in precious metals. There was no consideration whatsoever to pleasing numismatists who might later collect such coins.

The sharpness of a Lincoln cent depends on the technician's adjustment of the press as well as on the weight of the planchet and how it was prepared. If the dies were fit precisely the right distance apart, and a planchet was of precisely the correct weight and had been annealed to the proper softness, a coin with every detail needle sharp was the result. I like to call this a coin with Full Details (FD).

While the above represents an ideal situation, problems will occur if an overweight planchet is introduced. Bearing in mind that a weight latitude of 2 grains is permitted by law, and while the statutory weight is 48 grains, a planchet can weigh from 46 to 50 grains and still be legal. Planchets are not weighed individually but are processed in bulk and the weight averaged. Accordingly, some planchets can be outside the limits just mentioned. If a too-heavy planchet is fed into the press, the metal will have nowhere to go inside the squeezing dies and will be forced out at the edge, creating a wire rim (called a "fin" in mint jargon) and wearing the die in the process—or, worse, cracking the die. This did not happen very often with Lincoln cents, the lowest-value coin of the realm, because little effort was made to adjust the presses to make sharp coins. Further and as noted, a planchet that was improperly annealed (and thus was too hard) would not strike up properly.

The obvious answer is to space the dies slightly farther apart than optimum, so that slightly overweight planchets can be accommodated and coined at high speed without attention. Under this arrangement, only overweight planchets will produce perfectly struck coins (assuming the planchets have been annealed properly and are soft), while correct-weight and underweight planchets will create coins with areas of weakness. This is precisely what has happened since the beginning of the series—not often at first, but becoming the rule about 1916, with the Denver and San Francisco mints being the most egregious offenders in this regard.

Wide spacing of dies causes details on the high parts of the coin to be weak or missing. Sometimes, this has been incorrectly attributed to die wear. Deep parts in the die, however, were the last to wear. Worn dies are best identified by grainy fields with ridges and by weakness most evident on areas nearest the rims.

As also noted above, extreme hardness of the planchets if improperly annealed, poor metal flow, and design peculiarities contribute to weakness in some cases. In addition, work hardening, or the hardening of the planchet/coin during the striking process, seems to have varied over the years, depending on the planchet stock and, probably, the annealing.[16] Mechanical "play," or looseness of a die in its chuck, especially the lower or anvil die, may have played a part in certain instances.[17] Moreover, the alloy of cents was apt to vary, as were processes such as cleaning with acid, rinsing, and drying. Some years and mints in the series seem to have coins that toned quickly—1926-S being an example. On the other hand, Mint State coins of 1921 usually kept much of their original brilliance. Peculiarities such as these are discussed under the individual date and mintmark listings in chapter 11.

WHY QUALITY IS ELUSIVE

With this information, you now know that whether coins with Full Details exist for a given variety depends on several factors. First is the planchet itself, its weight and hardness—the latter influenced by the annealing process. Second, the spacing of the dies plays a part. Numismatists have found that in certain runs, such as for nearly (but not completely) all 1918-D, 1925-D, and 1925-S cents, this being but a short list, the dies were spaced significantly too far apart, and the resulting coins were very poorly struck. Improper annealing may have been a factor as well. Worn dies produce coins with mushy or indistinct features, most noticeable at the periphery, in addition to having grainy and otherwise unsatisfactory fields. In the numismatic marketplace you might examine 10, 20, or even more of these varieties before finding a Full Details coin.

Adding insult to injury, coins with shallow or light details often have areas of the original planchet that are not flattened out, and nicks, scratches, and other marks on the planchet remain visible on the completed coins; the key spot for this being on Lincoln's shoulder, as noted earlier, but sometimes it is seen on the head and other areas. Reading this book may spoil you: It is likely that you will never look at a Lincoln cent casually again!

Although the process has been changed in recent years, for most of the production era of Lincoln cents, after the little bin or hopper (called a *trap box*) receiving newly minted cents at the back of the coining press was filled, it was inspected by an attendant. If the coins were found to be satisfactory, they were dumped into a larger container with other cents. Afterward the coins, still mixed together, were run through a mechanical counting machine, then put into cloth bags and tossed into a vault, to be shipped away to the various Federal Reserve Banks (this beginning after the implementation of that system in 1913). In the early days some cents were bagged and then packed into wooden kegs. These were used for all denominations of coins shipped in quantity to a distant destination. Kegs were easy to roll around, without special equipment, whereas rectangular wooden crates would have been much more difficult to move.

As mentioned, in modern times a riddler machine has been added to the process, before counting, to prevent certain mint errors escaping. Such machines add more abrasions. At no time, past or present, has any care been taken to prevent nicks, marks, or other damage, including during the bagging, shipping, and delivery processes.

The result of this is that very few production-run Lincoln cents from the early years, prior to 1934, were ever in any high grades such as MS-66 or higher after such handling. A banker viewing a bag of cents in, say, 1924, might find few coins any nicer than MS-64 or so. If it is a consolation, heavier coins such as nickels, quarters, and higher denominations, including gold in the years before 1934, show even more marks.

When the Treasury Department sold coins to collectors, including Mint sets of circulation strikes in the 1940s, often the coins were nicked and marked. Seemingly, little or no effort was made to select "nice" ones. Commemorative coins were often handled in the same manner. The typical Carver-Washington half dollar of 1951 to 1954 is peppered with tiny marks—some from the original planchet, which was not struck up properly.

A quick glance at a modern presidential dollar (of the program launched in 2007) will show the typical coin has many small marks and scuffs. I once examined a roll of 25 John Adams dollars and found most of them would grade MS-63 or MS-64, with dozens of tiny marks, plus some with sizeable nicks or cuts. With cents, not only are marks fewer, but because hundreds of millions or even billions are coined, by the luck of the draw a bag of them will usually contain some in ultra-gem preservation.

MINTS AND THE DISTRIBUTION OF LINCOLN CENTS
QUANTITIES MINTED

Until recent years Lincoln cents cost less than a cent to produce. As such, they were once an important source of profit to the Mint, as were nickel five-cent coins. The profit, called *seignorage* (pronounced *senior-idge*) contributed heavily to the operating surplus of the various mints and, accordingly, the production of such pieces was highly encouraged. This was quite unlike the situation for silver and gold coins in the early days of the Mint, when gold was of full intrinsic value, and for a long time silver was likewise, resulting in little if any margin translating to the bottom line. From the 1790s until well into the nineteenth century much of the Mint's operating profit was derived from minting copper cents (and half cents too, from 1793 to 1857).

The aspect of seignorage profits has been largely overlooked in numismatic accounts, but in the early nineteenth century it was a major factor affecting the mintage quantities of minor coins. During the early era of the Lincoln cent, although a nice profit was derived from making them, the mintages depended upon the call for such coins in commerce. The recession of 1921 and 1922 and the Depression of the early 1930s each resulted in lower demand for cents and lower mintage quantities for current coins.[18]

By the time the Lincoln cent made its debut in 1909, "pennies" were highly important in commerce—in vending machines and elsewhere. Within a few years the implementation of a federal war tax, plus the increased popularity of odd prices requiring cents in change, such as 39¢, $1.29, and the like for merchandise, increased the demand. Beginning in the 1930s various state sales taxes and, in more recent times, regional or local taxes, have called for cents to make change in transactions. This is very puzzling to economists, university professors, and others, who consider the "penny" to be obsolete and of no use in commerce.

THE PHILADELPHIA MINT

By the time Lincoln cents were first made in 1909, the Philadelphia Mint was located in the third building to bear that name, first occupied in autumn 1901. Much new apparatus had been installed, and operations, some of which had been conducted by steam power until the early 1890s, were completely electrified. This structure, known by

The third Philadelphia Mint as illustrated in the era in which the Lincoln cent was first made there.

historians as the third Philadelphia Mint, remained in use until the fourth Philadelphia Mint was inaugurated in 1967.

During these transitions the Philadelphia Mint remained the center for creating designs and making dies. Later, in the 1990s, some die making was assigned to the Denver Mint. The Engraving Department was and is headquartered in Philadelphia. The Mint Collection, also called the Mint Cabinet, was on view at the Philadelphia Mint until the spring of 1923, when it was transferred to the "Castle" building of the Smithsonian Institution. Today known as the National Numismatic Collection, it is in the Museum of American History building. An expert curatorial staff cares for the treasures, and the facility is a magnet for researchers who are cordially welcomed by, perhaps, the finest staff in the department's history.

THE DENVER MINT

The present Denver Mint was constructed beginning in 1904 and struck its first coins in 1906, these being in silver and gold. It was not until 1911 that the first Lincoln cents were made there. The facility was enlarged in 1937. Today the same structure is in use, although with many improvements in technology. In recent years limited die-making operations have been set up there, but not involving the design process.

Throughout the annals of the Lincoln cent the Denver Mint earned the lowest marks for the quality of its coins for selected periods, primarily from 1916 through the late 1920s. Today as a class the Denver Mint coins present the greatest numismatic challenge for anyone seeking coins with Full Details.

The Denver Mint as it appeared in the early twentieth century. Lincoln cents were first struck there in 1911.

THE SAN FRANCISCO MINT

The San Francisco Mint struck its first Lincoln cents in July 1909, after which it produced them nearly continuously through 1955, but often in lower numbers than did the other two mints. On the West Coast neither cents nor nickels were in wide use at the time. In fact, no nickels were struck at San Francisco until 1912, and then

The San Francisco Mint as it appeared in the early twentieth century when Lincoln cents were first struck there. Nicknamed the "Granite Lady," the building was opened for business in 1874 and remained in use until 1937.

only in small numbers. This gradually changed, and by the 1920s cents were everywhere in the West. In recent decades mintmarked cents struck at the San Francisco Mint have been limited to Proofs.

In 1909 the facilities were located in the second building to bear that name, which had gone into operation in 1874, an impressive structure nicknamed the "Granite Lady." During the April 1906 earthquake and fire the structure was spared by the actions of Superintendent Frank Leach and the workers, who drew water from the Mint's own well. Afterward it stood alone in its dis-trict, surrounded by rubble. (Later Leach went to Washington to become director of the Mint, in which position he supervised the creation and early production of the Lincoln cent as outlined in chapter two.) In 1937, on Duboce Street in the same city, a modern fortress-like structure, which looks more like a penitentiary than a center of coining and numismatic activity, was occupied.

The new San Francisco Mint on Duboce Street went into production in 1937 and is the facility used today. Among other coins, Proof sets have been struck there since 1968. (*Modern Lithographers*)

In 1955 the Treasury Department announced that the San Francisco Mint would close its coining operations forever. It was more economical to strike coins in Denver and haul them to the West Coast than to continue a coining facility there. In that year 1955-S Lincoln cents and Roosevelt dimes were made, but no other coins. Later the Mint did resume coinage, including on a limited basis (compared to Philadelphia and Denver) cents and nickels for circulation as well as, beginning in 1968, S-marked Proofs of all denominations. Special Mint Sets (SMS) were made there from 1965 to 1967, but the coins had no mintmarks. Again, this was intended as a hindrance for the nasty numismatists who were blamed for creating and maintaining the nationwide coin shortage. From 1962 to 1982 the facility was known as the San Francisco Assay Office. The original name was restored in 1982 and is in use today.

THE WEST POINT MINT

In 1974 Mint Director Mary Brooks proposed that the Bureau of the Mint install presses at the West Point Bullion Depository. Located on the grounds of the United States Military Academy, the structure was well fortified, and in a secure area. The facility had been constructed in the late 1930s for the storage of silver, as a counterpart to the gold storage facility at Fort Knox in Kentucky.

Aerial view of the West Point Mint.

Soon presses were installed, and using planchets obtained on contract, the West Point Mint, as it became known in numismatics, commenced striking millions of Lincoln cents. No mintmark was used, giving the coins the appearance of Philadelphia Mint products. In time other coins were struck there, including American Eagle silver and gold bullion coins and certain commemoratives, some of which bore a W mintmark.

Cents were last regularly coined at the West Point Bullion Depository in 1985, although West Point coined the cent in three finishes in 2019. It would not be surprising if, in a future time of cent shortage, the denomination would be made there again. Today the facility is known as the West Point Mint.

CHAPTER SEVEN

PROOF LINCOLN CENTS, 1909 TO DATE
PRODUCTION, DISTRIBUTION, NUMISMATICS

INTRODUCTION

Proof coins with special finishes were made for collectors from 1909 to 1916 and again beginning in 1936. Because these represent a different method of manufacture and different distribution from circulation strikes, I have set them aside in this chapter.

Proofs made in the early range were designed as Matte Proofs: The finish had a minutely granular or matte surface, not unlike minutely fine sandpaper in appearance. Later Proofs minted from 1936 onward were usually called *brilliant* Proofs in their day, but now *mirror* Proofs is more descriptive, since a mirror Proof can become toned and therefore no longer "brilliant."

When Matte Proofs were issued in the early years of the Lincoln series they were extremely unpopular with collectors. In many instances a newly struck Matte Proof, with a bright but minutely granular surface, could not be distinguished from a circulation strike, especially if the latter had other than a frosty, lustrous surface. Today such coins are far more popular, with most specialists smartly opting to acquire only certified coins to be sure the coins are, indeed, Matte Proofs—as distinguished by minute details observable under magnification. Even among Matte Proofs certified by the *leading* services, there are some that I do not consider to be Matte Proofs. The attribution of certain Matte Proofs is a matter of opinion. Minute die markers or characteristics can help, but they are not the last word.

After the production of Matte Proof cents was discontinued in 1916, no more Proofs were struck, although Walter Breen has suggested that some were made in 1917, an assertion not endorsed by the leading certification services, which will not label them as such.

Then in 1936 the Philadelphia Mint decided to produce Proof sets, now of the mirror-finish type, again. These were sold in sets at $1.81 each, or individual coins could be ordered. This single-coin option continued through 1942. In that year the emphasis on strategic manufacturing for World War II and the need for more coins in circulation made it necessary to stop producing Proofs for collectors.

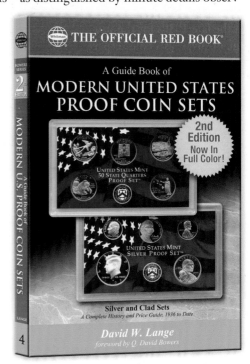

Lincoln-cent expert David W. Lange's *Guide Book of Modern United States Proof Coin Sets.* The Mint sells Proof Lincoln cents only within these special sets.

In 1950 production of Proofs was resumed, and coins were sold only as sets, at $2.10 each. These were put up in gray cardboard boxes, changed to flat packs partway through 1955. Production continued through 1964. At that time there was a nationwide coin shortage, and the Mint punished collectors by stopping the production of Proof coins. Production of Proofs was resumed in 1968, but at the San Francisco Mint for the first time, now with each piece bearing an S mintmark. Such sets have been produced down to the present day.

MATTE PROOF LINCOLN CENTS
BACKGROUND OF THE MATTE PROOF FINISH

Brilliant or mirror-finish Proof coins had been made in various denominations and types for many years by 1909, when the Lincoln cent was first coined. The typical mirror Proof in the Indian Head cent series, 1859 to 1909, was made from dies with deeply polished fields, giving them mirror surfaces, and with the Indian (actually Miss Liberty in the fanciful form of an Indian), wreath, shield, letters, and date, not polished. This imparted to the raised or relief surfaces a somewhat satiny or frosty appearance, often called *cameo* contrast today. This contrast added to the beauty of the coins in the eyes of collectors. Such pieces were widely appreciated then, and today they are still avidly sought by numismatists.

Matte Proof cent of 1916. Except under careful study, such coins are not much different in appearance from circulation strikes. (enlarged 1.5x)

Put into service in autumn 1901, the third Philadelphia Mint building had a special Medal Room, an improvement on the one in the earlier facility. This was equipped with two hydraulic presses, powered by electricity, that struck Proof coins, medals, and other special pieces (such as pattern coins) much more slowly than the electrified knuckle-action presses used for circulation coinage.

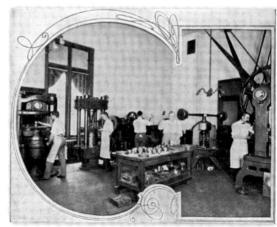

Chief Engraver Charles E. Barber of the Engraving Department and the staff in the Medal Room somehow concluded that matte or grainy surfaces on coins and medals made for collectors were preferable to the traditional mirror style with inscriptions and designs in satiny or frosty contrast. Moreover, artists in the private sector nearly all preferred this style. Matte-Proof-finish pieces, as they were called, had been made in France at the Paris Mint in the nineteenth century. Perhaps because Paris was the center of the art world at the time—what with the annual Salon, the

The Medal Room in the third Philadelphia Mint included hydraulic presses for the making of Proof coins. Such a device is the second machine from the left, by the window. (James Rankin Young, *The United States Mint at Philadelphia, Illustrated*, 1903)

Louvre, and world-class schools and studios—what the Paris Mint deemed desirable was thought to be ideal for the Philadelphia Mint as well.

In the 1890s the Philadelphia Mint was infected with Matte Proof fever and struck Assay Commission medals and certain other medallic issues in the Matte Proof format. This matte finish could be accomplished in several ways, and over a period of time each method was used. The dies could be given a matte finish by pickling them in acid or blasting them with minute particles of sand. Alternatively, carefully struck medals, from dies with regular finish, could be subjected to sandblasting and/or acid treatment.

Sand Blast Proof Gold Coins Disliked

For American gold coins, the traditional mirror finish had been used for many years, dating back to at least 1820. Although earlier single Proofs survive, the earliest known Proof set surviving today, a treasure of the National Numismatic Collection at the Smithsonian Institution, is dated 1821. (The Proof process was hardly new by 1820. It had been used in Europe for decades by that time; the 1746 silver Proof set of England is but one of many examples.)

Continuing into the twentieth century, Proof gold denominations, then consisting of the $2.50, $5, $10, and $20 values, were made from dies with the fields or flat areas polished to a mirrorlike finish and the lettering and designs untouched, giving them a satin or frosty finish. The contrast was very attractive, and Proofs of this style were eagerly sought by numismatists and still are.

In 1908 the new Indian Head design by Bela Lyon Pratt was introduced for the $2.50 and $5 gold coins, and in the $10 and $20 series the motto IN GOD WE TRUST was added to the new designs by Augustus Saint-Gaudens introduced in 1907. (Proofs of the 1907 Saint-Gaudens gold coins were not made, except for patterns and a few special strikings.) The Mint decided to issue the Proofs of 1908 with what it and numismatists called the Sand Blast Proof finish. Somehow, this terminology became lost in the second half of the twentieth century, and today many incorrectly call these Matte Proofs. This is probably a matter of marketing. To the uninitiated, "Matte Proof" may sound more elegant. Sand Blast Proof is proper, however.

A great hue and cry rose from the numismatic community because collectors and dealers found Sand Blast Proofs to be dull (appearing similar to fine-grain sandpaper), uninteresting, and not at all attractive. The Mint changed direction slightly in 1909 and 1910 and produced what are called today Satin Finish Proofs (alternatively, Roman Finish Proofs), with a bright yellow (not dull and grainy) finish, quite attractive at least to my eye, but not at all pleasing to numismatists at the time. These, too, bore no resemblance to the highly appreciated mirror Proofs of earlier years. In fact, in 1910 the ANA sent an official complaint to the Mint, requesting that this process be stopped immediately and the old mirror Proof style resumed. Collectors voted with their pocketbooks and refused to buy either Sand Blast or Satin Finish Proofs. Philadelphia dealer Henry Chapman, who had close connections to the Mint, told collector Robert Garrett that he doubted if more than five 1909 gold Proof sets had been bought by collectors.[19]

This complaint had the effect of discontinuing the Satin Finish Proof used in 1909 and 1910, returning in 1911 to the even more detested Sand Blast Proof style. Collector interest, already low, declined further. The nadir was touched in 1914 when just 50 Sand Blast $10 coins were made, and it is likely that not even these were all sold. In 1915 the production of Sand Blast Proof gold was given up completely.

The Mint, where many numismatic inquiries were handled through Chief Engraver Charles E. Barber, was not responsive to most collector interests at the time. Barber inherited the post after his father, Chief Engraver William E. Barber, died in 1879. His competence as an artist was generally regarded as average to poor (Augustus Saint-Gaudens called his work "wretched"), and his Liberty Head or "Barber" silver coins of 1892 were widely condemned by collectors and the public.

If the Mint had taken heed of numismatic concerns with the gold Proofs, perhaps they would have been popular and would have sold in larger numbers and for a longer time. Admittedly, the designs of the Indian Head $2.50 and $5 coins in particular, with the fields being the highest part of the coins and with the designs recessed or incuse (Bill Fivaz suggests the term *sunken relief*), would have presented a technical challenge to make in mirror-Proof form.

Concerning the perceived poor artistry of the Barber silver coins made since 1892, collectors, bypassing the Mint, took matters into their own hands and sent appeals to Congress. This grassroots campaign had the dramatic effect of inspiring the new "Mercury" dime, Standing Liberty quarter, and Liberty Walking half dollar of 1916—using outside artistic talent and ignoring Barber. Indeed, this had already been done with the 1909 Lincoln cent and the 1913 Indian/Buffalo nickel.

By way of further explanation, designs that were despised in one era often became admired in another. Today Barber silver coins are avidly collected. Many mintmark varieties in particular are very rare, since collectors at the time did not seek or save them. Similarly, in the first chapter of this book I quoted a contemporary nasty review of the 1793 Chain cent, a coin which just about anyone would give an eye tooth to own today!

STRIKING AND DISTRIBUTING MATTE PROOF CENTS

In 1909, when the Lincoln cent was introduced, production of Proof Indian Head cents of the mirror style had concluded. It was decided to make the Lincoln cents in the Matte Proof style, emulating the admired French process in use for medals since the 1890s and recently introduced in the Sand Blast Proof gold coins of 1908, as noted above.

For the Lincoln cent Matte Proofs this was done by taking the faces of the obverse and reverse dies and etching them so as to give a minutely grainy surface. I believe this was done by blasting them with minute sand particles, the sizes of which differed slightly over a period of time, or perhaps the duration of the blasting time varied, creating some slight differences in the finishes. Alternatively, the dies could have been lightly pickled in acid.

Planchets were carefully selected for these Matte Proofs, polished, and put into a medal press that struck the coins at slow speed so as to bring up all details of the design. The collars of the Matte Proofs were polished, giving the Matte Proofs a mirror surface when viewed edge-on (not visible in certified holders today, except for certain designs that permit this). The polishing of the planchets before striking may have been a factor in producing this effect as well.

The rims on the obverse in particular, but also on the reverse, were *flat*, rather than rounded, this being a key point, in my opinion, for attributing a Matte Proof as authentic today. Some certified "Matte Proofs" lack this feature. As to the surface of the Matte Proofs themselves, they did not appear to be much different from circulation strikes, especially certain circulation strikes that did not have deep luster. The variation was so subtle that many numismatists could not tell the difference between a sharply struck circulation strike and a Matte Proof.

These Matte Proofs were sold as part of what were known as minor Proof sets, containing the two denominations not made in precious metals: the cent and the nickel five-cent piece. In 1909 the nickel was of the Liberty Head design, as had been used since 1883. Proofs were continued in the mirror-finish style, including through the end of the Liberty Head series in 1913. Buffalo or Indian Head nickels, introduced in 1913, were made from lightly sandblasted dies in the Matte Proof style, They were carefully struck and had mirror edges and flat rims, similar to the Lincoln cents.

The price for a minor Proof set was just 8¢ plus postage, with no limit on the number that could be ordered. This charge was raised to 12¢ in 1912. Separately, silver Proof sets with the dime, quarter, and half dollar could be ordered. Gold coins were available separately on a single-coin basis, but could be ordered in sets as well.

Freshly minted Matte Proof cents were wrapped in a very thin but hard (not cottony soft) tissue paper to protect them. This tissue had sulfur content and soon toned the cents a rich, attractive brown and gave the nickels a whisper of a pleasing, delicate gray-blue tint.

MATTE PROOFS VIS-À-VIS CIRCULATION STRIKES

Collectors and dealers had great difficulty in telling Matte Proofs from certain circulation strikes with satiny (rather than richly frosty) surfaces. Particularly problematical was the 1909 V.D.B. cent, circulation-strike examples of which were often very well struck and with square or flat rims similar to the Proofs. Viewed edge-on, however, the circulation strikes were not mirrorlike, but rather had tiny vertical lines. The 1916 Matte Proof, the last year of issue, had a very finely grained surface and was not much different at all from circulation strikes of this year.

The staff of ANACS, then at Colorado Springs at the headquarters of the ANA, studied Matte Proofs carefully, including examples taken from full Proof sets preserved since those years, and came up with a list of minute die distinctions that could be used in authentication. Leonard Albrecht was the chief researcher on the project. These findings were published in *The Numismatist* and reprinted in book form as *Counterfeit Detection, volume 2*, 1986. Today much of this information, plus useful observations and new information, can be found in the essential texts by David W. Lange (*The Complete Guide to Lincoln Cents*) and John Wexler and Kevin Flynn (*The Authoritative Reference on Lincoln Cents*). These guidelines are not absolutely definitive, but are largely correct. As an example of a deviation from the norm, Lot 78 of the Childs Collection, which I cataloged and which was sold on August 30, 1999, was described as follows and was from an original Proof set kept intact since the time of issue:

> **1911 Matte Proof-65RB.** Deep satiny orange luster with very faint lavender toning. Die markers normally associated with the 1911 Matte Proof Lincoln cents are not readily apparent, however, there is no question of this coin's status.

Today we have the situation that most experienced collectors and dealers still have great difficulty differentiating Matte Proofs from circulation strikes, especially for the 1909 V.D.B. and 1916. Sam Lukes, long-time specialist in Lincoln cents, related that some years ago he submitted several "Matte Proof" 1909 V.D.B. cents, which he had obtained from as many different dealers, to ANACS. "I had a gut feeling that they were all very early circulation strikes, even though they exhibited square edges and matte surfaces. None were verified as being Proof!"[20]

Today the several leading certification services—NGC and PCGS—are well trained in the subject, and Matte Proofs they certify have the die distinctions first described by ANACS. David W. Lange is a key executive at NGC and continues his research and observations. Other certification services may well perform similar studies, but I suggest that before buying any "Matte Proof" you have it independently evaluated as to authenticity, if you are dealing with other than the services just mentioned. Even if it is certified by one of these highly regarded companies, be sure the coin has *flat* rims on both sides. At least, that is what I would do.

RECEPTION IN THE MARKETPLACE

After 1916 Matte Proofs languished in the marketplace. Many were simply spent because their appearance was not much different from a circulation strike that had toned brown. Others were kept with Buffalo nickels in two-piece minor Proof sets. They had hardly any market value and were not worthwhile for most dealers to keep in stock or offer in price lists. Nearly everyone kept these in their original tissue paper, or tucked them into 1.5 x 2–inch paper coin envelopes, there being no albums, folders, or holders available at the time.

Even in the 1930s, when collecting Lincoln cents became all the rage as "penny boards" and Raymond albums were vigorously marketed, few collectors sought Matte Proofs. This indifference continued for many years afterward. To those collecting by date and mint, a brilliant Uncirculated 1909 V.D.B. was infinitely preferable to a chocolate brown Matte Proof with original surfaces.

Around 1954 and 1955 I bought large numbers of pristine Matte Proof cents, all in original Mint tissue paper, from William L. Pukall, who had operated a mail-order coin business in Union City, New Jersey. He had been in the trade since 1914, or even earlier, but it was in 1914 that he began acquiring current Proof minor and silver coins and bank-wrapped rolls of the same denominations for store stock. These included mintmark varieties, a specialty that most other dealers ignored at the time. Later he purchased from another dealer, probably Henry Chapman, *more than a thousand* Matte Proof Lincoln cents that had been acquired, years earlier, as unsold remainders from the Philadelphia Mint. The tissue paper must have had an effect upon the surface

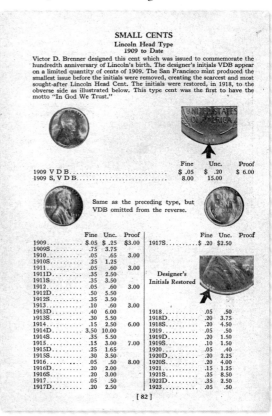

The first page of Lincoln cents from the first (1947) edition of *A Guide Book of United States Coins*, released in 1946. Matte Proofs, simply listed as "Proofs," were valued from $3 to $8 each.

of Matte Proofs from which the paper had been removed, for pieces kept out of the paper but with original sets always became toned, often light brown, but with yellow-orange at the center. I have never seen a fully brilliant *original* Matte Proof cent, and probably no such thing exists. Matte Proof "RD" cents that have been dipped and slightly retoned are usually yellow-orange from rim to rim, often with some hints or flecks of magenta.

Even though most dates in the hoard of Matte Proof cents cost me just $2 to $3 each from Pukall, they did not sell quickly. In the mid-1950s I mostly sold to private customers who submitted "want lists," but I also used catalogs and display advertisements. According to Walter Breen (who sometimes stated opinion, giving it as fact), David U. Proskey, another old-time dealer, purchased many unsold pieces from the Mint. Many of these later passed to Wayte Raymond, again per Breen. What happened to these, I do not know. Perhaps they never existed in the first place. In any event, after the passing of Raymond on September 23, 1956, most of his numismatic estate went through John J. Ford Jr., who cherrypicked what he wanted for his personal collection, then sold the rest through the New Netherlands Coin Co. After Raymond's death I would occasionally visit with his widow, Olga, who had an apartment overlooking the East River in New York City. Once, in the 1960s, I was in town with my family, and she had F.A.O. Schwarz send two stuffed animals over to the Plaza Hotel for my young sons, Wynn and Lee. By that time Mrs. Raymond still had a lot of residual inventory, such as Philippine Proof sets (made at the Philadelphia Mint from 1903 to 1908), but she had no Matte Proof cents at all. I didn't think to ask her if she previously had any, but I doubt if many were in her husband's estate.

As the coin market developed and expanded in the 1950s, many numismatists specialized in collecting only Proofs, and not circulation strikes. Collections of Barber dimes, quarters, and half dollars from 1892 onward would be formed by finding one of each Proof date; but a mintmark issue, not even a rarity, was of no interest to such specialists. It was natural to collect Lincoln cent Proofs as well. Matte Proof listings in *A Guide Book of United States Coins* beckoned, this being the book that, perhaps, 99 percent of collectors used when determining what to collect. Specialists sought one of each Matte Proof but had no interest in such things as the 1909-S V.D.B. or 1914-D.

In the 1960s Matte Proofs became very popular, even warm or perhaps hot in the marketplace. Many if not most were dipped to make them bright, and offerings of "brilliant" Matte Proofs were common. There were exceptions, but they were few and far between. There was hardly any market for Matte Proofs with original brown toning.

I recall an interesting incident in 1966, I believe it was, when I needed to reinforce our stock of Matte Proof cents and contacted Fred Vollmer, an Indiana dealer who was active in the field and employed a Teletype machine. Fred had delivered reliable quality before and was one of just a few dealers who were savvy enough to distinguish an authentic Matte Proof. After a telephone discussion, he agreed to review his stock of Matte Proofs and send me ones that were up to my "fussy" standards. He did not know how many of each he had, so we agreed on a price I would pay for each coin, 1909 V.D.B. through 1916, to be multiplied by the number of coins he could find of each date. They arrived in due course. I inspected them, found they were all just dandy, and mailed off a check, totaling into four figures, to him.

He soon called, asking where the rest of his money was, and stating I had paid only about half of what I had agreed to. This came as a surprise to me! I reviewed the paperwork at my end, and shared it with him—I had paid completely, in full, the amount agreed upon. "There were *more coins* than those," he said! After some going back and forth and checking with one of his employees, he concluded that after making up my main package and wrapping in brown paper, a clerk had placed additional coins he or she had later found on the outside of the brown wrapper, then put another wrapper around everything. At my end, these extra coins had been tossed in the trash! We chatted and, agreeable to both of us, split the difference for the missing coins.

With the advent of the Professional Coin Grading Service (PCGS) in 1986, followed by the Numismatic Guaranty Company of America (NGC) in 1987, certified coins encased in plastic "slabs" became very popular. These included Matte Proofs checked as to authenticity. By this time many dipped coins had acquired light toning, or sometimes even vivid rainbow toning (never seen by me on any *original* Matte Proof), and spotting. These were sometimes rejected by these and other grading services that went into business. More often, it seems, they were simply given lower numbers in the grading scale. It has been my experience that pristine undipped Matte Proofs, always with *some* brown toning and most often completely brown, are rarely stained or spotted, although they may have tiny flecks. (Coins with these can be avoided by cherrypicking for quality.) Perhaps the brown patination helped protect the surface against further chemical activity. When spotting is seen today, it is usually on coins with some red-orange surface.

Today Proofs certified by the leading services are very popular. Those most in the limelight are the pieces with very high numbers assigned by PCGS and entered in its Registry Set competition, an innovation by David Hall, the main founder of PCGS. The services assign a numerical grade, such as from 60 to 70 at the Mint State level, for Uncirculated cents, and also assign a color description—as explained in chapter eight.

There is not much market for BN (brown) coins because naïve buyers often avoid this color completely! RB (red and brown) pieces are also betwixt and between, with low demand. It is RD (red) coins that are most desired. Concerning BN examples, Sam Lukes offered this comment:

> Over the years I have viewed certified examples of Matte Proofs described as "BN" in color, which is really a shame, because some have original blends including aqua, sea green, magenta, yellow, and rose colorations which can hardly be described as being "brown."[21]

BEING A SMART BUYER OF MATTE PROOFS

If you are a true Lincoln specialist and want one of everything, then by all means a set of Matte Proofs, consisting of the 1909 V.D.B., regular 1909, and one of every date through 1916, should be a goal. If I were forming such a set, I would give as a goal a Matte Proof-65 or better grade, perhaps 66, with light-brown original toning or with brown original toning with some orange and red, but without even the slightest trace of a fleck or spot.

As mentioned, a very pleasing aspect of this formula is that the term BN is often a signal that investors and naïve collectors won't buy such coins, and, accordingly, prices can be remarkably inexpensive. *I view this as a wonderful advantage.* Ditto for Matte Proofs that are described as RB, providing that the colors are nicely blended and not blotchy or spotted. Pieces described as full RD, if with no toning at all, are in my opinion pieces that have been dipped, but certainly others may feel differently, and I respect this.

In my opinion a "poster example" of a RD Matte Proof should show delicate brown toning with abundant areas of slightly subdued, *original* red-orange color. There should be no blotches, flecks, or spots.

My recommendation is only to consider Matte Proofs certified by the leading services, such as NGC and PCGS, but use these as a *starting point*, looking for surface quality as described above. If a coin is found certified by a service other than these, have it independently verified as to die characteristics. Never, but absolutely never, buy a "Matte Proof" that has not been authenticated in this manner. This rule is true for any and all Internet offerings—the Web is a playground for smart and experienced fraudster wolves seeking investor and collector lambs.

Beyond all of the above, when you do find a Matte Proof with a BN, RB, or RD surface, be sure it has good eye appeal. This can vary considerably. If you are not a Lincoln cent specialist, remember this: A beautiful gem circulation-strike MS-65RD or finer cent of any of these dates will cost just a fraction of the price of a Matte Proof-65RD or finer coin, and may be just as visually appealing, if not more so. If you are the slightest bit skeptical about this, track down a nice image of a high-grade 1916 circulation strike and also a high-grade Matte Proof cent, and see for yourself.

David W. Lange, of NGC, states in his book that the *majority* of Matte Proofs on the market "have been cleaned at some point." He also reiterates that "matte surfaces . . . found little favor with collectors of the time," and that "current market value seems a bargain given the small number available; the general unpopularity of Matte Proofs is likely to blame." More from the same writer (now with emphasis added):

> While deeply toned Proofs were once a common sight on the bourse floor and in auctions, most have since been cleaned in some manner and then retoned to varying degrees. When done properly, the result is a very attractive coin which will qualify for certification *by the grading services*. If cleaned using harsh chemicals or abrasives, as were many during the 1950s, 1960s and 1970s, the result is an unnatural appearance which leaves these coins difficult to grade and impossible to have certified. With the restorative processes for coins becoming ever more sophisticated, however, there may yet be hope for these orphans.

My view is that today you have the choice of either a lustrous brown *original* Matte Proof, wonderful in that it is likely to be inexpensive, or a "gem" coin with "RD" surface by virtue of modern coin doctoring.

As you can see, the Matte Proofs are an arcane specialty! I've enjoyed them for many years, but as you have just read, I recommend them only to specialists and sophisticated buyers.

MIRROR-FINISH PROOF LINCOLN CENTS, 1936–1942

PRODUCTION AND DISTRIBUTION OF 1936–1942 PROOFS

Mirror-finish Proofs of 1936 were made from dies polished completely, including the portrait and other features, quite unlike the frosty or cameo contrast used in the Indian Head cent series from 1859 to 1909, which were also mirror Proofs. Pieces struck early in 1936 were not completely polished and have a hybrid appearance—sort of a satiny finish with elements of polish. Complaints ensued, and the dies for later coins were more thoroughly polished. The effect is much different from the mirror Proofs of the Indian Head cent series of 1859 to 1909, when only the field or flat part was polished.

Proof 1936 of the mirror type, with all parts of the die deeply polished, including the portrait. (enlarged 1.5x)

In 1936 director of the Mint Nellie Tayloe Ross described the new issues:

> Proof coins being struck at the Mint at the present time are made in every detail exactly as they have been made in the past, namely, the planchets are carefully selected and each one struck individually on a hydraulic press, and handled so that one coin cannot mar another. The dies are polished to a mirror finish at frequent intervals.
>
> The difference between the recent Proofs and those struck in the past is due to the difference in the design and the method used in preparing the master dies. All the present coins are made from sculptured models without retouching with a graver in any way, in order to preserve the exact quality and texture of the original sculptor's work. This gives a more or less uneven background with less sharpness in the details. In other words, they are produced the same as small medals might be struck.
>
> The master dies for the gold coins struck previous to 1907, and the silver coins struck prior to 1916, were prepared in the older and entirely different method, being lower in relief and much greater sharpness in detail by re-engraving, even though the original design was reduced from a sculptured model. The inscriptions were usually put into the master dies by means of punches. In addition, they were prepared with a "basined" background or field, that is, the field was polished to a perfect radius on a revolving disc, which again produced a much clearer definition between motif and field, and this gave an entirely different appearance to the coin.
>
> With the present coins, the models were never prepared with the intention of "basining," and it could not be done without many radical alterations in the relief of the present designs.

From 1936 through 1942 the dies were polished overall, as noted, although sometimes this was not completely done in the portrait and other design elements, with the result that the higher areas can have a satiny appearance, called *cameo* by the certification services. To merit this designation, the cameo feature must be present on *both sides*. Such distinctions were not widely noticed until 1991, when Rick Jerry Tomaska published his *Cameo and Brilliant Proof Coinage of the 1950 to 1970 Era*, which applied to Proofs of later years. In the marketplace notice was taken, however, of the early 1936 to 1942 Proofs, and mention of them can be found in David W. Lange's *Complete Guide to Lincoln Cents*.

Proofs were offered by the Mint at $1.81 per set of five coins (Lincoln cent, Jefferson nickel, "Mercury" or Winged Liberty Head dime, Washington quarter, and Liberty Walking half dollar), plus 8¢ shipping if sent by mail. Alternatively, Proof coins could be ordered singly as desired, with cents priced at 16¢ plus 8¢ postage. In 1936 most were ordered of the cents (5,569) and fewest of the quarter (3,389). This necessarily defines the number of complete *sets* at 3,389, but in actuality some collectors ordered quarters and ignored certain of the other denominations. These Proofs were put up in thin cellophane envelopes with glued seams. (The glue later turned a light yellow color.) Sometimes, multiple envelopes were stapled together at the top.

In 1936 the coin market was abuzz with the commemorative craze—the passion to buy low-mintage commemorative half dollars that had ignited in the summer of 1935 when collectors found that the new Hudson Sesquicentennial halves, advertised at $1 each, and with just 10,000 minted, had been sold out by the time most orders were received. Those in charge of the Hudson program feared that there would be no demand and dumped the vast majority to New York dealer Julius Guttag before the advertisements appeared in print. Pandemonium reigned, and the market price zoomed to $4 and $5—this in the middle of the Depression!

Enter C. Frank Dunn, the official distributor of Boone Bicentennial half dollars, first coined in 1934, then in 1935, and sold to a lukewarm reception. Why not make a *really rare* coin? Since the 1935-dated Boone sets were already made, he came up with the thought of creating another special variety, one with a tiny date "1934" on the reverse in addition to the regular 1935 date. Just 2,003 of these additional 1935 with "small 1934" coins were made at the Denver Mint and 2,004 at San Francisco, the smallest mintage of any silver commemorative in the history of U.S. numismatics. Offered at $3.70 per pair in *The Numismatist* in November 1935, the coins were presented to collectors who had no choice but to buy them in order to have their collections be complete. Hardly anyone, perhaps *no one*, was able to have an order filled. Dunn said that they were already "sold out," because advance notice had appeared in New York City papers. The market price skyrocketed to $50, then to $80! Somehow, Dunn just happened to find more sets to sell at the higher valuations.

In early 1936 these and other investment sensations hogged the spotlight, and scarcely any attention was paid to the opportunity to order new Proof coins!

In 1937, with the market for commemorative coins in free-fall collapse and speculation ended, more attention was turned to Proof coins, and quantities increased. In 1939 Congress pulled the plug on allowing private individuals and groups to have their own commemorative issues, ending widespread abuses in distribution and pricing. Proof coin mintage continued through 1942, after which year production stopped, as the Philadelphia Mint turned its attention to producing record numbers of circulating coins to satisfy the expanding domestic wartime commercial scene.

BEING A SMART BUYER OF 1936–1942 PROOFS

The glue in the cellophane envelopes of issue imparted toning or even spotting to some of the coins, as did, apparently, careless handling by those who packaged them at the Mint. An employee who touched either side of a coin would leave body acids or oils on the surface, not at all noticeable until a passage of time, when these developed into distinctive fingerprints or carbon spots. If an employee talked while packaging coins, little drops of moisture fell on the pieces, latent at first, but years later creating flecks and spots. In a more disastrous scenario of the same sort, in the early 1950s when the Royal Canadian Mint began selling special sets to collectors, it turned out that several years later the dark fingerprints of Mint employees were common on the coins.

In other instances, collectors enjoying their coins exposed them to the open air, including minute moisture that was expelled when people spoke, similarly producing tiny flecks on the coins. In still other instances, probably the majority, pieces that naturally toned a light brown were dipped to make them brilliant, after which the surface became especially chemically active and tended to become mottled in rainbow colors, or blotchy, or spotted, or all of these variables. This is especially true of 1936 coins, less so for 1937, and progressively less in later years. The result is that today relatively few pristine, undipped Proof Lincoln cents of the early 1936 to 1942 era survive.

Pristine, undipped mirror Proofs of 1936 to 1942 will always have delicate toning. Any fully bright coin, as brilliant as new, is that way by virtue of dipping. Tiny flecks are common for the reasons outlined above, but coins with these can be avoided easily enough. Relatively few pristine Proofs of this era are actually "BN" in color. Toning is usually somewhat light, with iridescent hues.

Many if not most Proofs sold in the marketplace in later years, up to the beginning of the present generation, were dipped if they were the slightest bit toned or spotted. Various conservation techniques, or doctoring (usually viewed as an unkind word), have been developed to remove spots—such as by putting a tiny drop of acid or other agent on the spot by means of the tip of a toothpick, watching it under high magnification, and repeating the process. This has worked for many coins but is revealed by tiny whitish or non-mirror areas where the flecks used to be—again, visible under magnification.

Not as important, but worth considering, is that a few Proof dies were overly polished, reducing some detail, but most people would not notice. Significant cameo contrast can be viewed as a plus when it occurs, sometimes on just one side and more often seen toward the end of this year span.

If I were buying high-quality Proof cents of this era I would opt for those lightly but very evenly toned, without any spots or flecks. Such coins might be certified as RB. If I were to seek an RD coin, I would be sure it had at least a hint of original toning. Otherwise, you and I could buy BN and RB coins and dip them ourselves! As is the case with the earlier discussed Matte Proofs, lightly toned mirror Proof Lincoln cents of the 1936 to 1942 era are delightfully inexpensive in comparison to full RD coins.

A run of the seven Proofs of the 1936 to 1942 era can make a very attractive display. Protect them well, if they are not in holders.

MIRROR-FINISH PROOF LINCOLN CENTS, 1950–1964
PRODUCTION AND DISTRIBUTION OF 1950–1964 PROOFS

In 1950 the Mint began selling Proof coins once again. This time they were available only in sets of five coins—the current designs being the Lincoln cent, Jefferson nickel, Roosevelt dime, Washington quarter, and Franklin half dollar. These sets were sold for $2.10 each. The coins were put in cellophane envelopes, stapled at the top, and placed in a square box of gray cardboard, stuffed with tissue paper to keep the

Proof 1954 cent. Note the general lack of details on the portrait due to extensive wear, occurring since this feature was last strengthened in 1916, of the hub and master dies. (enlarged 1.5x)

coins from moving around. The boxes were then wrapped in each direction by two strips of glue-backed brown tape, allowing the gray corners to be visible. In 1950 an ordering limit of five sets per person was placed, to be waived later if the Mint found that it had the capacity to make more sets. Buyers played games by having country cousins and others send in orders. These capers became more creative in later years when restrictions still applied, and investors and dealers wanted to buy more than just a handful of sets.

In 1950 sales amounted to 51,386 sets. Certain early strikings, especially of the Lincoln cents, were a hybrid between mirror and slightly grainy surfaces. Complaints were voiced, and the Mint commenced polishing the dies more vigorously. As was done in the 1936 to 1942 era, the entire die was polished, including the design features. Sometimes when polishing was incomplete on the portrait (in particular), coins with satiny contrast, called *cameo* as before, were created.

NEW PROOF SET PACKAGING

Partway through 1955 the Mint converted to the flat pack arrangement, with each coin sealed between layers of Pliofilm, consisting of two layers of inert polystyrene bonded to an inner layer of cellophane to add strength. Coins packaged this way tended to retain their original brightness for many years, but there were exceptions.

These sets were placed in envelopes with a cardboard stiffener and a printed slip of paper. Addresses and postage were added to the outside.

Quantities of Proof sets varied over the years, increasing in a general trend and peaking in 1957, when for the first time more than a million (1,247,952) were ordered. This record resulted from the momentum of the 1956 Proof set investment market bubble, which by the end of 1957 had collapsed. This cast a wet blanket on 1958 sales, which dropped to 875,652. The slump in interest did not last for long, and from 1959 onward it rose, to a peak of 3,218,019 in 1962; then slightly backslid in 1963 to 3,075,645; then jumped to 3,950,762, the last being accelerated by the 1964 inclusion of the first Kennedy half dollar in the set.

Proof sets were shipped by mail, and in nearly all instances they arrived safely. There were exceptions when certain employees of the U.S. Post Office proved to be sneak thieves. At one station in Chicago the toilets were jammed to overflowing, revealing that employees broke open quantities of Proof sets, swiped the coins, and attempted to destroy the evidence. In Springfield, Massachusetts, large numbers of Proof sets that reached the Post Office never left it, except in the pockets of workers. Such situations were speedily fixed when discovered, but they resulted in some stray Proof coins reaching circulation, to be reported now and then by alert collectors who found them.

By 1964 a nationwide coin shortage had developed. In a move viewed unfavorably by numismatists—said to have been responsible for the shortage—Mint Director Eva Adams ordered that production of Proofs be suspended beginning in 1965, and mintmarks be removed from coins struck at branch mints. She later relented, but the damage was done, and no Proof sets were produced in 1965, 1966, or 1967, although Special Mint Sets (SMS) were made. These had satiny or even partially mirrorlike surfaces and were sold at an even higher price than Proof sets, unsurprisingly resulting in more collector ill will toward the Bureau of the Mint. Relations between the collecting community and the Mint touched bottom. It was not until 1968 that Proof sets were again made, and then at the San Francisco Mint.

As the years rolled on from 1950 to 1964, cameo contrast Proofs were made with increasing frequency, but still in the minority, and those with today's highly prized deep cameo contrast were made in even fewer numbers. Scant notice was taken of such differences back then, until the 1980s—and especially after the 1991 publication of Rick Jerry Tomaska's *Cameo and Brilliant Proof Coinage of the 1950 to 1970 Era*, a little book that had a big effect on the coin market.

Special Mint Set (SMS) 1967 Lincoln cent. (enlarged 1.5x)

CHEMICAL AND OXIDATION CONSIDERATIONS

In an article in the May 1958 issue of *The Numismatist*, "The Preservation of Coins," Dr. F. Stevens Epps commented (excerpt):

This short essay is not to be construed with the worn out subject of how to clean coins. Rather it tells how to take a brilliant Uncirculated or Proof coin and keep it that way. The writer, for 10 years, has been a student of chemistry as it pertains to metals, and coins are metals. All metals are subject to oxidation unless they are airtight (sealed) in inert covering. Some metals will oxidize more quickly than others. For example: copper oxidizes more quickly than nickel, and nickel more readily than silver. These three basic metals, or combinations thereof, make up the content of most of our coinage today.

Now just what does the word "inert" mean? It means a substance which is not affected by oxygen, or which contains no oxygen. There are very few liquids or solids that are inert, so few that we can name them readily. In the liquids, there are benzene and ether; in the solids, paper that contains no sulphur and in the plastics ethylcellulose, polystyrene, and polyethylene. Even Plexiglas is questionable because it contains polymethacrylic acid.

Any chemical that attacks tarnish on a coin will later attack the metal itself. Butyrate is one of the most volatile plastics and acetate is not much better. They are commonly esterified together and dangerous for the protection of a mint coin.

If collectors are willing to learn and observe the rudiments of chemistry, and protect their mint and Proof coins in the proper manner each year as they receive them, there would be no need for future worry about restoring them to their mint condition.

But, the collector says, "This is all very good advice, but what am I to do?"

Since all paper contains sulphur, take those Uncirculated coins out of the bank wrapper, as it has about 5% sulphur content. Take your Proof coins out of the cellophane Mint-sealed package because all cellophane contains nitrate. The new Mint-sealed Proof package [flat pack] does not contain the percentage of nitrate that the usual run of cellophane coin envelopes do, very true, but it still contains some nitrate. . . .

In the plastics, stay with polystyrene, polyethylene, or ethylcellulose, and again you are safe. Collectors have written me and said, "I have done these very things and still ruined some Uncirculated coins." This is a true statement, so what happened?

Some foreign element was on the coin when it was covered with the inert covering. . . . Each coin, whether copper, nickel or silver, must be carefully inspected, or should be, before you place it in an inert covering of your choice. If this grease is removed within 30 to 60 days from the time of minting, or before it "sets" on the metal, you are safe. Use a clean pocket handkerchief, and then if you are still not sure, immerse the coin in medical benzene and buff it with lamb's wool, then place it in . . . any of the three mentioned plastics, and you can forget it for your lifetime. It will stay brilliant.

Today the "buff it with lamb's wool" is something I would avoid, but Dr. Epps' long-ago advice otherwise reads well. In a later (1960) article Epps commented, in part: "Anyone who buys a proof set through 1954 without looking at it should be subjected to a psychiatric examination."

In 1954 a different quality of plastic was adopted, notes David W. Lange in his book: "Softer to the touch, it was less abrasive to the coins, but it also accelerated the pace of unattractive toning."

Toward the end of this era, and even continuing to the present day, flexible clear polyvinyl chloride (PVC) envelopes have been used by collectors and dealers (but not by the Mint) to store and display coins. Over a period of time PVC transfers liquid goo to the surface of coins, which will etch and corrode copper and nickel. On silver and gold it is likely to simply remain on the surface, without causing damage. PVC traces can be removed by the careful application of acetone (inflammable and volatile). I haven't tried the "medical benzene" recommended by Dr. Epps, though this might be as good or better.

PVC, being soft and pliable, does not impart slight friction to the surface of coins, as cellophane can do when the coins are moved around a lot—such as in a dealer's stock, or traveling, or auction lot viewing. Use of PVC should be avoided like the plague, although it is used by most auction houses to minimize problems during the lot-viewing process. Such auction lots *must be removed instantly* from such holders by the new owners. Repeat: *Must be removed instantly.*

The Koin-Tain holders have been around for more than 50 years, contain no PVC, and are held in high regard, and the newer product, Saflip, of Mylar, is likewise esteemed. Other worthwhile products are on the market. Ask the advice of experts regarding any specific brand you may select.

Being a Smart Buyer of 1950–1964 Proofs

After reading the preceding, I imagine that without my giving any more details, you are already aware enough to be a smart buyer. My advice is about the same as for the mirror Proofs of 1936 to 1942, except that with Proofs from 1950 to 1954 staining and spotting is much less common. Brilliant coins, almost as bright as the day they were minted, can be found, although many from the early 1950s have been dipped. If examination under high-powered magnification reveals *any* tiny hairlines, you are holding a dipped or cleaned coin.

The presence of cameo contrast is a plus and always commands a premium in the marketplace, since this aspect is widely known. There are some doubled-die varieties of Proof coins described in the Lange and Wexler-Flynn texts. Certain of these command little if any premium. The Small Date and Large Date varieties of 1960 are essential for inclusion in a set of Proof Lincoln cents, with the Small Date being the rarer, but still very affordable.

Buy with care, examining each coin intently and selecting only Proofs with good eye appeal. There are many around, so the task is not at all daunting.

If you collect Proof *sets*, it is good practice to examine any that might be in the original wrappings, per the warning of Dr. Epps above. Sometimes, slightly impaired Proofs can be renewed by *expert* conservation, but don't practice this on valuable coins. Also, the use of any solvent, even an inert one, on a coin's surface, tends to "strip" the surface and make it very susceptible to atmospheric influences, which can cause spotting. Numismatic Conservation Services (a division of NGC) offers conservation for a fee and might be worth investigating.

As a caveat, in the market of the 1960s more than just a few crooks had their own flat-pack Proof set envelopes printed and filled them with their own versions of Pliofilm-sealed coins, but of common non-Proof issues or even blank metal washers! These often came to light after they had passed around among dealers and investors and were finally opened by a collector—by which time it was usually impossible to trace the line of previous ownership. If you buy a Mint-sealed Proof set, I'd advise that you open it for inspection soon after you acquire it.

MIRROR-FINISH PROOF LINCOLN CENTS, 1968 TO DATE

PRODUCTION AND DISTRIBUTION

Production of Proof sets was resumed in 1968, now at the San Francisco Mint, with each coin bearing an S mintmark. These were made on old-fashioned knuckle-type presses, but driven slowly. Each piece was struck twice before it left the dies, this to bring up the details in full (or with as much detail as the dies had). As a visitor to the Mint I saw these being made by employees who did not know much about numismatics, but who wore gloves. In a 1976 visit, however, I saw that as Proofs were carefully taken from the presses, they were stacked on top of each other in little piles! Presumably, that procedure was changed later.

Proof 1968-S cent, in the last year of the old hub lacking details in Lincoln's portrait. (enlarged 1.5x)

The offering price in 1968 was $5 per set, including delivery by registered mail. This coincided with a slump in investment interest: The hot market that had developed in a strong way in 1960 (catalyzed by the launching of *Coin World* as the first weekly coin publication and by the discovery of the "rare" and well-publicized 1960, Small Date, cents) had crashed by 1965. Few investors wanted to touch such things, but collectors and dealers found them to be immensely appealing (I ordered some myself), and 3,041,506 were reported as being sold. The actual production figure was slightly higher for this and later years because the Mint regularly makes some extras to fill orders

Obverse changes: Proof 1969-S cent with strengthened details. Proof 1993-S cent with additional adjustments to the portrait, and with recessed shoulder. (enlarged 1.5x)

that were either lost or for which there are quality problems. What happened to these extra sets is anyone's guess. When I endeavored to find out in the early 1990s, it seems that no one knew anything about them.

The 1968-S sets were packaged in attractive rigid holders of clear polystyrene plastic, with the coins mounted in a plastic insert. The whole arrangement was very nice, a great improvement over anything earlier. Coins tended to remain pristine in their original packaging, the only occasional problems being the development of flecks if moisture or another substance touched the surface during the minting or packaging process.

In 1973 Eisenhower dollars were included in Proof sets for the first time, although special Proof strikings in silver (instead of clad composition) had been available since the inception of the design in 1971. The price was raised to $7 per set, then in 1977 to $9. Prices were adjusted upward on several later occasions, and in some instances beginning in 1983 "Prestige" and "Premier" Proof sets were made, including other coins such as commemoratives, and strikings of certain higher denominations in silver instead of clad metal, etc.—a subject beyond the scope of the present text. (See David W. Lange's 2010 book, *A Guide Book of Modern United States Proof Coin Sets*, second edition, for details.) In any event, you and I are concentrating on individual Proof Lincoln cents here, and not sets.

Beginning in 1975 *circulation strike* Lincoln cents coined at San Francisco had no mintmark, another "punishment" to numismatists, this time by Mint Director Mary Brooks, who was wrestling with yet another nationwide coin shortage. *Proof* cents continued to have the S mintmark, with the pleasing numismatic result that later cents are "Proof only" issues—with no equivalent pieces made for circulation.

The new copper-coated zinc composition, introduced on circulation strikes in 1982 and Proofs in 1983, caused problems. David W. Lange commented:

> The San Francisco Mint struck nearly four million Proof cents for collectors [in 1982], but these were all of the traditional composition. It was found that the underlying zinc broke through its thin copper plating under the repeated impressions given to Proof coins. This problem was solved in 1983 and subsequent years by furnishing each Proof planchet with a second copper plating.[22]

In 1983 a fiberboard insert replaced that of plastic, and this style has continued. David W. Lange reported that "while there have been some problems of corrosion associated with the fiberboard inserts (the 1984 sets being particularly susceptible), they've been generally satisfactory provided that one's sets are not stored in a moist environment or where they may experience extremes of temperature."

In 1990 a few Proofs were made without the S mintmark. How many actually left the San Francisco Mint, nobody knows, but likely no more than a couple hundred, if indeed that many. David W. Lange suggests 100 to 150, which seems about on target in view of the great rarity of these today—although a population as high as 200 has been advanced by others. In the early 1990s a new rotary polishing system for planchets, giving them a better finish for Proof production, was introduced.[23]

Proof 1990 Lincoln cent without the S mintmark. (enlarged 1.5x)

Proof sets are popular collectibles today. Annual mintages have been hovering around the one million mark, and the San Francisco cents have continued to be "Proof only" issues. Modern sets are attractive and well worth owning.

BEING A SMART BUYER OF 1968-S TO DATE PROOFS

Nearly all Proof cents from 1968-S to date survive in superb gem preservation today. Simply avoid any with flecks, stains, or other problems, or any that do not have eye appeal. A gem Proof of this era should fairly shout, "Buy me!"

Cameo contrast Proofs are available for all dates, but deep cameo contrast Proofs can range from scarce to rare in the early years. After about 1977-S they are the rule, not the exception. The Bureau of the Mint responded

Details of a 1998-S Proof with the typical deep cameo contrast. This effect was made by sandblasting the portrait and other incuse features of the dies, while giving the fields a high mirror polish.

to collector preferences and began deliberately making them this way. Population reports are inconsistent because such terms as Cameo and Deep Cameo were not used by all grading services until after many had been certified without these words. By implication, there is no need at all to pay any more for a post-1977 Proof marked Cameo or Deep Cameo, since nearly all have that finish. In chapter 11 the certification populations of Proofs that are unspecified, Cameo, and Deep Cameo are all combined for 1978 and later years.

Today Proof coins are made with great care, using carefully selected and prepared planchets. Dies are chromium plated for extra mirror depth (as some have been since the late 1920s), and the deep cameo effect is gained by light sandblasting of the devices that are in relief on the finished coin.

Before jumping into higher-priced early deep cameos, study the populations and also the current market. Interest levels and prices have varied over the years.

In 1985 the S mintmark was made part of the Proof master die for the first time, a process continued to the present day. (This procedure was adopted for circulation strikes in 1990.) This eliminated different positions of the mintmark as well as any doubling of the letter. The earlier-mentioned 1990 Proof without a mintmark is an anomaly.

There are some Proof doubled-die varieties described in the Lange and Wexler-Flynn texts. There are quite a few differences, usually very subtle, but interesting when viewed under magnification. Often, there is no premium attached to them.

There is also the matter of variable spacing of AM in AMERICA on certain issues. John Wexler is credited for discovering these, after which time others have made further finds. These can be briefly described as follows:

Wide AM: Bottoms of letters spaced apart. FG close to building with F almost touching. *Standard* for all Proofs, except 1993, and circulation strikes from 1958 to 1992.

Close AM: Bottoms of letters almost touch. FG distant from building. *Standard* for circulation strikes since 1993. Standard on Proofs of 1993 only.

Such varieties can and do cause excitement, often sensational at first, then fading as more coins are examined and an orderly market develops. *Numismatic News*, May 3, 1998, carried a lengthy and informative article by Ken Potter, a consummate student of die varieties of modern coins, which began with this:

1998-S Proof Cent Latest to Show Close AM

A 1998-S Proof cent with a business-strike [circulation-strike] Close AM reverse design has been discovered and, additional reports of 1999-S Proof cents with the Close AM business-strike reverse trickle in and are now known in both silver and clad Proof sets. Lightning has struck twice for owners of modem Proof sets seeking potentially rare Lincoln cent varieties. Michelle Smith of Don's Coin Exchange in Enid, Okla., has reported the discovery of a Proof 1998-S Lincoln cent struck with a reverse die of a style intended for circulation strikes. The discovery follows right on the heels of our report of the same type of die pairing on a 1999-S Lincoln cent, which was featured as the lead story in the April 12 issue of Numismatic News. An example of that coin has already traded for a price exceeding $750 on eBay.

Except for 1993, all years of Proof Lincoln Memorial cents typically carry a reverse design style that exhibits the AM of AMERICA spaced wide apart (along with other differences) while their business-strike counterparts from 1993 to date have exhibited a design style with the AM almost connected. These variations in design style were first described by variety coin specialist and author John A. Wexler in January 2001. He announced that research had revealed that since 1994, the Mint had been using two different die designs concurrently for the reverse of the Lincoln cent.

The same article included this on Proof dies:

According to Ronald E. Harrigal, PE, assistant director for design, quality, research and development at the U.S. Mint:

"Proof cent dies average 3,000 coins per die. Dies are made in lots of 25, up to a batch quantity of 300, depending on the order. If the wrong hub was used, the range of coins that could be generated would be 75,000 to 900,000."

His figures are based on entire batches of dies being affected and not one or a few dies slipping in by mistake, which is also possible. For example, the 1999 circulation strike with a Wide AM Proof style reverse is only known struck from one die pair.[24]

Harrigal also said that, "Separate master dies for Proof and circulation are made for the cent only. This was done to enhance circulation coinage die life while retaining high image quality on the Proof variety. On all other coins, the Proof coin is used as a basis for master die approval and circulation varieties are made from the Proof die master."

CHAPTER EIGHT

GRADING LINCOLN CENTS
THEORY AND THE MARKETPLACE

GRADE AS A DETERMINANT OF VALUE
STANDARDIZING DESCRIPTIONS OF CONDITION

The grade assigned to a coin, reflecting the amount of contact or wear a coin has received, is an important element in determining a coin's value. A pristine Lincoln cent or other coin, in "new" condition, in recent times has been called Mint State, although the term was used as early as the nineteenth century.

For many years, dating back to the 1850s, various systems have been proposed to describe coin grades. All, including the ANA system most of us use today, have struggled with the subjective nature of such classification. A dealer or collector attending the sale of the John F. McCoy Collection, cataloged by W.E. Woodward, held in New York City in May 1864, pondered such descriptions as these:

A well-worn 1914-D cent designated VG-8 on the ANA Grading Scale.

> **Lot 355. 1801 [silver dollar].** Very fine, or perhaps uncirculated.
>
> **Lot 654. A set of Three Cent Pieces,** from 1851 to 1859 inclusive, with duplicates from '51 to '54 inclusive, all good, and mostly very fine, thirteen pieces.
>
> **Lot 670. 1799 [cent].** One of the finest existing, the best ever offered at auction, excessively rare.

At that time it would have been difficult for anyone to bid without actually inspecting the coins. Lot 355 is in some sort of a high grade, but it seems that Woodward himself, generally considered to be the most astute professional numismatist of his time, was not certain if the coin was Very Fine, or if it was Uncirculated. Or, perhaps very fine meant "nice" or "desirable" in this instance, although it was a distinct coin grade in the hobby at the time.

For the set of silver three-cent pieces, we have little clue as to the preservation of the coins offered. Lot 670, the rare 1799 cent, must have been very nice, but not much information is given about the grade.

In ensuing years descriptions of grades became more clear across the hobby, but there was still the matter of interpretation. What to J.W. Scott in 1880 might have been a Proof, to the eyes of Henry Chapman might have been a buffed-up Extremely Fine. Again, in-person inspection of auction lots was mandatory. This was usually done by dealers who obtained commissions from collectors to bid on their behalf.

A 1913 GRADING PROPOSAL

In March 1913, in *The Numismatist*, H.O. Granberg of Oshkosh, Wisconsin, one of the most prominent collectors and (part-time) dealers of his day, proposed a grading system, here excerpted. His introductory comments can be used today in the early twenty-first century, with little change:

> Since assuming the office of secretary of this Association many members have asked me to inaugurate some scheme for a uniform standard of classifying the condition of coins. It can be safely said that every member has some standard by which he judges the condition of coins, and it can be safely said that no two of these standards is exactly alike. Now, no two persons can think and see exactly alike in all respects, but if some standard were given the utmost publicity there is no reason why everyone concerned would not think nearer alike. My experience has been that the holder or owner of a coin is inclined to overestimate its condition, and the non-owner of a coin is apt to underestimate its condition. In other words, the condition of the coin varies if you own the coin or if someone else owns it. It is human nature. This will be the hardest phase to adjust, but if some descriptive standard was down in black and white, this variance of opinion could be reduced.
>
> These remarks apply to collectors as well as dealers. My experience has been that no two dealers judge condition exactly alike, but I think the dealer holds to his standard more consistently than the collector who, to bid intelligently, has got to learn the standard of each dealer. This is another phase to be taken up. The condition of wear as "Fine," "Good," "Fair," etc., is not enough. Some qualifying word should be employed as well, such as "bright," "scratched," "tarnished," etc. A good many dealers object to calling attention to faults, defects, and other imperfections in coins, as the mentioning of these defects in cold type tends to make the coin appear worse than it really is. This is partly true, or rather has become so, for only marked defects are stated, and whenever a coin's bad points are mentioned, the general supposition is that the coin is pretty bad.

The preceding paragraph is especially important, for Granberg realized that for truly effective communication, to describe a coin simply as Fine "is not enough." A further description is needed. Today we have numbers for grades, but as abundantly discussed in this book, smart buyers need much more, which now, nearly a century later, we still do not have. Continuing with Granberg in 1913:

Proposed Grading Standards

Proof: Coins struck by a hand press from new and sharp dies that are polished. Any defects in striking, or imperfection in the planchet should be noted. If the coin has suffered since striking, the blemish should be mentioned. The word "Proof" should be qualified by such word as "brilliant," "dull," "tarnished," "haymarked," "finger-marked," "scratched," "rubbed," etc.

Uncirculated: Struck for circulation, but not worn in any way. Any defects, such as scratches, nicks, bruises, fingermarks, spots, tarnish, etc. should be mentioned, also poor striking and defects in planchet. Copper coins that have dulled or have changed color but show no signs of wear, may be termed Uncirculated, but no corroded coin should be termed Uncirculated.

Very Fine: The condition but little below Uncirculated, with imperceptible wear, or showing only under close scrutiny. Lightly tarnished coins may be placed under this classification, but the fact should be mentioned. Badly tarnished coins should never be called Very Fine nor should coins marred in any way other than in a slight change of color.

Fine: Showing very slight traces of wear only in the parts in the highest relief. Any blemishes should be noted.

Very Good: A worn coin but every part distinct, nothing but very marked defects need be mentioned.

Good: Everything distinct but somewhat worn.

Fair: Much worn but all outlines showing.

Poor: Everything below Fair.

Other Aspects of Grading

Nicks, scratches, corrosion, tarnish, marks, faults in striking and in the planchet, file marks, discoloration, spots, etc., should be stated in the description of every coin above Good. These remarks do not necessarily apply to very cheap coins when put in lots, but these coins should not be given a high rating. Holes, partial or complete, solder marks, rings and loops should be stated in all coins above Fair.

If coins have been scoured or cleaned or plated (when they should not be) the fact should be mentioned. The color of the coins, especially copper coins, should be stated if the piece is of any value. Coins brightened by chemicals should not be called bright, but should be termed "cleaned." If obverse and reverse are markedly different in condition, both sides should be described. If the coin is a cheap coin, however, the average of the two sides may be stated. "Bright" and "brilliant" are terms defining the natural condition of the coins, not an artificial rendering of the surface.

The terms, "evenly struck," "off center," "weak," or "strong impression" should be used in every case where the value of the coin warrants the additional description.

It would be difficult to improve on the things he said were needed. In my opinion, if Granberg's 1913 suggestions were adopted today, we would all benefit!

Down through the years, many other grading systems were proposed, intermediate grades were added (not a jump from Very Fine to Uncirculated as in 1913, but with Extremely Fine and About Uncirculated in between), and other changes were made. The idea of describing a coin beyond "Very Fine," "Extremely Fine," or another set of adjectives, however, was never accepted by either collectors or dealers. Today, as in 1913, if a 1911-D cent graded MS-65RD has been dipped, it is not mentioned. If an EF-40 1909-S V.D.B. cent has a cut on the rim, this generally is not mentioned either.

In theory, most everyone agreed back in 1913, and nearly everyone seeking to *buy* a coin agrees today, that it is a good idea, but those *owning* coins are reluctant to go beyond the basics. The supposition in the marketplace in 1913, as it is today, is: "This coin is Extremely Fine. Now, you have to see for yourself if it has been cleaned, or has scratches, or if there are any other problems."

Continuing the chronicle of grading standards, *Photograde*, a photographic guide to grading by James F. Ruddy, was a big step and was widely used after its introduction in 1970. Later the idea was copied by others.

THE ANA GRADING STANDARDS

The ANA decided to get into the grading game, set up a grading committee, and in 1977 published *The Official ANA Grading Standard for United States Coins*, largely supervised by dealer Abe Kosoff, and compiled by Kenneth E. Bressett, successor to Richard S. Yeoman as editor of *A Guide Book of United States Coins*. I wrote the general introductory material.

The system was one of numbers, building upon a scheme devised by Dr. William H. Sheldon in 1949 and published in his *Early American Cents* book. The number 1 was assigned to a coin that was worn so smooth as to be barely identifiable. Sheldon's term for this was Basal State-1, which would correspond to the modern grade *Poor-1*. The number 70 represented absolute perfection.

In case you wonder why the scale does not go to up to 100 for perfection, here's the reason: the system is based solely on the market formula once used to determine the retail price for large copper cents minted between the years 1793 and 1814. At that time the market for cents was far different from what it is now, and an MS-60 coin was worth just twice as much as a VF-30 one. By assigning a *Basal Value* (another Sheldon concept) to a cent—say, a Basal Value of $2—you could then calculate that a VF-20 coin was worth $2 x 20, or $40; that an EF-40 coin was worth $2 x 40, or $80; an MS-60 $120; and so on. The system soon proved unworkable, however, because prices in the market were not so neatly arranged.

Today there is a huge difference between VF-30 and MS-60, and the system is even more absurd, or perhaps beyond absurd. The concept of using numbers lives on, however, and today we have them.

At first the ANA Grading Standards of 1977 mirrored the Sheldon system of 1949, more or less. In subsequent editions, however, the ANA board of governors added intermediate grades of Mint State listings, such as MS-63 and MS-67. Then were added the full range of Mint State possibilities, creating a total of 11 grades from MS-60 to MS-61, to MS-62, and so on, all the way to MS-70. On the other hand, the grade of Very Fine starts at VF-20 and runs until we reach Extra Fine at EF-40, or a range of 20 numbers, not all of which are used. Perhaps some day we will have VF-21, VF-22, etc. I hope not. The ANA book became well accepted and has gone through multiple editions, now at the eighth.

Below are given the guidelines as outlined in *The Official ANA Grading Standards for U.S. Coins*, eighth edition. These criteria represent an adaptation and distillation of information and opinions gathered from many leading experts in the field.

While they and any other standards are subject to interpretation, those propounded by the ANA are the most widely used in the marketplace, including by all of the leading grading services. Understanding them is the *first step* to being able to evaluate the grade of a coin. It is not the be-all and end-all, and it is by no means the final answer to smart buyers. It is, however, the final answer to perhaps 90 percent or more of the buyers of coins today. I do not mean to be iconoclastic, just realistic.

What is the grade of this lovely Proof 1987-S cent (enlarged 1.5x)? Most would agree it is "RD," for red color. One expert might call it Proof-67, however, and another 68, and perhaps 69 or 70. Grading is now, has been in the past, and probably always will be a matter of opinion.

OFFICIAL ANA GRADING STANDARDS
LINCOLN CENTS 1909 TO DATE
(ADAPTED)

MINT STATE (MS)

Absolutely no trace of wear. Abbreviations of BN (brown surface toning), RB (mint red-orange mixed with brown), and RD (mint orange-red) can be added to the numerical grades, as appropriate, as MS-63BN, MS-65RD, etc.

MS-65RD Lincoln cent

MS-70 A flawless coin exactly as it was minted, with no trace of wear or injury. Must have full mint luster and natural color.

MS-67 Virtually flawless, but with very minor imperfections.

MS-65 No trace of wear; nearly as perfect as MS-67 except for some small blemish. Has full

MS-65RB Lincoln cent

mint luster but may be unevenly toned or lightly fingermarked. A few minor nicks or marks may be present.

MS-63 A Mint State coin with attractive mint luster, but noticeable detracting contact marks or minor blemishes.

MS-60 A strictly Uncirculated coin with no trace of wear, but with blemishes more obvious than in higher grades. May have dull mint luster; color may be uneven shades of brown.

ABOUT UNCIRCULATED (AU)

Small traces of wear are visible on highest points.

AU-58 (Very Choice) Has some signs of abrasion: high points of cheek and jaw; tips of wheat stalks.

AU-55 (Choice) OBVERSE: Only a trace of wear shows on the highest point of the jaw. REVERSE: A trace of wear shows on the tops of the wheat stalks. SURFACE: Much of the mint luster is still present.

AU-58 Lincoln cent

AU-50 (Typical) OBVERSE: Traces of wear show on the cheek and jaw. REVERSE: Traces of wear show on the wheat stalks.

EXTREMELY FINE

Very light wear on only the highest points.

EF-45 (Choice) OBVERSE: Slight wear shows on hair above ear, on the cheek, and on the jaw. REVERSE: High points of wheat stalks are lightly worn, but each line is clearly defined. SURFACE: Some of the mint luster may show.

EF-45 Lincoln cent

EF-40 (Typical) OBVERSE: Wear shows on hair above ear, on the cheek, and on the jaw. REVERSE: High points of wheat stalks are worn, but each line is clearly defined. SURFACE: Traces of mint luster may show.

VERY FINE

Light to moderate even wear. All major features are sharp.

VF-30 (Choice) OBVERSE: There are small flat spots of wear on cheek and jaw. Hair still shows details. Ear and bow tie are slightly worn but show clearly. REVERSE: Lines in wheat stalks are lightly worn but fully detailed.

VF-30 Lincoln cent

VF-20 (Typical) OBVERSE: Head shows considerable flatness. Nearly all the details still show in hair and on the face. Ear and bow tie are worn but bold. REVERSE: Lines in wheat are worn flat and show very few details.

FINE

Moderate to heavy even wear. Entire design is clear and bold.

F-12 OBVERSE: Some details show in the hair. Cheek and jaw are worn nearly smooth. LIBERTY shows with no letters missing. The ear and bow are visible. REVERSE: Most details are visible in the stalks. Top wheat lines are worn but separated.

F-12 Lincoln cent

VERY GOOD

Well worn. Design is clear but flat and lacking details.

VG-8 OBVERSE: Outline of hair shows but most details are smooth. Cheek and jaw are smooth. Most of bow tie is visible. Legend and date are clear. REVERSE: Wheat shows some details and about half of the lines at the top.

VG-8 Lincoln cent

GOOD

Heavily worn. Design and legend are visible, but faint in spots.

G-4 OBVERSE: Entire design is well worn with very little detail remaining. Legend and date are weak but visible. REVERSE: Wheat is worn nearly flat but is completely outlined. Some grains are visible.

G-4 Lincoln cent

ABOUT GOOD

Outlined design. Parts of date and legend are worn smooth.

AG-3 OBVERSE: Head is outlined with nearly all details worn away. Legend and date are readable but very weak and merging into rim. REVERSE: Entire design is partially worn away. Parts of wheat and motto are merged with the rim.

Notes: Lincoln Memorial cents, struck from 1959 to date, can be graded using the obverse descriptions.

The following characteristic traits will assist in grading, but must not be confused with actual wear on the coins:

Matte Proof cents of 1909 through 1916: Often spotted or stained.

Branch mint cents of the 1920s: Usually not as sharply struck as are the later dates.

Many early issues are weakly struck on the obverse and/or the reverse, especially the following: 1911-D, 1914-D, 1917-D, 1918-D, 1918-S, 1921, 1921-S, 1922-D, 1923, 1923-S, 1924, 1924-S, 1925-D, 1925-S, 1926-S, 1927-D, 1927-S, 1928-S, 1929-D, 1929-S, 1930-S, 1935-D, and 1935-S.

1922 No D cent: Weakly struck at the head. Has a small I and joined RT in LIBERTY. The most sought-after variety has a weak obverse and a strong reverse. On two other varieties that sometimes show a weak D, the wheat heads are weak on the reverse.

1924-D: Usually has a weak mintmark.

1931-S: Sometimes is unevenly struck.

1936 Proof: Early strikes are less mirrorlike than are those struck later that year.

1955 Doubled Die: Hair details are less sharp than are those found on most cents of the period.

Pre-1935 Uncirculated cents: Should not be expected in bright, red condition. They are usually toned to various shades.

MS-63 cents in general: Copper coins of MS-63 and lower may have diminished luster, but must have non-porous clean surfaces, and good eye appeal and strike, to qualify for the corresponding grade.

MS-60 cents in general: Coins will not always have the exact stated amount of mint luster, strike, or absence of marks. Overall eye appeal and appearance may also influence the stated grade. Significant corrosion or rough, porous surfaces may detract from the grade. Intensity of the coin's color, ranging from red to brown, has a bearing on desirability and value.[25]

SCIENTIFIC OR NOT?

For a grading system or any other system to be truly scientific, it should be able to be used at a distance by a qualified person having the guidelines in hand. The worldwide system of weights and measures is scientific. A 1910-S Lincoln cent weighing 48.0 grains, if sent from Wolfeboro, New Hampshire, to the ANS in New York City, will be found to weigh 48.0 grains there as well, not 46.3 or 51.2 grains. A 1943 zinc-coated steel cent measured as 19.1 mm in Shamokin, Pennsylvania, on May 12, if put to calipers or a ruler in Basking Ridge, New Jersey, on September 24 will measure 19.1 mm then and there as well.

In contrast, if a 1924-D Lincoln cent certified as MS-64RB by PCGS (or NGC, or another service) were to be taken from its holder by an owner in Wolfeboro and sent to a buyer in New York City, it is very possible that the buyer might grade it as MS-63RB or MS-65RB. If returned to PCGS, or sent to NGC or ANACS, it is possible it might come back in a "body bag" with a notation that it cannot be certified because of "environmental damage," "cleaning," or whatever. It is also possible if this coin is sent back to PCGS, which graded it in the first place, it may be re-evaluated and returned as an MS-65RB. Indeed, the last is such a great possibility that thousands of collectors and hundreds of dealers play the "resubmission game," sending back coins to see if they can be upgraded.

If grading were at all scientific, that 1924-D cent, not in a certified holder, but unlabeled, could be sent to Chicago, Los Angeles, Tampa, St. Louis, and Memphis, and at each stop it would be graded precisely as MS-64RB.

At the risk of redundancy, I mention two of countless examples that actually happened:

A dealer sent a group of high-grade double eagles to a leading service a few weeks before cataloging them for an auction sale. An attractive 1853 came back as AU-58. The coin was sold, and the buyer took it out of the holder and sent it back to the same service. It came back as MS-62. Here we have the situation, *not at all uncommon*, that a coin first classified as worn, not Mint State at all, quickly and magically became Mint State! Scientific or not? You answer the question.

A rare 1804 silver dollar from the Amon Carter Jr. Collection was sent to a leading grading service and was encapsulated as EF-45. Later the same coin was sent to the same grading service and became AU-58, an improvement of 13 points! Scientific or not? What do you think?

Moreover, even within the ANA guidelines—and the same can be said for any other guidelines—two people can read the same words and come up with different opinions. Let's revisit the descriptions for these two grades for Lincoln cents:

> **MS-65** No trace of wear; nearly as perfect as MS-67 except for some small blemish. Has full mint luster but may be unevenly toned or lightly finger-marked. A few minor nicks or marks may be present.
>
> **MS-63** A Mint State coin with attractive mint luster, but noticeable detracting contact marks or minor blemishes.

Dealer Jones might look a coin and find it has "some small blemish" and "a few minor nicks or marks." Thus, it is an MS-65. Buyer Smith might find those "few minor marks or minor blemishes" to be worse than that, and may consider them "noticeable," thus calling it MS-63.

As if this were not enough, what are a *"few* minor marks or minor blemishes"? Four minor blemishes? Six? No two coins have the same marks and blemishes. A cent might have seven minor (whatever that may be) marks and three minor blemishes, and another might have just one minor mark, no blemishes, but a tiny scratch.

If you aspire to be a smart buyer (see chapter nine), you need more information. Since the holder does not provide this, it is up to you to learn more.

Many of us are too close to the system of grading numbers to look at the situation objectively. In reality, Lincoln cents are very complex, with many variables. If the real estate industry were to establish a system from 1 to 70 to grade summer vacation condos, would you buy a Grade-65 condo in Aspen without seeing it? Or, would you request a photographic tour or an in-person visit? As to a Grade-20 condo in Wildwood Crest, you know that it is hardly new. In fact, it has endured extensive use. But do you want to buy it without seeing its actual condition?

I am not satirizing the ANA Grading Standards. In fact, I've spent much time, with Kenneth Bressett and dozens of consultants, refining them—with changes in each edition. I do, however, realize that they are not scientific, and *The Official ANA Grading Standards for U.S. Coins*, eighth edition, states this clearly.

Advantages of the ANA Standards

That said, there are multiple distinct *advantages* the ANA Standards have to offer. Here are some that come to mind:

1. *Grades are easy to compare:* It is instantly obvious that an MS-67 coin is in a higher grade than an AU-55, and the latter coin is better than a VF-20, which in turn is in a higher grade than G-4. As you investigate coins offered in advertisements, auctions, Internet listings, etc., you can hone in on what you are seeking. If you want a gem Mint State coin, then a listing from, say, MS-65 upward will catch your eye. You can then evaluate it further, as described in chapter nine, "How to Be a Smart Buyer."

2. *No information is given about quality:* Yes, this is an *advantage* for you. It means that if you become a connoisseur and seek, for example, a 1925-D MS-65RD Lincoln cent that is sharply struck with Full Details, even though these are much rarer than weakly struck ones, you will probably not have to pay much more for it! This is called cherrypicking.

3. *Numbers appear to be very scientific:* Here is another advantage for you. As you set about being a smart buyer and looking here and there for superb quality coins in whatever grade you choose, your competitors in the marketplace will not disturb you. In fact, they may consider you to be quite unusual, if they are aware of you at all. These people have precision in other areas of their lives: The ABC Corporation bonds in their portfolio are graded AAA, their Toyota gets 28.3 miles per gallon on the Interstate, and so on. Collecting rare books, or prints, or furniture is imprecise and scary. Not so with coins. There is great confidence in knowing that experienced dealers have graded this coin as precisely AU-53, or MS-65BN, or some other number. No need to look at the coin itself. Just read the holder. This lessens competition for you, as does No. 2 above.

4. *Undesirable coins sell to most buyers:* Yes, this is yet another advantage for you, and it is a godsend for dealers. A 1925-D MS-65RD cent might have a couple of carbon spots, lack detail on the high points, and have grainy fields

resulting from worn dies; but if it is offered at a slight discount, it will find a wide and enthusiastic market with nearly everyone—perhaps not with you or me, but with nearly all others. This keeps overall market values strong.

5. *Buying opportunities occur more frequently:* The more emotional capital you have invested in collecting coins, the longer you will keep the coins you acquire. Specialists who spend ten years finding a rare object of desire are likely to cherish it for a long time. On the other hand, many if not most buyers, and certainly most investors, know little about the coins in certified holders and just read the labels. A new purchase soon loses its novelty value, and soon goes back on the market. The advantage is that you have more coins from which to choose. In contrast, in the 1950s most buyers of scarce and rare coins would hold on to them for years.

CERTIFIED COINS

DIFFERENT SERVICES

In the 1970s the ANA Certification Service (ANACS) set up in the business of grading coins for a fee. A submitted coin would be assigned a grade, photographed for identification, and sent back with a certificate showing the coin and its evaluation. In time the ANA sold ANACS to Amos Press, parent company of *Coin World*, which later sold it to Anderson Press. In December 2007 ANACS was acquired by Driving Force, LLC, and the grading company was relocated to Colorado.

In 1986 PCGS popularized the encapsulation of coins in a plastic holder, soon popularly called a "slab." NGC followed suit in 1987, and soon ANACS developed its own holder. Later more than 100 services were born, but most died. Today NGC and PCGS have the lion's share of the business, with ANACS and ICG joining them in terms of acceptance and reputation. There are, no doubt, other fine services as well. There are also a lot of exploitative and fly-by-night services, some of them with "official" or high-sounding names. My advice: On your own, approach several different dealers and collectors and ask about the grading services. Just say something like: "If you were buying a Proof-65RD 1936 cent for your own collection, which certification service would you prefer?" The services are continually discussed, and you'll soon become well informed as to which labels are worthwhile and which should be ignored.

The certification services use the same ANA Official Grading Standards that you have just read. Because the standards are not scientific, a given Lincoln cent or other coin can be assigned a different grade if resubmitted, or the grade can remain the same.

That said, some services have "tighter" interpretations than do others. If an MS-64BN Lincoln cent from Certification Service A is listed at $1,000 in the *Certified Coin Dealer Newsletter*, and the same coin from Certification Service B is posted at $900, it means that the dealer community values A's coins slightly higher than B's, meaning that they are perceived as being of slightly higher quality. It is important to remember that even with such differences, there are likely some MS-64BN coins graded by B that are of higher quality than some of those certified by A. Stated another way, each leading service has some coins that are apt to be finer than those of a competing service, and some that are to be lesser in quality.

ENCAPSULATED COINS

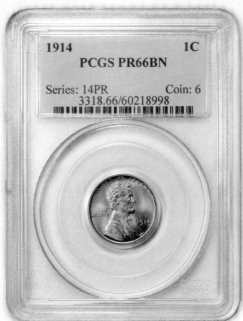

A selection of certified holders. From upper left, clockwise: ANACS, NGC, and PCGS. Each of these services has altered the style of its holders over a period of time. The typical "slab" has basic information on the face, as illustrated. The back usually contains a bar code, a holo-gram or related security strip, and serial information. Some repeat that on the front.

REGISTRY SETS

Some years ago David Hall, prime founder of PCGS, came up with the idea of the PCGS Registry Set. This developed into a very popular program whereby collectors and investors can form a set or collection in just about any series, and register it with PCGS. The total of the numbers (ANA grading numbers) in each set is added up, more weight is assigned to rarer issues, and a score is assigned.

For participants, this is like owning a stable of race horses. When one coin is improved, your score rises, and perhaps with the improvement of a half dozen coins, you will move from fourth-best set to third. As an auctioneer I know that when PCGS coins that are the highest graded are offered, there is a lot of excitement. Such coins do not need to be at all rare at lower levels. A Registry Set leader at MS-69 might be one of just three graded at that level and may be very expensive, while a very nice MS-65 may be valued at a very nominal and affordable sum.

My advice is that Registry Set participation can be exciting—just like betting in Las Vegas or on the Kentucky Derby, or buying options in the stock market—but there are losers as well as winners. Keep your eye on the series in which you are involved, and watch out for the real possibility that a coin, which today may have just three graded at MS-69, might have ten at that level, or even some at MS-70, a few years hence.

POPULATION REPORTS

In a word, *beware!* From the inception of PCGS in 1986 and NGC in 1987, the values of certain certified coins have been driven by the numbers appearing in their periodic population reports. As more and more coins are sent into the services, the populations expand: This is particularly true for the "ultra" grades such as MS-68 to 70 and Proof-68 to 70. *Populations never get smaller. They usually get larger, often much larger.* Take heed of this when buying, and you'll pay for the price of this book many times over!

If you are a Registry Set participant, or if you have a lot of money and want the best, then ultra grades are for you. For the rest of us, gem MS-65 and 66RD coins will be just fine, if selected with care.

COMMON SENSE WHEN ANALYZING REPORTS

Further, the population reports for Lincoln cents are heavily biased toward ultra-grade coins. One of the most common of all Lincoln cents of its era is the 1944 Philadelphia coin, of which 1,435,400,000 were struck. Today tens of millions of worn examples exist as do millions of Mint State coins. One recent population report reads:

> **1944 Cent population totals:** VF-20BN: 14, EF-40BN: 6, EF-45BN: 1, AU-50BN: 2, AU-53BN: 2, AU-55BN: 7, AU-58BN: 17, MS-60RD: 1, MS-61RD: 0, MS-62RD: 1, MS-63RD: 25, MS-64RD: 339, MS-65RD: 1,111, MS-66RD: 2,940, MS-67RD: 307, MS-68RD: 2, MS-69RD: 0, MS-70RD: 0.

What do these numbers mean? What do they not mean?

A newcomer to the hobby might read these numbers and think, "The most common grade of a 1944 cent is MS-66RD. Really rare is an EF-40, with only six certified." Then he or she would think: "How can this be, if more than a billion were minted? Why are more worn coins *rare?*" A eureka moment would then suggest that since it typically costs the best part of $10 or so to certify a cent, there would not be much point in submitting a potential EF-40 coin, which in bulk is worth perhaps just ten cents.

Instead, the submitted cents, with many obvious exceptions, are mostly those sent in with the hope of being graded MS-67RD (which sell for much more than the grading fee). No MS-69 has been certified yet, but perhaps the *first* one will be worth, say, $500 or $1,000 at auction, perhaps far more. The reports *leave much unsaid* and simply give a single element of value: how many have been certified in the highest Mint State RD grade. All other numbers, including those for such worthwhile and affordable grades as MS-64RD and MS-65RD, are completely meaningless in terms of the number of coins actually in existence. Even in the quest for MS-67RD or higher coins, I doubt if even 1 percent of the rolls of Mint State 1944 cents in existence have been examined for such possibilities.

Because of the above, it would be a waste of time and space to give population reports for Lincoln cents except in the very highest Mint State and Proof grades.

WORDS OF WISDOM FROM BILL FIVAZ

Near the beginning of this chapter, I quoted words that H.O. Granberg wrote in 1913 and stated that his recommendations, most of which were never implemented, still make good sense today. If they were put into use now, the hobby would benefit immensely.

It is perhaps a fitting close to this chapter to quote some words from my fine long-time friend Bill Fivaz, a true gentleman and one of the most knowledgeable numismatists in the hobby. They appeared a generation ago in *The Numismatist* of June 1982. I believe you will agree that his advice, excerpted here, is still relevant today—and, for what it may be worth, generally parallels what you have read in this book:

Developing Grading Skills

To be sure, many coins are purchased at the correct grade and are good investments, but there is only one person upon whose judgment you can rely completely, and that is you! The question is, what can you do to gain the necessary confidence?

First, take some time and study proper grading techniques, perhaps concentrating on just one series and learning all you can about the striking characteristics, the high points of wear, etc. Learn what issues are habitually weakly struck, what characteristics distinguish a weak strike from wear, and which dates exhibit good luster. Assimilate this information and then apply that knowledge to other series.

Next, choose a reputable dealer, one who grades coins properly. Avoid the dealer who tends to downgrade each coin offered him, refusing to acknowledge that some are legitimate MS-65s or whatever, even though many of the coins in his display cases are graded as such and are visibly inferior to those he has declined to buy. Unfortunately, double-standard grading is extremely prevalent in the hobby, and although some grading is based on the old "ownership is worth up to five points" principle, most of it is not. We must learn to live with this as a fact of life—it will never change.

Another fact is that the more coins you look at and grade, the more proficient you'll become. This is extremely important. Once equipped with the knowledge of how to grade, you must put this knowledge to practical use.

Join a coin club. Many clubs sponsor educational programs on grading, complete with color slide presentations on just about every type of coin actively collected. Discussions on grading can stimulate some excellent dialogue and you will soon become acquainted with knowledgeable individuals from whom you can seek advice.

Aaron Feldman, the late sage of numismatics, is credited with the statement, "Buy the book before the coin!" This is vitally true in learning grading practices. Three excellent books for your grading library are *ANA Grading Standards for United States Coins*, *Photograde: A Photographic Guide for United States Coins*, and *A Guide to the Grading of United States Coins*. The first 26 pages of *ANA Grading Standards* are particularly informative.

Get together with a collector friend or two on a regular basis to compare grading procedures. Jot down how you feel a particular coin should be graded and why, then compare notes. Discuss your differences, calling in a third party if necessary.

Never hesitate to question a dealer as to why he assigned a particular grade to a coin. Explain that you are trying to develop confidence in your own grading skills and would appreciate any help he might offer. Generally speaking, if a dealer is not busy and does not feel he must justify his grading, he will be glad to help you. Eventually you will decide for yourself which dealers grade accurately and which are a bit "sloppy."

The bottom line is that you are responsible for buying properly graded coins for your collection or portfolio, so spend some time building confidence in your ability to select the right coin. Don't depend on someone else to "do right by you"—too often it just doesn't turn out that way.

CHAPTER NINE

HOW TO BE A SMART BUYER
YOU CAN BE AN EXPERT!

WHAT TO LOOK FOR
INTRODUCTION

Now, to buying coins for your collection and enjoyment. Most Lincoln cents in the marketplace are simply described as MS-64BN, MS-66RD, or some other designation. Certified coins may be listed as MS-65 (NGC), MS-60BN (ANACS), MS-63RB (ICG), MS-67RD (PCGS), or similar.

Never but never, or almost never, will you see something like this: "MS-65RD, with a light spot on the obverse, several flecks on the reverse, and with flatness on the rims on both sides." Or, "MS-65RD, satiny, almost matte surfaces, probably from cyanide treatment which dulled the 'flash' and frost of the luster, but created a coin that is still attractive."

Once again, this is an advantage. You can be *very pleased* that there are so few smart buyers out there. Otherwise, coins such as the two above MS-65RD pieces would have no buyers at all, except perhaps at the MS-60 price level. In the meantime, you can peruse offerings of MS-65RD or any other grade coins and cherrypick for quality.

Be warned that such connoisseurship will limit what you will want to buy in auction or other offerings. I recently reviewed an offering of a nearly complete set of MS cents, 1909 to 1933. The 1909 V.D.B. cent was very nice, and some of the later P-Mint coins were nice as well. Every other coin had some flecks, or weakness, or some other problem. Situations such as these can be turned into a fascinating challenge for you.

ASPECTS OF SHARPNESS

Lincoln cents were made to be used in everyday commerce. To meet demand, the various mints were charged with turning out as many as possible, as efficiently and cheaply as possible. To accomplish this and to minimize problems with the coining presses, dies were often spaced slightly too far apart to create sharp coins, but ideally for prolonging their life. In addition, if planchets were not properly annealed (softened by heating, then cooled slowly), they would be too hard for the details to strike up properly.

A very weakly struck 1926-S cent certified as MS-63RD by a leading service, apparently building the weakness into the assigned grade. Both dies are extremely worn, with the reverse showing a "ghost" outline of the obverse. In addition, either the dies were spaced too widely apart or the planchet was too hard, from improper annealing.

Probably, any connoisseur would rather have a sharply struck AU-55 coin than this shallow low-end strike, never mind it being called RD. It is seen in this instance that a certified holder marked "1926-S MS-63RD" has no real meaning for a smart buyer.

The following tests may seem daunting upon first reading, but with some experience in the field—such as at coin shows and visiting coin shops—you will be able to make these determinations very quickly. Moreover, these tests, while applicable to all eras, are most important for the earlier dates from 1909 to 1933.

For Lincoln cents of the 1909 to 1958 years with the wheat ears reverse, sharply struck coins (Full Details) from new (not worn or tired) dies will have these characteristics:

OBVERSE WEAKNESSES

Weakly struck 1919-S. The LI in LIB-ERTY is weak, as are the beard and hair details and the mintmark. (enlarged 1.5x)

Weakly struck 1929-S from tired dies and with the dies too widely spaced and/or an improperly annealed planchet. (enlarged 1.5x)

Detail of the obverse of a high-grade 1921 cent with RD color, classified as a gem, but with many nicks and marks on Lincoln's shoulder. The fields are deeply lustrous and virtually mark-free.

Detail of the obverse of a high-grade 1927-S cent with RD color, classified as a gem, but with many nicks and marks on Lincoln's face and shoulder, these being the deepest areas of the die. The fields approach perfection, with scarcely a microscopic mark. Grading certification is by the field, not the portrait!

Obverse: The portrait of Lincoln should be sharp on the hair and beard. These features were sharp when the design was created in 1909, but as dies were made, the masters and hubs that created them became slightly worn, reducing the detail somewhat. In 1916 the details were sharpened, after which the details became progressively less sharp through the end of the type in 1958, and slightly beyond. For that reason you cannot expect the hair and beard details to be as good on a well-struck 1944 cent as on a 1909 or 1916 cent. To determine how sharp a 1944 cent can be under ideal circumstances, familiarize yourself with general sharpness of coins over the years, including of Proof coins of certain years (which are usually sharper than circulation strikes). You will begin to see the possibilities.

The shoulder of Lincoln is a "secret spot" hardly ever mentioned in print. When the dies were not closely spaced, and the higher parts did not strike up sharply, Lincoln's shoulder became weak. This is not immediately obvious because the die is quite smooth there. The secret is that if it is weakly struck, under magnification you will see little nicks and marks from the original planchet; that is, planchet abrasions that were not flattened away during the coining process. This checkpoint for sharpness is often ignored, and the certification services do not consider it at all. Accordingly, a cent in an ultra-high Mint State grade can be weakly struck on the shoulder and have planchet abrasions. In reality, two certified Lincoln cents, say of 1931-S, can be described as MS-67RD, but in reality, *you* can examine each and find that one has the shoulder of Lincoln fully struck, and the other has countless planchet abrasions. The prices are apt to be the same because other buyers are clueless about these nicks and marks.

REVERSE WEAKNESSES

1922-D cent from an overused or "tired" die, with a ridge between the bottom wheat ends, wavy surfaces, and graininess. This coin was certified as a high-level gem. (enlarged 1.5x)

Detail of the reverse of a 1914-D cent struck from an overly worn die. The top part of the rim is weak, the field is wavy, and there is a ridge connecting the bottoms of the wheat stalks. (enlarged 1.5x)

Weakly struck AM in AMER-ICA on a 1926-D cent. Such problems are not disclosed on certified holders.

Detail of the reverse of a "gem" 1917-S cent, struck from a very worn die, and with areas indistinct.

Weakly struck S in STATES on a 1931 cent.

The letters comprising IN GOD WE TRUST and LIBERTY should each be sharp. Look at the letters under magnification to be sure they were completely filled in the die. A quick glance won't do.

The rim should be sharp, with the flat field of the coin ending, then the upward curve of the outer part of the field continuing to the rim, which should be raised and full, either rounded or flat at the top. The rim should be consistent—not thick at one point around the coin and thin at another. When certified coins are photographed for illustration on the Internet or in catalogs, the rim is often obscured by the holder. In such instances, query the seller on this aspect of sharpness.

Worn or tired dies can be recognized by having a graininess to them, and/or a slight waviness in the field. Deep, rich, frosty luster may be impaired. Usually, worn dies are more noticeable on the reverse than on the obverse.

Reverse: Check all lettering for sharpness, using low-power magnification, say, 4x to 8x. Each letter should be fully formed. The wheat ears are usually strong, including the parallel lines at the top, but check. Often there is a slight ridge, curved downward, connecting the bottom tips of the wheat ears.

The rim should be sharp, similar to that on the obverse, except that for some issues the reverse rim is less prominent (although fully struck up). Worn dies are a big problem. Coins struck from these can be determined by holding the reverse so that the field is at an angle to the light, reflecting the light into your eye. If there is any waviness, rounded ridges, or anything other than a smooth, consistent flat surface, then reject the coin. Some Lincoln cents of the 1909 to 1919 years have a nicely textured, somewhat matte finish to the reverse, as struck. These are desirable, provided that other aspects of the coin are satisfactory.

For Lincoln cents from 1959 to date with the Lincoln Memorial reverse, sharply struck Full Details coins from new (not worn or tired) dies and/or on soft (properly annealed) planchets should have these characteristics:

Obverse: Check the portrait, including Lincoln's shoulder as described above, the last often showing pesky planchet marks when viewed under magnification. Due to hub wear, the details on the portrait will not be sharp; but within that context, select as nice a strike as you can find. *Proofs* of the various years usually show what detail can exist. Check a Proof of, say, 1962, to see what you might expect in a well-struck circulation example of the same date. Because the obverse die was modified several times, beginning significantly in late 1969, the typical cent became more sharply struck after that time. In 1984 the relief of the shoulder was lowered dramatically, after which the problem ceased to be important. Worn dies are less of a problem, but check that the fields are smooth and even. The rim should be clearly defined, raised, and evenly struck.

Reverse: The sharpness of details on the Lincoln Memorial varied over a period of time as hubs and masters evolved. Places to check include the shrubbery near the steps and, most obviously, the tiny statue of Lincoln near the center. Worn dies are not much of a problem, but check that the fields are smooth and even. The rim should be clearly defined, raised, and evenly struck.

ASPECTS OF PLANCHET QUALITY

The planchets or blank disks used to strike coins were typically of high quality, fairly consistent in weight, and of well-mixed alloy. As noted in the text, the planchets for the 1909 San Francisco cents and some of the 1910 cents were made from an alloy that streaked after being run through a rolling mill. After a few years these planchets developed a normal light "wood grain" effect in the toning. San Francisco planchets of the era, continuing to the early 1920s, are usually also more yellowish than those used at Philadelphia.

In later years the planchets were of more uniform consistency, resulting in coins of an orange-red color. There are some exceptions in which certain cents are a warmer red.

Sometimes during the strip rolling process, surface flakes or loose metal became what are known as *laminations*—chips of metal or tiny strips separated in part from the main planchet. Although collectors of mint errors might like to own some representative examples, mainstream specialists in cents usually avoid coins with this feature.

The copper-coated zinc planchets introduced in 1982 caused all sorts of problems. Many coins became discolored, or bubbles or blisters erupted on the surface, or the coins became blotchy. This problem extended through 1983 but was corrected in later years, although on occasion some unattractive coins were minted. Cents showing flaking of the copper coating or sections with the copper missing are not unusual and are in the category of mint errors.

"Light colored" cents were reported in the Collectors' Clearinghouse column of *Coin World* on May 23, 1983. Not long afterward, nearly 20 were sent in by readers:

Planchet lamination on the reverse of a 1930-S cent, detail. Also, the die is "tired" and shows traces of a raised ridge connecting the wheat stems.

> Mint officials say that the brass-colored plating is composed of 10% zinc and 90% copper rather than 100% copper. "That's why they are light in color," they explained. They believed that as time went on, those cents would turn a "mustard" color.

David W. Lange suggests that such coating, or an alloy close to it, has been used since 1983. "It adheres better and reduces blistering."[26] The color of finished cents can vary slightly, however.

Zinc proportions can vary among modern cents, caused by zinc planchets getting trapped in the copper plating tank and dissolving into the solution. Authentic cents with this variant feature have been reported by Ken Potter to also include 1985-D (most often encountered), 1997, 1997-D, and 1998.[27] Doubtless, others will be found. This metallic content can be simulated artificially, so authentication is recommended if a high enough price is asked for a coin to merit this. Otherwise, buy from a respected seller. Although there is not an active market in these, Ken Potter and other specialists have offered them for sale and have found many interested buyers.

In summary, except for 1982 and 1983 copper-coated zinc cents, planchet quality, although it should always be checked, is not much of a problem. The streakiness and yellow hue of the early San Francisco coins is not a negative and is recognized as a hallmark of the coins of that era. Dipped or brightened coins will not show this feature.

ASPECTS OF ORIGINAL COLOR

When a Lincoln cent left the coining press in, say, 1920, it had a bright, shiny orange-red color on both sides and on the edge (as viewed edge-on). Since the minting process created heat, the newly made coin was warm, even hot to the touch. Immediately, it was subjected to the atmosphere, which in any mint consisted of the normal nitrogen-oxygen composition, plus traces of human breath, heating or industrial fumes, various suspended particles, and more. Copper is a chemically active metal, and the cent began to acquire normal light toning—at first hardly perceptible.

At the Mint the coin was run through a mechanical counting machine, then put into a canvas bag for shipping. No care was taken to keep the bag from moisture, and in storage, handling, and shipping some dampness was probably acquired. This and other cents then went to the Federal Reserve System, and then to various banks, and sometimes they were wrapped in paper rolls (which always contain sulfur) of 50 coins each.

After that, the typical coin was paid into circulation, or perhaps it was saved in a piggy bank, or maybe it was acquired by a numismatist. As the years went by, the cent acquired more toning. If carefully kept in a dry environment away from heat and light, the cent's toning would be minimized. Otherwise the coin would acquire a tinge or whisper of light brown, with a pleasing softening of the orange-red color overall. If kept in a coin cabinet tray or in a paper envelope, it would typically acquire a deeper brown toning.

This same hypothetical 1920 cent, if viewed by an expert today, would be certified as MS-65RD or higher, if it had just a whisper of toning, but was otherwise a slightly subdued orange-red. If brown toning had crept over, say, 20 percent to 30 percent or so of the surface—and there being no particular grading rules on this—it would likely be called MS-65RB. If brown toning defined the entire surface, with no orange-red at all, or with just a small amount, it would be called MS-65BN.

Advance to, say, the year 1950. By this time the saving of bank-wrapped rolls of Lincoln cents had been popular with collectors and investors since the 1930s. Such rolls were often kept in dry places, such as bank safe-deposit boxes, Army surplus metal cartridge boxes (readily available at the time, and inexpensive), or tucked away somewhere else. Not long afterward, clear tubes of plastic became available. Coins stored in these tubes tended to remain nearly fully brilliant, with many coming down to the present day with full original orange-red color. On some kept in bank rolls, the edge (when viewed edge on) will have a light brown tint from the paper wrapper. Single coins in collections are usually toned on the edge from the careful fingers of numismatists.

Early issues from the San Francisco Mint are apt to have a distinctive coloration, as noted in the David W. Lange commentary quoted below.

Coins that match the above can be properly designated as having *original* color or toning, further described as RD, RB, or BN, depending on the extent of the toning.

BN, RB, AND RD: COLOR AND PRICE

In today's price hierarchy, coins certified as RD (red) with full brilliance command prices in many instances far in excess of those with the same number, but called BN or RB. And yet, from the standpoint of eye appeal and general desirability, a BN coin can often be nicer than an RD coin. Nowhere is this more evident than in Matte Proofs from 1909 to 1916.

Moreover, *original* RD-color cents from the early years can be *very rare*. There is no lack of certified coins labeled "RD," but many reached that state from conservation or doctoring.

In the marketplace if you make it your business to look at Internet or catalog pictures, or the coins themselves, and examine ten pieces certified as Proof-65BN and ten certified as Proof-65RD, you will find that the RD pieces have more problems—specks, spots, and the like, while the BN pieces can be pristine. For my money, I'd far rather have a much cheaper and much nicer BN or RB coin than a non-original RD coin at a far higher price. I've said this before, but the point is so important it is worth driving home.

A past issue of *Rare Coin Market Report*, which is no longer published, gave values for PCGS-graded coins as follows:

1911 Proof-65BN: $475, Proof-66BN: $775, Proof-67BN: $850
1911 Proof-65RB: $1,100, Proof-66RB: $1,400, Proof-67RB: $1,750
1911 Proof-65RD: $5,000, Proof-66RD: $11,000, Proof-67RD:
No price given

Isn't this dramatic! A Proof-66RD at $11,000 was more than 23 times more expensive than a Proof-65BN at $475. To me, such a difference is like finding money in the streets—if you are a connoisseur. Of course, if you can find a Proof-66RD that has no flecks or spots, and if you have a lot of money in your checking account, then by all means buy one.

Somewhat similarly, the same publication gave pricing for the 1936 Proof cent with mirror finish:

Details of a Mint State "RB" 1909-S cent with spots. In my opinion, an RB coin should be nicely blended red and brown, not red with spots.

Details of a Mint State "RB" 1923-S with a fingerprint in the obverse field.

A 1909-S V.D.B. certified as MS-65BN by a leading service, a handsome coin. (enlarged 1.5x)

RD, RB, AND BN COLOR

A gem Mint State RD 1910 cent with *original* color. On the obverse some natural fading is seen, especially at the rims, and a few flecks are present. The reverse is similar. Some nuances of an old fingerprint, hardly visible, can be seen to the left of the C in CENT. The striking is quite good, save for a hint of irregularity to the left of the L in LIBERTY. All things considered, this is an excellent example of a pristine cent of this early date, perhaps not the finest available, but very acceptable to most advanced specialists. (enlarged 1.5x)

A 1928-S cent with red and brown (RB) surfaces. The RB term has many interpretations in the marketplace, with some coins being RD coins with carbon spots or blotches. Finding attractive RB cents without distracting spots, stains, or other problems can be a challenge. Beauty is in the eye of the beholder, and some buyers might like this 1928-S, while others might prefer one with nearly complete brown (BN) toning. A recent PCGS price report valued a PCGS MS-65BN at $600, 65RB at $1,750, and 65RD at $5,250. For many connoisseurs, MS-65BN, cherrypicking for Full Details, would be an obvious choice for a 1928-S. For those involved in Registry Set competition, MS-65RD or higher would be the only way to go, and who cares whether it has Full Details. Such aspects and possibilities contribute to the challenge and pleasure of forming a set of high-quality Lincoln cents. (enlarged 1.5x)

A Mint State 1921-S cent, of a quality that might be certified as MS-65BN or 66BN, with rich, lustrous, attractive brown surfaces. Such a coin offers a nice meeting ground between high quality and low market price. An issue of the *Rare Coin Market Report* magazine, which is no longer published, once valued a PCGS MS-65BN at $500 and 65RD at $23,000. Of course, the 65RD would be nicer to have, assuming that it had a decent strike and good eye appeal, but the cost differential is tremendous. (enlarged 1.5x)

1936 Proof-65BN: $625, Proof-66BN: $910, Proof-67BN: $1,250
1936 Proof-65RB: $1,200, Proof-66RB: $2,250, Proof-67RB: $3,000
1936 Proof-65RD: $2,900, Proof-66RD: $8,000, Proof-67RD: $12,500

If I had been seeking a 1936 Proof cent, admittedly the most difficult issue to find from the mid-twentieth century, I would have opted for Proof-65RB at $1,200 because a gem at this level typically reflects a lightly but pleasingly toned example, never dipped. A Proof-67RD is nicer, but the difference between $1,200 and $12,500 is not to be sneezed at.

For good measure, this historical pricing from *Coin Dealer Newsletter* illustrates the same thing:

> **Matte Proof Lincoln cent 1909 to 1916,** any date, for type, NGC certification.
> Proof-65BN: $235, Proof-65RB: $445, Proof-65RD: $1,030

Among regular-issue cents, scan valuations to determine where the differential breaks are. For coins after 1934, you might as well go for RD in whatever Gem category you prefer, 65, 66, or whatever, but perhaps keep away from ultra-high grades, for these are mostly purchased by speculators and people who are working on Registry Sets—a fine sport, to be sure, but not for those with light wallets. For coins of the 1930s onward, *original* RD coins are easily enough found, in contrast to earlier issues.

For earlier Lincoln cents from 1909 to 1933, again look at the price charts. Here I am discussing posted prices for grades only, without respect to connoisseurship. A recent PCGS price guide has these values for PCGS-certified coins:

1914-S MS-65BN: $1,850, MS-65RB: $2,600, MS-65RD: $6,500
1925-S MS-65BN $1,000, MS-65RB $3,150, MS-65RD $22,000

If I were forming a set of Lincoln cents I would opt for BN or RB, and, in addition to nicely blended color, would insist upon a sharp strike, which would take some doing. I would be in the minority, however. Most people who could afford it would opt for the $6,500 1914-S and $22,000 1925-S coins, seeking to buy one certified with that number. They would not even *look* at the coin to see if it was sharply struck (which it probably would not be). I find this to be highly amusing.

INTERESTING OBSERVATIONS BY DAVID W. LANGE

In an article in *Numismatist*, "San Francisco Mint Cents 1908–24," August 2002, David W. Lange commented on the distinctive color seen on *original* (undipped, uncleaned) Lincoln cents of that era, and of brightness of color in relation to sharpness of strike:

One thing I've noticed while examining uncirculated bronze coins produced by the San Francisco Mint from the onset of coinage there in 1908 through roughly 1924 is that they have some very distinctive features. These often enable one to identify them as "S" Mint products before seeing the mintmark. Though the alloy used for United States cents was prescribed by law, there are peculiarities seemingly unique to cents made at San Francisco.

When entirely untoned, "S" Mint bronze coins have a very pale, brassy color unlike that of the more reddish or coppery cents from the Philadelphia and Denver Mints. For the period described, however, "S" Mint cents are seldom seen untoned. The only issues commonly encountered in that condition are the widely hoarded 1909-S cents, both with and without the designer's initials "V.D.B." Subsequent dates through the mid-1920s are typically toned to various degrees, though many have survived with partial mint color.

Examples having just light toning often display a pattern of tan or light brown streaks across obverse and reverse, the so-called "woodgrain" pattern. This resulted from impurities in the alloy or concentrations of pure copper that did not properly blend with the 5% tin and zinc added to it. When these less than perfect ingots were rolled into strip, from which blanks would later be punched, the concentrations were flattened and stretched into the patterns seen on the finished coins. Invisible when first struck, these flaws appeared only after the coin was exposed to atmospheric agents that caused the copper concentrations to tone more quickly than the properly mixed portions of the planchet.

Woodgrain toning is commonly seen on "S" Mint cents through 1923–24, after which time it is encountered only occasionally. Examination of the U. S. Mint Director's annual reports for the period in question reveals that cent planchets were alternately made in-house (at the various mints) and purchased from outside vendors.

After the mid-1920s, the U. S. Mint gradually phased out the production of both cent and nickel planchets in favor of ready-made ones, and this seems to have standardized the characteristics of planchets used at all the mint facilities.

Though most collectors favor bronze coins that are fully "red," I find this distinctive toning quite charming, and it further serves as an aid to authentication. I've never seen a 1909 cent from the Philadelphia Mint that was brassy and displayed woodgrain toning, so the presence of such distinctive features almost guarantees that a cent's "S" mintmark has not been added to a Philadelphia coin. This is true of both Indian and Lincoln cents.

As noted above, with the exception of 1909-S and 1909-S V.D.B. Lincolns, early "S" cents are seldom seen with all their original color. Most have toned to brown or retain just partial mint red. One peculiarity I've noticed about all copper and bronze coins is that sharply struck pieces tend to tone down more readily than weakly struck ones. This is true regardless of date or mint, and I suspect that the relative degree of work-hardening experienced by the planchet determines its resistance to atmospheric toning. This phenomenon is not unique to "S" Mint cents, but it is more critical with them due to their greater overall rarity. It extends even to the bronze one-centavo pieces made there 1908–20 for use in the Philippine Islands. Having collected this series for years, I almost never encountered a sharply struck coin having full mint color, while the well struck pieces I've owned were always brown or displayed light, woodgrain toning.[28]

COIN CLEANING AND DOCTORING

CLEANING AND DIPPING COINS

Lincoln cents began to be widely collected in the 1930s, with 1934 being the jumping-off date for widespread enthusiasm generated by the launching of the *Standard Catalogue;* the availability of inexpensive "penny boards" to store and display a collection as it grew; and, for the serious collector, the availability of cardboard album pages with clear slides on each side, as marketed by Wayte Raymond.

By this time the philosophy "brilliant is best" had been adopted by nearly all dealers and by many collectors. A bright coin was preferable to a toned one, the last often called *tarnished,* a nasty term no one liked. The solution was to brighten coins by the use of various chemicals and abrasives. The situation was hardly new and antedated the first Lincoln cent. In August 1903 in *The Numismatist,* dealer Farran Zerbe told of visiting the third Philadelphia Mint (opened for business in autumn 1901) and viewing the Mint Collection, a display that had commenced in June 1838 and had been added to continually ever since. The condition of certain U.S. coins was less than ideal, as Zerbe related:

> I found many of the silver Proof coins of late years partially covered with a white coating. On inquiry I learned that an over-zealous attendant during the last vacation months when the numismatic room was closed took it on himself to clean the tarnished coins, purchase some metal polish at a department store, and proceed with his cleaning operation. Later a coating of white appeared on the coins, which was now slowly disappearing. I expressed my displeasure at this improper treatment of Proof coins, and the custodian explained, "That is nothing. I have been here eight years and they have been cleaned three or four times in my time."

Zerbe speculated that should this cleaning continue, in the future one would have nothing left except plain planchets and badly worn coins!

In the 1930s and 1940s numismatists continued with the "brilliant" philosophy. Advertisements for Uncirculated Lincoln cents published in *The Numismatist* and the *Numismatic Scrapbook* offered "BU" or "brilliant Uncirculated" cents, hardly ever "Uncirculated with natural brown toning" or "Uncirculated with a mixture of red and brown color."

The wildly popular "Penny Collector" boards introduced in the mid-1930s by J.K. Post of Neenah, Wisconsin (products soon acquired by Whitman Publishing Company), had this advice printed on them: "Clean your specimens with a soft eraser or a little vinegar."

J. Henry Ripstra, president of the ANA, gave unfortunate advice in *The Numismatist* in April 1939, stating that there was no use for anyone to have "tarnished" coins in their collections, when some processes using acid, baking soda, and for some, a bristle brush, will work magic, "and you again have a brilliant coin." You can imagine what a 1909-S V.D.B cent subjected to dipping in acid, rubbing with baking soda, and, for good measure, treatment with a bristle brush might look like: brilliant as can be, with most, if not all, of the "flash" or frost of the luster gone, and now with sort of a matte or satiny surface.

To the January 1949 issue of *The Numismatist* G.R.L. Potter contributed an article, "Let's Keep It Clean!" The author recommended that cleaning should be considered a legitimate practice, but that coins should be cleaned once and once only. Further:

> Of the desirability of "clean" coins there can, I think, be no doubt. The most casual scrutiny of catalogues or dealers' lists shows that "brilliant Uncirculated" is the condition commanding the highest price, and it must follow that anything that will maintain or restore such a condition is desirable. It is my contention that such restoration and maintenance is often a very simple matter, and that the procedure is well within the capacity of any collector of average intelligence—which, of course, means all of us!

Potter recommended that numismatists use potassium cyanide. To be sure, he noted that it is a deadly poison, but then he went on to say:

> If the procedure . . . is carefully followed, no contact with the cyanide solution will occur. But accidents will happen, and if you do happen to get any cyanide solution on your skin wash it off immediately in running water until the greasy feel at point of contact has entirely disappeared. Cyanide is like a great many other things in life— fire, electricity, motor cars, or what have you—very dangerous if not properly used, but both safe and useful in careful hands.

Not everyone was apt to agree that using cyanide was similar in danger to driving a car or plugging lamp into the wall. There was the unfortunate tragedy involving J. Sanford Saltus, a wealthy numismatist, who on June 20, 1922, was in a hotel room with a glass of potassium cyanide on a table, together with a group of toned coins he had recently purchased. There was also a glass of ginger ale. Mistaking one glass of liquid for the other, he sipped the wrong substance. His body was found on the floor, and the coroner ruled "death by misadventure."

In the early 1960s I had occasion to pay a visit to James F. Kelly, the well-known Dayton, Ohio, dealer, who by that time had moved his office to the lower level of his home in nearby Englewood. In a comfortable suite paneled in warm knotty pine, he supervised a lively trade by mail, plus hosted in-person visitors by appointment. We knew each other very well as professionals and engaged in some dealer-to-dealer talk.

Jim asked me if I had ever used cyanide to clean coins. I responded that I had not, but was aware of the process through reading. He then proceeded to demonstrate. Lincoln cents with reddish-brown surfaces, even with light spots, became "brilliant Uncirculated," with the spots hardly noticeable except under magnification as light flecks. Cyanide was absolutely the best for silver coins, he said, with Liberty Seated coins benefiting immensely. On those, rubbing on the higher areas of Miss Liberty would be dissolved into a light matte surface showing no wear at all. In the process, such coins became not fully bright and brilliant, but a light silver-gray color. Today there are many certified "choice" and "gem" Liberty Seated coins with minutely granular matte surfaces on the market, never mind that when first struck, such pieces had deep frosty luster.

Almost alone in the trade, the New Netherlands Coin Company often mentioned the use of cyanide in auction listings, such as for its 51st Sale in June 1958. Lot 377, a red and brown 1909-S V.D.B. cent with a spot on the obverse and a fingerprint on the reverse, was accompanied by this comment: "More desirable than the cyanided examples commonly offered [as] 'Brilliant Uncirculated.'"

To this day I have not tried cyanide, and I don't suggest that you do either! That is, if you want to be around to read my *next* book—which I hope you will be. It continues to be okay, however, to drive a car and plug lamps into the wall.

The April 1960 issue of *The Numismatist*, published the same month that *Coin World* was founded, had multiple advertisements for lotions and potions to "improve" coins, including Lincoln cents.

"Brilliantize," a potion "Safe for Proof Coins," to "make copper, silver, other coins brilliant instantly" was available in regular size for $1, medium for $2, and large for $5. Testimonials were given, such as this from California: "This is the best cleaner I have ever used on all coins."

The Coin Care Corporation of Long Beach, California, offered "Copper Coin Cleaner," described as "useful for cleaning all kinds of coins, but particularly adapted to cleaning coins of copper or nickel. . . . brings out original color, including original brilliance, if it is still there under tarnish or coating. Dull or dark Uncirculated coins become brilliant Uncirculated coins in seconds. This result of years of experiment can be safely used on valuable coins to improve their appearance and increase their value." Just $1 per bottle.

Further in the same issue of *The Numismatist*, "E-Z-EST Jeweluster," was described as "the perfect coin cleaner" that "removes tarnish and oxidation instantly. Will not harm the most delicate Proof. Easy and fast to use; just dip, rinse, and dry." $2 a bottle.

Common silver dip was used to clean copper. In one of the periodicals a cleaning kit for cents was offered, including a brush with brass wire bristles.

A complete listing of advertisements, recommendations, and other misinformation for "improving" Lincoln cents would occupy hundreds of pages. With such messages coming month after month, year after year, collectors and dealers cleaned and dipped their Lincoln cents, and when they retoned, repeated the process. Collectors assumed that these processes must be very desirable, or else *The Numismatist* and other periodicals would not have run advertisements for them.

THE EFFECTS OF CLEANING AND DIPPING

Recall that in 1903 the silver coins in the Mint Collection had been cleaned "three or four times" in the most recent eight years, and who knows how many times before then— perhaps dozens of times. The result is that most of the once-pristine nineteenth-century silver Proofs in that display, now known as the National Numismatic Collection at the Smithsonian, are deeply hairlined and dull, although many remain brilliant. Elsewhere in numismatics, *any* Proof coin that today is brilliant, whether it was struck in 1822, 1942, or 1962, but shows even a few hairlines (and is thus apt to be graded Proof-60 to 64 or so), is brilliant by virtue of cleaning with friction. Proofs were not minted with hairlines! Not even one hairline! There is comfort in assigning a single number to such coins—sort of like the classic tale of the emperor who had no clothes. For a silver Liberty Seated coin, each of these descriptions could be given of the same coin:

> **Description 1.** 1864 Liberty Seated half dollar. Proof-63. Brilliant.
> **Description 2.** 1864 Liberty Seated half dollar. Dipped multiple times in the past, and also cleaned with silver polish or some other abrasive(s). Now fully brilliant. Hairlines on the obverse and reverse.

Description 1 will sell the coin. Description 2 will drive a buyer or bidder away: he or she will keep searching until a coin with Description 1 is found! Of course, both coins are *really* the same.

From experience in buying coins in the marketplace, I estimate that probably 90 to 95 percent of "brilliant Uncirculated" Lincoln cents sold in the marketplace in 1960 were brilliant by virtue of dipping, if they were dated from 1910 through the late 1920s.

Then as now, the fact that coins were dipped and cleaned was scarcely ever talked about. The facts of life are that any fully brilliant, bright-as-new Lincoln cent of the early era, through the 1920s, is that way because of dipping.

Cents that were gem Mint State, but toned brown, if dipped to become "RD" can be very attractive.

Silver dip preserves most of the luster and frost. Cyanide dipping tends to give the coins a slight matte finish, combined with reduced mint luster. If cyanided multiple times, the coin is likely to be completely matte, not unlike a Matte Proof at quick glance. Cyanided "brilliant Uncirculated" cents that were graded AU or low-level Mint State have little depth to the luster.

The dipping of coins in various potions and silver dips makes the surface "raw" and particularly susceptible to toning again, this time often with tiny or large spots or blotches. Rainbow color, hardly ever seen as *original* toning except on some Proof cents of 1936 to 1942, is nearly always a giveaway that the coin was dipped and then recolored.

How do you determine if a Lincoln cent has been dipped? This is a key question and is only answered by the experience of examining coins in the marketplace—in person, not via pictures or on the Internet. Most experienced dealers, if they are inclined to do so, can also help explain. Many dealers have little or no *numismatic* knowledge, so even if they wanted to, they couldn't tell the difference. They have a box of certified coins in one hand, a list of prices on a computer screen on their desk, and a telephone in their right hand—with which to sell naïve buyers "great investments" in "rare" coins.

Certified holders are of no help unless a coin has been *obviously* dipped or cyanided. The services are unconcerned with the cleaning of most silver coins—as evidenced by thousands of fully brilliant nineteenth-century silver Proof coins in lower Proof levels, displaying hairlines. If certification services were to reject cleaned coins, there would be absolutely no "brilliant" copper, silver, or gold coins in holders, if the coins had hairlines. Most buyers are unaware of this and think if they buy a coin certified by a leading service, it cannot have been cleaned. As quoted above, David W. Lange found that "early 'S' cents are seldom seen with all their *original* color." As a *smart buyer*, please take heed!

Sam Lukes tells of an acquaintance who has specialized in turning BN (brown) and RB (red and brown) Mint State Lincoln cents into ones that certified as RD (red). This was done by dipping the coin into a solution, then freezing it for a day, and then wrapping it in a special bag and freezing it again, after which he would leave it on a counter for several hours to return to room temperature.

Many of these were sent to grading services and certified as RD. Some were even crossed over to other services for even higher Mint State RD grades. Unfortunately, some of these "gems" later became spotted within their holders.[29] Some services, perhaps all, make no guarantees against coins becoming blotchy or spotted after certification. In my own experience, this does *not* happen to coins with *original* mint red-orange color.

For Lincoln cents, you have now been made aware of the effects of cleaning and dipping. In the marketplace such practices typically affect coins dated before the 1940s as well as some valuable and rare later varieties, such as the 1955, Doubled Die Obverse, cent.

I am well aware that the temptation to dip or brighten a coin seems to be a part of human nature, at least for numismatists. If *you* want to try it, experiment with modern Lincoln cents from pocket change—not a beautifully toned scarce or rare early date!

Gain some experience before buying early Lincoln cents, described as MS-64RD or higher, and you should have no problem determining what is original color and what is not. It is perhaps important to note that this can, indeed, be a difficulty for anyone who is colorblind. About 10 percent to 15 percent of males have color perception deficiencies.[30]

ASPECTS OF EYE APPEAL

Beauty is in the eye of the beholder. To me, a richly lustrous 1909 Matte Proof-65BN coin, if carefully selected, can be very attractive, as can an MS-65BN 1914-D cent. To someone else, a coin graded or, better yet, certified as MS-65RD is the only way to go, and one with brown toning would not be acceptable—all of this as noted above.

In any scenario, whether a coin is called BN, RB, or RD, the presence of flecks or spots is a minus. No question about it. In my opinion, blotchy and mottled coloration is a negative as well, but someone else might think that such a coin is a rare and beautiful find.

As you examine Lincoln cents in your exploration of the series, you will come to like the coloration and appearance of some, and not to like others. If you are contemplating a coin and cannot determine if it is beautiful, or if you find it borderline, simply wait for another opportunity. Lincoln cents are plentiful in nearly all grades, and an opportunity passed today will likely recur next month or next year.

At coin club meetings, at viewing sessions for auctions, at displays of copper coins at conventions, likely there will be an opportunity to find several collectors who are experienced in the field of Indian Head and Lincoln cents. Both series have essentially the same aspects of quality and connoisseurship. Discuss color, eye appeal, and anything else. You will find that most experienced collectors are very willing, even enthusiastic, to help anyone seeking to learn.

As to dealers in stores and at shows, some are as friendly as can be, while others have little or no time for idle chat that does not result in an immediate sale. Simply find a dealer who appreciates your growing interest. When you do, take caution if he or she is busy with another customer to ask when it might be convenient to return when the pace is more leisurely. It is also good etiquette to buy *something* if you take up a lot of time—perhaps a numismatic book or magnifying glass or the like.

While beauty is in the eye of the beholder, I am sure that with experience, a group of Lincoln cents you pick out as having good eye appeal will be found to be attractive to others as well.

A DEALER'S PERSPECTIVE

Littleton Coin Company, which probably sells as many Lincoln cents to collectors as any firm, and which endeavors to deliver quality coins to clients by mail, uses the following guidelines when buying Lincoln cents. I invited my long-time dealer friend David Sundman, CEO of Littleton, to share the basic guidelines his buyers use:

> What are the key factors Littleton's experts use when buying and/or grading Lincoln Head cents? What are the qualities they look for?
>
>> A coin that is conservative/accurate for the grade assigned
>> A coin that is original with attractive problem-free surfaces
>> A coin with no corrosion or unattractive spots and no heavy scratches
>
> Littleton Coin customers are advised whatever grade range they choose to collect, to make sure each coin is nice for the grade and has good eye appeal. Our staff selects coins for our stock that will please our customers every time they look at them in their collection. This means they are seeking coins that are accurately graded—not "pushed." While price is always a consideration, the starting point is that the coin surfaces must be original, attractive and problem free with no corrosion or unattractive spotting and no distracting scratches.
>
> As with all earlier U.S. copper coins, finding problem-free Lincoln cents is tougher than you'd think. Problem surfaces are endemic. Lincoln cents are prone to corrosion. Through the mid-1930s Lincolns often exhibit a reddish oxidation on the surfaces that we consider unattractive. This red oxidation can be easily missed if the coin is not rotated back and forth, side to side on its axis in a good light. Green coins and black oxidized coins are the more obvious forms of oxidation and corrosion that are seen often on earlier Lincolns and are rejected by our staff. Based on Littleton's more than 60 years of experience buying and selling Lincoln cents, we estimate that as many as a quarter to a third of the existing early Lincolns 1909–1939 are technically "damaged." They are worth considerably less than a nice problem-free coin.

David M. Sundman, CEO of Littleton Coin Co., with a Whitman "Penny Collector" board of 1935 and, on the nearby wall, another early "penny board."

When we are examining Uncirculated Lincolns we avoid buying coins with fingerprints or spotting, heavy scratches or corrosion. Corrosion spots are common on Uncirculated coins, because copper is so reactive.

Some Lincoln varieties require special attention. When looking at a 1922 "Plain" we only accept die pair #2, which exhibits a strong reverse strike with no trace of the "D" mint mark. Die pairs #1 and #3 exhibit a "shadow" of the "D" under proper lighting and we do not purchase them.

A special word about lighting: At Littleton we use a 100 watt incandescent bulb and hold coins 12 to 16 inches away from the light source. Our staff uses the same lights when we travel around the country to coin shows. We bring our own lighting with us to ensure lighting conditions are consistent with our normal office conditions.

By this time in the text, you've learned just about everything I know, plus advice and suggestions from many contributors to this book.

This information can be organized into the steps given below.

BUYING LINCOLN CENTS: FOUR STEPS TO SUCCESS

A SIMPLE SYSTEM

Variations of the Four Steps to Success have been used in some of my other Whitman books, and reports from readers and users have been enthusiastic across the board. In fact, *all* have been positive. I am confident that *you* can be among the best buyers the field of Lincoln cents has ever known!

By now in the present text you have read about grade, striking sharpness, cleaning, eye appeal, and many other things—certainly a lot to absorb. Add the element of time and a few field trips—visits to coin stores and conventions—and you will turn theory into practice. The fact that you have progressed this far in the book shows you have the interest. Don't rush. Lincoln cents are one of the most *complex* series in American numismatics, in respect to locating truly choice coins.

Most buyers of Lincoln cents—at least 90 percent, perhaps more than 95 percent—buy Lincoln cents only by considering the grade and price. A simple 1.5 x 2–inch coin holder, displaying a cent with a cellophane center, may be marked "MS-65RD." Or a certification service plastic "slab" may be so marked. The coin itself can be any Lincoln cent in any grade—a common 1910 in Good-4 grade, or a 1960, Small Date, in MS-67RD, or anything else. This information leads the buyer to consult a price guide, or multiple guides—price information is everywhere.

Under the above scenario, Mr. Average Buyer will see that he has an MS-65RD cent offered at, say, $400, and prices listed in *Coin World, Numismatic News*, the *Red Book*, and other places range from $500 to $600. Obviously, the $400 price is a great bargain!

Or, *Coin World, Numismatic News*, the *Red Book*, and other places will indicate a range of $250 to $325. Obviously, the $400 coin is vastly overpriced!

Mr. Average Buyer is price-driven. The actual appearance of the coin is of little concern. The MS-65RD marking in an XYZ Grading Service holder is all he needs. No research needed. The coin *must be* great, or it wouldn't have been certified in such a high grade!

This is not the way I would think, and I hope it is not the way you would think either. Let us suppose that instead of simply being marked MS-65RD, the coin is further described by the seller as "weakly struck on the head and rims, as usual." It probably won't be. *You* as a smart buyer will have to add this description on your own, after looking at it. With this new information, it would seem that if the coin were listed in guides at $500 to $600, this coin would not be worth buying for $400. No longer is it a bargain.

Now, let us suppose that a coin is marked as MS-65RD and further described as "needle-sharp strike on both sides, a rarity as such—in fact, the only coin of this sharpness I have seen in the past ten years." With this new information, it would seem that if price guides listed it at the range of $250 to $325, it would be a bargain at $400!

If you agree with this, you are on your way to being a smart buyer!

In short, if you want to be a connoisseur and form a truly outstanding collection of Lincoln cents, there is much more than just the grading numbers to consider. My opinion is that numbers, while important, are not necessarily any more significant than other aspects such as quality and eye appeal. I would rather have an MS-65RB cent with Full Details and attractive original toning than an MS-67RD with planchet abrasions and weak features. To me, the first, if rare in that form, would be worth double catalog value, while the second I wouldn't buy at half catalog price. I have mentioned this elsewhere in this book and will mention it again.

If I were forming a set of Lincoln cents and wanted superb coins, I would learn what and what not to expect in the marketplace, and then go through the process outlined below (some of which summarizes information I have given earlier). Lincoln cents are a very complex, sophisticated series, so my commentary is necessarily quite a bit more extensive than if I were discussing, say, Washington quarters or Saint-Gaudens double eagles:

Step 1: Numerical Grade Assigned to the Coin

When you visit a coin shop or a convention, or contemplate a catalog or Internet offering, have an approximate grade in mind for each coin you are seeking. If you are looking for a rare 1914-D Lincoln cent and have $1,000 or so to spend, there is no point in asking, except as an education, to look at Mint State coins. You will want to ask for coins in the Extremely Fine and About Uncirculated categories. At the same time there is no particular reason to waste your time looking at well-worn pieces in G-4 or VG-8 grades. These are the prices from the 2023 *Guide Book of United States Coins:*

> **1914-D Lincoln cent:** G-4: $145, VG-8: $165, F-12: $200, VF-20: $240, EF-40: $650, AU-50: $1,400, MS-60RB: $2,000, MS-63RB: $3,000

At a coin show, or in sending a "want list" to a dealer, ask to see coins in the range of EF-40 to AU-50 or so, because these are more or less in the price range you want to pay. Also, if I were buying a 1914-D and contemplating the above prices I might think: "Hmm. For not too much more money I could buy a Mint State coin." I would probably do this, but at the MS-60 level I would have a lot of cherrypicking to do for quality. There is a lot of "hidden value" to be found in the AU-58 grade, a favorite with at least two contributors to this book, Bill Fivaz and Bob Shippee. Poignantly, Lincoln cents graded AU-58 or MS-60 usually have fewer problems (stains, spots, etc.) than do higher-level pieces.

This prompts me to include *Red Book* prices for a 1926-S cent, which would seem to require a different mindset when making a buying decision:

1926-S Lincoln cent: G-4: $9, VG-8: $11, F-12: $13, VF-20: $17, EF-40: $35, AU-50: $75, MS-60RB: $165, MS-63RB: $375

Considering that, unlike the case with the 1914-D cent—which is costly in all grades—the 1926-S is very cheap at lower levels, you will have to think carefully. An AU-50 coin is more than three times the cost of an EF-40, and an MS-60 is more than double the value of AU-50. Because the 1926-S is a key date and a Mint State coin is listed at $325, I'd probably opt for that grade.

Before you begin buying the early series it would be a good idea to map out a strategy to determine in which grades you want to buy each of the different dates and mintmarks. Coins of 1935 and later are a cinch (except for rare die varieties). I'd opt for MS-65RD or MS-66RD and buy each one with care. The expensive earlier issues will have different requirements, depending on your budget.

Now, you are at a coin show or in a dealer's shop or at a club meeting. You are holding a Lincoln cent in your hand. Should you buy it? Your first step is to look at the assigned grade of the coin or, if you are familiar with grading, to assign your own number. Experienced collectors and dealers will often share their opinions with you, and without being an annoyance, see if you can "ask around" for help. The chances are excellent that if you are aspiring to collect Lincoln cents that are scarce and valuable from the early years, 1909 to 1933, most offered to you will be already graded and in certified holders. Due to the expense of certification, most of the later coins will be in other holders—perhaps 1.5 x 2–inch cardboard, or Koin-Tains, or small plastic holders. These holders will have just a number—such as MS-63, MS-65, or whatever—and will tell you little if anything more. Aha! Herein lies *your* opportunity! Of course, by now in this text you already know this.

If you are just entering numismatics, you would do well in the Lincoln cent series to only consider rare and expensive coins that have been certified by the leading grading services: Numismatic Guaranty Company (NGC) and the Professional Coin Grading Service (PCGS). NGC and PCGS publish population reports delineating the coins that have passed through their hands. There are other grading services, and you might want to check them out. At present, however, the above seem to be the most widely used by advanced collectors. Price information for many commercially graded coins can be found in many places, in particular, in *The Certified Coin Dealer Newsletter* and either the standard or the deluxe edition of *A Guide Book of United States Coins*.

You will want to learn about grading not only for Lincoln cents but also to become acquainted with general guidelines applied elsewhere—in order to gain a comprehensive view. Read *The Official ANA Grading Standards for U.S. Coins*, an adaptation of which is given in chapter eight in the present text. That book also has valuable introductory material, including the history and evolution of the grading process.

Spend time, preferably in person, looking at Lincoln cents—perhaps with this book in your hand. If you do this at a show or in a shop, it is good form to advise the dealer what you are doing—seeking education—and, as I've mentioned, to make a courtesy purchase of a coin or a book or two. In less time than you realize, you will learn the fundamentals of grading. Forming warm relationships with several friendly dealers will be an asset throughout your collecting career.

I do not want to overdo anything I say here, but paying attention to grade, color, and price, and the different variables can make the difference between having a beautiful collection that is numismatically desirable, or an extremely expensive collection that may also be desirable, but not worth the additional percentage of price involved.

In summary, Step 1 is to determine what grade range you wish to buy for a given Lincoln cent, and then examine coins offered in that range. Chances are good that expensive coins will be certified—but later dates will not—unless you seek ultra grades such as MS-67 or higher.

Now, with a Lincoln cent offered in the grade you are seeking, you have a candidate *for your further consideration.*

STEP 2: EYE APPEAL AT FIRST GLANCE

I discussed eye appeal earlier in this chapter, so there is no need to reiterate it here. Simply make sure that the coin is pleasing to your eyes and seek *original* color. If you feel you are not yet skilled enough to tackle the latter, enlist the advice of a trustworthy dealer or friend who has had extensive experience in the field, or seek the advice of several people. As you can imagine, this process is more relevant to buying a 1909-S V.D.B. cent, or a high grade *expensive* variety, and would not be practical if you are seeking a 1955-S or 1961-D. For common modern coins that are very inexpensive, a dollar or two each or less (except certified coins, which necessarily include the price of the holder), you can examine hundreds of coins. Soon, on your own you will know which have superb eye appeal and which do not. If in doubt, ask an expert about a sample or two you have selected (not a box with 200 coins in it.)

I advise that you go slowly and buy later dates, the issues from 1934 to the present, first. In that way any mistakes you make will be inexpensive. There is absolutely no need to compromise on the aspect of eye appeal. I am not aware of even a single date or mintmark that does not exist, and in multiples, with excellent eye appeal. In contrast, if you were a collector of Vermont copper coins of the 1785 to 1788 era by die varieties, there are some for which the finest known specimens might be Fine or Very Fine, with a rough surface—about as beautiful as a toad (but still appealing for what they are).

If the coin is attractive to your eye, then in some distant future year when time comes to sell it, the piece will be attractive to the eyes of other buyers, an important consideration. Now, with an attractive coin in hand, you have a candidate *for your further consideration.*

STEP 3: EVALUATING SHARPNESS AND RELATED FEATURES

At this point you have a Lincoln cent which you believe to be in the numerical grade written on a coin holder or printed on a slab certified by NGC or PCGS, or if you are in the fast lane, determined by your own experience. You also have for consideration one that is in the grade you seek and has passed your test for excellent eye appeal.

The next step is to examine the cent for sharpness, using the extensive information I gave earlier in this chapter and also checking the individual date and mintmark listings in chapter 11. Aspire to acquire a coin that has Full Details on both sides—including the portrait, lettering, and rim, and that has been struck from fresh dies. *This is the single most difficult problem for pre-1934 cents.* While, again, I hope you *aspire* to find coins with Full Details, for some you may have to compromise—but do this only after a period of time, and do not compromise significantly. For some, such as the 1926-S, you may have the choice of either Full Details or significant amounts of original mint red remaining, but not both. A complete collection of Full Details cents will inevitably have some that are RB or BN, not completely *original* RD.

Photographs can be useful for determining sharpness if the pictures are clear and of high resolution. For some series such as Morgan dollars, gold coins, and the like, pictures in auction catalogs and on the Internet can be very useful. For Lincoln cents, however, I would be very careful in this regard. Even if the brilliance or toning has good eye appeal, you need to be sure it is *original*.

In-person examination is usually required to be certain. If you are bidding after viewing an illustration, talk with the seller and have a discussion about originality. In the 1950s I used to do this by telephone with a leading dealer. I was a fairly good buyer, so he would run over the listings at his end, and say something like, "This one is not for you." We did not discuss further, but simply moved on to the next lot.

Also check for surface quality. Is the luster satiny or frosty, with full sheen—or is the coin struck from overused dies showing metal flow and granularity? Again, assigned numerical grades reveal nothing about this. Is the planchet of good quality, or is it rough? Generally, Matte Proofs of 1909 to 1916 and later mirror Proofs of 1936 and beyond have Full Details and are on good planchets.

If the Lincoln cent you are considering buying has passed the preceding tests, it is ready *for further consideration*. Chances are good that you are holding a very nice coin in your hand!

STEP 4: ESTABLISHING A FAIR MARKET PRICE

If you've done everything right, you have a Lincoln cent that is correctly graded, of superb eye appeal, with original brilliance or natural toning, and sharply struck. Now, to the price you should pay.

For starters, use one or several handy market guides for a ballpark estimate. Unlike many other series, all Lincoln cent date and mintmark issues are actively traded, and there is no lack of information. This book will be a good start, but since prices often change, it is best to get current values and updates.

Now comes the fun part: If the coin is common enough in a given grade, with sharp details, fine planchet quality, and good eye appeal, then the market price is very relevant, because you can shop around. To find out how easy or difficult it is to find a particular coin sharp, see chapter eleven. As an example, an MS-66 1943 zinc-coated steel cent is easy to find sharply struck and with superb eye appeal. Such coins are common, so you should pay in the range of current market price.

On the other hand, if at this point you have a sharply struck, beautiful Denver or San Francisco cent from the 1920s that is usually found weakly struck, don't become obsessed with the market price. If you have to pay a 50 percent premium to get it, do so. More often than not, however, you will be able to buy at current market or just slightly above, for the seller will not be concerned with sharpness, and may not care about original color either. In all circumstances, even with a common gem 1943 steel cent, a coin in the hand is worth two in the bush. There is something said for simply finalizing a transaction and moving on to the next coin you need.

Congratulations. You now own a *wonderful* Lincoln cent!

CHAPTER TEN

WAYS TO COLLECT LINCOLN CENTS
GENERAL AND SPECIALIZED

INTRODUCTION

There is no single best way to collect Lincoln cents. Dates and mintmarks are popular, as are varieties that can be discerned only under magnification. Proofs are another possibility. In this chapter I discuss some of the popular ways to form a nice collection of the series.

BY TYPE

Collecting U.S. coins by design types is a very popular pursuit. For many series, dates and mintmarks are expensive to collect if completion is desired, but a type set offers an attractive alternative. Examples include early silver dollars and gold coins.

With Lincoln cents there are more types than you probably realize. There is the type of 1909 with V.D.B. on the reverse, then the second type of 1909 without V.D.B. on the reverse and with no initials anywhere, used through 1917. Next comes the type with the V.D.B. initials on the shoulder, continued to 1958. To these can be added the 1943 steel cent, perhaps the most distinctive coin in the series. Then comes the 1959-to-date Memorial reverse, the Bicentennial reverses of 2009, and the Shield reverse from 2010 to the present.

A type set of Lincoln cents is extremely inexpensive, with the 1909 V.D.B. being the "rarity" in the series, but actually extremely common in an absolute sense. Figuring a nice but well-worn 1909 V.D.B. cent at $10, more or less, the remaining pieces will cost less than another $10, or, perhaps $15 or so for a full type set of Lincoln cents. Move up to Mint State and the 1909 V.D.B. is priced at $20 or so; the second type, from late 1909 through 1917 without initials on the shoulder, might cost another $20 or so, after which the remainder are almost pocket change. Even a set of superb brilliant gems will cost in the very low three figures. This arrangement has very little appeal, since there is no challenge involved. In fact, although I have worked with many people in forming complete or nearly complete type sets of all U.S. coins, I do not recall anyone at all ever concentrating only on Lincoln cents.

That said, a type set of Lincolns can no doubt be ignored. There is an exception: If you are not at all involved with Lincoln cents and would like to be, but are not sure—form a type set. If you go further, the coins will simply become part of your specialized collection.

BY DATES AND MINTMARKS

This is the number one way to collect Lincoln cents—the path that many people followed years ago when coins were available in circulation. This is still the most popular method. A date-and-mintmark set begins at 1909 and continues to the present day, and includes one of each date and mint. Beyond that, varieties such as doubled dies are optional, and most collectors either ignore them or pick favorites, such as those listed in *A Guide Book of United States Coins*. Die varieties are discussed separately below.

A full date-and-mintmark set is fairly easily assembled in grades up to low Mint State levels, say MS-63, or if brown (BN) and red and brown (RB) coins are added, up to MS-65. I make these comments strictly with regard to grade and not to aspects of striking, discussed above, which can add a tremendous challenge to certain varieties.

Gem Mint State with full red (MS-65RD) has been the ideal for many. A full set of these can be formed, with a list of the more expensive issues including the famous 1909-S V.D.B.

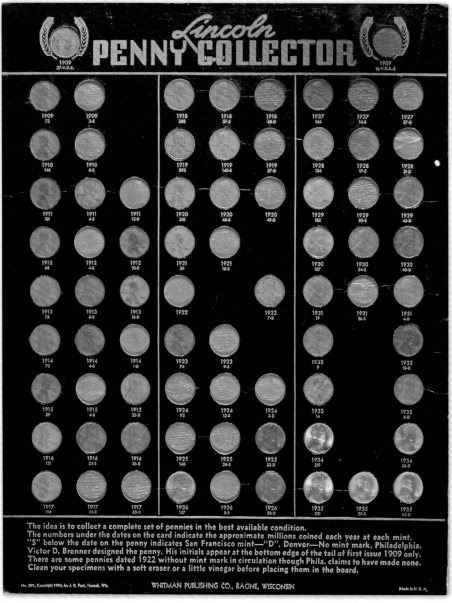

A 1935 "Penny Collector" board marketed that year by Whitman Publishing Company, which acquired the rights to the product from J.K. Post of Neenah, Wisconsin. Buyers found it very exciting to fill in the empty spaces one by one. Here, a nice beginning has been made by finding coins in pocket change. Collecting Lincoln cents by date and mint became very popular the 1930s and continues so to the present day.

and the 1914-D. Interestingly, in the late 1920s the 1914-S was considered to be the most elusive and valuable Lincoln cent in Mint State at $2, handily eclipsing the 1909-S V.D.B., which was obtainable for 50¢ or less, and the 1914-D at $1 or so. Today hardly anyone considers the 1914-S when contemplating the key issues (although gems remain elusive).

In Mint State the 1914-D is the rarest regular date and mintmark variety of Lincoln cent.

If you, as a connoisseur, would want to assemble a basic set of dates and mintmarks in MS-65RD and with original color, sharp strike, and excellent eye appeal, get set for a fascinating challenge.

If I were personally assembling a set, I would opt to acquire MS-65 to MS-66RD coins for all issues of the 1930s and later, and for those from 1909 to 1929 I would go for MS-65RB or RD, insisting upon Full Details for each issue. For many of the mintmarked issues, MS-65RB is at once affordable and practical. I would select Matte Proofs in Proof-65 or 66BN, and mirror Proofs in Proof-65RD or slightly higher. In terms of value for the price paid, a 1909-to-1929

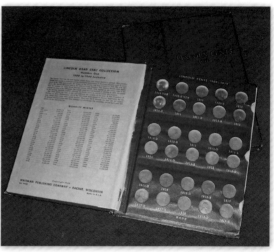

The Lincoln cent collection of Robert W. Rusbar. He started in the 1930s with a "penny board," then moved the coins to green "Popular" albums by 1952 when the writer viewed his coins, then to two Whitman bookshelf-type albums in 1964, these being shown here.

set of MS-65RB cents, patiently selected for Full Details coins, has to be one of the greatest bargains in numismatics.

Short Sets: The time was when many numismatists began their collections of *Mint State* coins with the year 1934, going up to the present day. In MS-65 or 66RD grade, including sharply struck pieces, such a "short set" is very affordable and quite interesting. Amazingly, it now extends to more than 200 coins, and still grows. For a short set, earlier dates can be ignored (but they rarely are) or earlier issues can be purchased in affordable grades ranging from Good to Mint State, depending on the cost involved.

A very inexpensive, yet extensive collection of gem circulation-strike Lincoln cents can be formed by obtaining one of each date from the inception of the Memorial Reverse (1959) and continuing to the present. If you add the San Francisco Mint Proofs, which I would do, the cost rises considerably, but still such coins are very affordable—a few dollars being typical for each.

COLLECTING BY VARIETIES

For each Lincoln cent, obverse and reverse dies were made. Often, during the process of creating working dies from multiple blows from a master die, a later impression could be slightly off-register. This created a doubling effect, most visible on the letters at the periphery, for that is where the rotation was the greatest. Coins struck from such dies

Julian Leidman, who attends more than a dozen shows each year, examines a new purchase.

Well-known collectors, dealers, and authors are enjoyable to meet, and coin shows provide opportunities. Shown are J.T. Stanton (left), Bill Fivaz, and Ken Bressett at an autograph event.

Part of the dealers' bourse at a coin show.

David W. Lange, for whom Lincoln cents have been a specialty for a long time, at the authors' table at an ANA convention.

The American Numismatic Association, located in Colorado Springs, has more than 20,000 members worldwide, and offers many membership benefits.

are known as doubled-die coins, a term originated by Kenneth Bressett in the late 1950s for use in *A Guide Book of United States Coins*, and since widely adopted. Hundreds of different doubled dies, the best known being the 1955 followed by the 1972 and the 1995 (the last being very plentiful in the marketplace), are known among Lincoln cents. The 1958 doubled die is an extraordinary and mysterious rarity, with just two or three known.

Until 1990, coins struck at the Denver and San Francisco mints and intended for circulation had a D or S mintmark added to the die. This was done by hand in the Engraving Department of the Philadelphia Mint, where all dies were made. Some mint-marks were slightly tilted, while others were punched twice, the second impression slightly off-register. In 1944 two dies with S mintmarks were overpunched with D mintmarks, creating the 1944-D, D Over S, overmintmark. Proofs of 1979-S and 1981-S occur with Clear S, with sharply delineated characteristics; and Filled S, with the center appearing solid or as a blob on the 1979-S and somewhat differently filled in on the 1981-S.

Styles of numerals used on Lincoln cents varied over the years. Note the 0 in these two dates.

Variations in the style and relative size of the numeral 3.

Beginning in the 1990s circulation strikes, known as the Close AM and the Wide AM, were for some years made with a slightly different reverse die style than were Proofs, the former having AM in AMERICA so closely spaced as to almost touch, and the latter having A and M distinctly separated.

Essential companions in the quest for such varieties are, alphabetically by author, books by Charles D. Daughtrey, the duo of Bill Fivaz and J.T. Stanton, David W. Lange, and the team of John Wexler and Kevin Flynn, the last listing a particularly large number of varieties. (See the selected bibliography for details.) While doubled and tilted mintmarks are a thing of the past due to changing die preparation techniques, doubled dies can occur anytime. Who knows, perhaps *you* will be the first to discover a new one.

For good measure, a bit of history: Commodore W.C. Eaton was the first collector to study and report variations in mintmark positions on Lincoln cents. After nearly two years of collecting information, he contributed this to *The Numismatist*, April 1911:

Varieties of the 1909 Lincoln Cent.

To the editor: The question as to the minor varieties of the San Francisco 1909 Lincoln cents having been referred to twice of late in *The Numismatist*, I assumed that the matter is of sufficient importance to have additional light thrown upon it. The first note was to the effect that these cents existed in two sub-varieties, in one of which the S is directly under the 0 of the date and in the other under the space between the 9 and the 0. The query was then made as to whether these minor varieties existed in the cents both with and without the V.D.B., and I am now in a position to say that they do exist in both.

On looking over twenty-five of these 1909s with the V.D.B. as received from the mint I found them to be about equally divided between the two varieties, but my twenty-five without V.D.B. were all alike, *i.e.*, the S below the space only.

Thinking the matter of sufficient interest I then took up the matter with the mint officials and, as the replies cover not only this but other points, I consider them of sufficient interest to quote them in full, as it is always well to have even small points officially decided.

My first letter was principally an inquiry as to whether these different positions of the S existed in both types. To this I received the following reply.

The Mint of the United States at San Francisco
Superintendent's Office
February 2, 1911.
W.C. Eaton, Commodore, U.S. Navy, Hamilton, N.Y.

Sir: The mintmark is put on dies by hand. The difference in location of the S on the specimens you possess was no doubt due to a misplacing of the initial when the die that eventually struck your pieces was being perfected. We do not know that any other issues exhibit this peculiarity.

The mints carry only current issues of coins struck by them and we cannot supply you with specimens issued prior to 1911.

The 1911 one cent pieces are ready for distribution. We do not manufacture nickels; half and quarter dollars, and dimes will be issued during the year.

Respectfully, (Signed) E.D. Hawkins, Chief Clerk.

On receiving this reply, in sending for the new cents, I made a few more inquiries bearing upon the case, especially as to whether the same dies were used for the cents without initials, by erasing the initials, or whether new dies were used. To this I received the following answer:

Sir: In return for your remittance of February 7, 1911, I am enclosing to you herewith, by registered mail, 25 Uncirculated, Lincoln-head design, one cent pieces issued by the San Francisco Mint during 1911.

Entirely new dies were made for the coinage of the non-initialed one cent pieces of the Lincoln-head design of 1909.

We do not make proof coins of any denomination.

The life of a die for one cent pieces is about 150,000 coins. The number of dies used depends upon the demand for the coin and cannot be definitely answered at this time.

From the above I made two deductions. First, as entirely new dies were made for the 1909 cents without initials we need not look for the differences that exist on those with initials. Second, that as the S was put on by hand we might find not only that difference in position but any other. As a matter of fact, I have today received from a Western dealer the looked for variety, no V.D.B, S directly under the 0, so am in a position to positively state that these minor varieties exist both with and without the initials. I may add that two other dealers had looked over their stocks of hundreds of these cents without finding any differences but, nevertheless, as 150,000 were made from each die they can not be so very rare. Of course as new dies were made the existence of these differences in both can only be a coincidence.

Neither my twenty-five 1910s nor my twenty-five 1911s show any differences, but as the S was put on by hand such differences may occur at any time. In my 1910s the S is always practically below the 1, though a trifle to the left. In my 1911s it is below the space between the 9 and the 1. Should other collectors find other positions I would be glad if they would let me know.

Very cordially,
W.C. Eaton, Commodore, U.S. Navy.
Hamilton, N.Y., Feb. 24, 1911.

His correspondence is of historical interest today. The varieties mentioned are also collectible today, but few pay any attention to mintmark positions. Sharply double-punched mintmarks, not noticed by Eaton, are another story. Interestingly, the dramatic 1909-S with S over an earlier horizontal S, so eagerly sought today and scarce, not rare, did not fall under his view.

COLLECTING PROOFS

Proof Lincoln cents can be a specialty unto themselves. See chapter seven for extended comments. Matte Proofs, minted from 1909 to 1916, including both the 1909 V.D.B. and regular 1909 types, have not been popular with collectors. They sometimes appear almost identical to circulation strikes, and a magnifying glass is needed to distinguish them. The pleasing side of this is that Matte Proofs tend to be inexpensive today, particularly in numismatically desirable shades (opinion here) of BN and RB.

More in the mainstream are the mirror type Proofs from 1936 to date. These can be collected in simple date progression: 1936 to 1942 continuously, 1950 to 1964 continuously, and 1986 (actually 1986-S) to the present time. A landmark from our own generation is the 1990 Proof without S mintmark, of which very few were coined. Whenever one is offered at auction or elsewhere, there is a lot of excitement.

While certain Proofs, especially of modern years, have been certified in ultra grades such as 68, 69, and 70, there is little actual difference among them. A high quality Proof-67RD of a modern set is just about perfection, and if it were my money being spent, I would not stretch and pay much more for two or three additional points. The terms *cameo* and *deep cameo* are used with some certified coins, but not all. Again, see chapter seven. Deep cameo Proofs are the rule for sets since the 1970s, and there is no sense paying any additional price for them.

A set of the mirror-finish Proofs, whether begun with 1936, 1950, or 1968, can be a very attractive and interesting possession. Make sure that your coins are housed and stored with care.

ANALYSIS AND MARKET GUIDE TO LINCOLN CENTS
COMPLETE 1909 TO DATE

INTRODUCTION

The following pages discuss and analyze dates, mintmarks, and especially significant varieties of Lincoln cents from 1909 to date. Again, you are cautioned that coins from 1934 to date exist by the tens of thousands in Mint State, and those of more recent dates by the many millions, and that those submitted to grading services are only a tiny fraction of those in the hands of collectors, dealers, and investors. A coin for which, say, ten have been certified at the MS-68RD level today may well have 20, 50, or 100 certified a decade from now. Use caution when paying a large premium for a coin that is "rare" in terms of certified high grades, but very common in such collectible grades as gem MS-65RD and 66RD. Poignant remarks from Sam Lukes:

> I remember that many years ago a client, unbeknownst to me, purchased the very first 1909 V.D.B. cent that PCGS had graded as MS-67RD. At the time no other grading service had certified this variety at such a high level. A prominent dealer convinced my client that this was a "Population 1, one-of-a-kind" coin, and consummated a sale for $3,250. In time, more than 100 more MS-67RD coins were certified by PCGS, and the market value dropped to about $350. Today as I write this, there are 183 MS-67RD 1909 V.D.B. cents in the PCGS population report alone, not even considering other services![32]

Lincoln cents, the most familiar of U.S. coins, were minted in response to the demand for them in banking and commercial circles. When small change was scarce, such as during both World Wars, cent mintages rose to high levels. When the country was in a recession or depression, as in 1921 and 1922 and 1930 through 1933, there were adequate stocks of "pennies" on hand, and new mintages were small. The "In America" story line, for each year listed below, reflects economic, social, and other trends and often explains why the demand for new cents changed. The text is necessarily extensive for the beginning year, 1909, to set the scene. The "In Numismatics" commentaries give a general view of coin collecting in each year. "News About Lincoln Cents" includes current and later information relevant to the cents of that particular year. Other listings include production, mintage, and variety notes for the various dates and mintmarks.

For most scarce and rare varieties, sophisticated die-struck fakes exist. These are endemic on the Internet and other places, usually offered by private individuals or dealers who are not recognized as *responsible* professional numismatists. For this reason I strongly recommend that you only buy certified examples, evaluated by a leading service, of scarce and rare issues. These services keep track of the earmarks of fakes and nearly always catch them.

IMPORTANT: ABOUT MARKET PRICES

The market prices of Lincoln cents represent evaluation and averaging of data collected from a panel of active dealers and experts, some with more than 50 years of experience in the field.

Prices of about $100 and higher are for coins certified by respected third-party grading services. Generally, PCGS coins will command prices slightly higher than those graded by other services. In all instances, prices are for *average quality* within the grades listed, which means that such cents as 1918-S, 1925-D, 1925-S, and many others will not have Full Details. Fortunately for you, when a Full Details coin is found, you may not have to pay a premium for it, since most buyers are not aware of these aspects of *quality* among Lincoln cents and focus solely upon the assigned grade.

Prices for coins below $100 are for "raw" or uncertified coins. This is a matter of practicality. As an illustration, another information source, the 2008 *Guide Book of United States Coins* gives a retail price of 25¢ each for dozens of different dates and mints of Lincoln cents in MS-65RD, dating back to the mid-1970s. Among these, a 2006 cent, of which more than 4 billion were made, is listed for 25¢. Most of this price reflects the dealer's handling cost, including adding it to stock, placing in a holder of some kind, displaying it for sale, and selling it. If you offered the dealer a $50 bag of face value (5,000 coins), they would have a total retail value, at 25¢ each, of $1,250. The dealer, however, would likely pay only slightly more than $50. Conversely, if you wanted to buy a bag of these cents, the dealer would not charge much more than face value.

Lincoln cents with market values up to several dollars each also include a significant percentage for stocking and handling. In contrast, a $1,000 coin reflects current net numismatic value, since at this level handling is not important. Likely, a dealer who needed a rare coin for stock would pay 70 percent, 80 percent, or more of that price to buy it from you.

A 2006 Lincoln cent certified as MS-65 by PCGS is likely to cost $6 or so, while one graded as MS-67 might cost $40. The concept—and I hope I am explaining it clearly—is that many modern coins are sent to PCGS (and other services) in the hope that some will come back in ultra-high grades, such as 67RD. When one does, a home run is hit, for likely the coin was acquired at face value from a bank roll. In the illustration the MS-65 coin available for $6 represents a slight loss for the owner: it cost more than that to certify it. It is hoped that the owner gained several MS-67RD coins among a group of coins certified.

Further, if a 2006 MS-67RD is offered for sale at $20 but is not in a holder, it would not sell to most buyers, even though it might seem to be half price. The reason is that the buyer could not be sure if PCGS agrees with that grade.

In summary: For most, if not all, Lincoln cents valued at below $100 or so, there is a two-tier market—a cheaper price, often *much* cheaper, for raw or uncertified coins, and, for coins certified by specific highly regarded services, prices that are significantly higher.

COMMENTARY

By now you know that forming a high quality collection of Lincoln cents is, indeed, complex, requires knowledge, and can be very exciting. For self-satisfaction, you can contemplate that it takes more skill to determine the quality of 1926-S cent than it does an 1804 silver dollar, the latter being worth into the millions of dollars. The thrill of the chase awaits you!

DATE-BY-DATE ANALYSIS

THE YEAR 1909

In America: When the Lincoln cent was launched in 1909, America was prosperous. The Panic of 1907, which caused financial distress, was now mostly history. William Howard Taft occupied the White House, having won the 1908 election. Outgoing President Theodore Roosevelt and an entourage headed to Africa for a game-hunting expedition. Automobiles were beginning to be popular but were still expensive, typically costing several thousand dollars or more for a well-equipped model. Horsepower in the literal sense provided most private and public transportation in towns and cities, supplemented by trolley and railroad lines. Airplanes were still a curiosity, and when one flew overhead or was shown at a county fair, it attracted a lot of attention.

Public entertainment was provided by amusement parks, often located at the end of a trolley line, so as to keep the cars busy on weekends. Every park had its penny arcade, as did most medium-sized towns and all cities. A cent, which everybody called a "penny," was the ticket to hearing a tune on a phonograph, or seeing a striptease or auto race on a hand-cranked Mutoscope flip-card machine. Strength testers, fortune tellers, and other devices grabbed pennies as well. Penny scales were common sights in stores and on streets. Indian Head cents were the style of the era, having been coined since 1859.

The nickelodeon or 5¢ theater was a recent craze, and since about 1904 thousands had been set up all across America. For a nickel a moviegoer could see an hour or more of comedies, travelogues, and mini-dramas. Most films were 1,000 feet in length and took about 12 minutes to see. Circuses, vaudeville troupes, Wild West shows, Chautauqua groups, and stage companies regularly visited the typical medium-sized town, while school and amateur plays and concerts filled in what was usually a year-round schedule of inexpensive entertainment. With a pocket full of pennies or nickels, a youngster, or an adult for that matter, could have an afternoon or evening of fun just about anywhere in America.

Most fine homes had a piano or reed organ, considered a mark of refinement and distinction—a family's second-most expensive asset after a house, unless there was a car parked outside, in which unlikely instance the piano ranked third. Music boxes were popular, and Edison, Columbia, and other phonographs were even more so. Only well-to-do families were apt to have such amenities. The typical factory worker earning $15 to $20 a week, or even less, had a lot to do just to keep food on the table. A loaf of bread cost 6¢, but with a half-dozen mouths to feed in a typical family, it disappeared quickly. Thousands of children worked as sorters in coal-processing collieries, as loom-tenders in textile mills, and tending animals and crops on farms. Most Americans had no more than an elementary-school education. All cities and many towns were wired for electricity, but rural homes were lighted with kerosene or candles.

In the marketplace in 1909 current coins included the ubiquitous Indian Head pennies and Liberty Head nickels, Barber and Liberty Seated dimes, quarters, and half dollars, and occasional silver dollars. The last were not widely used except in the West. Gold coins of the $2.50, $5, $10, and $20 denominations were readily available at banks but were not generally used east of the Rocky Mountains. San Francisco in particular was a gold-coin economy, with scarcely a $10 or $20 paper bill in sight. Currency was of a bewildering array of designs and issues, including Legal Tender Notes, Silver Certificates, Gold Certificates, Treasury or Coin Notes, and currency bearing the imprints of more than 5,000 different National Banks.

In Numismatics: Collecting federal coins by date and mintmark was not popular, and probably not more than several dozen numismatists endeavored to obtain one of each new mintmark variety of the Barber dime, quarter, and half dollar, although Augustus G. Heaton's 1893 monograph, *A Treatise on Mint Marks*, had influenced some to follow this specialty.

Minor Proof sets sold in early 1909 contained the Indian Head cent and Liberty Head nickel, and silver sets the Barber dime, quarter, and half dollar. Except for Proofs, Barber silver coins were not popular, and ditto for Morgan silver dollars (of earlier dates; none had been struck since 1904, and anticipation was that with hundreds of millions in Treasury storage, no more would ever be struck). Gold coins dated from 1795 to 1834 were popular and always attracted attention in the auction room. There was relatively little interest in Liberty Head gold issues of the $5, $10, and $20 denominations, and virtually no demand for mintmarks. Gold dollars were an exception, and building sets of these was popular with those who could afford it. Quarter eagles and $3 gold coins were mildly popular. In April 1909 C.W. Cowell sent a letter to *The Numismatist*, suggesting that collectors of gold coins could benefit from visiting their banks because "C and D mintmarks could be found easily, and usually in Fine condition." Few took heed.

The Numismatist, the journal of the ANA, had been published since 1888. The ANA itself was formed in November 1891. In 1909 it was deeply embroiled in controversy. Farran Zerbe, president of the association, a numismatic promoter and, some said, a charlatan, had visited the widow of Dr. George F. Heath, founder and publisher of *The Numismatist*, following Heath's recent death. He sought to acquire ownership of the magazine for the ANA. It had been the official ANA journal for more than a decade, but Lucy Heath held title. Surprise! Zerbe did buy it, but *for himself*. Now in 1909, although it was still the journal of the association, he was owner and publisher. Moreover, the impending election pitted Frank Higgins, an established collector and scholar in New York City, against Dr. J.M. Henderson, an Ohioan who was "Zerbe's man." Elections were done by proxy, with each member allowed to either mail in his or her vote, or give proxy to someone attending the annual convention. At the annual convention in August, 447 members were represented by proxy, including a lot of "new members" signed up by Zerbe at a discount to get their votes (for a hitherto unavailable *six-month* term), bringing the membership up to 621. The "Credentials Committee" reviewed the ballots cast, qualified slightly more than 450 of them, and announced that about 400 were for Henderson. In disgust, Virgil M. Brand, owner of the largest coin collection in the country, resigned from the ANA, never to rejoin, and many others became disenchanted. On the plus side, Zerbe turned out a much-improved magazine, with new features and more interesting articles. Zerbe was an expert numismatist and also smart, entrepreneurial, and enthusiastic; but he could be devious and not worthy of trust.

The new (introduced in 1908) Indian Head $2.50 and $5 coins were nearly universally condemned by collectors. In contrast, the MCMVII (1907) double eagle was widely liked and available for $28 or so in Uncirculated grade. Many numismatists owned one, even if gold was not their specialty. Sand Blast Proof gold coins, introduced in 1908, were detested, as were the new Satin Finish (or "Roman Finish") Proofs that replaced them in 1909. In the following year (1910) the ANA sent an official complaint to the Mint, requesting that the old-style mirror Proofs be resumed (see chapter seven for details). Most numismatists who collected the American series concentrated on colonial coins first and foremost, followed in no particular order by early copper cents (1793 to 1857), Indian Head cents by date, and early silver. Tokens and medals were very popular. More collectors specialized in Hard Times tokens (1832 to 1844) than did in Morgan silver dollars, minted from 1878 to 1904. As will be seen in the present narrative, collecting U.S. coins by date and mintmark did not become widely popular until the 1930s, and in the meantime, not many people saved such coins at the time of issue— accounting for the rarity in high grades of many Lincoln cents today.

New York City was the numismatic focal point of the country. Thomas L. Elder ran a store and conducted auctions. Lyman H. Low, who had been in the trade for decades, was active, as were the Scott Stamp & Coin Co., William Brown, and several others. The American Numismatic Society (ANS) offered a museum and library in its new (1908) building at 155th Street and Broadway. The recently formed New York Numismatic Club caught on quickly and was an enthusiastic group.

In Philadelphia, probably the number two city as a coin center, the Chapman brothers, S. Hudson and Henry, had offices and conducted sales, each on his own since their partnership was dissolved in the summer of 1906. Henry maintained a large retail stock of coins, one of relatively few such holdings in America. Chicago was a hotbed of activity, with the Chicago Coin Club being perhaps the best-known group in the country other than the national associations. Ben G. Green and Fred Michael & Bro. were active dealers there. In Fort Worth, Texas, B. Max Mehl, who began advertising as a coin dealer in 1903 when he was still a teenager, was by 1909 very well known—a prolific advertiser who also issued premium catalogs (inspired by the success of William von Bergen in Boston, who had profited a long time by selling "premium lists" to the public) and conducted mail bid sales. The St. Louis Stamp & Coin Co. was another active dealer, as was William Hesslein in New Haven, Connecticut. Around the country several dozen dealers did business by mail, and in various towns and cities many curiosity shops stocked coins along with stamps, minerals, prints, and other collectibles, but did not advertise or issue price lists.

Professional numismatists had to be knowledgeable to be successful, as did collectors. There were no grading services or even standards, no authentication bureaus, no equivalent of the Professional Numismatists Guild (formed in 1953, formalized in 1955) from which to seek redress for misdeeds and problems, such as counterfeits. Dealers had to know how to grade (although each had different ideas on the subject), how to tell the genuine from the false, and what current values were. Further, there were no reference books listing the mintages, values, and rarity of U.S. coins. The only sources for pricing were advertisements, auction realizations, and, most of all, judgment based upon experience. Because of this, numismatists who hoped to form worthwhile collections had to be knowledgeable—just as I am encouraging you to be, *today*, if you collect Lincoln cents!

News About Lincoln Cents: Released on August 2, 1909, the new coins were a sensation. Supplies were soon exhausted. Production of coins with V.D.B. was halted at the direction of Secretary of the Treasury Franklin MacVeagh. The hubs were revised to eliminate the artist's identification (but for expediency it seems that some working dies were made usable by simply grinding the initials off). The reverse rim was made less prominent. Production of the second version, without initials, was underway at the Philadelphia Mint by August 12. The novelty had passed by this time, and these attracted little public interest. Within a year or two most of the cents kept as souvenirs were spent. (For details, see chapter two.)

In fiscal year 1909 the average cent obverse die produced 183,751 impressions, and the average reverse die 144,314.

1909, V.D.B.

CIRCULATION MINTAGE: 27,995,000

MATTE PROOF MINTAGE: 1,194[33]

Enlarged 1.5x
(actual size 19 mm)

MARKET VALUES • 1909, V.D.B.

G-4	VG-8	F-12	VF-20	EF-40	AU-50	MS-60BN	MS-63BN	MS-65RD
$6	$7.50	$10	$12	$15	$18	$30	$35	$200

MARKET VALUES • 1909, V.D.B., Matte Proof

PF-63RB	PF-64RB
$12,500	$20,000

Key to Collecting: Readily available in any and all grades from well worn to gem Mint State, the last usually with original orange color, either full or partial. Luster varies from frosty to matte, the last often mistaken for Matte Proof finish. MS-65RD and higher certified coins abound, giving you a wide choice if "slabs" are your preference. We are all fortunate that this very short-lived type, certainly one of the greatest "story coins" in American numismatics, is the most affordable of all early Lincoln cents. There should be room for one in *every collection:* This is at once a landmark coin and inexpensive.

Striking and Sharpness: Most are well struck with Full Details, with excellent definition of Lincoln's hair, lettering, and other features. Some have the V.D.B. initials weakly defined, usually at the top. These should be avoided.

Matte Proofs: Proofs of this year are of the grainy or Matte Proof style, completely unlike the mirror Proofs in the predecessor Indian Head cent series, struck from dies the faces of which were lightly etched. The rims on both the obverse and reverse are perfectly flat (not rounded) and do not have the matte finish. Viewed edge-on, the edges are *mirrorlike,* unlike circulation strikes. Chapter seven gives details. Today, since most are encapsulated, you need to take the word of a grading service that a Matte Proof is indeed such. At the same time I recommend that you only buy a coin certified by one of the top several services, and then have it checked by another expert. As to the frequency of misattributed "Matte Proofs," under Lot 375 in New Netherlands' 51st Sale, June 1958, this comment was given: "Nine out of every ten offered will not stand up to critical examination." To the casual glance, many Matte Proofs do not look distinctive, and for this reason they were unpopular at the time of issue. Years ago coins with full *original* Mint color were almost unheard of. Today more than two dozen have been certified. Makes one wonder!

The mintage of the 1909 V.D.B. Matte Proof has been stated as 420 for many years. As researcher Roger W. Burdette and others have reported, figures for Proof mintage of this era, particularly for the cent, nickel, and gold coins, are subject to question. The mintage of 1,194 Matte Proofs has been suggested by Kevin Flynn.[34] Although Mint data supports this suggestion, surviving examples, including the number seen by certification services, suggest that far fewer ever reached numismatic channels.

A pristine (undipped) Matte Proof usually will have light brown toning overall, but some have mint red-orange at the centers. Any Matte Proof that is bright overall is virtually always a cleaned or dipped coin. I have never seen an *original* bright red-orange coin.

1909-S, V.D.B.

CIRCULATION MINTAGE: 484,000

Enlarged 1.5x
(actual size 19 mm)

MARKET VALUES • 1909-S, V.D.B.

G-4	VG-8	F-12	VF-20	EF-40	AU-50	MS-60BN	MS-63BN	MS-65RD
$725	$800	$900	$1,050	$1,200	$1,450	$1,850	$2,250	$7,750

Key to Collecting: This is the be-all and end-all object of desire in the Lincoln cent series, the Holy Grail (as David W. Lange suggests). It is by no means the rarest Lincoln cent. Certain of the die varieties (but not basic dates and mintmarks) are more elusive.

In Mint State the 1909-S V.D.B. is the most plentiful mintmark issue of its era, a record it does not yield until the late 1920s. It is much easier to find than the regular 1909-S made later, although the regular 1909-S has a much higher mintage (see 1909-S entry). High quality 1909-S V.D.B. cents certified by the leading services run into the thousands; more than 1,000 are MS-65RD or higher. The *demand* for this coin is incredible, and in comparison to the number of people seeking it, the 1909-S V.D.B. is indeed a key issue.

Examples are available in just about any grade desired, although attractive well-worn coins in grades such as VF and EF are rarer than are AU and Mint State coins. Most Mint State coins have original color, which is a yellowish-orange (different in color from the Philadelphia version; David W. Lange calls it "brassy") due to a slightly different alloy mix. The same distinctive color is seen on pristine (undipped) 1908-S and 1909-S Indian Head cents. On the other hand, an "RD" 1909-S V.D.B. that is orange, without the yellow tint, is most certainly a candidate for having been dipped and processed. There are quite a few of these dipped "beauties" around, including in certified holders.

The ownership of a 1909-S V.D.B. cent in *any* grade is a badge of accomplishment. Congratulations! You have obtained one of the greatest "story coins" in American numismatics, and, indeed, the most famous popular rarity.

Caveat: There are thousands of fakes on the market. Some of these have been made by adding an S to a Philadelphia coin, but some are die struck. Insist on buying an example certified by one of several leading certification services. Avoid buying *any* "raw" coin, such as on the Internet, or "from an old-time collection," etc., and be suspicious of bargains. See the introduction to this chapter.

Striking and Sharpness: The typical 1909-S V.D.B. cent is very well struck with Full Details, but some have the V.D.B. initials slightly weak, usually at the top. Avoid the last. Sam Lukes relates the instance in which someone paid $92,000 for a PCGS-graded MS-67RD example, although "the most important part of the coin, the designer's initials, were weakly struck and mushy."[35] This serves to illustrate that some people will buy just about anything if the label on a holder is appealing, never mind the coin itself! Likely, the typical reader of this book would rather pay $5,000 or so for an MS-65RD with Full Details. Or, at least I would. Matters such as this provide lively points for discussion at coin club meetings and anywhere else that collectors gather.

George J. Fuld told of a story from John Zug, the Bowie, Maryland mail-order dealer, who stated that he obtained 25,000 coins at face value from the San Francisco Mint at the time of issue, then sold them around 1918 for 1-3/4¢ each. Although it is certain that John Zug, Henry Chapman, and some other dealers had working stocks of such pieces, I am not aware of any single hoard running into the tens of thousands of pieces. If such an arrangement by Zug took place, it should be verifiable by Mint correspondence, none of which has come to light thus far. Likely, Zug was simply telling a "big story," as old-time dealers liked to do.

In *The Numismatist,* July 1910, these and other cents of the era were offered in quantity:

> For Sale. . . . Pennies in lots of 500 each kind. Lincoln V.D.B.-S, cir. and unc., 6¢; all unc., 8¢. Lincoln 1909-S, no initials, unc., 3¢.; 1910 do., 2¢. Indian 1908-S, cir. and unc., 6¢.; all unc., 8¢. Indian 1909-S, cir. and unc., 7¢.; all unc., 10¢. In lots of 100 each kind 1¢. each additional. California Loan Office, Oakland, Cal.

Mehl's Numismatic Monthly, January 1916, included this from a correspondent:

> The variations of the late issues of one and five cent pieces was brought to my attention through the catalog of a dealer who priced two 1909 Lincoln V.D.B. cents of the S mint, one of which had the S. mint mark under the 0 of the date and the other had the S between the first 9 and the 0. As a collector of the cent series and being in the part of the country where the S mint mark is most frequently seen, I began a search for the above two varieties with remarkable results. The number of different varieties that I found before I finally got the ones I originally started out to find have made a very large collection for me, not only in the Lincoln head but the Indian head cents as well.

As implied, in 1916 the 1909-S V.D.B. cent was easily enough found in circulation. Thus far, except for the public excitement when they were first issued, little or no numismatic attention was paid to such pieces, and no record has been located of anyone rescuing quantities from circulation.

Arthur M. Kagin related:

> In early 1952 I received an inquiry from a California collector asking for an offer on an Uncirculated roll of 1909-S, V.D.B. cents, I offered him $500 per roll. Each roll had 50 coins in it. About 10 days later five rolls arrived. About two weeks after sending him the check another five rolls arrived. In sending him the check I stated that I would buy all he had at the same price as I didn't want him to break the market by offering a large quantity at one time. About four or five months later a number of ads appeared in the *Numismatic Scrapbook Magazine* offering Uncirculated 1909-S V.D.B. cents at $12 to $15 each. Apparently, he had sold more rolls to other people.[36]

The S mintmark punch on early San Francisco Lincoln cents has a tiny raised-dot flaw within the upper loop, noted David W. Lange. This S punch was used in later years, into 1917, when a slightly larger letter replaced it.

1909, No V.D.B.

CIRCULATION MINTAGE: 72,702,618

MATTE PROOF MINTAGE: 2,618

Enlarged 1.5x
(actual size 19 mm)

MARKET VALUES • 1909, No V.D.B.

G-4	VG-8	F-12	VF-20	EF-40	AU-50	MS-60BN	MS-63BN	MS-65RD
$3	$4.50	$5	$6	$8	$12	$17	$25	$160

MARKET VALUES • 1909, No V.D.B., Matte Proof

PF-63RB	PF-64RB	PF-65RD
$750	$1,000	$2,000

Key to Collecting: Readily available in just about any desired grade, but in high grades only a small fraction exist compared to the widely saved 1909 V.D.B.

Striking and Sharpness: Most are well struck and have Full Details *except for* minute planchet marks on the shoulder.

Matte Proofs: These are scarce today. Most pristine (undipped) coins are a rich light brown color. Some have original red-orange color on one or both sides but are *never* fully brilliant in my experience—never mind that many dozens have been certified as such.

Three obverse dies were used to coin 1909 Matte Proof cents of this variety, one of which had been used for the V.D.B. Proofs. Two reverses were employed.

1909-S, No V.D.B.

CIRCULATION MINTAGE: 1,825,000

Enlarged 1.5x
(actual size 19 mm)

MARKET VALUES • 1909-S, No V.D.B.

G-4	VG-8	F-12	VF-20	EF-40	AU-50	MS-60BN	MS-63BN	MS-65RD
$90	$105	$115	$145	$160	$225	$350	$400	$1,500

Key to Collecting: Scarce in any and all grades from well worn up, this in the context of the Lincoln cent series. Beginning in the 1930s the low mintage of the regular 1909-S attracted many, who plucked them from circulation—usually in grades of Fine to VF and wearing down to G-4 by the early 1950s. MS-65RD and slightly higher coins are easy enough to find and are usually quite attractive. Undipped coins will have a slightly yellowish tint, similar to the 1909-S V.D.B.

Striking and Sharpness: Usually very well struck with Full Details.

Notes: One of the obverse dies used on the 1909-S V.D.B. cents was also used for 1909-S, No V.D.B., as were five new obverses. I've only seen one bank-wrapped roll offered, and that was owned by David Nethaway in the 1950s. Some reverses are said to show traces of the V.D.B. having been filed off (Breen *Encyclopedia* 1978). If so, then part of the field toward the rim would have had to have been filed away as well, a curious procedure.

1909-S, S Over Horizontal S: This is one of the more interesting die varieties in the series. While they are scarce, a nice example can be found with some persistence, including in grades of MS-65RD or higher. The mintmark was first punched erroneously in a horizontal position, then finally corrected. The variety was not publicized until the 1970s and is still not widely known today, although it is listed in the *Guide Book*. As the die continued in use, the under-type erroneous S and other punchings became less visible. Find a decent strike, as most are, but don't hold out for perfection.

1909-S, Repunched Mintmark, S Over Slightly Smaller S: A clear, well-formed slightly smaller S was overpunched with the regular S mintmark. Very clearly defined under low magnification.

THE YEAR 1910

In America: Prosperity continued in America, although the unemployment rate was 5.9 percent, considered to be slightly high. Halley's Comet was bright in the sky and attracted much attention (on its next return in 1986 it was faint).

In Numismatics: Likely, the total community of customers for dealers, buyers of current Proof sets, and others active in the hobby was about 5,000 to 10,000. Collecting current coins from circulation was not popular, and only a handful of numismatists were interested in mintmarked varieties.

News About Lincoln Cents: Minting took place at Philadelphia and San Francisco. Large quantities of the 1909 cents with V.D.B. were spent, as the public tired of the novelty, and by now there were ample coins of the new design in circulation. Production this year reached a record of 152,846,218, the most of any year since copper cents were first struck in 1793. The record would be broken in 1916 and again multiple times after that.

1910

CIRCULATION MINTAGE: 146,801,218

MATTE PROOF MINTAGE: 4,083

Enlarged 1.5x
(actual size 19 mm)

MARKET VALUES • 1910

G-4	VG-8	F-12	VF-20	EF-40	AU-50	MS-60BN	MS-63BN	MS-65RD
$0.75	$0.80	$1	$2	$4	$10	$18	$30	$230

MARKET VALUES • 1910, Matte Proof

PF-63RB	PF-64RB	PF-65RD
$675	$1,000	$1,850

Key to Collecting: Cents of this date are common in worn grades. Mint State coins are plentiful as well, but examples that are MS-65RD or higher, with *original* color, are slightly scarce. When evaluating populations of this or most any other Philadelphia Mint cent, remember that they are usually severely underreported, since these coins are not as valuable as the branch mint issues.

Striking and Sharpness: Nearly all are well struck on obverse and reverse. Close to Full Details coins can be found for this and most early dates, *except* for graininess on Lincoln's shoulder. To find one with truly Full Details, some patience and the use of a medium-strength magnifying glass are all you need.

Matte Proofs: Most pristine (undipped) coins are a rich light brown color. Some have original red-orange color on one or both sides but are never fully brilliant—never mind that dozens of "RD" gems have been certified in recent decades. In the context of Matte Proofs, this is one of the more plentiful issues in the marketplace. The first delivery of Matte Proofs was on January 7, 1910, and consisted of 483 acceptable coins from 498 struck. The Mint is said to have kept quantities of these on hand after 1910, eventually selling them to dealers including William L. Pukall. *All* of these remainder coins were toned a rich brown with hints of blue; no exceptions.[37]

Notes: One striking with barely discernible vestiges of the first 1909 die was described in *Coin World*, June 7, 2004:

> The unique Matte Proof 1910 Lincoln cent with traces of V.D.B. on the reverse, discovered in 1991 by Bill Fivaz, sold for $2,400 in the Society of Lincoln Cent Collectors' recently concluded 121st mail-bid sale. The reverse does not match that of other Matte Proof 1910 Lincoln cents. It does have abrasion lines near the lower rim (where the initials V.D.B. were on certain 1909 cents) and a spot where the reverse die used for Matte Proof 1909 Lincoln, V.D.B cent had a die chip.[38] [Graded Proof-65BN by ANACS][39]

Charles Daughtrey, in *Looking Through Lincoln Cents*, comments:

> A number of [1910 cents with traces of V.D.B.] have been reported to me for examination, but none of them showed anything more than die scratches or hits on the coin that wore to give the appearance of relief. Photographs of these reported "1910 V.D.B." cents have been published, but none of them show anything definite and convincing. Obviously, the jury is still out on this phantom's existence.

1910-S

CIRCULATION MINTAGE: 6,045,000

Enlarged 1.5x
(actual size 19 mm)

MARKET VALUES • 1910-S

G-4	VG-8	F-12	VF-20	EF-40	AU-50	MS-60BN	MS-63BN	MS-65RD
$15	$18	$22	$30	$55	$85	$110	$145	$650

Key to Collecting: In all grades this is slightly scarce, as the mintage implies. Mint State coins are seen with some frequency and usually have light toning. Carbon spots and flecks are usually not a problem, except on coins dipped decades ago and now slightly retoned. A blazing gem with original color is scarce if sharply struck and with good eye appeal. On such coins, the rims and edges will have light toning. Mint State coins with *original* color have distinctive hues (see chapter nine).

Striking and Sharpness: Typically well struck, but with the usual exceptions.

Notes: Obverse mintmark positions vary slightly, as they do on all branch mint coins of this era. Some are said to have traces of a V.D.B. having been removed (Breen *Encyclopedia* 1978); whether such pieces, if they exist, would stand up to modern scrutiny by experts can only be conjectured.

1910-S, Repunched Mintmark: The 1910-S, S Over S, variety is dramatically repunched, the earlier mintmark being partially visible in a slightly higher vertical position with enough traces remaining that the horizontal elements of the undertype are very distinct. Most are in circulated grades.

THE YEAR 1911

In America: Trust-busting, which was a trademark of the Theodore Roosevelt administration, was continued by William Howard Taft after he became president in 1909. In 1911 the Supreme Court found the Standard Oil Company (the Rockefeller interests) and the American Tobacco Co. in violation of the Sherman Antitrust Act.

In Numismatics: In an article in *The Numismatist* in May, William H. Woodin included this:

> I am very desirous of proving that the science of numismatics is a paying investment if a collection be formed with some judgment. An important and scientific collection of anything cannot be formed unless the collector is intensely interested in the subject and willing to devote much time to the study of all matters closely connected to the line he has selected. He must be an enthusiast . . . I have the deepest sympathy for people who cannot find some fad in which they can at times forget all the worries of life and spend refreshing hours.

News About Lincoln Cents: The Denver Mint struck Lincoln cents for the first time, inaugurating a policy (which would continue for decades with some exceptions) of striking cents at three mints each year.

The superintendent of the San Francisco Mint reported, "The life of a die for one-cent pieces is about 150,000 coins." Uncirculated coins were available directly from the Mint to interested collectors for face value plus a nominal postage and handling charge.

1911

CIRCULATION MINTAGE: 101,177,787

MATTE PROOF MINTAGE: 1,725

Enlarged 1.5x
(actual size 19 mm)

MARKET VALUES • 1911

G-4	VG-8	F-12	VF-20	EF-40	AU-50	MS-60BN	MS-63BN	MS-65RD
$0.75	$0.80	$1.50	$2.50	$8	$12	$20	$50	$450

MARKET VALUES • 1911, Matte Proof

PF-63RB	PF-64RB	PF-65RD
$675	$1,000	$2,500

Key to Collecting: Common in worn grades and in Mint State up to the 64 or 65 level, with brown or brown with tinges of red. Full *original* red (actually orange) gems are scarce.

Striking and Sharpness: Varies from quite sharp (including the shoulder of Lincoln), these being Full Details coins; to fairly sharp (with some original graininess on Lincoln's shoulder, but other features well defined); to light in areas. A sharp one can be found without great difficulty.

Matte Proofs: At least two qualities of surface exist on Matte Proof cents of this year, some are more satiny, and later examples less so. Most pristine (undipped) coins are a rich light brown color. Some have original red-orange color on one or both sides but are never fully brilliant, although about three dozen have been certified as Proof-65RD or higher—some of which might be duplicate listings of the same particular coin. An example from the Childs Collection, Lot 78, August 30, 1999, was purchased directly from the Mint by the Childs family in 1909 and held in the same family since, but has different die characteristics from those described in the Lange and Wexler-Flynn texts. Cataloged by the author, it is an unquestioned Matte Proof.

1911-D

CIRCULATION MINTAGE: 12,672,000

Enlarged 1.5x
(actual size 19 mm)

MARKET VALUES • 1911-D

G-4	VG-8	F-12	VF-20	EF-40	AU-50	MS-60BN	MS-63BN	MS-65RD
$7	$8.50	$12.50	$30	$65	$85	$100	$150	$1,000

Key to Collecting: Common in worn grades, as the mintage suggests. At any Mint State level this is a scarce issue, although this is not generally recognized. Mint State coins that are sharply struck with Full Details (see Striking and Sharpness) and without defects are especially scarce, and ones with full original red are very rare. This is a poster example of a coin to be cherrypicked. Most collectors are not aware of how elusive they are.

Striking and Sharpness: Most have light striking in one area or another, such as the higher parts of the Lincoln portrait, and the rim may be weak in areas. Poignantly, David W. Lange observed:

> Although most examples are rather softly struck, a few very sharp specimens may be found. When found in Mint State, these sharper coins are almost always brown or with minimal red. It seems that most of the fully red pieces fall into the softly struck category. This is true of many early Lincoln cents and can be quite frustrating to collectors.

It appears that the smoother surfaces of softly struck cents actually imparted some preservative quality to them which is lacking in the more textured coins with fuller strikes. Cleaned and retoned coins are also very common for this date. Although nearly all of these are rejected by the major grading services, a few of the most professional jobs may slip past.

Notes: In *Looking Through Lincoln Cents*, Charles D. Daughtrey illustrates a 1911-D cent, his variety 1911D-10M-001, with what appears to be a vestige of an earlier S mintmark below it. He notes that while he considers it an *overmintmark*, other authorities do not.

1911-S

CIRCULATION MINTAGE: 4,026,000

Enlarged 1.5x
(actual size 19 mm)

MARKET VALUES • 1911-S

G-4	VG-8	F-12	VF-20	EF-40	AU-50	MS-60BN	MS-63BN	MS-65RD
$32	$42	$50	$65	$85	$115	$200	$350	$2,500

Key to Collecting: This is a key date in all grades. Circulated examples, many of which were picked out of circulation in the 1930s and 1940s, are readily available at coin shows and in shops. Similar to many other low-mintage issues, most were gone from pocket change by the 1950s, with only widely scattered examples remaining to be found. Mint State coins at the 65RD and higher levels come on the market with some frequency, but some have flecks or spots. Finding a truly great coin combining quality surfaces and sharp detail will take some time. Mint State coins with *original* color have distinctive hues (see chapter nine).

Striking and Sharpness: Striking is usually somewhat light on the higher points, but Full Details pieces do exist. Since most collectors are not aware of the difference, once again you, as a knowledgeable collector, have an advantage when buying.

Notes: The repunched mintmark variety is often sought by specialists. This shows slight repunching left to right.

THE YEAR 1912

In America: On April 12 the "unsinkable" *Titanic* went to the bottom of the sea on its maiden voyage, the most sensational news of the year. In November Woodrow Wilson was elected president on the Democratic ticket, as Republicans split their votes between William H. Taft and Theodore Roosevelt, the last running independently on the Progressive or so-called Bull Moose Party ticket.

In Numismatics: An advertisement of the United States Coin Co. included this:

> Coins as an Investment: Many harsh words are said about collectors who interest themselves in an actual speculation as to whether or not the coins they are buying today will have appreciated in value 10 years from now. Numismatists of the

old school said the true collector is not interested in any such appreciation in the value of his collection but derives his entire profit and pleasure from the coins while in his hands. We feel however that the average American collector, while he greatly enjoys his coins, also feels very pleased if on disposing of his collection he realizes profits.

News About Lincoln Cents: Average number of cents struck per die, fiscal year figures (Wexler-Flynn text)—Philadelphia, 345,136 obverse, 355,880 reverse; Denver, 381,075 obverse, 323,337 reverse; San Francisco, 221,152 obverse, 192,305 reverse.

1912

CIRCULATION MINTAGE: 68,153,060

MATTE PROOF MINTAGE: 2,172

Enlarged 1.5x
(actual size 19 mm)

MARKET VALUES • 1912

G-4	VG-8	F-12	VF-20	EF-40	AU-50	MS-60BN	MS-63BN	MS-65RD
$1.75	$2.75	$3.50	$5.50	$15	$30	$35	$50	$500

MARKET VALUES • 1912, Matte Proof

PF-63RB	PF-64RB	PF-65RD
$675	$1,000	$3,000

Key to Collecting: This is a common date in worn grades. Mint State pieces are scarce, and gems with full *original* color and without carbon spots or flecks are *extremely rare*. In 1981 Stephen G. Manley, in *The Lincoln Cent*, stated without qualification: "The 1912 is the biggest sleeper of the Lincoln cent series in the upper grades." Today hundreds have been certified as MS-65RD or higher, but I don't know how Manley would evaluate them. Modern viewing reveals that quality coins without spots and with original color are elusive.

Striking and Sharpness: Most are fairly well struck, although there are exceptions.

Matte Proofs: Most pristine (undipped) coins are a rich light brown color and have a finely granular surface. Some have original red-orange color on one or both sides but in my experience are never fully brilliant. This date is quite *rare*, more so than the low mintage suggests.

1912-D

CIRCULATION MINTAGE: 10,411,000

Enlarged 1.5x
(actual size 19 mm)

MARKET VALUES • 1912-D

G-4	VG-8	F-12	VF-20	EF-40	AU-50	MS-60BN	MS-63BN	MS-65RD
$11	$13	$15	$35	$85	$115	$175	$300	$1,250

Key to Collecting: Slightly scarce in circulated grades. Mint State coins are seen with some frequency, but gems with full *original* color and with sharply struck surfaces in all areas, including the borders, are rare.

Striking and Sharpness: Often well struck at the center, but weak or slightly "fuzzy" at the periphery, due to use of worn dies. David W. Lange: "While most 1912-D cents are well struck in their centers they tend to have an 'expanded' look to them . . . The lettering and numerals, including both date and mintmark, appear larger than normal. This is a form of die wear that seems to be peculiar to the Denver Mint issues."

Notes: W.C. Eaton contributed this to *The Numismatist*, March 1912:

> I have to now report that the Denver Mint is already using, or has used, three differ-
> ent dies for the cents of 1912, at least the "D" has been cut in three slightly differing
> places. In the first two a prolongation of the "1" downward would cut the right edge
> of the "D" but in one case the "D" is perceptibly nearer the "9" than in the other. In
> the third variety the "1" prolonged would miss the "D" altogether and the "D" is
> smaller than in either of the first two varieties. These three varieties were all mixed
> in one lot of 25 I have just received from the Mint.

1912-S

CIRCULATION MINTAGE: 4,431,000

Enlarged 1.5x
(actual size 19 mm)

MARKET VALUES • 1912-S

G-4	VG-8	F-12	VF-20	EF-40	AU-50	MS-60BN	MS-63BN	MS-65RD
$18	$23	$25	$45	$80	$115	$185	$285	$2,500

Key to Collecting: Scarce in all grades. Gems with full *original* color and free of flecks are rare. David W. Lange acutely observes: "The fact that most of the surviving high grade examples have been dipped at some point is not clearly reflected in the certified population data, as some leeway seems to have been given for this very scarce date." This comment is a reality check for many, perhaps the majority of collectors "out there" who read the labels on holders but are clueless about such aspects as originality of color or, for that matter, quality of strike. The idea that *leeway* is given in certifying some dipped coins should not come as a surprise to you by this point in my text. Mint State coins with *original* color have distinctive hues (see chapter nine).

Striking and Sharpness: Usually seen fairly well struck. A Full Details coin is a reason-able expectation.

THE YEAR 1913

In America: The Federal Reserve System was established with 12 branch banks. The 16th amendment to the Constitution provided for an income tax. The *New York World* published the first crossword puzzle. Ragtime was the sensation of the popular music world, as it had been since the turn of the century. Coin-operated pianos and orchestrions (automatic orchestras) were all the rage in saloons, bordellos, and other places of entertainment. X-ray machines began to be widely installed in hospitals and clinics.

In Numismatics: H.O. Granberg, a Wisconsin industrialist and occasional dealer in coins, proposed a set of grading standards (see chapter eight). The Indian Head / Buffalo nickel was introduced.

News About Lincoln Cents: Average number of cents struck per die, fiscal year figures (Wexler-Flynn text)—Philadelphia, 337,752 obverse, 323,621 reverse; Denver, 501,364 obverse, 391,309 reverse; San Francisco, 218,275 obverse, 160,835 reverse.

1913

CIRCULATION MINTAGE: 76,532,352

MATTE PROOF MINTAGE: 2,983

Enlarged 1.5x
(actual size 19 mm)

MARKET VALUES • 1913

G-4	VG-8	F-12	VF-20	EF-40	AU-50	MS-60BN	MS-63BN	MS-65RD
$1.25	$1.35	$3	$4	$25	$35	$40	$65	$450

MARKET VALUES • 1913, Matte Proof

PF-63RB	PF-64RB	PF-65RD
$675	$1,000	$1,750

Key to Collecting: Well-worn examples picked out of circulation from the 1930s onward are plentiful. As is true of most Lincoln cents after 1909, up to the early 1920s, EF and AU coins—which might have been picked out of circulation in the teens and 1920s if there had been a widespread interest, but there was not—are scarce. Mint State coins are plentiful in the context of the series, including MS-65RD and higher.

Striking and Sharpness: Most are well struck, although there are exceptions.

Matte Proofs: Most pristine (undipped) coins are a rich light brown color. Some have original red-orange color on one or both sides but are never fully brilliant, although dozens have been certified Proof-65RD or higher. This is the most plentiful date of the Matte Proof Lincoln cents.

1913-D

CIRCULATION MINTAGE: 15,804,000

Enlarged 1.5x
(actual size 19 mm)

MARKET VALUES • 1913-D

G-4	VG-8	F-12	VF-20	EF-40	AU-50	MS-60BN	MS-63BN	MS-65RD
$3.25	$3.75	$5	$10	$60	$75	$115	$225	$1,650

Key to Collecting: Relatively plentiful in worn grades. Many Mint State coins exist, including 120 certified as 65RD and 10 as 66RD (up from just 48 and 6, respectively, when David W. Lange wrote his book on the subject in 1995). A gem RD coin with sharp strike is a rarity: a quest for the cherrypicker.

Striking and Sharpness: Most have areas of weakness. Full Details examples are hard to find.

1913-S
CIRCULATION MINTAGE: 6,101,000

Enlarged 1.5x
(actual size 19 mm)

MARKET VALUES • 1913-S

G-4	VG-8	F-12	VF-20	EF-40	AU-50	MS-60BN	MS-63BN	MS-65RD
$11	$13.50	$18	$35	$65	$115	$200	$300	$3,000

Key to Collecting: This is a scarce issue in all grades, in the context of the early Lincoln series. Most in existence were picked out of circulation from the 1930s onward and tend to grade from Good to Fine or so. Mint State coins are elusive, and gems with original color and sharp strike are rare. The advantage of being a smart buyer and cherrypicking is implied by David W. Lange's comment that many coins certified as RD "just barely make the cut." Words to heed, I would say! Mint State coins with *original* color have distinctive hues (see chapter nine).

Striking and Sharpness: Most show some lightness, but not as egregiously as for the 1913-D.

THE YEAR 1914

In America: After ten years of construction the Panama Canal opened to traffic. The Federal Trade Commission was established. Prosperity continued in America despite an unemployment rate of 7.9 percent. Automobiles were in wide use, and many who could afford them enjoyed pleasure excursions to the mountains or seashore. Airplanes were no longer a novelty. Interurban or electric railroads connecting cities were popular, and in many areas of America trips of hundreds of miles could be taken by changing at different stations. Pullman cars on regular trains hauled by steam locomotives furnished elegant service for long-distance trips. In August the World War began in Europe. Although the United States did not officially join the conflict until 1917, America provided vast supplies of munitions and other supplies to England, France, and other countries, with the result that nearly all manufacturers were busy, often working around the clock. Wages and prices rose.

In Numismatics: In New York City the ANS held a grand exhibition of coins with displays on loan from many collectors. There were 579 members in the ANA.

News About Lincoln Cents: Collector dislike of Matte Proofs continued, and the mintage declined to half of what it was in the preceding year.

1914

CIRCULATION MINTAGE: 75,238,432

MATTE PROOF MINTAGE: 1,365

Enlarged 1.5x
(actual size 19 mm)

MARKET VALUES • 1914

G-4	VG-8	F-12	VF-20	EF-40	AU-50	MS-60BN	MS-63BN	MS-65RD
$1.25	$1.35	$2	$6	$20	$45	$65	$80	$650

MARKET VALUES • 1914, Matte Proof

PF-63RB	PF-64RB	PF-65RD
$675	$1,050	$1,750

Key to Collecting: Considered to be common in worn grades. Mint State pieces, including gems with the RD suffix, are seen with frequency. Although careful buying is always advised, finding a sharply struck gem with original color will be easier for the 1914 than for most of the issues to either side of this year. This is contrary to the sometimes-encountered comment that the 1914 is especially scarce among Philadelphia Mint cents.

Striking and Sharpness: Most are very well struck—a pleasant surprise. Full Details coins, while not plentiful, will not be hard to find.

Matte Proofs: These are scarce today. Most pristine (undipped) coins are a rich light brown color. Some have original red-orange color on one or both sides but are never fully brilliant in my experience with pristine coins, despite dozens having been certified as such.

Notes: Several decades ago a group of mirror-style "Proofs" appeared on the market but were quickly proven fake. Occasionally, examples still come on the market.

1914-D

CIRCULATION MINTAGE: 1,193,000

Enlarged 1.5x
(actual size 19 mm)

MARKET VALUES • 1914-D

G-4	VG-8	F-12	VF-20	EF-40	AU-50	MS-60BN	MS-63BN	MS-65RD
$170	$200	$250	$300	$700	$1,450	$2,500	$3,750	$15,000

Key to Collecting: The 1914-D is a rarity in all grades. Notice of this low-mintage issue was not widespread until albums and folders became popular in the 1930s, by which time many coins had been worn down to levels of Fine and Very Fine. From that time onward the search was on, and many were retrieved from circulation, but far fewer than for other issues except the 1909-S V.D.B. Mint State coins are rare, and gems with *original* color, and with no flecks or spots, are very rare. Nearly all have carbon spots of varying sizes, unless they have been dipped or cyanided. A gem with good eye appeal and sharp strike will be a prize when found.

Striking and Sharpness: Most are fairly well struck, but many have some lightness on the Lincoln's hair details and shoulder, and at the tops of the letters. Others are flat at the rims. Six obverse dies were used and perhaps as many as seven reverses.

Notes: An example described as "beautiful light red Uncirculated with several delicate hints of toning, and only separated from perfection by a few microscopic reverse flecks. . . . One of the finest extant if not the finest," was sold in New Netherlands' 50th Sale, December 1957, for $210. This description of a pristine, undipped coin is unusual for its mention of negatives, as is the catalogers' (John J. Ford Jr. and Walter Breen) comment that it might be the *finest known* (in view of later, fully brilliant pieces appearing on the market, usually as the result of "improvements" via chemistry).

As to the relative number of 1914-D cents in circulation in 1938 and their quality, *The Numismatic Scrapbook Magazine* printed this:

> Goldblatt Bros. department stores started in business in 1914. They recently offered a "soda" to anyone presenting a 1914 cent at their fountains. Kenneth D. McQuigg inquired as to how many were presented and received a letter stating that 2,463 were turned in. Of these, 29 were D mint and 40 S mint. McQuigg states that most of the coins were worn and over 95 percent were below Good.

In the 1970s two rolls of Uncirculated coins, 100 pieces total, turned up in Hawaii (another account says the Philippine Islands). I examined several pieces said to have been from that source, and they were spotted red and brown. Walter Breen wrote that a "hoard of at least 700 Uncirculated specimens existed until the early 1950s."[40] In the 1970s I bought a half-roll of Uncirculated coins from a New Zealand source.

Caveat: Fakes of the 1914-D cent abound. Until sophisticated die-struck forgeries came on the market in quantities, 1960s to date, most were crude. Many were made by altering the first 4 of a 1944-D cent (which, unlike a real 1914-D cent, has tiny initials V.D.B. on the shoulder).

1914-S

CIRCULATION MINTAGE: 4,137,000

Enlarged 1.5x
(actual size 19 mm)

MARKET VALUES • 1914-S

G-4	VG-8	F-12	VF-20	EF-40	AU-50	MS-60BN	MS-63BN	MS-65RD
$18	$26	$28	$40	$95	$150	$325	$500	$5,000

Key to Collecting: The 1914-S is scarce in lower circulated grades and is rare at the EF and AU levels. Mint State coins are few and far between. Nearly all are toned BN, or are RB. The bronze planchets used at San Francisco this year and the next seem to have been prone to toning quickly. MS-65RD coins with *original* color are very difficult to locate, especially if well struck. This is one of many early Lincoln cents where you, as a connoisseur and cherrypicker, can have a great advantage—but patience is needed (see Notes). Mint State coins with *original* color have distinctive hues (see chapter nine).

Striking and Sharpness: Most are fairly sharp, but others are weak.

Notes: In the early 1930s the 1914-S was recognized as one of the two key issues in Mint State, ranking in price with the 1914-D (and earlier ranking higher than the 1914-D) and valued higher than the 1909-S V.D.B. Later this distinction faded, and while the 1914-S is still regarded as scarce, it is no longer a subject of publicity in this regard. Beware gem "RD" cents that have been dipped. David W. Lange noted:

> Mint State coins which have not been cleaned at some point (and these are few in number) will be fairly dark, precluding the designation MSRD in all but a few instances . . . A deterrent to finding a desirable coin is the conflict between strike and color. It seems that sharply struck coins are invariably dark, while the few bright examples tend to be mushy.

THE YEAR 1915

In America: The World War in Europe continued to rage, bringing more prosperity to America, the supplier of many goods, although overall unemployment here was 8.5 percent. An anti-German sentiment arose in the United States, with the announcement that Germany had used poison gas against its enemies. Universal City opened in Los Angeles, reflecting the moving of the center of film production to California. The Ford Motor Company turned out its millionth automobile, with the Model T being one of America's favorites.

In Numismatics: In January Thomas L. Elder presented a paper at the ANS, noting in part:

> There are perhaps several thousand coin collectors in America. Only a few of these are numismatists or well-posted students who have given the subject serious study, or have really important collections. Of this latter group there are surely not over 500. But there are many who take some kind of an interest in coins and in the collecting of them. There are in America perhaps 25 persons who advertise themselves as coin dealers.

News About Lincoln Cents: In 1915 there were no basic books on collecting U.S. coins, no references with mintage figures and prices, and no grading standards—a situation unchanged from previous times. There was very little interest in collecting Lincoln cents by date and mint, and no notice was taken of the recent 1914-D being scarce or desirable. This is *key* to understanding the rarity of such coins today.

1915

CIRCULATION MINTAGE: 29,092,120

MATTE PROOF MINTAGE: 1,150

Enlarged 1.5x
(actual size 19 mm)

MARKET VALUES • 1915

G-4	VG-8	F-12	VF-20	EF-40	AU-50	MS-60BN	MS-63BN	MS-65RD
$2.65	$3.75	$5	$18	$55	$70	$100	$105	$750

MARKET VALUES • 1915, Matte Proof

PF-63RB	PF-64RB	PF-65RD
$850	$1,250	$4,000

Key to Collecting: Although the mintage of the 1915 is low for a Philadelphia Mint cent, it is nonetheless common in all grades up to and including gem Mint State. Many "RD" coins are either that color by virtue of dipping, or have flecks and spots. Truly choice *original* pieces, sharply struck, are scarce.

Striking and Sharpness: Usually sharp. David W. Lange noted:

> The obverse master die for the cents of 1915 from all three mints appears to have been manually enhanced. The cents of this date are similar to those of earlier years yet, when coined from fresh working dies, they possess superior detail in Lincoln's hair and beard. This reworking proved so successful that for the cents of 1916 a new master hub was prepared incorporating these changes, but to an even finer state of detail.

Matte Proofs: These are rare today. Most pristine (undipped) coins are a rich light brown color. Some have original red-orange color on one or both sides but are never fully brilliant.

1915-D

CIRCULATION MINTAGE: 22,050,000

Enlarged 1.5x
(actual size 19 mm)

MARKET VALUES • 1915-D

G-4	VG-8	F-12	VF-20	EF-40	AU-50	MS-60BN	MS-63BN	MS-65RD
$2.65	$4.25	$7.50	$15	$35	$55	$85	$125	$1,000

Key to Collecting: Common in the context of early branch mint Lincolns, these were plentiful in circulation into the 1950s. Mint State coins are seen with frequency in the marketplace, but gems with *original* color, no spots, and sharply struck are rare.

Striking and Sharpness: Many are lightly defined on the higher areas due to tired dies and/or the dies being spaced too far apart in the press.

1915-S

CIRCULATION MINTAGE: 4,833,000

Enlarged 1.5x
(actual size 19 mm)

MARKET VALUES • 1915-S

G-4	VG-8	F-12	VF-20	EF-40	AU-50	MS-60BN	MS-63BN	MS-65RD
$16	$21	$30	$35	$80	$125	$275	$600	$3,250

Key to Collecting: The 1915-S is scarce in all grades, especially at higher levels, these including from EF-40 upward. Mint State coins are seen with frequency but are usually toned and sometimes blotchy. The bronze used this year, and in 1914 at San Francisco, seemed to turn dark quickly. Many if not most "brilliant" coins on the market in recent generations have been dipped or processed. Gem coins with *original* mint red-orange, and without flecks or spots, are rare. Mint State coins with *original* color have distinctive hues (see chapter nine).

Striking and Sharpness: Most are fairly well struck, but there are many exceptions. Full Details coins can be found with some persistence.

THE YEAR 1916

In America: Wartime prosperity continued, and unemployment sank to 5.1 percent.

In Numismatics: The New York Coin Club in December 1914 launched a movement that soon included Edgar H. Adams (editor of *The Numismatist*), William H. Woodin, Thomas L. Elder and others, to change the Barber dime, quarter, and half dollar, the artistry of which had been generally viewed as miserable for a long time. In 1916 this became a reality with the introduction of the "Mercury" dime, Standing Liberty quarter, and Liberty Walking half dollar—all done by artists outside of the Mint.

News About Lincoln Cents: In 1916 a Proof set of the minor denominations consisted of just two coins: the Buffalo nickel and Lincoln cent, both in matte finish. Collectors had been critical of Matte, Sand Blast, and Satin Proofs from the beginning, and orders were so small that they were no longer worthwhile for the Mint to strike.

Average number of cents struck per die, fiscal year (Wexler-Flynn text)—Philadelphia, 378,786 obverse, 371,400 reverse; Denver, 180,690 obverse, 103,669 reverse; San Francisco, 484,658 obverse, 484,685 reverse.

The master hub for the obverse of the cent was sharpened this year, giving more detail to Lincoln's hair.

1916

CIRCULATION MINTAGE: 131,833,677

MATTE PROOF MINTAGE: 1,050

Enlarged 1.5x
(actual size 19 mm)

MARKET VALUES • 1916

G-4	VG-8	F-12	VF-20	EF-40	AU-50	MS-60BN	MS-63BN	MS-65RD
$0.75	$0.80	$0.85	$3	$9	$15	$20	$35	$325

MARKET VALUES • 1916, Matte Proof

PF-63RB	PF-64RB	PF-65RD
$2,750	$3,500	$10,000

Key to Collecting: Plentiful in all grades including choice and gem Mint State. Sharply struck coins with original mint red-orange and no flecks or spots are scarce, however.

Striking and Sharpness: Many are found with exquisite sharpness from the strengthened hub this year. Full Details coins await your discovery. There are also, however, many from dies spaced too widely apart or which were overly worn.

Matte Proofs: Authentic Matte Proofs are rare. Often, circulation strikes fool even the experts, unless die characteristics are examined under a microscope. True Proofs should have a *flat rim*. Most pristine (undipped) coins are a rich light brown color. Some have original red-orange color on one or both sides but are never fully brilliant.

1916-D

CIRCULATION MINTAGE: 35,956,000

Enlarged 1.5x
(actual size 19 mm)

MARKET VALUES • 1916-D

G-4	VG-8	F-12	VF-20	EF-40	AU-50	MS-60BN	MS-63BN	MS-65RD
$1.15	$1.85	$3	$6	$15	$35	$100	$135	$1,350

Key to Collecting: Plentiful in all grades, but rare in *high quality* MS-65RD and above. Be careful about original color, avoid spotted pieces, and insist on a sharp strike.

Striking and Sharpness: Sharpness varies due to the use of worn dies and the presence of too much space between dies in the press. Improperly annealed planchets may have been a factor as well. Many sharp examples exist, however, the desirability of which is enhanced by the modified hub this year.

1916-S

CIRCULATION MINTAGE: 22,510,000

Enlarged 1.5x
(actual size 19 mm)

MARKET VALUES • 1916-S

G-4	VG-8	F-12	VF-20	EF-40	AU-50	MS-60BN	MS-63BN	MS-65RD
$2	$2.35	$3.50	$15	$30	$65	$115	$200	$6,500

Key to Collecting: Common in nearly all grades. Pristine Mint State coins will nearly always show some light fading and, often, a wood-grain effect. A 100 percent brilliant coin, including the edges, has been dipped. Mint State coins with *original* color have distinctive hues (see chapter nine).

Striking and Sharpness: Often seen well struck, but there are many exceptions.

THE YEAR 1917

In America: On April 6 the United States declared war against Germany, an action backed by most citizens, in view of the sinking by a U-Boat of the passenger liner *Lusitania*. Unemployment fell to 4.6 percent as factory production increased. It was a time of great prosperity, but few celebrated that fact because of the suffering in Europe.

In Numismatics: The coin market was mixed, with the war in Europe, in progress since August 1914, causing disruptions overseas. The international price of gold and silver rose, gold coins disappeared from circulation, and most banks would not pay them out at par.

News About Lincoln Cents: The obverse master hub die began to show signs of wear, which would continue for decades through 1968.

1917

CIRCULATION MINTAGE: 196,429,785

Enlarged 1.5x
(actual size 19 mm)

MARKET VALUES • 1917

G-4	VG-8	F-12	VF-20	EF-40	AU-50	MS-60BN	MS-63BN	MS-65RD
$0.50	$0.65	$0.75	$2	$5	$15	$18	$35	$475

Key to Collecting: Common in all grades including choice and gem Mint State with original red-orange. A no-problem date, although usual care should be exercised to avoid spotted and dipped coins.

Striking and Sharpness: Many Full Details coins exist, rivaling certain 1916 cents. There are many unsatisfactory strikes, however, and it will pay to ignore these.

1917, Doubled Die Obverse: Slight but unmistakable doubling is shown on the date and IN GOD WE TRUST. These are scarce, but not widely known except to readers of specialized texts. No doubt some still may be found among "raw" coins. In 1998 Sam Lukes bought a small group of these, the finest of which was subsequently graded as MS-65RD by PCGS, and sold for $18,750.[41]

Caveat concerning the so-called 1917 "Matte Proof": Walter Breen in his 1988 *Encyclopedia* states that an unknown number of Proofs were "clandestinely made." These started coming on the market in the 1960s, along with "Satin Proof" 1921 Peace silver dollars, and a lot of other impostors (opinion here) not earlier called Proofs. I have found no early references to such coins at all, either in Mint data or in reliable market listings, and remain skeptical. Examples seen have had nice matte-like surfaces, sometimes on just one side, but have lacked the vital combination of broad, flat rims on both sides and a mirror Proof edge (when viewed edge-on from the side). *The leading certification services do not recognize Proofs of this year.*

1917-D

CIRCULATION MINTAGE: 55,120,000

Enlarged 1.5x
(actual size 19 mm)

MARKET VALUES • 1917-D

G-4	VG-8	F-12	VF-20	EF-40	AU-50	MS-60BN	MS-63BN	MS-65RD
$1.15	$1.65	$3.50	$5	$50	$60	$80	$145	$1,500

Key to Collecting: Common in grades of G and VG, progressively less common as the numbers rise. Mint State coins are plentiful, but most are weakly struck (see Striking and Sharpness), and many have spots from earlier cleaning. A sharply struck original-color gem is a rare bird indeed! Again, certification service numbers do not reflect either sharpness or eye appeal, leaving many opportunities for alert buyers.

Striking and Sharpness: Most range from below average to wretched in terms of sharpness. Exceptions exist but are very rare, especially in higher grades.

1917-S

CIRCULATION MINTAGE: 32,620,000

Enlarged 1.5x
(actual size 19 mm)

MARKET VALUES • 1917-S

G-4	VG-8	F-12	VF-20	EF-40	AU-50	MS-60BN	MS-63BN	MS-65RD
$1.15	$1.35	$2.00	$2.50	$15	$30	$85	$165	$6,000

Key to Collecting: Common in worn grades, less so in higher levels. A sharply struck MS-65RD or higher coin, without spots and with excellent eye appeal, is a *rarity*, although few non-specialists know this. Mint State coins with *original* color have distinctive hues (see chapter nine).

Striking and Sharpness: Substandard is the rule for sharpness this year in San Francisco, similarly to the situation at Denver. There are exceptions.

Notes: Dies made early this year had the S mintmark added by the same punch used since 1909. Later this year a new punch with a slightly larger S was placed into use.

THE YEAR 1918

In America: The Boston Red Sox won the World Series for the fifth time but afterward ran into a long losing streak, perhaps exacerbated by trading away George Herman "Babe" Ruth in 1920. The Red Sox didn't win the World Series again until 2004. Peace was declared in November, and the World War came to an end. Members of the American Expeditionary Force (AEF) looked forward to returning home. Prosperity was at its height, with unemployment at only 1.4 percent.

News About Lincoln Cents: In this year the initials V.D.B. were restored to the cent, now in tiny letters on the edge of Lincoln's shoulder.

1918

CIRCULATION MINTAGE: 288,104,634

Enlarged 1.5x
(actual size 19 mm)

MARKET VALUES • 1918

G-4	VG-8	F-12	VF-20	EF-40	AU-50	MS-60BN	MS-63BN	MS-65RD
$0.75	$0.80	$0.85	$1.50	$5	$10	$16	$30	$500

Key to Collecting: Common in all grades through gem Mint State with original color.

Striking and Sharpness: Usually well defined, but there are exceptions.

1918-D

CIRCULATION MINTAGE: 47,830,000

Enlarged 1.5x
(actual size 19 mm)

MARKET VALUES • 1918-D

G-4	VG-8	F-12	VF-20	EF-40	AU-50	MS-60BN	MS-63BN	MS-65RD
$1.15	$1.35	$2.50	$4	$20	$40	$80	$150	$3,500

Key to Collecting: Common in lower grades, but fairly scarce in Mint State. Gems with original color and sharp strike are very rare. Several dozen have been certified as MS-65RD or higher, but likely the number of sharp strikes in this group can be counted on the fingers of one hand.

Striking and Sharpness: Lack of detail is the rule. While worn dies are part of the cause, it seems likely that the Denver Mint in particular, and the San Francisco Mint to a lesser extent, spaced the dies slightly too widely apart. This same situation exists for many branch mint coins of other denominations from the World War era through the 1920s.

1918-S

CIRCULATION MINTAGE: 34,680,000

Enlarged 1.5x
(actual size 19 mm)

MARKET VALUES • 1918-S

G-4	VG-8	F-12	VF-20	EF-40	AU-50	MS-60BN	MS-63BN	MS-65RD
$0.75	$1	$2	$4	$15	$40	$85	$200	$5,000

Key to Collecting: Common in worn grades. Mint State coins are not rare in lower numerical levels, or with brown or red and brown toning. MS-65RD coins are rare, as certification data shows. If you are a connoisseur, and want one that is sharply struck and with no flecks, be prepared for a challenging search. Mint State coins with *original* color have distinctive hues (see chapter nine). As is true of most mintmarked issues of this era and the 1920s, Full Details coins are more likely to be found among BN and RB coins.

Striking and Sharpness: Usually poorly struck. Exceptions are few and far between.

THE YEAR 1919

In America: On January 16 the Volstead Act was ratified as the 18th amendment to the Constitution. Accordingly, prohibition of the social and casual (but not medicinal) use of alcoholic beverages, simply called Prohibition, went into effect in 1920. By this time ragtime, heard in public places since the 1890s, faded in popularity, and jazz or Dixieland music was played everywhere.

In Numismatics: Among the leading dealers of the era were Henry Chapman, S. Hudson Chapman, B. Max Mehl, Thomas L. Elder, John Zug, and Wayte Raymond. The coin market was quiet and did not participate in the inflation that characterized many aspects of the American scene.

News About Lincoln Cents: The imposition of a luxury tax required the payment of cents in change for many transactions, thus causing a shortage of these for a time. Production continued at record high levels as compared to the prewar years.

1919

CIRCULATION MINTAGE: 392,021,000

Enlarged 1.5x
(actual size 19 mm)

MARKET VALUES • 1919

G-4	VG-8	F-12	VF-20	EF-40	AU-50	MS-60BN	MS-63BN	MS-65RD
$0.50	$0.55	$0.65	$1	$3	$5	$15	$25	$250

Key to Collecting: Common in all grades through gem MS-65RD and higher. Spots are not much of a problem. A nice gem will be an easy find, for a change. Hooray!

Striking and Sharpness: Most are well struck this year, due to careful adjustment of the coining presses and properly annealed planchets. A Full Details coin awaits your discovery in the marketplace.

1919-D

CIRCULATION MINTAGE: 57,154,000

Enlarged 1.5x
(actual size 19 mm)

MARKET VALUES • 1919-D

G-4	VG-8	F-12	VF-20	EF-40	AU-50	MS-60BN	MS-63BN	MS-65RD
$1.15	$1.50	$2	$4	$10	$35	$70	$125	$1,250

Key to Collecting: At a casual glance, the 1919-D is a common issue among cents from the Denver Mint—unless, that is, you desire a choice or gem specimen that is well struck and with original color. Such a coin is a rarity. Many pieces with original mint color are mottled or irregular.

Striking and Sharpness: Most show lightness of striking in some areas, particularly at the center of the obverse and the periphery of the reverse. Wavy surfaces from overused dies, particularly on the reverse, are often seen.

1919-S

CIRCULATION MINTAGE: 139,760,000

Enlarged 1.5x
(actual size 19 mm)

MARKET VALUES • 1919-S

G-4	VG-8	F-12	VF-20	EF-40	AU-50	MS-60BN	MS-63BN	MS-65RD
$0.75	$0.80	$1.50	$2.50	$6	$20	$60	$120	$5,500

Key to Collecting: The 1919-S is easily available in just about any grade desired. Sharply struck pieces with original color are in the minority, however, and finding one will be a challenge—but not on the order of certain other branch mint issues of the era. Mint State coins with *original* color have distinctive hues (see chapter nine).

Striking and Sharpness: Full Details coins are rare.

THE YEAR 1920

In America: Prohibition forced the closing of many fine restaurants, while at the same time private clubs and speakeasies, often complete with illegal slot machines, took up the slack. In Pittsburgh radio station KDKA produced the first commercial broadcast. Results of the November election, in which Warren G. Harding was elected president, were aired, among other news that year. The American economy became ever so slightly chilled, but optimism prevailed.

In Numismatics: In August the ANA membership stood at 603.

News About Lincoln Cents: The *Annual Report of the Director of the Mint* for the fiscal year ended June 30, 1920 noted:

> At the Philadelphia mint 357,000,000 cents were coined during this year; the average per pair of dies is more than 450,000 pieces. This result stands alone in our records, and such an average can only be obtained by the most painstaking care in the selection of the steel in every succeeding operation until the dies are set in the coining presses.

1920

CIRCULATION MINTAGE: 310,165,000

Enlarged 1.5x
(actual size 19 mm)

Market Values • 1920

G-4	VG-8	F-12	VF-20	EF-40	AU-50	MS-60BN	MS-63BN	MS-65RD
$0.35	$0.40	$0.45	$1	$2.50	$6	$20	$30	$250

Key to Collecting: This is a common date in the context of the era, and choice and gem examples are plentiful in the marketplace. Many have been dipped.

Striking and Sharpness: The strike is usually decent for 1920, but the dies were not made with the sharp detail seen a decade earlier in the series. Overused dies show graininess.

1920-D

CIRCULATION MINTAGE: 49,280,000

Enlarged 1.5x
(actual size 19 mm)

Market Values • 1920-D

G-4	VG-8	F-12	VF-20	EF-40	AU-50	MS-60BN	MS-63BN	MS-65RD
$1.15	$2.25	$3	$5	$15	$40	$85	$115	$2,000

Key to Collecting: Finding a *sharply struck* gem with *original color* is almost, but not quite, an impossibility. The 1920-D is another great challenge for the connoisseur. Most gems certified as "RD aren't really [and have] a subdued red bordering on red/brown or a peculiar pink color," notes David W. Lange, who concludes, that "for those who place more emphasis on the certified grade than on the coin itself, this may not matter, but experienced collectors will recognize the difference." The majority of buyers who look only at the label on a certified coin can be easily enough satisfied, as many more than 100 MS-65RD coins beckon. If you are a connoisseur, be prepared for a challenge, perhaps one lasting for a year or two or three. As always, you will benefit from the fact that most buyers are clueless on matters of sharpness and strike.

Striking and Sharpness: The typical 1920-D is a miserable strike, with a lack of detail on Lincoln's hair, the usual microscopic planchet marks on the shoulder, and an uneven field and indistinct edges of letters on the reverse. Probably, poor annealing of planchets and poor press adjustment combined to cause these problems.

1920-S

CIRCULATION MINTAGE: 46,220,000

Enlarged 1.5x
(actual size 19 mm)

Market Values • 1920-S

G-4	VG-8	F-12	VF-20	EF-40	AU-50	MS-60BN	MS-63BN	MS-65RD
$1.15	$2.25	$3	$5	$15	$40	$120	$185	$12,000

Key to Collecting: While average examples are easily enough found (because the 1920-S is not a key date), finding a choice or gem piece, sharply struck with original color, is a different matter entirely. Mint State coins with *original* color have distinctive hues (see chapter nine). As David W. Lange notes, "very few red examples are known for this date (aside from those which have been chemically, or mechanically assisted)." Original color for the 1920-S is either a rich red-orange or a golden yellow—probably resulting from different sources of metal.

If certification services add the sophistication of striking and original color to their evaluations, this is a date and mint that will break out of the charts as a formidable rarity.

Striking and Sharpness: Most 1920-S cents are poorly struck, with indistinct details on the higher areas on the obverse and with the reverse often blurry. Tired, overused dies seem to have been the rule at San Francisco this year. Finding a truly Full Details coin may be like tilting at a windmill, and this is one issue for which you may have to compromise. It is rather curious that only Lincoln cent specialists are aware of this. Most dealers would be surprised to learn of the rarity of a choice coin of this date and mint.

The Year 1921

In America: America experienced its first economic recession since the short-lived Panic of 1907, this just before the Lincoln cent era. Commerce paused to catch its breath. Prices and markets weakened, factory output diminished, and the outlook was grim. On August 16 the Department of Labor reported that 5,735,000 people were out of work. Many businesses failed, and even more had difficulties and experienced losses. Agriculture was especially hard hit.

In Numismatics: Demand for new coins fell and mintages were generally low, creating varieties that would be recognized as key issues by a later generation of numismatists. These elusive coins included dimes, quarters, and half dollars. Silver dollars were an exception and were made in quantity following special legislation, although such coins were neither wanted nor needed in commerce.

News About Lincoln Cents: In recent years coinage had reached record levels, and now it receded. Because of reduced demand no cents were struck at Denver.

1921

Circulation Mintage: 39,157,000

Enlarged 1.5x
(actual size 19 mm)

Market Values • 1921

G-4	VG-8	F-12	VF-20	EF-40	AU-50	MS-60BN	MS-63BN	MS-65RD
$0.50	$0.75	$1.25	$2.10	$12	$25	$55	$80	$600

Key to Collecting: Although sharply struck coins are rare on a relative basis, enough Mint State coins exist that finding one can be done with patience. In the 1950s this was the one date, among Philadelphia cents of the early 1920s, that occasionally was seen in roll quantities, one or two at a time—with the pieces typically being a bright yellow-orange in hue.

Striking and Sharpness: Most are weakly struck or from tired, overused dies. This is one of the most poorly struck Philadelphia Mint cents of the era.

1921-S

Circulation Mintage: 15,274,000

Enlarged 1.5x
(actual size 19 mm)

Market Values • 1921-S

G-4	VG-8	F-12	VF-20	EF-40	AU-50	MS-60BN	MS-63BN	MS-65RD
$2.50	$3	$5	$7	$40	$75	$140	$250	$10,000

Key to Collecting: Circulated examples are scarce in context, due to the low mintage. Choice and gem Mint State coins are very rare if with original color and sharply struck. Otherwise, there are many certified coins available. Some streakiness or graining may be evident. Many coins sold as Mint State over the years have been dipped and recolored. Mint State coins with *original* color have distinctive hues (see chapter nine). Connoisseurship combined with patience is needed to land a truly choice prize.

Striking and Sharpness: Most coins are struck with light definition of details on higher points and/or from worn dies. The S mintmark can be weak. Full Details examples are rare.

Notes: "All 1921-S cents were coined early in the year, before a nationwide recession slowed business activity. Due to a lack of demand from banks, the San Francisco Mint still had in its vaults on June 30, 1922 some 15,493,230 cents of earlier years awaiting distribution. Thus, no more were coined until the latter part of 1923." (David W. Lange)

The Year 1922

In America: The economy remained in the doldrums, although there was an uptick in automobile sales. The Midwest and other agricultural areas continued to suffer with many people out of work. Wages were cut by many employers.

In Numismatics: Demand for copper, nickel, and silver American coinage hit a low point for the era, except for Peace silver dollars, which were made in record numbers due to special legislation.

News About Lincoln Cents: With a nationwide slump in the economy, there was little need for new cents. Mintage was accomplished only at Denver.

1922-D

Circulation Mintage: 7,160,000

Enlarged 1.5x
(actual size 19 mm)

Market Values • 1922-D

G-4	VG-8	F-12	VF-20	EF-40	AU-50	MS-60BN	MS-63BN	MS-65RD
$21	$25	$30	$35	$45	$75	$115	$250	$1,350

Key to Collecting: The 1922-D has been a numismatic favorite for a long time, a date and mintmark widely saved in the 1930s when it became popular to look for key issues in circulation. Original Mint State coins are found here and there in the marketplace. I have never seen a roll of 50.

Today circulated coins are plentiful in an absolute basis, but among Lincoln cents are among the scarcer early issues. Gem high-grade Mint State coins with original color are very scarce, and some effort will be needed to find one in a combination of high quality, sharp strike, and good eye appeal. Curiously, poorly struck coins and/or those from worn dies are desirable (see next two entries). These have a weak D or no D mintmark at all, furnishing a substitute for a mintmarkless 1922 in a year when no coins were struck at the Philadelphia Mint. Advanced specialists may want to acquire a regular 1922-D and also one with a weak or, better yet, completely missing D.

Striking and Sharpness: Ranges from sharp to very weak (for the latter, see next two entries).

Notes: Twenty obverse dies were prepared for the coinage, but it is not known if all were used. Twenty-seven reverses were on hand, but, again, not all may have been used.

1922-D, Weak D

Circulation Mintage: Unknown

Enlarged 1.5x
(actual size 19 mm)

Market Values • 1922-D, Weak D

G-4	VG-8	F-12	VF-20	EF-40	AU-50	MS-60BN	MS-63BN
$26	$35	$50	$70	$160	$200	$350	$1,000

Key to Collecting: This variety is known from at least two pairs of dies, both of which became worn to a point where the D is barely visible. The rest of the obverse is weakly detailed as well. The reverse quality can range from weak to sharp: reverse dies were replaced as needed, and not necessarily at the same time as obverse dies.

Caveat: Some of these, with a little raised area or a hint of a D, have been certified as "No D" or "Plain" by the services. This is simply profiteering. The same coins were called "Weak D" or similar years ago. A coin that shows a hint of a D is *not* a 1922 "Plain" and is not particularly rare.

1922-D, No D ("Plain")

Circulation Mintage: Unknown

Enlarged 1.5x
(actual size 19 mm)

Market Values • 1922-D, No D ("Plain")

G-4	VG-8	F-12	VF-20	EF-40	AU-50	MS-60BN	MS-63BN
$475	$575	$600	$750	$1,500	$3,500	$9,500	$18,500

Key to Collecting: Some 1922-D cents were struck from obverse dies that were so weak that the D was not visible, or only barely visible. *Avoid these.* The most desired issue is from die pair No. 2, described below, with the D mintmark deliberately effaced (in the process of removing some die damage that occurred in the coining press). Buy only coins from die pair No. 2. Avoid all others, which are simply "Weak D" coins.

Caveat: Beware normal 1922-D cents from which unscrupulous people have removed the D mintmark. Buying a 1922 Plain from a leading certification service, and only from die pair No. 2, is strongly suggested.

Striking and Sharpness: When dies were first used, they produced regular 1922-D cents. Then, they weakened as the die became worn from extensive use. It is thought that the D was completely ground off of one die—that being from pair No. 2—when it was relapped or resurfaced to reduce surface roughness and extend its life. Cents of 1922-D struck without a mintmark *always* have a very weakly detailed obverse in other areas as well. The reverse can range from weak to fairly sharp, depending upon the die.

The ANACS staff, writing in *The Numismatist*, July 1982, consolidated comments and research by others and described the specific characteristics of die pairs used to strike 1922 cents with a weak or missing D. Die pair No. 2, with no D visible, was described as starting with a fresh pair of dies. The two dies clashed (met in the coining press without a planchet between them), causing clash marks on both sides. According to the ANACS scenario, the obverse die was lightly dressed or filed, to remove the clash marks, and in the process the D was removed completely. The reverse die was discarded and replaced by a new one. Thus were produced 1922 cents with no D whatever.

Notes: Many veteran collectors pooh-poohed the 1922 "plain" cent as nothing more than a defective coin. *The Numismatist* printed this in May 1945:

> In 1922 the U.S. Government coined 7,160,000 Lincoln head cents at the Denver Mint. None was coined at Philadelphia or San Francisco. Some of these cents are poorly struck and show only a faint outline or no sign of the D mintmark. That's all there is to the story. Collectors who feel they "must" own a 1922 cent with an obliterated mintmark should use a tack-hammer on the mintmark of a well struck specimen. With a little practice they will become as expert as the next fellow.

In *Looking Through Lincoln Cents*, 2005 edition, Charles D. Daughtrey commented: "It is my opinion that all 1922 'no D' cents are common, grease filled or worn out dies, and that none of them should have ever gained the attention or value they currently demand."

THE YEAR 1923

In America: President Warren G. Harding died on August 3, 1923, from a heart attack. Vice President Calvin Coolidge was sworn in as president. The economy gained strength this year.

In Numismatics: The numismatic market remained quiet in 1923, although the American economy was recovering—the prelude to what would soon become the "Roaring Twenties." Collecting current coins by date and mintmark varieties was not in vogue at all, and virtually nothing about them appeared in print.

News About Lincoln Cents: Coins were struck only at Philadelphia and San Francisco. Many but not all of the planchets were provided through a contract with the Scovill Manufacturing Co. of Waterbury, Connecticut.

1923

CIRCULATION MINTAGE: 74,723,000

Enlarged 1.5x
(actual size 19 mm)

MARKET VALUES • 1923

G-4	VG-8	F-12	VF-20	EF-40	AU-50	MS-60BN	MS-63BN	MS-65RD
$0.50	$0.60	$0.65	$1	$5	$10	$15	$30	$350

Key to Collecting: Common in all grades through and including MS-65RD. Finding a sharp specimen with good eye appeal will not be a problem.

Striking and Sharpness: Varies from Full Details to poor. Keep in mind that as the hubs and master dies were used during this decade, details in Lincoln's hair became less distinct. A 1923 cent struck from carefully spaced new dies will not be as detailed as a 1916 cent (the year the details were sharpened). The shoulder of Lincoln continued to be lightly struck on most cents of this decade. This is detected today by examining the area under high magnification to see if there are any minute nicks and marks from the original planchet.

1923-S

CIRCULATION MINTAGE: 8,700,000

Enlarged 1.5x
(actual size 19 mm)

MARKET VALUES • 1923-S

G-4	VG-8	F-12	VF-20	EF-40	AU-50	MS-60BN	MS-63BN	MS-65RD
$8	$11	$12	$15	$50	$100	$250	$475	$35,000

Key to Collecting: Somewhat scarce in all grades, although not generally considered a key date. This was one of the mintmark varieties that collectors saved in quantity during the 1930s, when looking through pocket change first became popular. The vast majority of "brilliant" coins have been dipped. A sharply struck gem "RD" coin with original color is a first-class rarity, although some exist. Once again, this affords a wonderful opportunity for cherrypicking because 90 percent of buyers will just see "MS-RD" on a holder and write a check—never mind that a connoisseur would not want that particular coin at all. Reflecting sophisticated thinking, David W. Lange stated that he would rather have a sharp AU example than a weakly struck Mint State coin. Mint State coins with *original* color have distinctive hues (see chapter nine).

Striking and Sharpness: Usually weak, sometimes *very* weak. Most connoisseurs who land a Full Details coin buy one toned brown or red and brown.

THE YEAR 1924

In America: Land speculation in Florida was the latest investment craze, and buyers rushed to buy or place contracts on properties, some of which were worthless swampland. The recession of 1921 was forgotten.

In Numismatics: A talk by Thomas L. Elder stressed that lack of ready information on U.S. coins was a deterrent to people joining the hobby:

> Badly we need books on American numismatics and paper money, especially books on our political medals and tokens and a convenient work on American colonial and Continental coins. There are plenty of neglected subjects in American numismatics. And an odd phase of this matter is that we have been 10 times more industrious in issuing works on the subject of ancient and foreign numismatics.

News About Lincoln Cents: It was back to business as usual, and for the first time since 1920, cents were struck at all three mints. Obituaries of the year included Lincoln cent designer Victor D. Brenner.

1924

CIRCULATION MINTAGE: 75,178,000

Enlarged 1.5x
(actual size 19 mm)

MARKET VALUES • 1924

G-4	VG-8	F-12	VF-20	EF-40	AU-50	MS-60BN	MS-63BN	MS-65RD
$0.35	$0.60	$0.65	$1	$6	$10	$25	$50	$500

Key to Collecting: Common in all grades including Mint State. Sharply struck gems with original color are not difficult to locate, but careful inspection is advised.

Striking and Sharpness: Many are weak, but many others are sharp. Quality is mixed, but there are enough around that this is not a problem.

1924-D

CIRCULATION MINTAGE: 2,520,000

Enlarged 1.5x
(actual size 19 mm)

MARKET VALUES • 1924-D

G-4	VG-8	F-12	VF-20	EF-40	AU-50	MS-60BN	MS-63BN	MS-65RD
$31	$40	$50	$55	$125	$165	$300	$600	$12,500

Key to Collecting: Registering the lowest mintage since 1914-D, the 1924-D has always been considered a semi-key issue. Many were saved from pocket change in the 1930s and later. Mint State coins are scarce, and higher level examples with original color, sharp details, and no spots are rare today.

Striking and Sharpness: Usually with weakness, often attributed to worn dies, but perhaps most likely from the dies being too far apart in the press. Sometimes the left and right borders are light, and on some strikes the D mintmark is not bold.

1924-S

CIRCULATION MINTAGE: 11,696,000

Enlarged 1.5x
(actual size 19 mm)

MARKET VALUES • 1924-S

G-4	VG-8	F-12	VF-20	EF-40	AU-50	MS-60BN	MS-63BN	MS-65RD
$2.25	$2.85	$3.50	$6	$40	$85	$135	$375	$20,000

Key to Collecting: Circulated coins can be found in just about any grade, but most are G or VG. Although the mintage of the 1924-S is multiples of its Denver cousin, in gem Mint State with original color, the 1924-S handily eclipses it in rarity, as well as nearly all other cents of this decade, the reason for this being unknown today. A recent PCGS population report shows that the 1924-S has only 11 examples graded MS-65RD—six fewer than the 1920-S has.

Striking and Sharpness: Usually weakly defined in areas. Exceptions are few and far between.

Notes: It is likely that these were not released into circulation until 1925.

THE YEAR 1925

In America: Prosperity was almost everywhere. This was the era of elegant limousines, new mansions, and living the good life, as epitomized in F. Scott Fitzgerald's new novel, *The Great Gatsby*.

In Numismatics: At the annual ANA convention held this year in Detroit the record membership of 970 was announced, plus 30 applications were being processed. On one evening, to the satisfaction of all, the exhibition room was set aside for "Dealers' Night." Recently, there had been much discussion as to whether commercial transactions should be allowed at such shows.

1925

CIRCULATION MINTAGE: 139,949,000

Enlarged 1.5x
(actual size 19 mm)

MARKET VALUES • 1925

G-4	VG-8	F-12	VF-20	EF-40	AU-50	MS-60BN	MS-63BN	MS-65RD
$0.35	$0.40	$0.50	$0.60	$3	$7	$10	$25	$125

Key to Collecting: Common in any grade you desire, including gem Mint State, sharply struck and with original color.

Striking and Sharpness: Most are well struck, but there are the inevitable exceptions.

1925-D

CIRCULATION MINTAGE: 22,580,000

Enlarged 1.5x
(actual size 19 mm)

MARKET VALUES • 1925-D

G-4	VG-8	F-12	VF-20	EF-40	AU-50	MS-60BN	MS-63BN	MS-65RD
$1.15	$1.50	$2.50	$5	$20	$35	$75	$125	$3,750

Key to Collecting: Common in all grades through Mint State. A gem that is sharply struck and having original mint color is a *rara avis*, per notes below. If you are a typical buyer, you'll find a choice or gem 64 or 65 quickly. If you are a connoisseur, perhaps a decade hence you will still be looking. Ease of collecting always leads to fading of enthusiasm. Seeking sharply struck Lincoln cents of the 1920s will keep you on your toes.

Striking and Sharpness: Usually weakly struck, embarrassing, one might think, to the Treasury Department—but no one cared. (During the decade, branch mint Buffalo nickels, Standing Liberty quarters, and Liberty Walking halves were also miserably struck in most instances.) An unhappy tie for first place here, per David W. Lange:

> 1925-D vies with 1925-S for the title of most poorly made issue in the entire Lincoln series. It's difficult to believe that the dies for the 1925-D cents were ever new, as sharply rendered specimens are essentially unknown. Gross distortion of the design elements (particularly toward the peripheries) is the norm for these coins. It's quite possible that the [dies were not properly hardened]. This would have led to premature erosion.

1925-S

CIRCULATION MINTAGE: 26,380,000

Enlarged 1.5x
(actual size 19 mm)

MARKET VALUES • 1925-S

G-4	VG-8	F-12	VF-20	EF-40	AU-50	MS-60BN	MS-63BN	MS-65RD
$1.15	$1.65	$2.50	$4	$15	$35	$115	$225	$20,000

Key to Collecting: Common in worn grades. Scarce in Mint State, and usually dipped when seen. Truly rare as certified MS-65RD. As to a specimen with Full Details certified MS-65RD, such a coin would be the find of the year. Good luck!

Striking and Sharpness: Poor striking, keeping the Denver cents company in this regard, was the order of the day for this issue.

THE YEAR 1926

In America: Prosperity continued. Building construction enjoyed boom times.

In Numismatics: The "Roaring Twenties" were not roaring at all in numismatics. A popular discussion of the year was how to get more people interested in coin collecting. Many ideas were expressed, but the ranks of numismatists remained small, as did the scope of the market. Inflation of prices, which characterized art, antiques, prints, old books, and other collectibles, did not include rare coins.

News About Lincoln Cents: Any desired date and mintmark could be purchased in brilliant Uncirculated grade for less than a dollar, most of them for less than 25¢.

1926

CIRCULATION MINTAGE: 157,088,000

Enlarged 1.5x
(actual size 19 mm)

MARKET VALUES • 1926

G-4	VG-8	F-12	VF-20	EF-40	AU-50	MS-60BN	MS-63BN	MS-65RD
$0.35	$0.40	$0.45	$0.50	$2	$5	$10	$12	$125

Key to Collecting: Common in all circulated grades. Plentiful in MS-65RD and higher, including well-struck examples.

Striking and Sharpness: Usually well struck. Hooray!

1926-D

CIRCULATION MINTAGE: 28,020,000

Enlarged 1.5x
(actual size 19 mm)

MARKET VALUES • 1926-D

G-4	VG-8	F-12	VF-20	EF-40	AU-50	MS-60BN	MS-63BN	MS-65RD
$1.65	$2.00	$3.50	$7.50	$15	$35	$125	$175	$2,500

Key to Collecting: Common in circulated grades. Readily available in Mint State as well, except that most brilliant coins have been cleaned. Sol Taylor and David W. Lange write that the 1926-D is usually unattractive, dull, and, per Lange, "Those coins graded MS-65RD by the grading services will not be equal in their aesthetic qualities to a 1926 in the same certified grade." (Again, an alert for naïve buyers who believe all certified coins in a given grade are the same!) Gems with original color and sharply struck are exceedingly rare.

Striking and Sharpness: Poor, as a rule. David W. Lange attributes this to a combination of "dies displaying advanced wear," poor die steel, and low-quality planchets; I suggest that improper die spacing was also a factor. Find a Full Details coin and you've hit a numismatic World Series home run with the bases loaded.

1926-S

CIRCULATION MINTAGE: 4,550,000

Enlarged 1.5x
(actual size 19 mm)

MARKET VALUES • 1926-S

G-4	VG-8	F-12	VF-20	EF-40	AU-50	MS-60BN	MS-63BN	MS-65RD
$11	$13	$15	$20	$45	$75	$250	$525	$115,000

Key to Collecting: The low mintage has hallmarked this as a key issue ever since collectors began plucking coins from circulation in the 1930s. Examples remain scarce in circulated grades in comparison to higher mintage issues. As to certified MS-65RD coins, when David W. Lange wrote his book in 1995, there was just one—count it—just one. This is *the* rarity among pristine (undipped) Mint State Lincolns. Recently Sam Lukes, a Lincoln cent specialist for many years, stated that *he* has never seen a 1926-S that he would call MS-65RD.[42]

Striking and Sharpness: Usually with indistinct areas: sub-par. Exceptions are rare. It seems likely that Full Details coins were struck on especially soft planchets and toned very quickly. Weak strikes that have much of the original color were probably struck on harder planchets, which tended to tone slowly.

Notes: A small cache of 14 red and brown Uncirculated pieces was sold, against a *Standard Catalog* valuation of $25 Uncirculated, in several lots in New Netherlands' 50th Sale, December 1957. They realized about $15 to $25 each. Some were described as weakly struck, but probably all were to some degree.

A well-known specialist in Lincoln cents, "S.B.," a connoisseur and careful buyer, mentioned to me some years ago that he had never seen an MS-65 cent with full *original* red, but he had had many red and brown ones offered to him and took detailed notes on each. Lo and behold! Some of those former red and brown coins somehow became "RD," were certified as such, and reoffered to him. These were easy to identify from small surface marks he had recorded earlier. Perhaps if "coin doctors" keep busy, MS-65RD 1926-S cents will become common!

THE YEAR 1927

In America: Charles Lindbergh, leaving Long Island at 7:55 a.m. on May 20 and arriving in Paris 33 hours and 29 minutes later, piloted *The Spirit of St. Louis* across the Atlantic. Ford Motor Co. introduced the Model A, successor to 15 million Model Ts on the road. In keeping with prosperity and spending on luxury items (by those who could afford to do so), automobiles were everywhere, especially in towns and cities, while horses remained a familiar sight in rural areas. As the Roaring Twenties continued many grand hotels, private mansions, and other structures were built in resort and scenic areas accessible by auto, but not by train. Skyscrapers sprouted in big cities. Radio was so popular that it was often played in public places.

News About Lincoln Cents: The detail in new dies continued to decline due to wear on the hubs. Still, in this context, many fairly sharp coins were made, especially at the Philadelphia Mint.

1927

CIRCULATION MINTAGE: 144,440,000

Enlarged 1.5x
(actual size 19 mm)

MARKET VALUES • 1927

G-4	VG-8	F-12	VF-20	EF-40	AU-50	MS-60BN	MS-63BN	MS-65RD
$0.35	$0.40	$0.45	$0.60	$2	$5	$10	$15	$125

Key to Collecting: Common in all grades including gem Mint State, well struck.

Striking and Sharpness: Usually well struck. Full Details coins are not hard to find.

1927-D

CIRCULATION MINTAGE: 27,170,000

Enlarged 1.5x
(actual size 19 mm)

MARKET VALUES • 1927-D

G-4	VG-8	F-12	VF-20	EF-40	AU-50	MS-60BN	MS-63BN	MS-65RD
$1.35	$1.85	$2.75	$3.75	$7.50	$30	$65	$100	$2,000

Key to Collecting: Common in all circulated grades, except at the gem level. Full red-orange coins are somewhat scarce.

Striking and Sharpness: Most have weakness in areas, but enough were well enough struck that Full Details examples are encountered with frequency in the marketplace.

1927-S

CIRCULATION MINTAGE: 14,276,000

Enlarged 1.5x
(actual size 19 mm)

MARKET VALUES • 1927-S

G-4	VG-8	F-12	VF-20	EF-40	AU-50	MS-60BN	MS-63BN	MS-65RD
$1.65	$2	$3	$5	$20	$50	$115	$185	$8,500

Key to Collecting: Common in circulated grades, and readily available (except for sharply struck coins) in Mint State. Virtually all specialists have had to make do with weakly defined coins. This situation is really amazing in that the absolute *rarity* of original Mint Red Lincoln cents with sharp details is almost completely unknown to the general collecting public!

Striking and Sharpness: Usually miserable. Full Details examples are rare. David W. Lange wrote that, for his collection, he sold a nearly full RD Mint State coin and kept "an attractive and original red/brown example which grades only AU-58, yet it possesses an absolutely needle-sharp strike."

THE YEAR 1928

In America: Republican Herbert Hoover, running against Democrat Alfred E. Smith, was elected president in a landslide in November. The stock market was a sure-thing investment for millions of Americans, who watched the value of their shares go up and up. "Wow! I'm rich!" In the booming economy nothing could go wrong.

In Numismatics: The ANA had slightly more than 1,000 members, of whom no more than 10 percent were regular attendees of conventions. M.L. Beistle, a manufacturer of cardboard and paper products in Shippensburg, Pennsylvania, launched his "Unique Coin Holders" album pages. Later these were marketed aggressively by Wayte Raymond and helped contribute to the coin boom of the mid-1930s. In the meantime, however, sales seem to have been slow.

News About Lincoln Cents: The economy was robust, and this called for extensive coinage of new cents at the three mints.

1928

CIRCULATION MINTAGE: 134,116,000

Enlarged 1.5x
(actual size 19 mm)

MARKET VALUES • 1928

G-4	VG-8	F-12	VF-20	EF-40	AU-50	MS-60BN	MS-63BN	MS-65RD
$0.35	$0.40	$0.45	$0.60	$2	$5	$10	$15	$150

Key to Collecting: Common in all grades, including well-struck gems with full original color just beginning to naturally fade.

Striking and Sharpness: Most are well struck. Full Details coins are plentiful.

1928-D

CIRCULATION MINTAGE: 31,170,000

Enlarged 1.5x
(actual size 19 mm)

MARKET VALUES • 1928-D

G-4	VG-8	F-12	VF-20	EF-40	AU-50	MS-60BN	MS-63BN	MS-65RD
$0.85	$1	$1.75	$3	$6	$20	$50	$80	$1,000

Key to Collecting: Common in all grades, including Mint State up to about MS-64. MS-65RD coins with original color are somewhat scarce.

Striking and Sharpness: Many are lightly defined, though others are sharp. Enough Full Details coins are around that finding one will not be a problem.

1928-S

CIRCULATION MINTAGE: 17,266,000

Enlarged 1.5x
(actual size 19 mm)

MARKET VALUES • 1928-S

G-4	VG-8	F-12	VF-20	EF-40	AU-50	MS-60BN	MS-63BN	MS-65RD
$1.15	$1.60	$2.75	$3.75	$10	$35	$100	$130	$8,500

Key to Collecting: Common in all grades up to about MS-64BN and RB. MS-65RD coins with sharp strike are rarities. This date and mint has never attracted much attention—however, the mintage was generous.

Striking and Sharpness: Usually weak. David W. Lange calls them "mushy."

1928-S Large and Small S Mintmarks: The difference is dramatic. The large S is the rarer of the two, according to Charles D. Daughtrey. A similar difference is found among 1941-S cents, these being better known than the 1928-S. The large mintmark has a very "fat" or heavy diagonal at the center and flat edges at the upper right and lower left to the serifs. The small mintmark is, of course, smaller and has blobs at the serifs. Also see the 1941-S with two mintmark sizes. Collector interest is minimal, and you should be able to buy either without paying a premium.

THE YEAR 1929

In America: All across America office buildings and towers were under construction. At B.F. Goodrich, polyvinyl chloride (PVC), a flexible plastic that would become wildly popular half a century later for the storage and display of coins, was developed. The stock market continued to capture the public imagination, and nearly everyone was a winner. September 3 became a day to remember: The Dow-Jones Industrial Average peaked at a record 381.17. Then prices wiggled, and in October seriously began to fall. By year's end $26 billion in value had been lost, precipitating what became known as the Depression. Buyers of stocks on margin were wiped out. For the time being, in late 1929, optimism prevailed, and those in the public eye were united in stating that the plunge was only temporary. In the meantime margin calls deepened the problems of speculators and nearly all financial institutions. The unemployment rate was just 3.2 percent.

In Numismatics: The temporary fall of stock prices was not felt in the rare coin market, and at the close of the year all was in good order. Membership in the ANA once again stood at an all-time high of 1,125, and the recent convention in Chicago had attracted a record attendance (103 members and 30 visitors).

News About Lincoln Cents: New coins began piling up in bank vaults, adding to limited supplies of 1927 and 1928 issues. Somehow, the demand for cents in commerce had slowed. When coin collecting became very popular in 1934 (see listing), some of these older rolls were found and saved.

1929

Circulation Mintage: 185,262,000

Enlarged 1.5x
(actual size 19 mm)

Market Values • 1929

G-4	VG-8	F-12	VF-20	EF-40	AU-50	MS-60BN	MS-63BN	MS-65RD
$0.35	$0.40	$0.45	$0.75	$3	$5	$8	$14	$130

Key to Collecting: Plentiful in all grades, including MS-65RD and beyond. Cents, of this year and the next several, have a deeper red-orange color than coins of later or earlier dates.

Striking and Sharpness: Usually sharply struck, but there are exceptions.

Notes: Newspaper accounts stated that certain 1929 cents, on which the head of Lincoln was "too small," turned up in Evanston, Illinois. These must have been counterfeits despite this report:

> Federal authorities were called in. They telegraphed the government mints and found that the pennies, instead of being counterfeit, were of imperfect coinage, and that they should never have been put into circulation. Mint officials asked that the imperfect coins be withdrawn from circulation at once. But Evanston coin collectors, learning of the situation, began bidding $1 each for the pennies. . . . The pennies bear the date 1929. The Lincoln head is considerably smaller than on other pennies, and the edges are rough.[43]

1929-D

Circulation Mintage: 41,730,000

Enlarged 1.5x
(actual size 19 mm)

Market Values • 1929-D

G-4	VG-8	F-12	VF-20	EF-40	AU-50	MS-60BN	MS-63BN	MS-65RD
$0.60	$0.85	$1.25	$2.25	$7	$15	$30	$50	$550

Key to Collecting: Common in all grades through Mint State. MS-65RD and higher are rare, if sharply struck, but otherwise readily available.

Striking and Sharpness: Usually with weakness in areas. Some are sharp, however. Full Details coins can be found.

1929-S

CIRCULATION MINTAGE: 50,148,000

Enlarged 1.5x
(actual size 19 mm)

MARKET VALUES • 1929-S

G-4	VG-8	F-12	VF-20	EF-40	AU-50	MS-60BN	MS-63BN	MS-65RD
$0.60	$0.90	$1.70	$2.35	$7	$15	$25	$30	$450

Key to Collecting: Common in all grades through gem Mint State RD. Sharpness adds a challenge, and well-struck coins are in the minority.

Striking and Sharpness: A mixed bag, with most having weakness to one degree or another. Full Details coins exist, however.

THE YEAR 1930

In America: The stock market plunge continued, and unemployment rose to 8.9 percent. Concerned citizens reduced purchases of real estate, automobiles, and other items, taking a wait-and-see attitude for the economy. By year's end matters did not get any better.

In Numismatics: The year closed on an optimistic note in the coin hobby. The ANA experienced membership gains. The Scott Stamp & Coin Co. launched its line of "National" albums, made by the Beistle Company. These soon replaced the clumsy procedure of displaying coins in flat open trays housed in coin cabinets.

News About Lincoln Cents: Coins were struck, for the last time until 1935, at the Philadelphia, Denver, and San Francisco mints. In 1930 a Mint State 1909-S V.D.B. Lincoln cent would have cost you 25¢: a price not much different from five years earlier or, for that matter, five years later.

1930

CIRCULATION MINTAGE: 157,415,000

Enlarged 1.5x
(actual size 19 mm)

MARKET VALUES • 1930

G-4	VG-8	F-12	VF-20	EF-40	AU-50	MS-60BN	MS-63BN	MS-65RD
$0.35	$0.40	$0.45	$0.50	$1.25	$3	$6	$10	$50

Key to Collecting: Common in any desired grade, including MS-65RD and beyond, sharply struck.

Striking and Sharpness: Most are fairly well struck, considering that the hub dies had been losing detail since 1916.

1930-D

Circulation Mintage: 40,100,000

Enlarged 1.5x
(actual size 19 mm)

Market Values • 1930-D

G-4	VG-8	F-12	VF-20	EF-40	AU-50	MS-60BN	MS-63BN	MS-65RD
$0.35	$0.40	$0.45	$0.55	$2.50	$4	$12	$30	$170

Key to Collecting: Common in all grades through gem Mint State, and sharply struck, but this is the scarcest of the three issues of this year.

Striking and Sharpness: Quality is mixed; sharp strikes are available, but in the minority.

Notes: Most seem to have a large D mintmark, but in the December 1953 issue of the *Numismatic Scrapbook Magazine*, Arlie Slabaugh reported a small D. In actuality, for the "large" D, the same D punch (normally employed from 1917 to 1932) was used, but punched more deeply into a working die. One rare variety has the 0 in the date filled in, due to the center breaking away from the working die.

1930-S

Circulation Mintage: 24,286,000

Enlarged 1.5x
(actual size 19 mm)

Market Values • 1930-S

G-4	VG-8	F-12	VF-20	EF-40	AU-50	MS-60BN	MS-63BN	MS-65RD
$0.35	$0.40	$0.45	$1.25	$1.75	$6	$10	$12	$100

Key to Collecting: Common in all grades, including gems with Full Details and original mint red-orange color.

Striking and Sharpness: Usually fairly well struck, making this issue a standout in comparison to the typical San Francisco cent of the 1920s. David W. Lange suggests that perhaps employees were fearful of losing their jobs in the Depression economy and decided to mind the presses more carefully and turn out sharper coins.

The Year 1931

In America: The economy continued its downward path, now with unemployment at 16.3 percent. The newly finished Empire State Building and other structures in New York City offered space that was hard to rent. In the entertainment world, radio and movies were going strong.

In Numismatics: As the Depression continued to sweep across America and, indeed, the world, optimism still prevailed among most numismatists. There were exceptions to be sure. George J. Bauer, president of the ANA, commented in September:

In the face of an economic condition that has not only strained the resources of individuals but governments as well and threatened the stability of our social structure, your Association has made steady progress and you will be pleased to learn that our membership in good standing has increased from 1,196 to 1,244, a net gain of 48. This is proof of the interest and efforts of our members and my fellow officers, also the committees, in their work in advancing the ANA.

News About Lincoln Cents: The 1931-S cent was only minted in small quantities—soon becoming a catalyst, a firecracker that helped set off the coin boom in 1934 (see listing).

1931

CIRCULATION MINTAGE: 19,396,000

Enlarged 1.5x
(actual size 19 mm)

MARKET VALUES • 1931

G-4	VG-8	F-12	VF-20	EF-40	AU-50	MS-60BN	MS-63BN	MS-65RD
$1.00	$1.25	$1.50	$2	$4	$9	$20	$35	$185

Key to Collecting: Common in all grades, including Full Details gems with original color. It is important to remember that "common" in this context is *rare* in comparison to *any* date and mintmark struck in 1934 or later. Cents of 1931 never were readily available in quantities of bank-wrapped rolls, and I do not recall ever handling one. (My activity as a dealer began in 1953.)

Striking and Sharpness: Usually well struck.

1931-D

CIRCULATION MINTAGE: 4,480,000

Enlarged 1.5x
(actual size 19 mm)

MARKET VALUES • 1931-D

G-4	VG-8	F-12	VF-20	EF-40	AU-50	MS-60BN	MS-63BN	MS-65RD
$7.50	$8	$9	$10	$15	$35	$60	$70	$1,300

Key to Collecting: Common in any and all grades, but a semi-key issue among cents of this decade. Readily available, but far scarcer than its lower-mintage cousin, the 1931-S, in gem Mint State with sharp details. Rolls and other quantities of the 1931-D were generally overlooked by dealers and collectors in this era, and few were saved.

Striking and Sharpness: Usually well struck.

1931-S

CIRCULATION MINTAGE: 866,000

Enlarged 1.5x
(actual size 19 mm)

MARKET VALUES • 1931-S

G-4	VG-8	F-12	VF-20	EF-40	AU-50	MS-60BN	MS-63BN	MS-65RD
$75	$85	$95	$100	$125	$145	$175	$225	$650

Key to Collecting: A key to the series, the 1931-S is a famous issue due to its low mintage. Plentiful in Mint State or close, rare in worn grades, it has attracted attention for a long time. This issue was not widely released in 1931 but was held by the Treasury. Specimens were later made available for face value to collectors and investors, probably resulting in at least half of them being saved in Mint State. Today these remain readily available in gem quality with good strike, but spotting can be a problem. Many have been dipped.

Striking and Sharpness: Varies, but usually above average. Full Details coins can be found but are in the minority.

Notes: Walter Breen reported that the Maurice Scharlack hoard contained "over 200,000 red Uncirculated specimens, many weak."[44] I have no confirmation of this quantity, which seems to be overly large for one dealer. In the mid-1950s I bought a cigar box full of rolls (more than a thousand coins) from Dayton dealer James Kelly. Until the coin market boom that began in 1960, rolls of 1931-S cents turned up more often than any other Lincoln cent before 1934.

David W. Lange supplied this letter written in 1985 by veteran dealer Norman Shultz, of Salt Lake City, Utah:

> The 1931-S cents were sent to the Federal Reserve Bank here in 1935—500,000 of them. One of the fellows working here called me and told me they had these, and how many did I want? In 1935 money was scarce with any coin dealer, and I took a $20 sack. I sold it to a lawyer for the Southern Pacific in Los Angeles for 40¢ each. A year later he sold them back to me for 30¢ each. This will give you some idea how tight money was. The bank would not lend me money to buy coins even when I offered to put up face value in rare coins.[45]

The 500,000 quantity seems overly large for the quantity remaining undistributed in 1935, but who knows?

Caveat: Many fakes exist with an S attached to a regular 1931 Philadelphia coin.

THE YEAR 1932

In America: The Dow-Jones Industrial Average touched bottom at 41.22 on July 28, 1932, the low point for the Depression years. This was in contrast to the record 381.17 reached on September 3, 1929, representing a drop of nearly 90 percent. Unemployment was at 24.1 percent, most banks were in trouble with uncollectible loans, many stocks were at fractions of their 1929 highs or had been delisted due to bankruptcy, and times were difficult everywhere. Those who were lucky enough to be employed took home an average weekly paycheck of $17, as compared to $28 in 1929. President Herbert Hoover, now widely viewed as an elitist who had little concern for the declining welfare of the average citizen, said, "Prosperity is just around the corner," which had a hollow ring to millions standing in breadlines and soup kitchens in the cities. Hoover lost his bid for reelection in November, while Franklin D. Roosevelt, with dynamic proposals to end the Depression, captured the hearts and votes of the nation.

In Numismatics: The Washington quarter was launched but attracted relatively little numismatic attention and, due to its face value, not much investment interest. The ANA experienced a slight dip in membership. Overall, the hobby remained strong while the nation suffered. At the Philadelphia, Denver, and San Francisco mints coinage production was at low levels, and some denominations, continuing the trend from 1931, were not produced at all.

News About Lincoln Cents: The Treasury Department accommodated collectors by offering recent as well as older issues of Uncirculated coins, in quantity if desired, from its stocks. The cost was just face value plus postage. Included were these Lincoln cents: 1929, 1929-S, 1930, 1930-D, 1930-S, 1931, 1931-D, 1931-S, 1932, and 1932-D. Alert collectors and dealers descended upon the opportunity, particularly focusing on the low-mintage 1931-S cents, of which at least several hundred thousand were purchased and squirreled away for investment and stock.

1932

CIRCULATION MINTAGE: 9,062,000

Enlarged 1.5x
(actual size 19 mm)

MARKET VALUES • 1932

G-4	VG-8	F-12	VF-20	EF-40	AU-50	MS-60BN	MS-63BN	MS-65RD
$2	$2.50	$2.75	$3.50	$6	$15	$20	$30	$115

Key to Collecting: The production this year hit an all-time low for a Philadelphia Mint Lincoln cent. Despite this, today there are enough examples around, having been picked from circulation or saved in rolls, to fill numismatic demand. Singles in MS-65RD with Full Details are easily enough found.

Striking and Sharpness: Varies, but enough sharp examples exist that finding one will not be a problem.

1932-D

CIRCULATION MINTAGE: 10,500,000

Enlarged 1.5x
(actual size 19 mm)

MARKET VALUES • 1932-D

G-4	VG-8	F-12	VF-20	EF-40	AU-50	MS-60BN	MS-63BN	MS-65RD

$2	$2.50	$2.75	$3.25	$4.50	$13	$19	$30	$250

Key to Collecting: Readily available in any desired grade, up to MS-65RD and beyond, sharply struck. Scarce, however, in the context of any and all issues 1934 and later.

Striking and Sharpness: Varies, but finding a Full Details example will not be difficult.

THE YEAR 1933

In America: In the deepest year of the Depression Franklin Roosevelt moved into the White House and soon launched the New Deal, a plan to revive the economy. He inherited, among other miseries, an unemployment rate of 24 percent and a deeply troubled banking system. Chosen as secretary of the Treasury was well-known numismatist William H. Woodin. America went off the gold standard, which, officially, it had been on since 1900, although de facto the standard had been in place generations earlier. Prohibition was repealed, to the joy of just about everyone; the "great experiment" had failed.

In Numismatics: Roosevelt stopped the production of gold coins and called for the surrender of those held by the public and banks, except for numismatic purposes. At the several mints the production of new copper, nickel, and silver coins was low, as it had been in recent years.

News About Lincoln Cents: Although by this time the 1931-S cent had attracted attention for its low mintage, scarcely any attention was paid to the new issues of 1933, the last year for which this would be true.

1933

CIRCULATION MINTAGE: 14,360,000

Enlarged 1.5x
(actual size 19 mm)

MARKET VALUES • 1933

G-4	VG-8	F-12	VF-20	EF-40	AU-50	MS-60BN	MS-63BN	MS-65RD
$2	$2.50	$2.75	$3	$7	$13	$20	$30	$125

Key to Collecting: Scarce in terms of mintage, but enough were saved, including in gem Mint State, that finding the coin of your dreams will be easy enough.

Striking and Sharpness: Often with Full Details, but there are exceptions.

Notes: A bank-wrapped roll of 50 coins was sold in New Netherlands' 50th Sale, December 1957, for $300. The catalog stated that L.S. Werner had contacted the Mint about cents in 1933 and was told that only 802,000 were released that year because of a lack of demand in that Depression era.

1933-D

CIRCULATION MINTAGE: 6,200,000

Enlarged 1.5x
(actual size 19 mm)

MARKET VALUES • 1933-D

G-4	VG-8	F-12	VF-20	EF-40	AU-50	MS-60BN	MS-63BN	MS-65RD
$5.50	$6.00	$6.50	$8	$15	$20	$23	$25	$150

Key to Collecting: Readily available, including well-struck gems with original color, on the numismatic market. Scarce or even rare, however, in comparison to issues of 1934 and later, a comment that can be made of nearly all cents after the V.D.B. issues of 1909, down to 1933, except for certain of the higher mintage Philadelphia dates.

Striking and Sharpness: Usually well struck. Full Details coins are easy to find. In this year a new larger D mintmark was used, which would remain the standard for decades.

THE YEAR 1934

In America: Despite New Deal programs instituted by President Roosevelt, the economy remained in a slump. The "dust bowl" Midwest was plagued by drought, bankrupting many farmers and prompting a migration to other places, especially California. Automobile sales showed an upward trend, and the Ford Motor Co. restored the $5 daily wage to 47,000 of its 70,000 employees. American Airlines and Continental Airlines were formed.

In Numismatics: Wayte Raymond, manager of the Coin Department of the Scott Stamp & Coin Co., New York City, launched the *Standard Catalogue of United States Coins*. At long last—generations in the waiting—a reference book was available with mintages and current market prices! It was about time. There was a stirring in the commemorative market as more collectors and dealers took up this specialty. Several new issues were announced. Membership in the ANA increased, and just about all in numismatics agreed that the hobby was headed onward and upward.

News About Lincoln Cents: This was the first year that bank-wrapped rolls of Uncirculated Lincoln cents were saved in large quantities. As demand for cents for circulation increased, stocks in Treasury and bank vaults, including some quantities dating back to the late 1920s, were tapped.

1934

CIRCULATION MINTAGE: 219,080,000

Enlarged 1.5x
(actual size 19 mm)

MARKET VALUES • 1934

G-4	VG-8	F-12	VF-20	EF-40	AU-50	MS-60BN	MS-63BN	MS-65RD
$0.15	$0.18	$0.20	$0.30	$1	$4	$7	$8	$45

Key to Collecting: This is a common date in any and all grades. Millions were saved at the time of issue, initiating the roll-investment interest in the hobby. The 3 in the date has a *long, pointed tail* at the bottom, unlike all other 3 digits in the series to date, and unlike the 3 used later in this decade; this pointed-tail style was again used in 1943 and has not been employed since.

Striking and Sharpness: Usually well struck. Full Details coins are readily available.

1934, Doubled Die Obverse: The working die was punched once, then rotated and deeply punched the final time, obliterating the earlier impression except for a slight trace of the right side of the 3 in the date, and the 4, both visible in the field below the date. Scarce. Not widely known.

1934-D

Circulation Mintage: 28,446,000

Enlarged 1.5x
(actual size 19 mm)

Market Values • 1934-D

G-4	VG-8	F-12	VF-20	EF-40	AU-50	MS-60BN	MS-63BN	MS-65RD
$0.20	$0.25	$0.50	$0.75	$2.25	$7.50	$20	$22	$100

Key to Collecting: Common in all Mint State grades, although this is the scarcest issue of 1934 and later. It is sufficiently scarce that some offerings of roll sets in the 1950s (when such were stock in trade on the market) started with 1935 rather than 1934.

Striking and Sharpness: Varies: some are weak, others strong. There are enough Full Details coins around that you can find a nice one.

The Year 1935

In America: The economy continued to be sluggish, but improvements were seen in many areas. The "dust bowl" remained a problem in the Midwest.

In Numismatics: By year's end, 1935 stood as the most dynamic 12-month period the numismatic hobby had ever known. Commemorative half dollars were all the rage, their prices soared, and buyers scrambled to get them. More than a dozen new commemoratives were planned for 1936. Lee F. Hewitt, of Chicago, announced the new *Numismatic Scrapbook Magazine*, which quickly became a runaway success.

News About Lincoln Cents: In Uncirculated grades, key issues were the 1913-D and S, 1914, 1914-D, 1914-S (especially hard to find and valued at about $2), 1915, 1924-D, and 1924-S. The 1909-S V.D.B. was still around in roll quantities and was apt to sell for 25¢ or so each. The Whitman imprint appeared on "penny boards" invented by J.K. Post of Neenah, Wisconsin. These sold like hotcakes. "Hmm. How long will it take me to fill in all of the holes?"

1935

Circulation Mintage: 245,388,000

Enlarged 1.5x
(actual size 19 mm)

Market Values • 1935

G-4	VG-8	F-12	VF-20	EF-40	AU-50	MS-60BN	MS-63BN	MS-65RD
$0.15	$0.18	$0.20	$0.25	$0.50	$1	$3	$5	$45

Key to Collecting: Common in all grades through gem MS-65RD and higher.

Striking and Sharpness: Although striking can vary, many sharp examples survive, including those with Full Details (meaning that *everything* is sharp, and with no planchet marks on Lincoln's shoulder).

1935-D

Circulation Mintage: 47,000,000

Enlarged 1.5x
(actual size 19 mm)

Market Values • 1935-D

G-4	VG-8	F-12	VF-20	EF-40	AU-50	MS-60BN	MS-63BN	MS-65RD
$0.15	$0.18	$0.20	$0.25	$0.50	$2	$5	$6	$65

Key to Collecting: This issue is common in all grades through gem MS-65RD and higher, although necessarily less often seen than its higher-mintage Philadelphia counterpart.

Striking and Sharpness: Striking can vary, and more than just a few are weakly struck. Full Details examples survive but constitute a tiny minority of coins in the marketplace. Finding one can be a challenge in comparison to most other cents of this decade.

1935-S

Circulation Mintage: 38,702,000

Enlarged 1.5x
(actual size 19 mm)

Market Values • 1935-S

G-4	VG-8	F-12	VF-20	EF-40	AU-50	MS-60BN	MS-63BN	MS-65RD
$0.15	$0.18	$0.25	$0.50	$2	$5	$12	$17	$85

Key to Collecting: Quality varies widely for the 1935-S, with some being weakly struck and others having irregular toning. Finding a choice gem is doable, but cherrypicking is advised—perhaps more so than for any other Lincoln cent in this *decade*.

Striking and Sharpness: Get set for an enjoyable treasure hunt for a Full Details coin.

THE YEAR 1936

In America: Citizens either loved or hated President Roosevelt, but enough felt positive about his programs to reelect him by a great margin. The unemployment rate was down to 14 percent, or 10 percent less than when Roosevelt took office in 1933. The "dust bowl" Midwest had another bad year. Margaret Mitchell's *Gone With the Wind* novel was published and soon became a sensation, *the* book to read.

In Numismatics: In 1936 the coin hobby was preoccupied with the commemorative boom. Speculation was rampant, and the market for these coins seemed poised to go upward forever—but by summer many prices had weakened, signaling a slump that would hit bottom in 1941. Meanwhile, with all of the commemorative excitement, few collectors were interested in ordering Proof coins, now available for the first time since 1916.

News About Lincoln Cents: Just 5,569 Proof Lincoln cents were made.

1936

CIRCULATION MINTAGE: 309,632,000

PROOF MINTAGE: 5,569

Enlarged 1.5x
(actual size 19 mm)

MARKET VALUES • 1936

G-4	VG-8	F-12	VF-20	EF-40	AU-50	MS-60BN	MS-63BN	MS-65RD
$0.15	$0.18	$0.25	$0.50	$1.50	$2.60	$3	$4	$15

MARKET VALUES • 1936, Proof

PF-63RB	PF-64RB	PF-65RD
$450	$750	$2,500

Key to Collecting: Common in all grades through gem MS-65RD and higher.

Striking and Sharpness: Although striking can vary, many Full Details examples survive.

Proofs: The earliest Proofs of this year had only partially mirrored surfaces and were satiny. Today these are called Type I issues. Soon the fully mirrored format, with the polished area on the dies including the portrait and other features, was used. Shane Anderson gives a mintage of 3,700 for the Type I and 1,869 for the Type II, although my own experience is that the Type II is more often seen today. Certification data would seem to agree with this.

1936, Doubled Die Obverse: Several varieties exist and are described in detail by John Wexler and Kevin Flynn in *The Authoritative Reference on Lincoln Cents*. The Bill Fivaz and J.T. Stanton *Cherrypicker's Guide* lists three of them. (FS-101 is illustrated here.) Most are well struck. These are very elusive, and gems, if found, are apt to be very expensive.

1936-D

CIRCULATION MINTAGE: 40,620,000

Enlarged 1.5x
(actual size 19 mm)

MARKET VALUES • 1936-D

G-4	VG-8	F-12	VF-20	EF-40	AU-50	MS-60BN	MS-63BN	MS-65RD
$0.15	$0.20	$0.30	$0.50	$1	$2	$3	$4	$20

Key to Collecting: Common in all grades through gem MS-65 and higher.

Striking and Sharpness: Usually seen well struck, but normal checking for sharpness is advised.

1936-S

CIRCULATION MINTAGE: 29,130,000

Enlarged 1.5x
(actual size 19 mm)

MARKET VALUES • 1936-S

G-4	VG-8	F-12	VF-20	EF-40	AU-50	MS-60BN	MS-63BN	MS-65RD
$0.15	$0.25	$0.40	$0.55	$1	$3	$5	$6	$25

Key to Collecting: Saved in large quantities at the time, the 1936-S is common today in any desired grade. Later mintages in the *billions* would make the 1936-S and other cents of the 1930s seem rare by comparison. In 1936 and today, the number of available gems exceeded the number of numismatists seeking them.

Striking and Sharpness: Full Details coins are plentiful.

THE YEAR 1937

In America: The economy, while hardly robust, was well on its way to recovery. The unemployment rate went down to 14.3 percent.

In Numismatics: On May 15 the new San Francisco Mint was dedicated.

News About Lincoln Cents: In *The Numismatist* in June, editor Frank Duffield noted:

> Anyone, without the expenditure of even a dollar, may start a collection of small cents. This makes that series of coins attractive to both sexes of all ages. Its attractiveness has been stimulated by the cardboard holders for the series placed on the market by novelty dealers.

A brilliant Uncirculated 1909-S V.D.B. cost about $2 in the marketplace, or nearly ten times its market price of a decade earlier and up from just 50¢ a few years before. Among other Lincoln cents in this grade were: 1909-S $1, 1910-S 50¢, 1911-S $1.75, 1911-D $1.25, 1912-S 90¢, 1912-D $1.75, 1913-S $2.75, 1913-D $2.25, 1914-S $2.75, and 1914-D $8.

The Whitman Publishing Company continued to offer its "Lincoln Head Penny" boards for 25¢—"developing . . . the numismatists of tomorrow," an advertisement noted.

1937

CIRCULATION MINTAGE: 309,170,000

PROOF MINTAGE: 9,320

Enlarged 1.5x
(actual size 19 mm)

MARKET VALUES • 1937

G-4	VG-8	F-12	VF-20	EF-40	AU-50	MS-60BN	MS-63BN	MS-65RD
$0.15	$0.20	$0.30	$0.50	$1	$2	$3	$4	$15

MARKET VALUES • 1937, Proof

PF-63RB	PF-64RB	PF-65RD
$65	$90	$350

Key to Collecting: Common in any and all grades desired.

Striking and Sharpness: Full Details coins are plentiful.

Proofs: These are readily available in proportion to the number minted. Many have been dipped, then later acquired spots, then were redipped. Pristine coins will always have gentle toning. No exceptions.

Notes: In 1941 at the ANA convention held that year in Philadelphia, Ira Z. Reed, well-known Philadelphia dealer, offered pairs of 1937 Lincoln cents and Buffalo nickels, with *reeded edges*, for sale. These were sold as novelties, not as Mint products. Somehow, the intent of these was forgotten, and in time both were later listed as rarities in *A Guide Book of United States Coins*. In March 1960, in the auction James F. Kelly conducted for the Penn-Ohio Coin Convention, an example of the cent was offered with this misinformation presented as fact:

> 1937 rare "milled edge" variety. Unc. bright red. This cent and the nickel (Lot No. 276) were purchased at the 1941 Philadelphia ANA Convention. There have been many conflicting stories regarding this coin but it has been verified by none other than the late F.C.C. Boyd that the late Ira Reed obtained 300 sets of these coins from the Mint just prior to the Convention. This information is first-hand as I was at the convention, was well acquainted with Mr. Reed and Mr. Boyd and can vouch for the above statements. It is a rare coin with auction records close to $100.

This phony description resulted in the "rare" cent bringing $35 and is perhaps a good lesson that a "first-hand" recollection can become erroneous when reported years later! Such stuff provides fodder for numismatic students and researchers, who now in the early twenty-first century are more numerous and enthusiastic than at any other time in the history of the hobby.

Writing in *The Numismatist*, April 1940, Stephen Teets commented: "There is a small 7 and a large 7 on our 1937 Lincoln cents. The former is very small and can be easily discerned. I have been able to locate only one specimen of the small 7 type." Perhaps this was from a relapsed die or other process which made a regular 7 seem small. Only one date size is recognized today.

1937-D

CIRCULATION MINTAGE: 50,430,000

Enlarged 1.5x
(actual size 19 mm)

MARKET VALUES • 1937-D

G-4	VG-8	F-12	VF-20	EF-40	AU-50	MS-60BN	MS-63BN	MS-65RD
$0.15	$0.20	$0.25	$0.40	$1	$3	$5	$6	$17

Key to Collecting: Easily found in gem preservation.

Striking and Sharpness: Full Details coins are plentiful. Overall, a high quality issue.

1937-S

CIRCULATION MINTAGE: 34,500,000

Enlarged 1.5x
(actual size 19 mm)

MARKET VALUES • 1937-S

G-4	VG-8	F-12	VF-20	EF-40	AU-50	MS-60BN	MS-63BN	MS-65RD
$0.15	$0.20	$0.30	$0.40	$1	$3	$5	$8	$20

Key to Collecting: Cents were struck at the old San Francisco Mint early in the year, then in the autumn at the new facility. Common today, including those in gem preservation.

Striking and Sharpness: Sharpness can vary.

THE YEAR 1938

In America: The unemployment rate rose to 19 percent, reflecting a setback in the economic recovery. This was due to a cut in government spending on Roosevelt's New Deal programs.

In Numismatics: On November 15 the new Jefferson nickel was placed into circulation. The coin market continued to be robust for just about all coins except commemoratives.

1938

CIRCULATION MINTAGE: 156,682,000

PROOF MINTAGE: 14,734

Enlarged 1.5x
(actual size 19 mm)

MARKET VALUES • 1938

G-4	VG-8	F-12	VF-20	EF-40	AU-50	MS-60BN	MS-63BN	MS-65RD
$0.15	$0.20	$0.30	$0.40	$1	$2	$4	$7	$15

MARKET VALUES • 1938, Proof

PF-63RB	PF-64RB	PF-65RD
$60	$80	$200

Key to Collecting: Common in all grades.

Striking and Sharpness: Usually well struck. Full Details coins are readily available.

Proofs: Plentiful in keeping with the mintage. Due to dipping and spotting (from glue in the cellophane envelopes of issue as well as from cleaning), pristine gems are scarce. These always have delicate toning.

1938-D

CIRCULATION MINTAGE: 20,010,000

Enlarged 1.5x
(actual size 19 mm)

MARKET VALUES • 1938-D

G-4	VG-8	F-12	VF-20	EF-40	AU-50	MS-60BN	MS-63BN	MS-65RD
$0.20	$0.30	$0.50	$0.80	$1.25	$3	$4	$7	$15

Key to Collecting: Plentiful in just about any grade desired.

Striking and Sharpness: No problem here.

1938-S

CIRCULATION MINTAGE: 15,180,000

Enlarged 1.5x
(actual size 19 mm)

MARKET VALUES • 1938-S

G-4	VG-8	F-12	VF-20	EF-40	AU-50	MS-60BN	MS-63BN	MS-65RD
$0.40	$0.50	$0.60	$0.75	$1.10	$3	$4	$6	$15

Key to Collecting: Despite the relatively small mintage, quantities were saved by collectors, dealers, and investors. Gems are readily available today. One variety shows the mintmark triple punched.

Striking and Sharpness: Full Details coins are found easily enough.

1938-S, Large S Over Small S: A slightly smaller S was first punched into the die, then overpunched with a larger mintmark. FS-501 is illustrated. Another variety, FS-502, shows a final S over garbled earlier punchings, perhaps from the same mintmark punch.

THE YEAR 1939

In America: World War II began in Europe as Germany invaded nearby lands. At the New York World's Fair the pavilion for stricken Czechoslovakia stood empty. A new miracle fiber, nylon, was introduced at the same event. Amidst great anticipation and excitement, *Gone With the Wind* played in theaters.

News About Lincoln Cents: Wayte Raymond offered a complete collection of Uncirculated Lincoln cents from 1909 to 1938 for $80.

1939

CIRCULATION MINTAGE: 316,466,000

PROOF MINTAGE: 13,520

Enlarged 1.5x
(actual size 19 mm)

MARKET VALUES • 1939

G-4	VG-8	F-12	VF-20	EF-40	AU-50	MS-60BN	MS-63BN	MS-65RD
$0.15	$0.18	$0.20	$0.25	$0.50	$1	$2	$3	$10

MARKET VALUES • 1939, Proof

PF-63RB	PF-64RB	PF-65RD
$55	$70	$180

Key to Collecting: Common in any grade desired.

Striking and Sharpness: Full Details coins are as common as can be.

Proofs: Readily available, but pristine undipped gems are in the minority. In one variety, the second 9 in the date appears smaller due to overpolishing of the die.

1939-D

CIRCULATION MINTAGE: 15,160,000

Enlarged 1.5x
(actual size 19 mm)

MARKET VALUES • 1939-D

G-4	VG-8	F-12	VF-20	EF-40	AU-50	MS-60BN	MS-63BN	MS-65RD
$0.50	$0.60	$0.65	$0.85	$1.25	$3	$4	$5	$11

Key to Collecting: Common in absolute terms, but scarce in the context of Lincoln cents of the era. This was widely recognized at the time, and large quantities of rolls were saved. Gems are available easily enough. By 1946 this continued to be well known as a key issue. In that year dealer R. Green, of Chicago, offered rolls of 50 Uncirculated coins "for investment" at $3.60—certainly a fortunate purchase for anyone at the time.

Striking and Sharpness: Varies, but finding a Full Details coin will be no problem.

1939-S

CIRCULATION MINTAGE: 52,070,000

Enlarged 1.5x
(actual size 19 mm)

MARKET VALUES • 1939-S

G-4	VG-8	F-12	VF-20	EF-40	AU-50	MS-60BN	MS-63BN	MS-65RD
$0.15	$0.20	$0.30	$0.75	$1	$2.50	$3	$4	$15

Key to Collecting: Although enough were saved that they are common today, most have unsatisfactory luster and are not from sharp dies, as Sol Taylor notes in his *Standard Guide to the Lincoln Cents.*

Striking and Sharpness: Cherrypicking is advised. Don't stop until you find one with Full Details.

THE YEAR 1940

In America: World War II was intensifying overseas as the Battle of Britain set much of central London afire. Meanwhile, it was déjà vu, and as in World War I, American factories worked overtime to supply war goods to England and her allies. Prosperity had returned, and big time, but perhaps for the wrong reasons. The Selective Service Act went into effect, providing for the drafting of American soldiers should this become necessary.

In Numismatics: The coin hobby remained strong in 1940, with continuing emphasis on starting out by collecting Lincoln cents from circulation. Dealers had smiles on their faces.

1940

CIRCULATION MINTAGE: 586,810,000

PROOF MINTAGE: 15,872

Enlarged 1.5x
(actual size 19 mm)

MARKET VALUES • 1940

G-4	VG-8	F-12	VF-20	EF-40	AU-50	MS-60BN	MS-63BN	MS-65RD
$0.15	$0.18	$0.20	$0.40	$0.60	$1	$2	$3	$14

MARKET VALUES • 1940, Proof

PF-63RB	PF-64RB	PF-65RD
$45	$60	$150

Key to Collecting: Very common, including well-struck gems. Hereafter, as the years go by, watch the present population report quantities expand for ultra-grade coins (an all-purpose comment applicable to nearly all varieties 1934 to date).

Striking and Sharpness: Full Details coins are easily located.

Proofs: Plentiful in proportion to the mintage. Pristine undipped coins are in the minority.

1940-D

CIRCULATION MINTAGE: 81,390,000

Enlarged 1.5x
(actual size 19 mm)

MARKET VALUES • 1940-D

G-4	VG-8	F-12	VF-20	EF-40	AU-50	MS-60BN	MS-63BN	MS-65RD
$0.15	$0.18	$0.25	$0.60	$0.75	$2	$3	$4	$15

Key to Collecting: Readily available in almost any grade desired.

Striking and Sharpness: A Full Details coin awaits you.

1940-S

CIRCULATION MINTAGE: 112,940,000

Enlarged 1.5x
(actual size 19 mm)

MARKET VALUES • 1940-S

G-4	VG-8	F-12	VF-20	EF-40	AU-50	MS-60BN	MS-63BN	MS-65RD
$0.15	$0.18	$0.20	$0.50	$1	$1.75	$3	$4	$15

Key to Collecting: Minted in large quantities, the 1940-S is easily obtainable today in just about any grade desired. A few were made with the reverse aligned in the same direction as the obverse, instead of with the standard 180° difference.

Striking and Sharpness: Full Details coins are common.

THE YEAR 1941

In America: President Roosevelt introduced his "Four Freedoms" in a message to Congress. The surprise attack by Japanese aircraft on Pearl Harbor on December 7 pushed America's entry into World War II. The economy went from cherry red to white hot. Big band and swing music was all the rage. Movie houses and radio sets provided the main entertainment.

In Numismatics: The *Handbook of United States Coins*, a listing of prices paid by dealers, by R.S. Yeoman, was issued by Whitman Publishing Co. Whitman introduced its three-panel folding blue cardboard coin albums, successors to the "penny board" sheets and related products. Commemorative coin prices, reeling from the 1936–1937 crash, touched bottom this year.

News About Lincoln Cents: In *The Numismatist* in January, "A Study of Lincoln Cents," an article by Louis I. Kane, discussed the variations in mintmark positions observed on such issues as the 1928-S, 1929-D, and 1930-S issues:

> The position of mintmarks seems to rove all along the year. In some years the mint-mark starts in the extreme left and continues horizontally to the end of the date, then it may start from the extreme left and drop diagonally, or it will begin at some point under the second numeral of the date and zigzag about. Very interesting, no?

1941

CIRCULATION MINTAGE: 887,018,000

PROOF MINTAGE: 21,100

Enlarged 1.5x
(actual size 19 mm)

MARKET VALUES • 1941

G-4	VG-8	F-12	VF-20	EF-40	AU-50	MS-60BN	MS-63BN	MS-65RD
$0.15	$0.18	$0.20	$0.30	$0.60	$1.50	$2	$3	$14

MARKET VALUES • 1941, Proof

PF-63RB	PF-64RB	PF-65RD
$40	$55	$150

Key to Collecting: Common as can be in just about any grade desired.

Striking and Sharpness: Full Details coins are plentiful.

Proofs: Readily available in proportion to the mintages. Pristine gems are in the minority but are more available than for issues in the 1930s.

1941, Thick Planchet: Some cents were made from planchet stock that was too thick. These are properly considered as mint errors, but since many were made, notice is made of them here. These turned up in Chicago later in the year. In the November issue of *Numismatic Scrapbook Magazine*, Superintendent of the Mint Edwin H. Dressel commented in part to Lee F. Hewitt, editor:

> In view of the extremely heavy demands for coinage, and the fact that we have a greatly augmented working force, mistakes, such as you mention, could be due to the inexperience of the new employee during his period of training.

John Dannreuther reports a thick planchet cent seemingly struck in brass.[46]

1941, Doubled Die Obverse: With slight doubling, best observed on the letters, such as the boldly doubled B in LIBERTY. Three varieties exist.

1941-D

CIRCULATION MINTAGE: 128,700,000

Enlarged 1.5x
(actual size 19 mm)

MARKET VALUES • 1941-D

G-4	VG-8	F-12	VF-20	EF-40	AU-50	MS-60BN	MS-63BN	MS-65RD
$0.15	$0.18	$0.20	$0.50	$1	$3	$4	$5	$15

Key to Collecting: Very common in all grades, although some are lightly struck.

Striking and Sharpness: Full Details coins are easily enough found for nearly all cents of this era.

1941-S

CIRCULATION MINTAGE: 92,360,000

Enlarged 1.5x
(actual size 19 mm)

MARKET VALUES • 1941-S

G-4	VG-8	F-12	VF-20	EF-40	AU-50	MS-60BN	MS-63BN	MS-65RD
$0.15	$0.18	$0.30	$0.50	$1	$3	$4	$5	$15

Key to Collecting: Gems are common, but cherrypicking is advised. Some are either weak in areas or lack eye appeal, or both.

Striking and Sharpness: Full Details coins can be found, but some scouting may be needed.

1941-S Large and Small S Mintmarks: The difference is dramatic. The large S is the rarer of the two, with David W. Lange suggesting that perhaps only 5 to 10 percent are of this variety. (A similar difference is found among 1928-S cents.) The large mintmark on the 1941-S is heavy at the upper left curve, thin at the center, and slightly heavier at the lower right. The edge of the top right serif is vertical, while the lower left serif is more of a blob. The small mintmark is, of course, smaller and is similar in general appearance to that of the 1928-S with small S. Although these have been discussed in print many times, collector interest is not strong. There should be room for one of each in your collection.

THE YEAR 1942

In America: The war effort galvanized citizens on the home front as servicemen deployed to fight the Axis powers (Germany, Italy, and Japan). Losses were heavy in the Pacific and European theaters (as scenes of action were called), but hopes were high. Factories that formerly made automobiles, tractors, refrigerators, jukeboxes, radios, and other consumer goods converted to produce jeeps, tanks, airplanes, and ammunition. Employees and employers accumulated cash, since the options to spend it were limited. Unemployment dropped to 4.7 percent, about half of the 1940 figure.

In Numismatics: With continuous production since 1936, Proof coins were suspended following the 1942 coinage because Mint facilities had a more important use in the war effort. Proof coinage would be resumed in 1950.

News About Lincoln Cents: Because copper was needed for military uses, production of cents was curtailed dramatically in July. In December it was discontinued entirely. Most of the cents of this year were struck in brass—an alloy of 95 percent copper and 5 percent zinc, with no tin. Experiments were made with other materials for coinage (see chapter two).

1942

CIRCULATION MINTAGE: 657,796,000

PROOF MINTAGE: 32,600

Enlarged 1.5x
(actual size 19 mm)

MARKET VALUES • 1942

G-4	VG-8	F-12	VF-20	EF-40	AU-50	MS-60BN	MS-63BN	MS-65RD
$0.15	$0.18	$0.20	$0.25	$0.50	$0.75	$1	$2	$14

MARKET VALUES • 1942, Proof

PF-63RB	PF-64RB	PF-65RD
$40	$55	$150

Key to Collecting: Common in all grades, although sharpness can vary. Other than by elemental analysis, there is no practical way the new alloy can be differentiated from the old for the cents of this year from the several mints.

Striking and Sharpness: Full Details coins are plentiful but are interspersed among many coins you would not want to buy.

Proofs: Available easily enough, but pristine undipped gems are scarce. Such coins will have light toning but can still be called RD by the services. This is the last year of Proofs until 1950.

1942-D

CIRCULATION MINTAGE: 206,698,000

Enlarged 1.5x
(actual size 19 mm)

MARKET VALUES • 1942-D

G-4	VG-8	F-12	VF-20	EF-40	AU-50	MS-60BN	MS-63BN	MS-65RD
$0.15	$0.18	$0.20	$0.25	$0.50	$0.85	$1	$2	$14

Key to Collecting: Very common, as the population report numbers suggest, in just about any desired grade, including ultra gems. As always, be careful when paying a high price for such a coin. Perfectly desirable MS-65RD and 66RD coins can cost just a fraction of the price and be 99.9 percent as satisfactory, or at least they would be to me if I were assembling a beautiful collection of Lincoln cents.

Striking and Sharpness: Full Details coins are plentiful.

1942-S

CIRCULATION MINTAGE: 85,590,000

Enlarged 1.5x
(actual size 19 mm)

Market Values • 1942-S

G-4	VG-8	F-12	VF-20	EF-40	AU-50	MS-60BN	MS-63BN	MS-65RD
$0.20	$0.25	$0.30	$0.85	$1.25	$5.50	$7	$8	$20

Key to Collecting: Again, this is an issue that can be found in nearly any grade desired, although in ultra grades past MS-67RD fewer have been certified than for 1942-D.

Striking and Sharpness: Die spacing and die wear resulted in many coins with traces of lightness, but some basic searching should enable you to find a Full Details example.

The Year 1943

In America: World War II continued overseas, with notable successes as well as losses. The Pentagon was completed. Air raid practices, with all lights extinguished so as not to aid potential enemy aircraft, were conducted in larger towns and cities. Food and gasoline were rationed. The train re-emerged as the main method of long-distance travel. The economy continued in overdrive, with the unemployment rate dropping to 1.9 percent. With cash plentiful, the price of available goods rose, depreciating the value of the dollar. To compensate for increased defense expenditures, the government increased taxes, taking more money from citizens.

In Numismatics: With cash aplenty in citizens' pockets, rare coins became an increasing focus of investment interest, making the market, even for commemoratives (which touched bottom in 1941), trend upward. Abe Kosoff's sale of the Michael F. Higgy Collection in September saw many twentieth-century coins sell for multiples of the latest catalog values. The market caught fire and would remain hot for the next several years.

News About Lincoln Cents: This is the year of the zinc-coated steel cent (see chapter two).

1943

Circulation Mintage: 684,628,670

Enlarged 1.5x
(actual size 19 mm)

Market Values • 1943

F-12	VF-20	EF-40	AU-50	MS-63BN	MS-65	MS-66	MS-67	MS-68
$0.30	$0.35	$0.40	$0.50	$2.50	$8	$45	$200	$3,000

Key to Collecting: These are very common in grades from VF to spotted Mint State. Opt for a pristine gem Mint State, and be "picky." There is not much money at stake. Such coins with no spotting are in the distinct minority, but when found are very beautiful. Coating pieces with clear fingernail polish to prevent oxidation was a common and effective practice; such can be removed harmlessly by acetone.

Striking and Sharpness: Full Details coins exist aplenty. Some show lightness in the higher areas. Some have a weak 4 in the date. Some have letters missing and are not rare.

1943 Struck in Bronze: This is numismatically classified as an off-metal error, not a regular circulation issue. For years there had been rumors that a few 1943 cents had been made in bronze instead of the zinc-coated steel standard. In November 1952 Lee F. Hewitt, in *The Numismatic Scrapbook Magazine*, wrote:

> While numismatists have kept their collective eagle-eyes open for that possibility of a stray bronze blank getting mixed in with the steel ones—to date no genuine 1943 cents in bronze have been reported.
>
> There are numerous "copper-plated" pieces floating around and there is a simple test to determine that they are copper-plated without cutting away any of the plating. A magnet will attract the steel cent but not a bronze one. As a further test have the doubtful piece weighed. The steel cents struck from January to May, 1943, weigh 41.5 grains and those struck in the latter part of year weigh 42.5 grains. A bronze cent weighs 48 grains.

Since that time many purported bronze cents, some from extremely deceptive counterfeit dies made by the spark erosion process or by high-speed impacting of a struck steel cent into a soft steel blank, then hardening it, have come to light. Even the experts differ on the authenticity of some of these. An *authentic* 1943 "bronze" cent should always come with certification from one of the major third-party grading services.

The first coin to gain some measure of credibility in coin periodicals was one found by a 14-year-old California lad, reported in March 1957 in the *Scrapbook*. Superintendent of the Mint Rae V. Biester stated it was the only one made and should be surrendered to the Mint—which the owner declined to do. R.S. Yeoman, editor of *A Guide Book of United States Coins*, advised that it would not be listed in that reference, "as it would mean cataloguing all off-metal coins."

In February 1958 the *Scrapbook* printed this from an Illinois numismatist:

> As all 1943 cents are made of steel they can be case hardened and pressed into a piece of soft polished steel. This die can then be hardened and pressed into another cent. No doubt all 1943 copper cents have been made in this manner.

After that, skepticism tended to vanish when additional pieces were reported. With the rise of certification services, dozens have been called genuine. In his 1988 *Encyclopedia* Walter Breen suggested, per information from ANACS, that about 40 had been found to be authentic—a quantity unsupported by any data of which I am aware.[47] One example, reportedly from a lady friend of the late Chief Engraver John R. Sinnock and graded Extremely Fine, sold at auction for $10,000 in 1981.

1943-D

CIRCULATION MINTAGE: 217,660,000

Enlarged 1.5x
(actual size 19 mm)

MARKET VALUES • 1943-D

F-12	VF-20	EF-40	AU-50	MS-63BN	MS-65	MS-66	MS-67	MS-68
$0.35	$0.40	$0.50	$0.75	$3	$10	$35	$185	$2,250

Key to Collecting: These are readily available in gem Mint State. Attractiveness varies, but finding a beautiful one will be no problem.

Striking and Sharpness: Usually fairly well struck, although there are exceptions.

1943-D, Repunched Mintmark: The light but very distinctive register impression of an earlier D is seen southwest of and partially under the regular D. One of the most dramatic double-punched mintmarks in the series—and a "must-have" variety for many who know about it.

1943-D Struck in Bronze: A mint error, an off-metal strike. The first was reported in the *Numismatic Scrapbook Magazine*, January 1958, by a Utah collector, who stated that a Secret Service agent had pronounced it to be genuine. After that, examples were reported one after the other. In his 1988 *Encyclopedia* Walter Breen stated, "about 24 known," a figure I consider far off base. An MS-64BN coin, examined and authenticated by ANACS, NGC, and PCGS, is believed to be unique. It was sold in 2010 for $1,700,000 by Legend Numismatics. David W. Lange reported that he examined it and concurred that it was genuine. It is said to have come from a former employee of the Denver Mint.

1943-S

CIRCULATION MINTAGE: 191,550,000

Enlarged 1.5x
(actual size 19 mm)

MARKET VALUES • 1943-S

F-12	VF-20	EF-40	AU-50	MS-63BN	MS-65	MS-66	MS-67	MS-68
$0.40	$0.65	$0.75	$1	$6	$20	$50	$200	$3,000

Key to Collecting: Comments similar to 1943 and 1943-D. Gems are common but are in the minority of extant specimens.

Striking and Sharpness: Usually fairly well struck, although there are exceptions.

1943-S Struck in Bronze: A mint error, an off-metal strike. Walter Breen's 1988 *Encyclopedia* states, "about 6 known." "Someone's experimenting to make 1943-S bronze cents," was reported in the *Numismatic Scrapbook Magazine* of December 1960. Any purported 1943-S bronze cent needs to be analyzed and certified by PCGS or NGC. There are countless 1943-S bronze cents in the marketplace that are not genuine. Only five examples are currently known to exist. Just one of those examples is in Mint State. The first example discovered was found in circulation by a 14-year-old boy in 1944, and it grades an estimated EF-45.

THE YEAR 1944

In America: World War II turned in favor of the Allies. In June the D-Day invasion of Normandy launched the reoccupation of Europe and the liberation of France and the Low Countries. In the Pacific Allied ships, planes, and troops, drawing closer to the Japanese homeland, gained control of one island after another. On the home front, on Main Street, towns displayed banners with blue stars for citizens in service and gold stars for those who had died in the war. Inflation marched on and prosperity was everywhere. At the polls in

November Franklin D. Roosevelt gained his unprecedented fourth term as president, beating Republican challenger Thomas Dewey (who would try again in 1948).

News About Lincoln Cents: Steel cents were discontinued and brass was used again, in an alloy of 95 percent copper and 5 percent zinc, as first employed early in 1942.

1944

CIRCULATION MINTAGE: 1,435,400,000

Enlarged 1.5x
(actual size 19 mm)

MARKET VALUES • 1944

VF-20	EF-40	AU-50	MS-63RB	MS-65RB	MS-65RD	MS-67RD
$0.10	$0.20	$0.35	$1	$5	$12	$150

Key to Collecting: Common as can be, as might be expected from its billion-plus coinage.

Striking and Sharpness: Varies, but sharp examples can be found with ease.

Notes: Apparently, quite a few 1944 cents were made on 1943 zinc-coated steel planchets, since dozens have been certified as genuine by ANACS. Some details are weak. Perhaps the first report of these was in the February 1959 issue of the *Numismatic Scrapbook Magazine*. Such pieces are classified as off-metal errors. One was reported to have come from a lady friend of Chief Engraver John R. Sinnock and was auctioned in 1981 for $3,500.

1944-D

CIRCULATION MINTAGE: 430,578,000

Enlarged 1.5x
(actual size 19 mm)

MARKET VALUES • 1944-D

VF-20	EF-40	AU-50	MS-63RB	MS-65RB	MS-65RD	MS-67RD
$0.10	$0.20	$0.35	$0.85	$4	$14	$100

Key to Collecting: Gems abound and lower-grade pieces are common.

Striking and Sharpness: Usually well struck. Full Details coins are readily available.

1944-D, D OVER S

CIRCULATION MINTAGE:
Estimated 500,000 (included above)

1944-D/S Variety 1
(FS-501)

1944-D/S Variety 2
(FS-502)

MARKET VALUES • 1944-D, D Over S

VF-20	EF-40	AU-50	MS-63RB	MS-65RB	MS-65RD
$100	$175	$235	$450	$700	$2,000

Key to Collecting: Only a tiny fraction of 1944-D cents have this feature, but still it is likely that thousands exist. More than 200 have been certified as MS-64RD or higher, with far fewer of BN and RB, simply because they are of lesser value, although more plentiful.

There are two varieties of the overmintmark. The more desirable and significantly rarer Variety 1 has the earlier S protruding above the D. The usually seen Variety 2 has the S under the D. Probably a couple hundred thousand to half a million of Variety 1 were coined (judging from typical die life), although the number could have been much smaller if the error was noticed and the die was retired from service. Variety 2 was made in larger numbers. Both were relatively unknown a generation ago. As is true of virtually all die varieties within the series, the opportunity for cherrypicking is excellent.

Caveat: Some coins were certified, by PCGS for example, simply as 1944-D, D Over S, before Variety 1 and Variety 2 were separately used on labels. Accordingly, population reports are not accurate with regard to these varieties.

1944-S

CIRCULATION MINTAGE: 282,760,000

Enlarged 1.5x
(actual size 19 mm)

MARKET VALUES • 1944-S

VF-20	EF-40	AU-50	MS-63RB	MS-65RB	MS-65RD	MS-67RD
$0.15	$0.20	$0.35	$0.85	$4	$13	$100

Key to Collecting: Common in all grades.

Striking and Sharpness: Often lightly defined in areas, so some looking will need to be done to find a sharp one.

Notes: Two styles of S mintmarks were used. The earlier has serifs and the later (and scarcer) has rounded ends and is more compact. This later style continued in use the next year.

THE YEAR 1945

In America: The Nazis surrendered in the spring. Most German cities were in ruins. Roosevelt died on April 12 while in Warm Springs, Georgia, and Vice President Harry S. Truman became president but was unaware of the development of the atomic bomb. Learning quickly, he authorized its use on August 6 on the Japanese city of Hiroshima, then again on August 9 on Nagasaki, actions that ended the war and are said to have saved the two million lives a land invasion would have cost. As the news of victory spread in war-weary towns and cities across America, celebrations knew no limits and lasted into the night. Inflation continued. The unemployment rate was 1.9 percent. The Dow-Jones Industrial Average registered a low of 155 and a high of 195, still far below the high of September 1929. The first completely electronic computer, using vacuum tubes, was completed: the ENIAC (for Electronic Numerical Integrator and Calculator); it would be dedicated in 1946 at the University of Pennsylvania. Citizens looked forward to a resumption of normal economic conditions and the availability of consumer goods.

Enthusiasm prevailed. Homecoming servicemen and their wives started what became known as the baby boom.

In Numismatics: Gold coins were as hot as a firecracker, with common-date double eagles selling for $80 and more, up from less than $40 when the war began. Prices of just about anything and everything went up, and up some more.

News About Lincoln Cents: Mintage continued at a high level due to the war in progress and the demand for more coins in circulation. The brass alloy was continued this year.

1945

CIRCULATION MINTAGE: 1,040,515,000

Enlarged 1.5x
(actual size 19 mm)

MARKET VALUES • 1945

VF-20	EF-40	AU-50	MS-63RB	MS-65RB	MS-65RD	MS-67RD
$0.10	$0.20	$0.35	$0.85	$2	$8	$225

Key to Collecting: Due to the quantity of surviving Mint State coins, a satisfactory gem can be found with ease, but many are blotchy. One variety displays a heavy die crack connecting the two wheat stalks on the reverse.

Striking and Sharpness: Varies, but mostly quite good.

1945-D

CIRCULATION MINTAGE: 266,268,000

Enlarged 1.5x
(actual size 19 mm)

MARKET VALUES • 1945-D

VF-20	EF-40	AU-50	MS-63RB	MS-65RB	MS-65RD	MS-67RD
$0.10	$0.20	$0.35	$0.85	$2	$9	$125

Key to Collecting: Common in gem grade, but some looking may be required because many are unattractive.

Striking and Sharpness: Varies, but many sharp strikes exist.

1945-S

CIRCULATION MINTAGE: 181,770,000

Enlarged 1.5x
(actual size 19 mm)

MARKET VALUES • 1945-S

VF-20	EF-40	AU-50	MS-63RB	MS-65RB	MS-65RD	MS-67RD
$0.15	$0.20	$0.35	$0.85	$2	$9	$75

Key to Collecting: Gems abound but are scarcer than for the higher mintage issues of the era. Eye appeal can vary.

Striking and Sharpness: Varies, with some weakly defined.

THE YEAR 1946

In America: Good times prevailed, with servicemen continuing to return from abroad and factories running full speed to convert to producing consumer goods, which were still hard to find. Inflation continued. Workers went on strike in steel, coal, and electrical industries. Prices rose across the board.

In Numismatics: *A Guide Book of United States Coins,* written by R.S. Yeoman with the technical assistance of Stuart Mosher, was published with a 1947 cover date. The ANA had about 6,000 members. The Roosevelt dime made its debut, designed by Chief Engraver John R. Sinnock. The 1946 Iowa Centennial and Booker T. Washington commemorative half dollars were issued, the first commemoratives made since 1939.

News About Lincoln Cents: David W. Lange points out: "The cents of 1946 from all three mints sport a broad and rakish numeral 4 in their dates, the only time that this style was employed during that decade."

1946

CIRCULATION MINTAGE: 991,655,000

Enlarged 1.5x
(actual size 19 mm)

MARKET VALUES • 1946

VF-20	EF-40	AU-50	MS-63RB	MS-65RB	MS-65RD	MS-67RD
$0.10	$0.20	$0.35	$0.60	$2	$14	$650

Key to Collecting: Repeating a familiar scenario, gems are common. Color varies from reddish to red-orange, with no difference in value.

Striking and Sharpness: Varies, but Full Details examples are common.

1946-D

CIRCULATION MINTAGE: 315,690,000

Enlarged 1.5x
(actual size 19 mm)

MARKET VALUES • 1946-D

VF-20	EF-40	AU-50	MS-63RB	MS-65RB	MS-65RD	MS-67RD
$0.10	$0.20	$0.35	$0.60	$2	$10	$175

Key to Collecting: Common, including gems with original color, in all grades.

Striking and Sharpness: Many were weakly struck due to wide die spacing, but sharp examples can be found.

1946-S

CIRCULATION MINTAGE: 198,100,000

Enlarged 1.5x
(actual size 19 mm)

MARKET VALUES • 1946-S

VF-20	EF-40	AU-50	MS-63RB	MS-65RB	MS-65RD	MS-67RD
$0.15	$0.20	$0.35	$0.60	$2	$10	$200

Key to Collecting: Gems are common, including those with original color, but sharpness can be a problem—easily enough overcome by cherrypicking.

Striking and Sharpness: Poor die spacing plus overused dies combined to create many inadequate pieces. Sharp examples can be found, however.

1946-S, S OVER D

MARKET VALUES • 1946-S, S Over D

VF-20	EF-40	AU-50	MS-63RB	MS-65RB	MS-65RD
$35	$75	$125	$225	$400	$650

Key to Collecting: This features an earlier D, small in size, that is unequivocally visible when examined under magnification but is not sharply defined. Some imagination may be required to see it. Accordingly, it is not widely collected. Most examples found so far have been in lower grades. MS-65RD pieces are rare, but probably many remain in numismatic hands as regular 1946-S cents that have not been examined.

John Wexler and Kevin Flynn commented in 1996: "This is an extremely difficult variety to find in any grade; very rare in Mint State." The listing of the variety in *A Guide Book of United States Coins* has focused attention on it. Today more than 50 MS-65RD coins have been certified. No doubt there are many others to be discovered, and still others that will not be submitted unless lower grades come to have higher market values. As to the total number known, perhaps an estimate of 500 to 1,000 would be realistic.

THE YEAR 1947

In America: The economy continued its strength. Consumer goods were finally becoming available again, but demand for automobiles, new types of washing machines, housing, and other products outran supply. Buyers often paid more than list price for goods, in order to get to the front of long lines. The unemployment rate edged up to 3.9 percent.

In Numismatics: All seemed to be well in the marketplace, at least on the surface. Privately, some dealers worried whether recent record auction prices would hold.[48] Membership of the ANA stood at 7,236.

News About Lincoln Cents: The alloy was modified slightly to add 1 percent tin to 95 percent copper and 4 percent zinc. This combination was used through 1961, after which zinc was not used until the entirely different cent stock of 1982.

1947

CIRCULATION MINTAGE: 190,555,000

Enlarged 1.5x
(actual size 19 mm)

MARKET VALUES • 1947

VF-20	EF-40	AU-50	MS-63RB	MS-65RB	MS-65RD	MS-67RD
$0.10	$0.20	$0.40	$1	$3	$12	$1,500

Key to Collecting: Gems with original color are in the distinct minority, but enough exist to fill the demand. A doubled-die variety has attracted interest among specialists.

Striking and Sharpness: Varies, but most are sharp. Full Details coins abound.

1947-D

CIRCULATION MINTAGE: 194,750,000

Enlarged 1.5x
(actual size 19 mm)

MARKET VALUES • 1947-D

VF-20	EF-40	AU-50	MS-63RB	MS-65RB	MS-65RD	MS-67RD
$0.10	$0.20	$0.40	$0.60	$2	$10	$200

Key to Collecting: Common in all grades. Gems, of course, are a tiny minority, but in absolute terms, enough exist to make them readily available.

Striking and Sharpness: Usually quite good.

1947-S

CIRCULATION MINTAGE: 99,000,000

Enlarged 1.5x
(actual size 19 mm)

MARKET VALUES • 1947-S

VF-20	EF-40	AU-50	MS-63RB	MS-65RB	MS-65RD	MS-67RD
$0.20	$0.25	$0.50	$0.85	$2	$12	$200

Key to Collecting: Common in all grades including gem, but cherrypicking is advised for strike.

Striking and Sharpness: Often shows weakness, with Full Details specimens constituting a small percentage.

The Year 1948

In America: In the presidential election, which pitted incumbent Harry S. Truman against Republican challenger Thomas Dewey, the latter was the favorite. Somehow, Truman won, surprising many. At the time political pundits and observers viewed him as having mediocre talent. Many modern historians disagree and admire his accomplishments.

In Numismatics: After having had a run-up in prices for several years, followed by a hint of chill in 1947, in 1948 the rare coin market caught a cold. Prices declined in many series, especially for expensive issues.

News About Lincoln Cents: Beginning this year and continuing through about 1951, fewer Uncirculated rolls were saved by investors because the coin market was in a slump.

1948

Circulation Mintage: 317,570,000

Enlarged 1.5x
(actual size 19 mm)

Market Values • 1948

VF-20	EF-40	AU-50	MS-63RB	MS-65RB	MS-65RD	MS-67RD
$0.10	$0.20	$0.35	$0.85	$2	$15	$1,850

Key to Collecting: Common in all grades, up to and including MS-65RD or higher. Mintages of this era were reduced from the immediately preceding years, but still the quantities were large.

Striking and Sharpness: Usually quite good. Full Details coins are common.

1948-D

Circulation Mintage: 172,637,500

Enlarged 1.5x
(actual size 19 mm)

Market Values • 1948-D

VF-20	EF-40	AU-50	MS-63RB	MS-65RB	MS-65RD	MS-67RD
$0.10	$0.20	$0.35	$0.60	$2	$11	$550

Key to Collecting: Common in all grades including original gems.

Striking and Sharpness: Varies—some are weak, others strong.

1948-S

Circulation Mintage: 81,735,000

Enlarged 1.5x
(actual size 19 mm)

MARKET VALUES • 1948-S

VF-20	EF-40	AU-50	MS-63RB	MS-65RB	MS-65RD	MS-67RD
$0.20	$0.30	$0.35	$1	$3	$9	$100

Key to Collecting: Common in all grades, but not nearly as common as higher mint-age issues of the era.

Striking and Sharpness: Many have weaknesses, but sharp examples can be found.

THE YEAR 1949

In America: The United States extended diplomatic recognition to Israel (established in 1948). Consumer goods were now widely available, but not in all models and styles. Although peace had prevailed in most areas of the world since 1945, the "Cold War" with the Soviet Union was a focus of national worry and attention. The Dow-Jones Industrial Average registered 161 and 200 as the low and high for the year.

In Numismatics: The coin collecting hobby in America was fraught with uncertainty. The ANA had a record high membership, but increased costs had resulted in a five-figure deficit the year before, and expenses continued to escalate. In the commercial arena some dealers were experiencing difficulties with a declining market. Many auction sales did poorly, realizing lower prices lower than for 1945 and 1946. At the Smithsonian Institution the Division of Numismatics was formally instituted, giving new recognition to the displays mounted and research conducted there. *Early American Cents*, by Dr. William H. Sheldon, was published. This introduced the Sheldon grading system, ranging from 1 to 70.

News About Lincoln Cents: Gilroy Roberts, chief engraver at the Mint, stated that since at least 1947 the typical die for the cent had been used for 800,000 to 1,000,000 impressions or more.[49]

1949

CIRCULATION MINTAGE: 217,775,000

Enlarged 1.5x
(actual size 19 mm)

MARKET VALUES • 1949

VF-20	EF-40	AU-50	MS-63RB	MS-65RB	MS-65RD	MS-67RD
$0.10	$0.20	$0.35	$1	$3	$15	$1,350

Key to Collecting: Common in all grades. David W. Lange notes: "Common are pieces having a pattern of shallow stains which has been described as 'cob webbing.' An unappealing feature which often affects every coin in a roll, it's common for many Philadelphia Mint cents dated 1949–52. It was almost certainly caused by some chemical treatment of the planchets prior to coining, but why it appears particularly for these years is not known." Such comments are a good reason for you to acquire his *Complete Guide to Lincoln Cents* book, if you make the series a specialty.

Striking and Sharpness: Usually well struck. Full Details coins are readily available.

1949-D

CIRCULATION MINTAGE: 153,132,500

Enlarged 1.5x
(actual size 19 mm)

MARKET VALUES • 1949-D

VF-20	EF-40	AU-50	MS-63RB	MS-65RB	MS-65RD	MS-67RD
$0.10	$0.20	$0.35	$1	$3	$14	$450

Key to Collecting: Common in all grades, but a bit scarce in terms of ultra-grade gems certified so far.

Striking and Sharpness: Usually sharp, but there are the inevitable exceptions.

1949-S

CIRCULATION MINTAGE: 64,290,000

Enlarged 1.5x
(actual size 19 mm)

MARKET VALUES • 1949-S

VF-20	EF-40	AU-50	MS-63RB	MS-65RB	MS-65RD	MS-67RD
$0.25	$0.30	$0.35	$2	$4	$16	$175

Key to Collecting: Common in all grades, but fewer rolls were saved than was the case earlier in the decade. This was recession time in the coin investment market.

Striking and Sharpness: Varies from weak to sharp.

THE YEAR 1950

In America: As the Cold War with the USSR (Union of Soviet Socialist Republics) escalated, President Truman authorized the making of the hydrogen bomb. Real war was underway in Korea, but Congress would not call it that—later designating it as a "police action" or "conflict." By 1953, 5,700,000 troops had served and 54,246 had died. Many Americans viewed the situation as unwinnable and poorly planned. The American economy reached an equilibrium, with many consumer needs filled with products. The unemployment rate was 5.9 percent.

In Numismatics: In 1950 the Philadelphia Mint produced 51,386 Proof sets, the first since 1942. The cost of a set was $2.10. These went on sale on July 17, with a limit of five sets per person. Interest was good, but there was little excitement.

The numismatic market was quiet, continuing the trend of 1949. Louis E. Eliasberg fulfilled his dream of obtaining one each of every basic date and mintmark of U.S. coin.

News About Lincoln Cents: The numeral 5 introduced on this date had a long tail at the bottom, quite unlike the compact 5 used earlier on years that ended in 5.

1950

CIRCULATION MINTAGE: 272,635,000

PROOF MINTAGE: 51,386

Enlarged 1.5x
(actual size 19 mm)

MARKET VALUES • 1950

VF-20	EF-40	AU-50	MS-63RB	MS-65RB	MS-65RD	MS-67RD
$0.10	$0.20	$0.35	$0.85	$2	$18	$950

MARKET VALUES • 1950, Proof

PF-65RD	PF-66RD	PF-67RD
$70	$100	$325

Key to Collecting: Common in all grades, but scarcer in Mint State than those issued recently before 1948 or after 1951. Saving bank-wrapped rolls lessened in popularity: Only contrarians did it. Gems with original bright color are slightly scarce.

Striking and Sharpness: Usually quite good. Finding a Full Details coin is no problem.

Proofs: The earlier Proofs of the year have a hybrid finish that is mirrorlike but with some satiny graininess. Later strikes, these being the majority, are from highly polished dies. Some of the deeply mirrored pieces have slightly satiny or "frosted" portraits. These are especially desirable to the specialists who seek them. The terms "Cameo" and "Ultra Cameo" are used by grading services, but in any event the cameo effect is much less distinctive than that found on modern Proof Lincoln cents (which are now deliberately made with cameo contrast).

1950-D

CIRCULATION MINTAGE: 334,950,000

Enlarged 1.5x
(actual size 19 mm)

MARKET VALUES • 1950-D

VF-20	EF-40	AU-50	MS-63RB	MS-65RB	MS-65RD	MS-67RD
$0.10	$0.20	$0.35	$0.60	$2	$17	$675

Key to Collecting: Common in all grades, with the highest production of any mint this year. Again, relatively few bank-wrapped rolls were saved. On a relative basis, gem coins with full original color are scarce today, but on an absolute basis, there are enough around to satisfy the needs of those who seek them.

Striking and Sharpness: Varies, but many Full Details coins are in the offing.

1950-S

CIRCULATION MINTAGE: 118,505,000

Enlarged 1.5x
(actual size 19 mm)

MARKET VALUES • 1950-S

VF-20	EF-40	AU-50	MS-63RB	MS-65RB	MS-65RD	MS-67RD
$0.15	$0.25	$0.35	$0.85	$2	$13	$300

Key to Collecting: Common in all grades, but scarce in comparison to Philadelphia and Denver cents of the era. Relatively few rolls were saved. David W. Lange notes that many of 1950-S and 1951-S cents have dark streaking, probably from some chemical, not thoroughly rinsed away, used in one of the processes. Enough gems survive, however, to fill numismatic needs. Increasingly, these are being picked through for submission of higher-grade pieces to the certification services.

Striking and Sharpness: Usually quite good.

THE YEAR 1951

In America: The Korean conflict occupied newspaper headlines. The unemployment rate was 5.3 percent.

In Numismatics: The coin market continued in the doldrums as 1951 began. The ANA membership stood at 7,323, a loss of 356 during the year. In 1950 the Denver Mint had produced only 2,630,030 nickels—the smallest nickel five-cent piece coinage since 1931. When the mintage figure was released in 1951, excitement prevailed. The hot-ticket coin of the decade! Still, there was no great widespread interest in most other modern coins, and prices remained low.

News About Lincoln Cents: Roll investing slowed for many investors, but the low face value of cents made them affordable, and larger quantities were saved than for recent years, as had been the case since 1934. The 1950-D nickel sizzle had a ripple effect on all rolls. A set of Mint State Lincoln cent dates and mintmarks from 1934 to 1950 cost about $2.50.

1951

CIRCULATION MINTAGE: 284,576,000

PROOF MINTAGE: 57,500

Enlarged 1.5x
(actual size 19 mm)

MARKET VALUES • 1951

VF-20	EF-40	AU-50	MS-63RB	MS-65RB	MS-65RD	MS-67RD
$0.10	$0.25	$0.35	$0.70	$2	$18	$700

MARKET VALUES • 1951, Proof

PF-65RD	PF-66RD	PF-67RD
$65	$100	$225

Key to Collecting: Common in all grades including gems with original color.

Striking and Sharpness: Sharp is the rule. Full Details coins abound.

Proofs: Most survive in choice to gem grades, although many have been dipped. Cameo contrast on the 1951 Proof is harder to find than on any other cent from 1950 to 1970, notes Rick Jerry Tomaska in *Cameo and Brilliant Proof Coinage of the 1950 to 1970 Era.*

1951-D

CIRCULATION MINTAGE: 625,355,000

Enlarged 1.5x
(actual size 19 mm)

MARKET VALUES • 1951-D

VF-20	EF-40	AU-50	MS-63RB	MS-65RB	MS-65RD	MS-67RD
$0.10	$0.12	$0.35	$0.60	$2	$9	$200

Key to Collecting: Common in all grades.

Striking and Sharpness: Usually very good.

Notes: Traces of what some consider to be an earlier S, in the form of what may be the outer upper-left curve of the S protruding slightly from the upright of the D, can be seen under high magnification. Per the Wexler-Flynn text, verification was mainly by a photographic over-lay. Otherwise, what seems to be the upper left of an S might be the heavy top-left serif of a D. Not especially collected until recent times, and then only by dedicated specialists. Not recognized by *A Guide Book of United States Coins.* Notwithstanding this, quite a few have been certified, including at the gem level.

1951-S

CIRCULATION MINTAGE: 136,010,000

Enlarged 1.5x
(actual size 19 mm)

MARKET VALUES • 1951-S

VF-20	EF-40	AU-50	MS-63RB	MS-65RB	MS-65RD	MS-67RD
$0.25	$0.30	$0.50	$1.00	$3	$11	$325

Key to Collecting: Common in all grades including gems with original color.

Striking and Sharpness: Varies. Many are weak, but you can find one with Full Details.

THE YEAR 1952

In America: Military leader Dwight D. Eisenhower scored an easy victory over Democratic opponent Adlai Stevenson. "Ike" would serve for eight years, 1953 to 1961, and would be widely viewed as a "nice guy," easygoing, and with little controversy, except for the seeming lack of real progress with the Korean conflict early in his administration.

In Numismatics: The slump in the coin market ended, activity became intense, and excitement prevailed. A new era of enthusiasm had been launched, catalyzed by the 1950-D nickels, rolls of other coins, and a growing interest in Proof sets. In Iola, Wisconsin, Chet Krause launched *Numismatic News* as a monthly paper oriented toward classified advertising. It caught on quickly and became very popular. The *Numismatic Scrapbook* remained the most popular periodical in the hobby, followed by *The Numismatist*.

News About Lincoln Cents: At the Mint, thought was given to changing the Lincoln cent to a design by James Earle Fraser, and pattern pieces were struck. The election of Eisenhower (a Republican, as Lincoln had been) and a strong demand for circulating coins of various denominations put an end to the idea.[50]

1952

CIRCULATION MINTAGE: 186,775,000

PROOF MINTAGE: 81,980

Enlarged 1.5x
(actual size 19 mm)

MARKET VALUES • 1952

VF-20	EF-40	AU-50	MS-63RB	MS-65RB	MS-65RD	MS-67RD
$0.10	$0.15	$0.35	$1	$3	$16	$1,450

MARKET VALUES • 1952, Proof

PF-65RD	PF-66RD	PF-67RD
$50	$75	$125

Key to Collecting: Common in all grades.

Striking and Sharpness: Usually quite good.

Proofs: Plentiful in proportion to the mintage. Cameo contrast Proofs are not "deep."

1952-D

CIRCULATION MINTAGE: 746,130,000

Enlarged 1.5x
(actual size 19 mm)

MARKET VALUES • 1952-D

VF-20	EF-40	AU-50	MS-63RB	MS-65RB	MS-65RD	MS-67RD
$0.10	$0.15	$0.25	$0.75	$2	$9	$300

Key to Collecting: Common in all grades. What were once believed to be two 1952-D, D Over S, varieties are now known to be one D Over S and one D Over D. Take a strong magnifying glass and go hunting.

Striking and Sharpness: Usually well struck. Full Details coins are readily available.

Notes: While the 1952-D, D Over S, has sometimes been suspected of being a repunched D mintmark, it is now largely agreed upon as a D Over S, with the S protruding from the bottom of the D. There is also a D Over D variety, which has contributed to the confusion.

1952-S

CIRCULATION MINTAGE: 137,800,004

Enlarged 1.5x
(actual size 19 mm)

MARKET VALUES • 1952-S

VF-20	EF-40	AU-50	MS-63RB	MS-65RB	MS-65RD	MS-67RD
$0.15	$0.20	$0.35	$2	$4	$13	$150

Key to Collecting: Common in all grades, although scarcer in circulated grades than are coins from the other two mints. Beginning in a strong way this year, rolls of S-marked coins became especially popular with investors, resulting in proportionately more being saved than of the Philadelphia and Denver coins. In absolute terms, however, there are more than enough to go around today.

Striking and Sharpness: Varies, with many weakly defined, although enough sharp coins were produced that you will easily find one with Full Details.

THE YEAR 1953

In America: There was a Communist lurking on every corner (the government might have you believe), and anyone suspected of having such leanings at one time was *persona non grata*. The Korean conflict wound down. *TV Guide* was published and soon became popular. Ditto for *Playboy* magazine.

In Numismatics: The hobby of coin collecting continued to grow, with enthusiasm everywhere. Prices rose, and many dealers offered to pay more than *Red Book* list prices.

1953

CIRCULATION MINTAGE: 256,755,000

PROOF MINTAGE: 128,800

Enlarged 1.5x
(actual size 19 mm)

MARKET VALUES • 1953

VF-20	EF-40	AU-50	MS-63RB	MS-65RB	MS-65RD	MS-67RD
$0.10	$0.15	$0.20	$0.50	$1	$18	$2,000

MARKET VALUES • 1953, Proof

PF-65RD	PF-66RD	PF-67RD
$30	$40	$100

Key to Collecting: Common in all grades.

Striking and Sharpness: Usually very good. Full Details coins abound.

Proofs: Easily available due to the high mintage. Examples with deep cameo contrast are rare.

1953-D

CIRCULATION MINTAGE: 700,515,000

Enlarged 1.5x
(actual size 19 mm)

MARKET VALUES • 1953-D

VF-20	EF-40	AU-50	MS-63RB	MS-65RB	MS-65RD	MS-67RD
$0.10	$0.15	$0.20	$0.50	$1	$11	$500

Key to Collecting: Common in all grades, as might be expected from such a high mintage figure.

Striking and Sharpness: Usually quite good.

1953-S

CIRCULATION MINTAGE: 181,835,000

Enlarged 1.5x
(actual size 19 mm)

MARKET VALUES • 1953-S

VF-20	EF-40	AU-50	MS-63RB	MS-65RB	MS-65RD	MS-67RD
$0.10	$0.15	$0.20	$0.60	$2	$12	$175

Key to Collecting: Common in all grades, but slightly scarcer than cents of the other two mints (particularly Denver). Some coins are discolored. Bank-wrapped rolls were saved with a passion because S-marked coins were a great favorite with investors.

Striking and Sharpness: Varies, but usually good.

THE YEAR 1954

In America: The economy was robust, and in most places there was enthusiasm and hope.

In Numismatics: The market was strong, as it had been since 1952, and was getting better each month. Proof sets and rolls were in strong demand, but all series did well.

1954

CIRCULATION MINTAGE: 71,640,050

PROOF MINTAGE: 233,300

Enlarged 1.5x
(actual size 19 mm)

MARKET VALUES • 1954

VF-20	EF-40	AU-50	MS-63RB	MS-65RB	MS-65RD	MS-67RD
$0.25	$0.35	$0.45	$0.60	$2	$27	$15,000

MARKET VALUES • 1954, Proof

PF-65RD	PF-66RD	PF-67RD
$20	$30	$60

Key to Collecting: Common in all grades, although on a comparative basis, well-struck coins with original red surfaces and superb eye appeal are few and far between. Most are somewhat dark, as made. The remarkably low mintage for a Philadelphia Mint cent of this era encouraged the saving of rolls by investors.

Striking and Sharpness: Striking is often poor, which is rather curious considering the technology available at the time and the general reputation of the Philadelphia Mint for turning out well-struck coins.

Proofs: Readily available in proportion to the mintage. Gems are easy to find, as are those with cameo contrast.

1954-D

CIRCULATION MINTAGE: 251,552,500

Enlarged 1.5x
(actual size 19 mm)

MARKET VALUES • 1954-D

VF-20	EF-40	AU-50	MS-63RB	MS-64RB	MS-65RB	MS-65RD
$0.10	$0.12	$0.20	$0.50	$1	$10	$400

Key to Collecting: Common in all grades including superb gem Mint State.

Striking and Sharpness: Varies, but many if not most were well struck. No problem finding one with Full Details.

1954-S

CIRCULATION MINTAGE: 96,190,000

Enlarged 1.5x
(actual size 19 mm)

MARKET VALUES • 1954-S

VF-20	EF-40	AU-50	MS-63RB	MS-64RB	MS-65RB	MS-65RD
$0.10	$0.12	$0.20	$0.50	$1	$8	$115

Key to Collecting: Common in all grades. Gem Mint State coins with original color and needle-sharp strike require some pursuit. Rolls were saved with a vengeance—thousands and thousands of them.

Striking and Sharpness: Varies, with many being poorly struck. Some have a die crack or defect linking the BE in LIBERTY, giving rise to the term "LIBIERTY," a variety that attracted modest attention at one time but now is mostly forgotten. Shane Anderson's *Complete Lincoln Cent Encyclopedia* makes special note of these.

The Year 1955

In America: The economy remained strong. Hurricane Diane raked across the Northeast on August 19, causing widespread flooding and more than $1 billion in damage. "Rock Around the Clock," by Bill Haley and His Comets, popularized rock and roll music, which quickly became a sensation. Disneyland opened on July 13. In Montgomery, Alabama, Mrs. Rosa Parks, a Black woman, refused to give up her seat to a White man and was arrested, precipitating a boycott that under Rev. Dr. Martin Luther King led to widespread civil rights reform. The first McDonald's restaurant was opened. An American U-2 spy plane piloted by Francis Gary Powers was downed over Russia. The first B-52 bomber was delivered to the Air Force. The Salk polio vaccine was announced.

In Numismatics: In this year the San Francisco Mint struck its final coins—cents and five-cent pieces—seemingly closing forever this chapter in history. Presses were removed, other government offices were installed. Eventually on July 11, 1962, the "Mint" title became "Assay Office."

In August the annual convention of the ANA was held in Omaha, Nebraska. At the time the membership of the ANA stood at 10,462. The convention had 528 registrants, an all-time high. At the auction, held by Bebee's, an Uncirculated 1914-D cent fetched a strong $85. The bourse comprised 45 dealers, one of whom was the author of this book.

News About Lincoln Cents: The announced closing of the San Francisco Mint caused a mad scramble for rolls of cents and dimes, the only denominations struck. Pennsylvania instituted a 1 percent sales tax to help pay for relief for victims of Hurricane Diane. This caused a shortage of cents for a time.

1955

CIRCULATION MINTAGE: 330,958,200

PROOF MINTAGE: 378,200

Enlarged 1.5x
(actual size 19 mm)

Market Values • 1955

VF-20	EF-40	AU-50	MS-63RB	MS-65RB	MS-65RD	MS-67RD
$0.10	$0.12	$0.15	$0.35	$1	$19	$650

Market Values • 1955, Proof

PF-65RD	PF-66RD	PF-67RD
$18	$30	$50

Key to Collecting: Common overall, although sharply struck gems with full original color are scarce in the context of the series. Cherrypicking is a necessity for smart buyers, including among certified gems. Many cents of this date and mint have die cracks at the center of the obverse, probably from improperly tempered steel dies. Such coins are sometimes called the "cracked skull" variety.

Striking and Sharpness: Usually below par.

Proofs: Common in the context of the series. Proof sets were a popular investment at the time. Cameo contrast coins are not hard to find.

1955, Doubled Die Obverse: By almost any evaluation the 1955, Doubled Die Obverse, cent is the most famous die error in the series. The date and all obverse lettering are dramatically doubled. As to how the coins were made, I inquired at the Philadelphia Mint and learned that, on a particular day in 1955, several presses were coining cents, dumping the coins into a box where they were then collected and mixed with the cents from other coining presses. Late in the afternoon a Mint inspector noticed the bizarre doubled cents and removed the offending die. By that time somewhat more than 40,000 cents had been produced, about 24,000 of which had been

mixed with normal cents from other presses. The decision was made to destroy the cents still in the box and to release into circulation the 24,000 or so pieces that were mixed with other cents. The Mint had no reason to believe that these would attract attention or have value with collectors. They were simply viewed as defective coins. It is likely that about 3,000 to 4,000 1955, Doubled Die Obverse, cents exist. All genuine pieces have the reverse die misaligned about 5 percent from the normal 180° rotation. Many counterfeits exist, so I recommend buying only coins that have been certified by one of the leading services.

MARKET VALUES • 1955, Doubled Die Obverse

VF-20	EF-40	AU-50	MS-63RB	MS-65RB	MS-65RD
$1,600	$1,750	$2,000	$3,500	$10,000	$30,000

1955-D

CIRCULATION MINTAGE: 563,257,500

Enlarged 1.5x
(actual size 19 mm)

MARKET VALUES • 1955-D

VF-20	EF-40	AU-50	MS-63RB	MS-65RB	MS-65RD	MS-67RD
$0.10	$0.12	$0.15	$0.35	$1	$9	$550

Key to Collecting: Common in all grades including gems with original color.

Striking and Sharpness: Often poor. Finding one with Full Details will be a challenge with this date and mint.

1955-S

CIRCULATION MINTAGE: 44,610,000

Enlarged 1.5x
(actual size 19 mm)

MARKET VALUES • 1955-S

VF-20	EF-40	AU-50	MS-63RB	MS-65RB	MS-65RD	MS-67RD
$0.20	$0.30	$0.40	$0.85	$3	$8	$115

Key to Collecting: Very scarce in circulated grades. Extremely common in Mint State, since millions of coins were snapped up by dealers and collectors. Cents for the year were last coined by March 24. Three years later in August 1958, during my visit there, the Oakland Coin Shop (of Leo A. Young and son Gary) had many bags of rolls stacked along one wall. Walter Breen (*Encyclopedia*, 1988) states that Robert Friedberg, operator of several dozen coin boutiques as leased facilities in department stores, had seven million.

Striking and Sharpness: Often with weakness in areas; few are needle-sharp.

THE YEAR 1956

In America: The economy was prosperous. Music was dominated by rock and roll, and cars by tail fins. The media and government continued to warn citizens that atomic war with the Soviet Union was a possibility.

In Numismatics: The coin market was very strong, with rolls and Proof sets leading the way. Lincoln cents remained the single most popular series to collect, most often inserted in blue Whitman folders, but for higher-grade collections, National, Popular, Meghrig, or other albums. Plastic holders were becoming increasingly popular, but mostly for use with series with fewer coins than Lincoln cents.

1956

CIRCULATION MINTAGE: 420,745,000

PROOF MINTAGE: 669,384

Enlarged 1.5x
(actual size 19 mm)

MARKET VALUES • 1956

VF-20	EF-40	AU-50	MS-63RB	MS-65RB	MS-65RD	MS-67RD
$0.10	$0.12	$0.15	$0.35	$1	$13	$450

MARKET VALUES • 1956, Proof

PF-65RD	PF-66RD	PF-67RD
$10	$25	$30

Key to Collecting: Common in all grades, although needle-sharp gems with original color are scarcer than one might expect due to poor workmanship at the Mint.

Striking and Sharpness: Varies, but many are sharp.

Proofs: Proofs are very common and are usually very attractive. Cameo contrast coins are in the minority but are readily available.

1956-D

CIRCULATION MINTAGE: 1,098,201,100

Enlarged 1.5x
(actual size 19 mm)

MARKET VALUES • 1956-D

VF-20	EF-40	AU-50	MS-63RB	MS-65RB	MS-65RD	MS-67RD
$0.10	$0.12	$0.15	$0.30	$1	$9	$325

Key to Collecting: Common in all grades.

Striking and Sharpness: Usually very good.

1956-D Doubled D Mintmark: Called "D Above Shadow D" in *A Guide Book of United States Coins.* The 1956-D cent variety with the mintmark sharply doubled, first punched too low (and now visible as a distinct but somewhat ghostlike image), was reported by several readers in the *Numismatic Scrapbook Magazine* in May 1962. Today the variety is extremely popular but  scarce, with early-die-state specimens selling at a healthy premium. Many gems have been certified. In my opinion, this is one of the most interesting repunched mintmarks in the entire series.

THE YEAR 1957

In America: Stunned by the launch of the Russian earth-orbiting *Sputnik* on October 4, America soon rushed to catch up in the space race. The Cold War standoff with the USSR continued.

In Numismatics: In the summer the ANA reported this was the first year the organization operated with a budget topping $100,000. Membership stood at 13,562. Long-time dealer B. Max Mehl died at his Fort Worth, Texas, home on September 27, ending a career that began in 1900. The final (18th) edition of the *Standard Catalogue of United States Coins* was published. The market for modern Proof sets crashed. Dr. Robert Bilinski promoted his *Guide to Coin Investment*, which he billed as "The most amazing report ever completed on investment practices within a hobby," which it may have been.

1957

CIRCULATION MINTAGE: 282,540,000

PROOF MINTAGE: 1,247,952

Enlarged 1.5x
(actual size 19 mm)

MARKET VALUES • 1957

VF-20	EF-40	AU-50	MS-63RB	MS-65RB	MS-65RD	MS-67RD
$0.10	$0.12	$0.15	$0.30	$1	$15	$1,850

MARKET VALUES • 1957, Proof

PF-65RD	PF-66RD	PF-67RD
$10	$25	$30

Key to Collecting: Common in all grades.

Striking and Sharpness: Usually excellent.

Proofs: Common, and usually attractive. Cameo contrast Proofs are scarcer, often with the contrast on only one side. During this era cameo Proofs were not deliberately made, but the Proof finish on some specimens resulted from early strikes from incompletely polished dies—before they self-polished from extended use.

1957-D

CIRCULATION MINTAGE: 1,051,342,000

Enlarged 1.5x
(actual size 19 mm)

MARKET VALUES • 1957-D

VF-20	EF-40	AU-50	MS-63RB	MS-65RB	MS-65RD	MS-67RD
$0.10	$0.12	$0.15	$0.30	$1	$9	$300

Key to Collecting: Common in all grades, as might be expected from a mintage that crossed the billion line.

Striking and Sharpness: Usually quite good. Full Details coins abound.

THE YEAR 1958

In America: The economy was in a short-lived slump. The first New York-to-London passenger jet flights were inaugurated by BOAC (British Overseas Airways Corporation) on October 4, but domestic jet travel was still two years away. The computer microchip was devised.

News About Lincoln Cents: In *The Numismatist* in September 1958 Daniel D. Wiseman of Austin, Minnesota, related that he and his wife had just finished an endeavor that occupied a full year: looking through a million cents. While they found no 1909-S V.D.B. coins, they picked out seven 1909-S, five 1914-D, "nearly a roll of 1924-D," and three 1931-S. Others included more than 35 Indian Head cents.

1958

CIRCULATION MINTAGE: 252,525,000

PROOF MINTAGE: 875,652

Enlarged 1.5x
(actual size 19 mm)

MARKET VALUES • 1958

VF-20	EF-40	AU-50	MS-63RB	MS-65RB	MS-65RD	MS-67RD
$0.10	$0.12	$0.15	$0.30	$1	$9	$400

MARKET VALUES • 1958, Proof

PF-65RD	PF-66RD	PF-67RD
$8	$20	$30

Key to Collecting: Common in all grades.

Striking and Sharpness: Varies, but most are well struck.

Proofs: Common and usually attractive. Cameo contrast pieces are less often seen, and those with deep contrast are rare.

1958, Doubled Die Obverse: The doubling on the date of this variety is very slight, but on the lettering it is dramatic. The "Collector's Clearinghouse" feature in *Coin World* observed that it was more dramatic than on the 1972, Doubled Die Obverse, but not comparable to that on the 1955, Doubled Die Obverse. It had been discovered about 1960 by a collector who looked

through a $50 face-value bag of 1958 cents. Walter Breen, in his 1988 *Encyclopedia*, noted that the doubling is plainest on LIBERTY and the motto, and that Charles Ludovico was the discoverer. In *Coin World*, October 17, 2005, editor Beth Deisher wrote:

> The finer of two known specimens of the 1958 Lincoln Doubled Die Obverse cent has been purchased by New York collector Stewart Blay in a private transaction for "in excess of $100,000," setting a record for a doubled die cent. Professional Coin Grading Service graded the coin Mint State-65 red in late September during the Long Beach Coin and Stamp Expo.[51]

The account noted that the other piece had been graded by ANACS, about the time it sold privately on July 12, 1996, for $25,025 as MS-64RD. In 2000 it was given the same grade by PCGS and it sold for $57,500.

It would seem that this would be a cherrypicker's dream coin. Despite much searching, this variety remains a great rarity, with just three reported. At the time the typical cent die was used for 800,000 to 1,000,000 impressions before being retired. Perhaps the doubling was noticed at an early time, and the die was removed from service.

1958-D

CIRCULATION MINTAGE: 800,953,300

Enlarged 1.5x
(actual size 19 mm)

MARKET VALUES • 1958-D

VF-20	EF-40	AU-50	MS-63RB	MS-65RB	MS-65RD	MS-67RD
$0.10	$0.12	$0.15	$0.30	$1	$8	$200

Key to Collecting: Common in all grades.

Striking and Sharpness: Varies, but most are well struck.

THE YEAR 1959

In America: Alaska (January 3) and Hawaii (August 21) joined the Union. Tail fins on automobiles reached their zenith in the Cadillac of this year, with the DeSoto and others mounting strong competition.

In Numismatics: 1958 and 1959 were good years for the collector, investor, and dealer alike. Anyone who purchased Proof sets at the reduced prices of those years would have no trouble in doubling or tripling his or her investment capital within the next five years, in the boom market of the early 1960s.

News About Lincoln Cents: The Lincoln cent was modified by Chief Engraver Frank Gasparro to the Lincoln Memorial reverse, replacing the "wheat ears" motif that had been in use since 1909. From this point on, when weakness is evident on cents, it will be evident on the portrait as before, but now also on the tiny figure of Lincoln within the Memorial and the shrubbery. Of course, it is important to check the rim and all other features as well.

THE MEMORIAL REVERSE TYPE INTRODUCED

Note to the reader: From 1959 to date, "Striking and Sharpness" aspects of coin quality are discussed within the "Key to Collecting" paragraphs.

1959

CIRCULATION MINTAGE: 609,715,000

PROOF MINTAGE: 1,149,291

Enlarged 1.5x
(actual size 19 mm)

MARKET VALUES • 1959, Proof

PF-65RD	PF-67RD	PF-67Cam	PF-68DCam
$3	$22	$55	$750

Key to Collecting: Common in all grades. First struck on January 2 and first released on February 12. Sharpness of strike varies, so cherrypick for sharpness.

Proofs: Common, and usually seen choice. Cameo contrast (better yet, deep cameo) coins are very popular and are often purchased in appropriately marked certified holders.

1959-D

CIRCULATION MINTAGE: 1,279,760,000

Key to Collecting: Common in all grades. Under magnification, many are found to have the mintmark repunched. This adds interest but typically not value, unless the repunching is spectacular. The same can be said for other Denver coins to follow, until the practice of adding mintmarks by hand was stopped. One variety has a triple-punched mintmark. Sharpness of strike varies, so cherrypick for sharpness.

A Curiosity: Beginning in the 1980s a purported 1959-D cent with the old-style "wheat ears" reverse made the news. A Secret Service agent who had taken a counterfeit detection course with the ANA suggested it was genuine, but his teacher, J.P. Martin, stated that while he had no specific evidence it was a counterfeit, his "gut instinct" was that it was not a Mint product.[52] PCGS founder David Hall stated he thought it was a fake. Others suggested it was genuine. Today the general opinion is that it is a fake.

THE YEAR 1960

In America: In a closely contested election for the presidency, John F. Kennedy beat Richard M. Nixon, ushering in a warm family-type aura to the White House, the first since the Theodore Roosevelt administration. The Cold War between the United States and the Soviet Union continued, with the latter's lead in the space race (landing the *Lunik II* on the moon) causing concern.

In Numismatics: On April 21 *Coin World*, the first weekly numismatic publication, was launched, with D. Wayne ("Dick") Johnson as editor. A year's subscription was $3. By August the ANA had more than 19,000 members, of whom 4,000 had been added in the preceding 12 months.

News About Lincoln Cents: At a New Netherlands Coin Co. sale on April 22, a "gem Uncirculated" 1909-S V.D.B. cent fetched $100, and a 1914-D brilliant Uncirculated cent, "with traces of tarnish," commanded $245. In May dealers Abner Kreisberg and Jerry Cohen offered a roll set (50 coins per roll) of Lincoln cents from 1934 to 1959 for $1,300.

Also in May, newspapers and television programs across America carried accounts of the fabulous, valuable, and rare 1960, Small Date, Lincoln cents. It was estimated that about two million of these were made in Philadelphia, and a much larger quantity in Denver. This electrified the numismatic community. Accounts were published of $50 face value bags (5,000 coins) selling for $12,000 or more. In August Mint Director William H. Brett pooh-poohed the idea that 1960, Small Date, cents would have any lasting value, noting that by August 23 some 235,915,000 cents had been produced at the Philadelphia Mint (strangely, without any reference at all to the Small Date variety).

The inauguration of *Coin World* on April 21 and in the next month the vast publicity and hoopla that developed for the 1960, Small Date, cent, plus an expanded interest in coins in general, served to ignite the market. Prices rose across the board, starting a boom that would last until 1964. Numismatics was a hot topic nationwide, and newcomers rushed to get in on anticipated large profits in the offing.

More About the Small Date Cents: The Small Date cents were made first. It was found at the Mint that the 0 in the date was too small and that the interior might break away on the die, causing the numeral to fill in (as it actually did on certain 1930-D Lincoln cents and 1960 Jefferson nickels). The date was made larger, but this was not announced. Soon Large Date cents replaced the Small Dates and were made in much larger quantities. At the Denver Mint the Small Date dies were used much longer before being replaced. The difference was not publicized until May, after which time Mint Director Brett, apparently acting on general policy and without specific knowledge, stated that all were from the same master hub and that there was no difference. Later the Mint admitted that, indeed, a change had been made. David W. Lange estimated the specific mintage of the Small Date:

> Some 2,075,000 cents were coined at the Philadelphia Mint in January before production was halted. None were struck in February, and then cents alone were coined in March and April as the mint attempted to make up for lost production. It's a reasonable assumption that the two million cents of January represent the total production of small-date 1960-P cents for circulation. The fact that the large date coins were found so early in the year tends to reinforce this theory. The balance of the 1960-P cent seems to have been of the large date variety.

Quick Test for Large and Small Dates: The Large Date has the top of the 1 in the date significantly lower than the top of the adjacent 9. On the Small Date the tops of 1 and 9 are at the same level.

Large Date (left) and Small Date Details

1960, SMALL DATE

CIRCULATION MINTAGE:
Estimated 2,075,000

PROOF MINTAGE: 1,691,602
(estimated 90 percent Large Date,
10 percent Small Date)

Enlarged 1.5x
(actual size 19 mm)

MARKET VALUES • 1960, Small Date, Proof

PF-65RD	PF-67RD	PF-67Cam	PF-68DCam
$22	$37	$55	$1,000

Key to Collecting: This is by far the more elusive of the two Philadelphia Mint varieties. The mintage estimate is that of David W. Lange. Many Small Date cents were saved by numismatists, with the result that examples, including well-struck choice and gem coins with original color, are readily available today. Circulated coins are very scarce. Most are well struck.

Proofs: Most examples survive as choice or gem specimens. With, say, an estimated mintage of 170,000 pieces, the Small Date is scarce in comparison to the Large Date. That figure is sufficiently large, however, that in the early twenty-first century there are enough in existence to give one to every unduplicated name in the ANA membership list and the subscriber lists to *Coin World* and *Numismatic News*. For a long time more Small Date than Large Date coins had been certified; this was because the Small Dates are worth more and thus more practical to have certified.

1960, LARGE DATE

CIRCULATION MINTAGE:
Estimated 586,405,000

PROOF MINTAGE: 1,691,602
(estimated 90 percent Large Date,
10 percent Small Date)

Enlarged 1.5x
(actual size 19 mm)

MARKET VALUES • 1960, Large Date, Proof

PF-65RD	PF-67RD	PF-67Cam	PF-68DCam
$2	$15	$25	$300

Key to Collecting: This is far and away the more common of the two Philadelphia Mint varieties. Sharpness of strike varies, so cherrypick for sharpness.

Proofs: These constitute the vast majority of Proofs, probably more than 1,600,000 coins. Most survive as gems today.

1960, Large Date Over Small Date, Proofs: These reflect overpunching of more than one Small Date die with a Large Date hub. Very slight doubling is seen at one side of the date numerals. Multiple dies have been identified. (FS-102 is illustrated.) These seem to be quite scarce, perhaps with a mintage of just 15,000 to 20,000.

1960-D, SMALL DATE

CIRCULATION MINTAGE:
1,580,884,000 (perhaps 30 percent Small Date, 70 percent Large Date)

Key to Collecting: Common in all grades including sharply struck gems. While these were made in lesser numbers than the Large Date, still hundreds of millions were certainly created. When the Small Dates were discovered, some thought that the Denver coins were nearly as scarce as the Philadelphia issues, but this did not prove to be the case. It might be conjectured that Small Date dies sent to Denver were kept in use until they were retired. There was no awareness, until May, of the date size differences, so coinage may have continued up to that time, or even longer. Sharpness of strike varies, so cherrypick for sharpness. Full Details coins are not hard to find.

1960-D, LARGE DATE

CIRCULATION MINTAGE:
1,580,884,000 (30 percent Small Date, 70 percent Large Date)

Key to Collecting: Very common in all grades. Sharpness of strike varies, so find one with Full Details.

1960-D, Large Date Over Small Date, Repunched D: Final D mintmark tilted slightly to the left, with earlier, smaller D mintmark appearing, ghostlike, mostly protruding above it. One of the most interesting varieties in the series—a "twofer" that shows the date and mintmark each with distinguishing features.

These constitute only a tiny fraction of the 1960-D, Large Date, mintage. Enough exist, however, including certified coins, that finding an example will be no problem.[53]

THE YEAR 1961

In America: The U.S. space program saw astronauts take sub-orbital space flights. The Kennedy family in the White House was a media delight, with wife Jackie being a favorite magazine cover subject. The covert Bay of Pigs operation, designed to topple Cuban dictator Fidel Castro, failed, and the government owned up to the responsibility.

In Numismatics: Two days after a September 21 nomination by President John F. Kennedy, Eva B. Adams was confirmed by the Senate as the new Mint director, succeeding William H. Brett. She soon viewed numismatists as adversaries to the Mint's interest and several years later made them shoulder the blame for a nationwide coin shortage. Still later she "got religion," learned about numismatics, and even gained a seat on the ANA board of governors.

News About Lincoln Cents: In a January message ANA president Admiral Oscar H. Dodson stated that 1960, Small Date, Lincoln cents were the "bottom rung of an adventurous and inspiring ladder." The excitement of the 1960, Small Date, cent had faded, but its effects remained since there were now tens of thousands of newcomers in the hobby, all eager to explore other series.

1961

CIRCULATION MINTAGE: 753,345,000

PROOF MINTAGE: 3,028,244

Enlarged 1.5x
(actual size 19 mm)

MARKET VALUES • 1961, Proof

PF-65RD	PF-67RD	PF-67Cam	PF-68DCam
$1.50	$23	$40	$300

Key to Collecting: Very common, since many rolls and bags were saved in this second year of the coin market boom. Sharpness of strike varies, so cherrypick to find one with Full Details.

Proofs: Common. Usually found at the gem level, and very attractive. Deep cameo Proofs are much less often seen.

1961-D

CIRCULATION MINTAGE: 1,753,266,700

Key to Collecting: Common in all grades including gem Mint State. Sharpness of strike varies, with some weakly struck and/or with poor luster. Not a problem if you search. There are many Full Details coins available.

1961-D, D Over Horizontal D: The first D was struck far on its side, to the left, not quite horizontal but dramatic in appearance. The second D was punched in the correct orientation. Scarce in comparison to regular coins, but likely hundreds of thousands were struck.

THE YEAR 1962

In America: The Cuban missile crisis confrontation between America and the USSR brought the nation closer than ever to the brink of nuclear war. The Soviets backed off and rerouted their ships on their way to Cuba, with weapons, back home. Unemployment had been inching up and now stood at 6.7 percent. The Seattle World's Fair, with its iconic Space Needle, attracted many visitors. The American economy suffered a setback, with market prices dropping in many areas, including stocks.

In Numismatics: On July 11, 1962, the government changed the designation of the San Francisco Mint to the San Francisco Assay Office. Contrary to the national economy, the coin market was on fire as the boom, ignited in 1960, continued to expand. Prices rose for almost all American series, from half cents to double eagles. Many coin shops opened, to the extent that within the next two years Chet Krause, publisher of *Numismatic News*, estimated that there were 6,000 or so nationwide. Just about every medium-size town had two or more, and large cities were apt to have more than a dozen.

In November hundreds of thousands of long-stored 1903-O Morgan silver dollars were released from a sealed vault in the Philadelphia Mint. These were the most valuable Morgan dollar variety at the time, cataloguing at $1,500 in the *Red Book*, with none higher. Collectors and dealers scrambled to acquire them, and at one point a bag of 1,000 coins could be bought for $4,000, equal to $4 per coin. This was like finding gold in the streets, and thousands more citizens rushed to discover the world of numismatics, further fueling the entire hobby.

News About Lincoln Cents: The alloy was changed this year from 95 percent copper, 5 percent tin and zinc (as it had been since 1946), to 95 percent copper, 5 percent zinc. The latter can be referred to as *brass*, because *bronze* is defined as copper with tin and, sometimes, other metals added, while brass is copper and zinc. Earlier, brass had been used intermittently for years, beginning in 1942.

1962

CIRCULATION MINTAGE: 606,045,000

PROOF MINTAGE: 3,218,019

Enlarged 1.5x
(actual size 19 mm)

MARKET VALUES • 1962, Proof

PF-65RD	PF-67RD	PF-67Cam	PF-68DCam
$1.50	$10	$15	$100

Key to Collecting: Common in all grades. Various die doublings and variations are found this year and for others of the era and are delineated in the Wexler-Flynn text. Most can be purchased without paying a premium. Full Details coins are readily available.

Proofs: Very common, including superb gems. Deep cameo Proofs are scarce.

1962-D

CIRCULATION MINTAGE: 1,793,148,140

Key to Collecting: Very common, but as David W. Lange notes, "Despite the large number of available specimens, true gems are difficult to find."

THE YEAR 1963

In America: In Washington on August 28, on the steps of the Lincoln Memorial, Rev. Dr. Martin Luther King gave his "I Have a Dream" speech as part of a rally attended by an estimated 200,000. On November 22 Lee Harvey Oswald fired a shot that killed President Kennedy. Vice President Lyndon B. Johnson was sworn in as chief executive the same day. The nation mourned.

In Numismatics: Teletype systems linked several hundred dealers by 1962 or 1963, and at one time the Professional Numismatists Guild even had its own network. The *Coin Dealer Newsletter* was launched and using Teletype data as a basis, listed bid and ask prices for rolls, Proof sets, and other items.

1963

CIRCULATION MINTAGE: 754,110,000

PROOF MINTAGE: 3,075,645

MARKET VALUES • 1963, Proof

PF-65RD	PF-67RD	PF-67Cam	PF-68DCam
$1.50	$10	$14	$55

Key to Collecting: Common in all grades. Hoarded in vast quantities by investors at the time, but many were probably cashed in later in the decade, when such passion subsided. Most are found well struck.

Proofs: Plentiful. Cameo contrast coins are easily obtained as well.

1963-D

CIRCULATION MINTAGE: 1,774,020,400

Enlarged 1.5x
(actual size 19 mm)

Key to Collecting: Common in all grades, although coins with good eye appeal are in the minority. Sharpness of strike varies: Perhaps most of the inferior strikes came from poorly prepared planchets (per David W. Lange). It is to be remembered that the obverse hub dies, slowly but surely over the decades, lost detail, with the result that a cent of 1963, or any other year in this era, will not hold a candle in detail to a cent of 1916 (when details were sharpened). A "good" strike in the modern era is one that, the hub considered, is good within the context of the era.

THE YEAR 1964

In America: The government announced that as of July 1 California became the most populous state, with New York now in second place. In the Gulf of Tonkin boats from North Vietnam were alleged to have attacked an American destroyer, prompting Congress, on August 7, to approve of military intervention in the area. Surely, the situation would be resolved quickly.

In Numismatics: This was one of the most pivotal years in numismatics. The government laid plans that would dramatically affect coinage, including Lincoln cents.

The great investment boom was still red hot early in 1964, but cooling winds of change soon arose. Counterfeits of key U.S. coins plagued the marketplace. The ANA published plans for a Headquarters building. (The location of Colorado Springs was decided upon and announced early in the next year.) In other ANA business, the Hall of Fame was instituted (and would become a very popular feature at Headquarters), and records were changed from paper files to IBM magnetic tape.

In the meantime the world price of silver metal was rising, despite the U.S. Treasury trying to maintain a uniform market value of $1.28 per ounce. The Treasury cache of older-date silver dollars, which had been draining since November 1962, became further depleted, until in March it was announced that only about three million were left, and no more would be paid out. In the same month the new Kennedy silver half dollar made its debut, and millions of coins were snapped up by the public—leaving none for general circulation. Citizens rushed to hoard ordinary silver dimes, quarters, and half dollars in circulation, and bank supplies became short. Soon the problem spread to common Lincoln cents, which virtually disappeared from pocket change, precipitating the worst coin shortage since the Civil War. The Treasury Department announced that the silver content of the dime, quarter, and half dollar would be reduced or eliminated entirely, in view of rising world prices of this precious metal. It became difficult for stores to make change, and some merchants advertised to pay premiums for rolls of common Lincoln cents to use in cash registers.

Eva Adams, director of the Mint, blamed this nationwide shortage on *coin collectors*, not the public, causing great consternation in numismatic circles. As punishment, mintmarks on coins were to be eliminated and the production of Proof sets was to be discontinued.

The market for rare coins remained very strong, although behind the scenes there were many worries about the price stability of rolls and Proof sets, these being investors' favorites.

News About Lincoln Cents: On September 28 the San Francisco Assay Office began to make planchets for cents and five-cent pieces. On September 1, 1965, the first time since 1955, the former San Francisco Mint began striking Lincoln cents. The dies were backdated to 1964 and did not have an S mintmark. Of the total mintage of 2,648,575,000 of mintmarkless 1964 cents, made in the style of the Philadelphia Mint, about 92 percent were struck in Philadelphia and 8 percent in San Francisco. The Denver Mint's 1964-D cents were all struck in Denver, in calendar year 1964.

1964

CIRCULATION MINTAGE: 2,648,575,000

PROOF MINTAGE: 3,950,762

Enlarged 1.5x
(actual size 19 mm)

MARKET VALUES • 1964, Proof

PF-65RD	PF-67RD	PF-67Cam	PF-68DCam
$1.50	$10	$11	$23

Key to Collecting: This is an extremely common issue, available in virtually endless quantities in just about any grade desired. Cents of the 1964 "Philadelphia" issue include some made in *1965 in San Francisco*, but without mintmarks (see The Year 1964, News About Lincoln Cents). Sharpness of strike varies, but so many were made that a relatively sharp example can be found easily. Keep in mind that by this time, many features of the portrait on the hubs had faded due to extensive use since modification in 1916.

Proofs: Usually seen in gem preservation, sometimes from dies that were too vigorously polished, removing design detail. Cameo Proofs, while in the minority, are plentiful. These are the last of the Philadelphia Mint Proofs. No Proofs were made until 1968, when the San Francisco Mint was employed in striking them.

1964-D

CIRCULATION MINTAGE: 3,799,071,500

Key to Collecting: Plentiful in all grades, although gems with good visual appeal are in the minority. Coins were struck from 1964-D dies in calendar year 1965 as well. Sharpness varies, and surfaces are often poor. Decent examples exist, however.

THE YEAR 1965

In America: College students protested against an assault, apparently undertaken with no plan of action and an uncertain outcome, against Communists in Southeast Asia (that by this time had become the Vietnam War). The surgeon general of the United States declared that smoking was dangerous to health and mandated that warnings be placed on cigarette packs.

In Numismatics: In January 1965 the coin market, to anyone reading *Coin World* or *Numismatic News,* seemed to be robust. Behind the scenes, however, seasoned collectors and dealers worried that the investment bubble, which began in 1960, would burst—the rate of price increases had been slowing. The bellwether roll of 40 1950-D nickels, now at $1,200, seemed to be vulnerable, as did many other rolls and Proof sets, these being investors' favorites. Special deals were being made to move such investment-type items. Buyers became scarce. All of a sudden, it was sell time. By the summer the 1950-D nickel roll was advertised for just $750 and headed further south. Meanwhile, the prices of scarce and rare coins remained strong, as reflected in price lists and auction results.

On July 23 President Lyndon B. Johnson signed the Coinage Act of 1965, which changed the metallic content of higher denomination coins and had other provisions, including making legal tender *any* coins previously struck at a federal mint.

Mint Director Eva Adams placed in operation her plan to mete out punishment to coin collectors for supposedly causing the nationwide shortage of circulated Lincoln cents and other coins. She eliminated mintmarks on coins struck at the Denver and San Francisco mints and stopped production of Proof sets. Moreover, she extended the date 1964 to December 29, 1965, for Lincoln cents and Jefferson nickels. These restrikes (for that is what they were) bore no special markings. Collectors were not completely overlooked—in the absence of Proof sets, the Mint made Special Mint Sets (SMS) with coins from specially polished dies (but not of full mirror Proof quality). New "clad" metal compositions were introduced for the dime, quarter, and half dollar. The San Francisco Mint, which had not been involved in coinage since 1955, resumed punching planchets for cents and nickels from metal strip. The planchets were shipped to Denver and San Francisco for coinage (but without D or S mintmarks).

News About Lincoln Cents: After the passage of the Coinage Act of 1965 the Treasury moved ten coin presses from the Denver Mint to the San Francisco Assay Office (earlier known as the San Francisco Mint), after which production of Lincoln cents commenced on September 1. The S mintmark was eliminated from these coins, and they were backdated 1964, to discourage hoarding. Production of cents with the 1965 date did not begin until December 29, 1965. Most of the cents of this date were struck in calendar year 1966 at the Denver Mint, and a lesser number at the San Francisco Mint, but without mintmarks. This production continued to July 1966. Only 1,085,000

1965-dated cents were actually struck in that year. Unfortunately, there is no die difference to distinguish these.

Special Mint Sets (SMS) were made and sold at a premium to collectors from this year through 1967, as a consolation for Proofs not being issued. These are well struck, from partially polished dies, and are usually very appealing. Some are quite mirrorlike.

1965

CIRCULATION MINTAGE: 1,497,224,900

SPECIAL MINT SET MINTAGE:
2,360,000 (about 62,000 unsold)

Enlarged 1.5x
(actual size 19 mm)

MARKET VALUES • 1965, Special Mint Set

PF-65RD	PF-67RD
$11	$55

Key to Collecting: Very common and struck at all three mints, mostly in calendar year 1966 (see The Year 1965, News About Lincoln Cents). Gems with good visual appeal are in the minority. Sharpness of strike varies, as does planchet quality.

Special Mint Set (SMS) coins: These are sharply struck and attractive, but normal planchets, instead of those carefully prepared and selected, were used. Most are not particularly distinctive, except for some that are prooflike. Some have handling marks, reflective of indifferent care taken at the Mint. Production from 1965-dated dies took place in early 1966. These are desirable and widely collected by specialists. Cherrypick for quality, and seek those that are somewhat prooflike.

THE YEAR 1966

In America: The unpopular Vietnam War continued to divide Americans, with nearly all men of draft age opposing it. The military effort seemed to be without a long-term strategy for winning.

In Numismatics: There were few happy numismatic campers. Long faces were everywhere. There was a nationwide scramble to pluck all pre-1965 silver coins from circulation, and not enough clad (no silver content) dimes and quarters had been struck so far to make up the shortage.

News About Lincoln Cents: Production of Special Mint Sets continued in lieu of Proofs. Striking of cents bearing this date took place at all three mints beginning in July 1966, as it had when the mints were restriking 1965-dated coins.

1966

CIRCULATION MINTAGE: 2,188,147,783

SPECIAL MINT SET MINTAGE:
2,261,583 (about 114,000 unsold)

Enlarged 1.5x
(actual size 19 mm)

MARKET VALUES • 1966, Special Mint Set

PF-65RD	PF-67RD
$10	$25

Key to Collecting: Very common in any desired grade, through ultra gem. Striking is usually excellent within the context of the faded details of the portrait during this era (corrected in 1969), but there are exceptions.

Special Mint Set (SMS) coins: SMS coins of this date were struck from polished planchets and from slightly polished dies, giving an improvement over the 1965 issues. Some show handling marks, usually minor. Nearly all are very attractive and closely resemble Proofs, yielding coins that are well worth owning, a significant improvement over the SMS of the previous year.

THE YEAR 1967

In America: The Vietnam War continued to alienate many citizens, who thought that the United States had no valid right or reason to be involved, while others stated that loyal Americans should support the military without equivocation.

In Numismatics: The fortunes of the ANA started looking up. On June 10 the headquarters building was dedicated, with more than 600 people on hand. On the same day a new ANA service, the Bureau of Numismatic Identification and Authentication, was launched. For a fee, coins could be submitted, and returned with a photograph and document of registration—useful as proof of ownership. The "Authentication" part was scheduled to come later, when facilities were expanded and experts hired.

The coin market continued to slump as buyers left the hobby. Investment-type coins remained out of vogue, but early issues, die varieties, and the like were in demand.

News About Lincoln Cents: This is the last year of Special Mint Sets, and also of placing no mintmark on coins struck at the Denver and San Francisco branch mints (although in the 1970s the practice would resume when San Francisco struck circulation cents without mintmarks). All Lincoln cents dated 1967 were actually struck in calendar year 1967, and no earlier-dated cents were made.

Mint Director Eva Adams supported Senate bill S.1008 to repeal the prohibition of mintmarks on U.S. coins. Some light was seen at the end of a dark numismatic tunnel. For the year, however, Lincoln cents and other coins remained mintmarkless.

1967

CIRCULATION MINTAGE: 3,048,667,100

SPECIAL MINT SET MINTAGE:
1,863,344 (about 27,000 unsold)

Enlarged 1.5x
(actual size 19 mm)

MARKET VALUES • 1967, Special Mint Set

MS-65RD	MS-67RD
$11	$42

Key to Collecting: Extremely common in any desired grade, as the mintage of more than three billion might suggest. The striking is usually quite good in the context of the era.

Special Mint Set (SMS) coins: Quality reached a high level, and most coins resemble full Proofs. Some have cameo contrast and are especially desirable.

THE YEAR 1968

In America: Civil rights leader Martin Luther King was assassinated in Memphis, and Senator Robert Kennedy met a similar fate in Los Angeles. President Johnson did not seek reelection, and veteran politician Richard Nixon was voted into the White House. On CBS *60 Minutes* was launched, becoming a staple for the network. Vast oil reserves were discovered in Alaska. The first ATM machine was placed in service. Credit cards were a way of life, with BankAmericard being perhaps the most popular. Other leading cards included Diners Club and Carte Blanche. *The Graduate* was a box-office hit.

In Numismatics: Proof set production was resumed, now at the San Francisco Assay Office (called this officially until 1988, but the San Francisco Mint in most popular usage), with each Proof being given an S mintmark. The San Francisco Mint also produced mintmarked circulation strikes for the first time since 1955.

News About Lincoln Cents: The mintage of Lincoln cents returned to normal in Philadelphia, Denver, and San Francisco, producing cents with a D mintmark, not seen since 1964, and S-marked coins, not seen since 1955. Proof cents, now with an S mintmark, were made for the first time since 1964.

The San Francisco Mint cents, struck for circulation, were eagerly sought and traded actively, usually in roll or bag quantities.

1968

CIRCULATION MINTAGE: 1,707,880,970

Key to Collecting: Common in any desired grade, into the gem category. Eye appeal can vary. Sharpness of strike varies, so cherrypick to find one with better-than-average sharpness—although by this year the portrait had many indistinct areas.

1968-D

CIRCULATION MINTAGE: 2,886,269,600

Key to Collecting: Common in all grades. Usually well struck in relation to the dies themselves, considering that by this time, the details on the master hub were often light.

1968-S

CIRCULATION MINTAGE: 258,270,001

PROOF MINTAGE: 3,041,506

Enlarged 1.5x
(actual size 19 mm)

MARKET VALUES • 1968-S, Proof

PF-65RD	PF-67RD	PF-67Cam	PF-68DCam
$1	$12	$16	$50

Key to Collecting: Common in all grades, although in circulation this and subsequent S-marked coins are seen infrequently in comparison to Philadelphia and Denver issues. Very popular with investors, bags of 1968-S cents found a ready market. Sharpness of strike varies; it is often weak because the portrait was "mushy" by this time.

Proofs: Usually attractive and seen at the gem level. Over-polishing of the dies removed lower-relief details on some. Cameo and deep cameo coins are especially desired. Certification figures are of little meaning, although those building Registry Sets can take note of what has been certified at Proof-68RD and higher—this comment holding true for later Proofs as well. Of the 3,031,506 Proof cents struck this year, fewer than one out of every 3,000 have been submitted to the several certification services combined. *Be careful of any Proofs of this era that are "rare" only because of low population report figures.*

THE YEAR 1969

In America: American astronauts Neil A. Armstrong and Edwin E. Aldrin Jr. became the first humans to walk on the moon. In Bethel, New York, near the town of Woodstock, a half million young people gathered in August for four days of drinking, drugs, music, sex, and other revelry.

News About Lincoln Cents: In 1969 the obverse was modified, with differences in several areas and sharpening of features. The relief of the obverse was lowered, permitting more consistent striking of details. A quick way to identify the modification is to check the highest wave of Lincoln's hair. On issues of 1969 and later it is directly under the W in WE. Earlier it was to the left, between GOD and WE. The modifications ended a generation of coins with lack of needle-sharp details due to wear on hub dies. A quick way to discern the differences in sharpness is by comparing a 1968-S Proof with one of 1969-S.

1969

CIRCULATION MINTAGE: 1,136,910,000

Key to Collecting: First year of the modified obverse portrait and features. Common in all grades including gem. Full details coins are common. 1969 Philadelphia Mint "Doubled Die" cents, details concerning which can be found in the Wexler-Flynn and Lange texts, are fakes (San Francisco issues are genuine).

1969-D

CIRCULATION MINTAGE: 4,002,832,200

Key to Collecting: Common in all grades including gem. Usually well struck.

1969-S

CIRCULATION MINTAGE: 544,375,000
PROOF MINTAGE: 2,934,631

Enlarged 1.5x
(actual size 19 mm)

MARKET VALUES • 1969-S, Proof

PF-65RD	PF-67RD	PF-67Cam	PF-68DCam
$1	$11	$13	$33

Key to Collecting: Common on an absolute basis. Popular with investors, and large quantities were saved in gem Mint State. Scarce in circulation, in comparison to Philadelphia and Denver coins. Usually well struck.

Proofs: Usually of high quality. Cameo Proofs, especially, are in demand. David W. Lange reported that some were struck from a broken die, and these are rare.

1969-S, Doubled Die Obverse: The date and lettering are well doubled on the obverse, not as dramatically as for the 1955, Doubled Die Obverse, but appearing especially clear under low magnification. Gems exist, as the population data indicate, but are rare. Discovery of this variety made front-page news in *Coin World*, July 8, 1970. The Secret Service went on a witch hunt for these, believing they were counterfeits in the style of fake Philadelphia Mint doubled dies (see 1969 entry). By the time these were acknowledged as legitimate, five genuine coins had been destroyed. (See the Wexler-Flynn text for dramatic details and identification of the cast of characters in this sorry situation.)

Caveat: Some 1969-S circulation strikes from regular dies, but with "machine doubling" or die chatter during the coining process, have been offered or even certified (but not by one of the top three or four services) as the Doubled Die Obverse. Machine-doubled coins will have the S mintmark doubled, whereas the Doubled Die does not.

THE YEAR 1970

In America: Increasingly, youths, particularly those of draft age, were disenchanted with the Vietnam War and engaged in many protests. The "drug culture," destroying the lives of many people, singers Janis Joplin and Jimi Hendrix among them, was almost everywhere. Events in New York the year before precipitated the formation of many gay and lesbian advocacy groups in 1970, as LGBTQ Americans coalesced in their desire for equal rights. Overseas the bar code and the LCD (liquid crystal display) went into use, and soon would reach the United States.

In Numismatics: Optimism was the byword in the hobby. The ANA continued its progress on its Authentication Trust development. Membership rose by 1,000 names and now stood at 24,780, and new strength was being felt in the coin market. James F. Ruddy launched *Photograde*, a photographic guide to grading coins, which became a runaway bestseller and inspired confidence in those who used it.

News About Lincoln Cents: Two hub varieties were made this year. The Large Date was used on Philadelphia and Denver cents, and both Large and Small dates on San Francisco cents. From the Wexler-Flynn text, *The Authoritative Reference on Lincoln Cents:*

1970 Philadelphia, Denver, and San Francisco Large Date: Thinner space between digits. Inside of 0 larger. Top of 7 below 9 and 0. Top of 0 comes to a point. Bottom of 7 comes to a point. LIBERTY has clear, distinct letters.

1970-S, Small Date: More space between digits. Inside of 0 smaller. Top of 7 even with top of 9 and 0. Top of 0 well rounded; bottom of 7 is squared. LIBERTY usually has mushy letters with the TY much weaker.

1970

CIRCULATION MINTAGE: 1,898,315,000

Key to Collecting: Large Date only. Common in all grades including gem Mint State. Usually well struck.

1970-D

CIRCULATION MINTAGE: 2,891,438,900

Key to Collecting: Large Date only. Common in all grades. Usually well struck.

1970-S

CIRCULATION MINTAGE:
690,560,004 (mostly Large Date)

PROOF MINTAGE:
2,632,810 (mostly Large Date)

Enlarged 1.5x
(actual size 19 mm)

MARKET VALUES • 1970-S, Small Date (High 7) Proof

PF-65RD	PF-67RD	PF-67Cam
$40	$65	$150

MARKET VALUES • 1970-S, Large Date (Low 7) Proof

PF-65RD	PF-67RD	PF-67Cam	PF-68DCam
$1	$15	$25	$65

Key to Collecting: Two date sizes, from this mint only, this year: Small Date (higher 7, level with the top of 0) and Large Date (lower 7)—the Small Date being rare in the context of the series. The Large Date is common in all grades. All S-marked cents of this era are few and far between in general circulation. Bags and rolls of the Large Date were widely hoarded, thus gems are easy to find in quantity. Usually well struck.

1970-S, Small Date: Certification numbers cannot be compared to those of the Large Date, since the valuable Small Dates were certified in proportionately larger numbers.

1970-S, Large Date: This is plentiful in numismatic hands.

1970-S, Large Date, Doubled Die Obverse: Slight doubling is seen on the date, and significant doubling is seen on the peripheral lettering. This issue, listed in *A Guide Book of United States Coins*, remains very rare, despite intensive searching through hoarded cents of this date.

Proofs: Made in Small Date and Large Date varieties as described, the Small Date being just a fraction of the overall mintage of Proofs.

1970-S, Small Date, Proofs: Certification numbers cannot be compared to the Large Date, as the valuable Small Dates were certified in proportionately larger numbers. Deep cameo Proofs are especially rare.

1970-S, Large Date, Proofs: Most Proofs are of this variety.

THE YEAR 1971

In America: The Vietnam War continued to cause civil dissension. Inflation was rampant, and in August the government clamped a freeze, for 90 days, on wages and prices.

In Numismatics: Although the market crash of 1965 was history, little buying energy was evident in Lincoln cents and other twentieth-century series. Sales of Morgan dollars, hyperactive since the Treasury release beginning in November 1962, cooled down a bit. Paper money, more or less quiet for years, became a hot spot in the market. Gold coins were in the spotlight with lots of action, a trend that would continue into the next year.

The Philadelphia Mint took delivery of an improved Janvier engraving machine, a precision device that made master hubs from artists' models. The Eisenhower dollar made its debut.

1971

CIRCULATION MINTAGE: 1,919,490,000

Enlarged 1.5x
(actual size 19 mm)

Key to Collecting: Common in all grades including gem. David W. Lange points out that, excepting San Francisco issues, some issues of this period may be "rare" in *bag* quantities, a situation not of much significance to the majority of numismatists. Usually well struck.

1971-D

CIRCULATION MINTAGE: 2,911,045,000

Key to Collecting: Common as can be, including gems. Finding Full Details coins is not a problem for most circulation strikes of this era.

1971-S

CIRCULATION MINTAGE: 525,133,459

PROOF MINTAGE: 3,220,733

MARKET VALUES • 1971-S, Proof

PF-65RD	PF-67RD	PF-67Cam	PF-68DCam
$1	$18	$30	$120

Key to Collecting: Very common because at the time San Francisco coins in rolls were especially appealing to investors. Usually well struck.

Proofs: Usually of superb quality, including with cameo contrast. *Deep* cameo contrast coins are scarce.

1971-S, Doubled Die Obverse, Proof: Slight doubling is especially noticeable on the letters. A detail showing LIBERTY is illustrated here. This variety forms only a small percentage of the total Proof issue. Its listing in *A Guide Book of United States Coins* has stimulated demand. Breen dismisses its importance: "Minutely doubled obverse dies exist; they command little premium over normal Proofs. Though very rare."

THE YEAR 1972

In America: President Nixon sought reelection in a campaign against Democratic opponent George McGovern and won, despite annoying allegations of what would develop into the Watergate scandal, by a landslide. In December large-scale bombing in North Vietnam was halted, in a reversal of Nixon's directive earlier in the year. On November 14, for its first time going over 1,000, the Dow-Jones Industrial Average closed at 1,003.16.

In Numismatics: Plastic holders were in vogue for storing and displaying individual coins as well as sets. Hooray! A new market and investment boom, focused on gold coins, was underway. Prices went up and up. Dealers and collectors again had warm feelings about the hobby. The ANA Certification Service (ANACS) was set up in Washington, D.C., with Charles R. Hoskins as director. The location was chosen so as to be near Secret Service and Treasury facilities as well as, for reference, the National Coin Collection at the Smithsonian Institution.

1972

CIRCULATION MINTAGE: 2,933,255,000

Enlarged 1.5x
(actual size 19 mm)

Key to Collecting: Common in all grades including superb gem Mint State. Usually well struck.

1972, Doubled Die Obverse: Creating a sensation soon after it was released, this variety became an instant "must-have" coin for thousands of collectors. John Wexler suggested that 75,000 were released, many more than the 20,000 estimated by Sol Taylor. No information has been seen as to why this die was removed from use. Today this is one of the most popular varieties in the Lincoln series. Multiple genuine obverse dies exist for this issue (see Fivaz-Stanton). Counterfeits are also common. My advice is to buy coins certified by the leading services.

1972-D

CIRCULATION MINTAGE: 2,665,071,400

Key to Collecting: Common in all grades including gem Mint State. Usually well struck.

1972-S

CIRCULATION MINTAGE: 376,939,108

PROOF MINTAGE: 3,260,996

MARKET VALUES • 1972-S, Proof

PF-65RD	PF-67RD	PF-67Cam	PF-68DCam
$1	$15	$20	$35

Key to Collecting: Common in all grades, although diluted in circulation by greater numbers of Philadelphia and Denver cents. Full Details coins are easily found.

Proofs: Common, including with cameo contrast.

THE YEAR 1973

In America: A cease-fire was declared in Vietnam on January 28. Throughout the year the Watergate affair consumed the media, as key administration people resigned or were fired. Following an unrelated corruption investigation, Vice President Spiro T. Agnew resigned, to be replaced by Representative Gerald Ford, speaker of the House, per Constitutional rules.

In Numismatics: ANACS expanded its service of inspecting coins and pronouncing upon their authenticity or lack thereof. The market continued its strength, and "trophy" rarities were very much in demand, with gold coins especially in the spotlight. Silver dollars were among the most actively sought series.

News About Lincoln Cents: The reverse hub was modified slightly, and the initials FG, for Frank Gasparro, were considerably enlarged and some design details were sharpened. In the next year the size of FG was reduced slightly.

1973

Circulation Mintage: 3,728,245,000

Enlarged 1.5x
(actual size 19 mm)

Key to Collecting: Common in all grades including gem Mint State. Usually well struck. On any of the cents of this era, check the high points of Lincoln on the obverse, and on the reverse check the tiny statue at the center of the Memorial, and the shrubbery.

1973-D

Circulation Mintage: 3,549,576,588

Key to Collecting: Common in all grades including gem Mint State, but scarce in MS-66RD and rare at MS-67RD, based on certified populations. Seemingly, this is a good coin for cherrypicking if you can find some original rolls. Usually well struck.

1973-S

Circulation Mintage: 317,177,295

Proof Mintage: 2,760,339

Market Values • 1973-S, Proof

PF-65RD	PF-67RD	PF-67Cam	PF-68DCam
$1	$13	$16	$30

Key to Collecting: Easily enough found today, since many millions were saved. In circulation, however, they are few and far between in comparison to the issues of Philadelphia and Denver. When these first came out, they were the object of wild and frantic speculation, with $50 face value bags selling for $700 or more because the Mint was slow in releasing them, and it seemed to some that a rarity was in the offing. With good judgment, Mint Director Mary Brooks directed that remaining stocks be mixed with Denver and Philadelphia coins and placed into circulation. This was mostly done in 1974 and effectively removed the possibility of anyone getting more $50 bags (while at the same time making the coins available to collectors looking through pocket change). Usually all are well struck.

Proofs: Common. Most, of this era and later, have deep cameo contrast, although labeling varies on certified holders.

The Year 1974

In America: The Watergate scandal continued to unfold, sweeping up many of the Nixon insiders in perjury and scandal. Nixon resigned on August 8, becoming the first president to take such a step. Gerald Ford was sworn in as president, becoming the first to hold the office without being elected as either president or vice president. In a controversial move, he completely pardoned Nixon on September 8.

In Numismatics: Gold coins were front-row center in the eyes of investors, and prices continued to increase. As of May 31 of that year, the ANA had a record 28,021 members.

News About Lincoln Cents: Throughout the year there was a shortage of cents in commercial and banking circles. With the price of copper rising, as an experiment the Mint struck some cents in aluminum (see 1974 and 1974-D entries). Otherwise, it was believed, record quantities of brass (or, familiarly but inaccurately, *bronze*) cents would need to be made, and if the price of metal continued to increase, cents would be hoarded. The price fell, however, the aluminum cents were almost (but not completely) forgotten, and the public turned its mind to other things.

In the summer the West Point Bullion Depository, with a staff of about 50 people, was marshaled into service as a mint to strike cents. Millions of coins were produced there, but since they bore no mintmark, they were not collectible as such. This was the last year that circulation-strike cents made at San Francisco bore an S mintmark.

The designer's initials were slightly reduced but remained larger than on the 1972 style (see 1973 entry). Two obverse hub changes were made: one with very sharp details, used only in 1974; the other with less detail, used through 1982. David W. Lange calls the first the Large Date and the second the Small Date, although he notes that the only *significant* distinction is that on the Small Date the date is farther from the border. These varieties have not attracted wide notice in the collecting community and are not listed in the *Guide Book*.

David W. Lange discussed the changes of this year:

> Of particular interest to collectors, at least those with sharp eyes, are the subtle changes that occurred during 1974. The obverse master hub created in 1969 and used thereafter through 1973 was replaced with a dramatically sharpened portrait for the 1974 cent coinage. In addition to more distinct lettering, numeral 7 of the date received a shorter horizontal segment and a long, curving arc to its diagonal segment. Finally, the Lincoln bust was given a more robust character, his wavy hair being bolder and more sharply delineated from his ear.
>
> Dies generated from this new and very attractive obverse hub were used by all four mints active at that time. This included West Point which, like Philadelphia, coined cents without a mintmark. Strangely, however, this obverse hub was replaced with another one midway through 1974, resulting in two subtypes for the Lincoln cents dated 1974. This hub, too, was used to sink dies for all the mints, resulting in a total of six collectable cent varieties for 1974. All of the 1974-S proofs appear to be from the first hub, as the proofs were made early in that year.
>
> The second obverse of 1974 differed from the first in being of faintly lower relief and having duller details in Lincoln's hair. A noticeable blending of Lincoln's ear with the surrounding hair further aggravated this loss of boldness. Finally, the new master hub had been mechanically reduced to a slightly smaller diameter than the first. This provided greater separation of peripheral elements from the coin's border, but it also made the entire design slightly smaller overall. This is perhaps most noticeable in the greater distance between the date and adjacent border on the revised hub.[54]

1974

CIRCULATION MINTAGE: 4,232,140,523

Key to Collecting: Common in all grades. Mintmarkless coins struck at West Point cannot be differentiated from Philadelphia issues. Usually well struck.

1974 Aluminum Cent: In late 1973 the rising price of copper prompted the Mint to investigate making cents in aluminum. Seven different alloys, combining various metals with 96 percent aluminum, were tested using 1974-dated dies. Mint Director Mary Brooks passed out samples, making no statement that they had to be returned. They went to nine congressmen and four senators, and some went to Mint staff. Others went to Treasury officials. Apparently, no account of the distribution was made because no one thought these pieces would become numismatically interesting, rare, or valuable. News of this excited collectors, and it was hoped that some would reach the market, where they certainly would become expensive rarities. Brooks sought to have the recipients bring their coins back, but 14 remained missing. The FBI and others got into the act and interviewed the congressmen, whose recollections were fuzzy at best—complete with denials that such coins had ever been received—and no more were returned. Mint records reveal that 1,571,167 such aluminum cents were struck in anticipation of their use.

Speculation arose in numismatic circles as to the legality of these aluminum cents should an example come to light. The matter was moot—none had been seen in the marketplace. Then in 2001 one surfaced and was featured in *Numismatic News*, in a February 20 article by Alan Herbert. The coin is said to have been found, after a congressman had dropped it on the floor of the Rayburn Office Building, by Albert Toven, a U.S. Capitol police officer. Seeking to return it, Toven was told by the congressman to keep it. In 2005 it was certified as AU-58 by the Independent Coin Grading Company (ICG). Less than two months later it had "graduated" from the AU level to MS-62 in a PCGS holder. A discussion printed in *Coin World* ("Aluminum 1¢ Changes Grade," by Paul Gilkes, October 17, 2005) quoted ICG founder Keith Love as saying, "The ICG graders were unanimous in calling the coin AU-58." David Hall, principal at PCGS, stated that graders there all pronounced it to be Uncirculated. (Readers who believe that grading is scientific, please take note!) Another example is in the National Numismatic Collection in the Smithsonian Institution.

Some experimental coins, in bronze-clad steel, were also made, as were strikings of approximately cent-sized coins from dies with "nonsense" descriptions, to test various compositions.

1974-D

CIRCULATION MINTAGE: 4,235,098,000

Key to Collecting: Common in all grades. Usually well struck.

Notes: An aluminum 1974-D exists, although a lawsuit between the heir of the owner and the U.S. government determined that the piece was struck and removed from the Mint without the proper authorization, making it the property of the U.S. government. The heir, Randall Lawrence, had contended that his father, former deputy director of the Denver Mint Harry Lawrence, had received the cent as part of a retirement gift from his superiors. This did not prove to be enough to sway the courts.

1974-S

CIRCULATION MINTAGE: 409,426,660

PROOF MINTAGE: 2,612,568

Enlarged 1.5x
(actual size 19 mm)

MARKET VALUES • 1974-S, Proof

PF-65RD	PF-67RD	PF-67Cam	PF-68DCam
$1	$13	$16	$30

Key to Collecting: Common in all grades due to hoarding. In circulation, these and other San Francisco cents of the era are scarce in proportion to those from Philadelphia and Denver. Many were released mixed with Denver and Philadelphia cents, as had been done with the 1973-S. Full Details coins are common.

Proofs: Cameo contrast is the rule, with deep cameos being in the minority but still plentiful. Proofs are from the new hub, used only this year, with the portrait details slightly sharper.

THE YEAR 1975

In America: Economic conditions, beset by inflation, continued to worsen. The unemployment rate was 8.5 percent. The Republic of South Vietnam collapsed, ending the war with not a decisive victory, but a whimper.

In Numismatics: Ownership of gold bullion became legal a wink after midnight on December 31, 1974. The price of the metal had been floating free on the market and had touched $200 per ounce. In the biennial ANA election, Virgil Hancock was the winner. In August president Hancock assigned dealer Abe Kosoff the task of coordinating the preparation of an official ANA coin grading system, to be published in book form. Work soon got underway. From his home in Palm Springs, California, Kosoff corresponded with collectors, dealers, and others to get their ideas.

News About Lincoln Cents: All told, the year was healthy in the numismatic hobby, except for the popularity of Mint Director Mary Brooks. Nearly 10 *billion* cents were struck this year. Circulation-strike cents, produced at the San Francisco Mint by the many millions, were made without S mintmarks, giving them the appearance of Philadelphia coins. Brooks thought that this would minimize the hoarding of such cents, which, no doubt, it did. Proofs were of the 1975-S variety.

1975

CIRCULATION MINTAGE: 5,451,476,142

Enlarged 1.5x
(actual size 19 mm)

Key to Collecting: Common in all grades, as the immense mintage indicates. Mintmarkless coins struck at West Point and San Francisco cannot be differentiated from Philadelphia issues. Usually well struck.

1975-D

CIRCULATION MINTAGE: 4,505,275,300

Key to Collecting: Common in all grades including gem Mint State. Usually well struck.

1975-S

PROOF MINTAGE: 2,845,450

MARKET VALUES • 1975-S, Proof

PF-65RD	PF-67RD	PF-67Cam	PF-68DCam
$3.50	$13	$16	$30

Proofs: Mostly made with cameo contrast, much less often with deep cameo contrast. Popular as a "Proof only" date. While the San Francisco Mint struck cents for circulation, these did not have a mintmark and appeared the same as Philadelphia issues. From this year onward, S-marked Proofs have this special cachet and are thus essential for the completion of a date-and-mintmark collection.

THE YEAR 1976

In America: President Ford, handicapped by public dislike of his pardon of Nixon, and Jimmy Carter faced each other in the November presidential election. Carter won. The economy continued to be ravaged by uncontrolled inflation. The Bicentennial was celebrated. In New York City harbor, a fleet of tall ships attracted attention. Many towns published small bicentennial histories.

In Numismatics: The national economy was in recessionary times, and the coin market was largely a fizzle—unusual, because the coin market often moves contrary to the economy. Gold had lost its luster, new faces were few and far between, and even rarities such as Proof gold were not exciting to buyers. In retrospect, this was one of the most favorable years to buy, for many prices were cheap. Numismatic interest in Bicentennial coins, including Proofs, fell short of expectations. In the autumn ANACS relocated from Washington, D.C., to ANA Headquarters in Colorado Springs. Association membership declined slightly.

1976

CIRCULATION MINTAGE: 4,674,292,426

Enlarged 1.5x
(actual size 19 mm)

Key to Collecting: Common in all grades including gem Mint State. Sharp strikes can be easily found. Mintmarkless coins struck at West Point cannot be differentiated from Philadelphia issues.

1976-D

CIRCULATION MINTAGE: 4,221,592,455

Key to Collecting: Common in all grades including gem Mint State. Sharp strikes can be easily found.

1976-S

PROOF MINTAGE: 4,149,730

MARKET VALUES • 1976-S, Proof

PF-65RD	PF-67RD	PF-67Cam	PF-68DCam
$3.20	$13	$16	$30

Proofs: Common with typical cameo contrast. Deep cameo cents are in the minority. Proof set production reached a high (to this point in time) this year due to demand for Bicentennial coins. By year's end, however, some sets remained unsold.

THE YEAR 1977

In America: Inflation continued to be out of control, with interest rates rising to dizzying heights—driving up costs and creating still more inflation. The average American household earned $13,572: not enough for many to maintain their standard of living.

In Numismatics: Following a launch ceremony on November 18, the Whitman Publishing Company distributed the *ANA Official Grading Standards for United States Coins* book.

1977

CIRCULATION MINTAGE: 4,469,930,000

Key to Collecting: Common in all grades including gem Mint State. Mintmarkless coins struck at West Point cannot be differentiated from Philadelphia issues. "Overdate" 1977, 7 Over 6, cents caused some notice this year but were found to be counterfeits. Full Details coins are common.

1977-D

CIRCULATION MINTAGE: 4,194,062,300

Key to Collecting: Common in all grades including gem Mint State. Sharp strikes can be easily found.

1977-S

PROOF MINTAGE: 3,251,152

Enlarged 1.5x
(actual size 19 mm)

MARKET VALUES • 1977-S, Proof

PF-65RD	PF-67RD	PF-67Cam	PF-68DCam
$2.50	$13	$16	$30

Proofs: Common. Usually found with cameo contrast, less often with deep cameo contrast.

THE YEAR 1978

In America: The Carter administration continued to be troubled with inflation, now at an annual rate of 8 percent, against a productivity increase, for the year, of only 0.4 percent, and reckless government spending. It was revealed that it cost $2 to deliver $1 in aid or public welfare.

In Numismatics: Under John Hunter and Ed Fleischmann, ANACS in Colorado Springs did a land-office business reviewing coins for authentication. The threat to the hobby from counterfeiting, a focal point of attention in recent years, was diminishing. ANA membership continued to slide and now was 29,369. The coin market was in fine shape, flying high, with auctions achieving record prices. Increased interest in bullion silver and gold brought more buyers into the market.

1978

CIRCULATION MINTAGE: 5,558,605,000

Enlarged 1.5x
(actual size 19 mm)

Key to Collecting: Common in all grades including gem Mint State. Mintmarkless coins struck at San Francisco and West Point cannot be differentiated from Philadelphia issues. Full Details coins are common.

1978-D

CIRCULATION MINTAGE: 4,280,233,400

Key to Collecting: Common in all grades including gem Mint State. Sharp strikes can be easily found.

1978-S

PROOF MINTAGE: 3,127,781

MARKET VALUES • 1978-S, Proof

PF-65RD	PF-67RD	PF-67Cam	PF-68DCam
$2.50	$13	$16	$30

Proofs: Common. Deep cameo contrast was the norm, not the exception, continuing from this year onward.

THE YEAR 1979

In America: America became increasingly dependent on foreign oil and had no control of the price charged for it by such "allies" as Saudi Arabia and Venezuela. In October the Federal Reserve, in an effort to control the money supply, raised the discount rate to 12 percent, causing stock and bond prices to drop. Many banks raised the prime rate to 14.5 percent. Fear of holding money increased, and people rushed to acquire tangible things, including gold and silver. The typical citizen was ill at ease—with the economic crystal ball cloudy. At year's end the Dow-Jones Industrial Average was at 838.

In Numismatics: The ANA Certification Service (ANACS) expanded into the grading of coins for a fee. Prices of silver and gold bullion rose to record highs, and the excitement carried over into the market for rare coins. Auctions realized record prices, and retail sales were excellent everywhere. Scarce and rare coins in many series soared to previously unheard-of levels—often several times the market values of a decade earlier.

1979

CIRCULATION MINTAGE: 6,018,515,000

Key to Collecting: Common in all grades including gem Mint State. Mintmarkless coins struck at San Francisco and West Point cannot be differentiated from Philadelphia issues. Full Details coins are common.

1979-D

CIRCULATION MINTAGE: 4,139,357,254

Key to Collecting: Common in all grades including gem Mint State. Sharp strikes can be easily found. Examples exist without the FG initials on the reverse, resulting from either weak striking or dressing the face of the die too harshly (most likely). In many other instances in this era, the FG initials can be weak in areas. These are of no commercial importance.

1979-S

PROOF MINTAGE: 3,677,175

Enlarged 1.5x
(actual size 19 mm)

MARKET VALUES • 1979-S, Filled S, Proof

PF-65RD	PF-67RD	PF-67Cam	PF-68DCam
$5	$11	$13	$17

MARKET VALUES • 1979-S, Clear S, Proof

PF-65RD	PF-67RD	PF-67Cam	PF-68DCam
$6	$17	$20	$30

Proofs With "Filled S": Variety with old-style S punch, filled in at the center, making it appear as a blob. Deep cameo contrast.

Proofs With "Clear S": Variety with new punch, well defined at the center. Scarcer of the two varieties, but not dramatically so. Deep cameo contrast. These S mintmark variations are known across the other Proof denominations and are considered scarce only for the Kennedy half dollar and the Susan B. Anthony dollar. This same punch was used in 1980.

THE YEAR 1980

In America: By November Republican contender Ronald Reagan wiped out President Carter's bid for reelection. In the meantime interest rates were at a record high for the twentieth century, and gasoline and energy costs were up. Ted Turner launched CNN, a round-the-clock news programming channel, in Atlanta. The movie *Coal Miner's Daughter* was boffo at the box office. On May 18 Mount Saint Helens exploded in a volcanic eruption, darkening the skies and spreading millions of tons of rock and ash. On November 21 a television viewership record was set with the "Who Shot J.R.?" episode of *Dallas.*

In Numismatics: By 1979 coin investment was one of the hottest things going, and by early 1980 prices were riding a crest. Numerous editors of newsletters, "hard money" advocates, and others proclaimed that anyone holding paper dollars was a fool, an idiot, or worse. Gold (and to a lesser extent, silver) was the only way to go. Early in the year gold hit an all-time high of $873 per ounce and silver $49.50 per ounce. By this time most *serious numismatists* were sitting on the sidelines and not buying any of the hot coins that investors were lapping up. In the spring dealers and investors zipped up their wallets, buyers of "investment grade" coins were nowhere to be seen, and the market for such coins plunged.

Soft clear polyvinyl chloride (PVC) envelopes had become a very popular way to store coins, and many collectors, dealers, and auction houses used them. Alarms were sounded, including this by Edward Cohen in *The Numismatist:*

> I am greatly concerned about long term storage of coins in vinyl flips. I, as well as a close friend, have noticed green corrosion developing on copper, copper-nickel, brass, and other base metal coins stored in these flips. We both use quality flips. Corrosion starts to appear after two years and is most evident after two years as a green circle on flip. After 10 years, corrosion is well into central surface of coin. Base metal coins within a few years lose their brilliance.
>
> For coins stored in Mylar, cardboard holders I have never had a problem. I get no sympathy from dealers in this matter. I believe collectors should know about the problem. Subsequently warnings about vinyl flips were issued in the hobby, but, curiously, the manufacturers and distributors of same remained silent on the subject. Countless coins, particularly those containing copper or nickel, were damaged.
>
> Many of these were rescued, at least partially, by dipping to remove the PVC, in solvents such as ammonia and acetone, then dipping, to restore brilliance, in another solution.[55]

The ANA board of governors expanded the official grading standards, in the Uncirculated range, to include intermediate grades MS-63 and MS-67. The Numismatic Bibliomania Society, a club for devotees of numismatic literature, was formed.

News About Lincoln Cents: Lincoln cents, ignored by nearly all investors, were not affected by the market crash.

In July 1979 Mint Director Stella B. Hackel revealed a new plan for mintmarks, noting that a P mintmark would appear on all coins from the cent to the dollar made at Philadelphia in 1980—except this:

In 1980, one-cent coins produced for circulation in Philadelphia, Denver, San Francisco, and the West Point Bullion Depository will bear no mintmarks. At present there is considerable withdrawal from circulation by collectors of "D" marked one-cent coins. Elimination of any distinction among coins struck at the four Mint locations should increase the circulating one-cent pool. With the exception of the one-cent coins, the "D" mintmark will continue to appear on all other denominations struck at Denver. All Proof coins, including the Proof one-cent coin, and the Susan B. Anthony dollar coins produced for circulation by the San Francisco Assay Office will bear the "S" mintmark.

The plan did not come to pass, and Denver Mint cents bore a D mintmark.

1980

CIRCULATION MINTAGE: 7,414,705,000

Key to Collecting: Common in all grades including gem Mint State. Sharp strikes can be easily found. Mintmarkless coins struck at San Francisco and West Point cannot be differentiated from Philadelphia issues.

1980-D

CIRCULATION MINTAGE: 5,140,098,660

Key to Collecting: Common in all grades including gem Mint State. A larger D mintmark was implemented this year. Sharp strikes can be easily found.

1980-S

PROOF MINTAGE: 3,554,806

Enlarged 1.5x
(actual size 19 mm)

MARKET VALUES • 1980-S, Proof

PF-65RD	PF-67RD	PF-67Cam	PF-68DCam
$2.50	$10	$11	$15

Proofs: Common. Made with deep cameo contrast.

THE YEAR 1981

In America: The inflation rate reached 14 percent in its third consecutive year of double digits. The unemployment rate was 7.4 percent. Sales of new cars plummeted, and airlines posted losses. A Supreme Court ruling allowed TV cameras in courtrooms. IBM marketed its first personal computer (PC). Nutrasweet™ was approved for use. The characteristics of an obscure disease, AIDS, were identified.

In Numismatics: The market slump continued. For the next several years many prices continued to nosedive to fractions of their former highs. In the meantime areas that were not hot investment spots did well—such as early and rare U.S. coins, tokens, medals, and paper money. Many cheered the return of emphasis to traditional numismatics and did not bemoan the failure or disappearance of various coin investment corporations.

News About Lincoln Cents: Lincoln cents were more widely used than ever in circulation. Although there were virtually no goods or services that could be bought for one cent alone, the coin was necessary in making change since all but a handful of states had sales taxes. Although mintages had reached record highs in recent times, in 1981, the Treasury stocks were alarmingly low. An inventory at the end of the year showed "only" 140 million held by the Mint and about 470 million by the Federal Reserve Bank system. In the most recent fiscal year (ending June 30), according to a report by Mint Director Donna Pope, the Mint was able to strike only about 13.32 billion, short of the 15.3 billion the Federal Reserve requested.

1981

CIRCULATION MINTAGE: 7,491,750,000

Key to Collecting: Common in all grades including gem Mint State, although examples with good eye appeal are in the minority (not a problem, since there are so many anyway). Full Details coins can be easily found. Mintmarkless coins struck at San Francisco and West Point cannot be differentiated from Philadelphia issues. David W. Lange notes that cents sold by the Bureau of the Mint, as part of Mint sets, are often discolored, probably due to some rinse used at the Mint.

1981-D

CIRCULATION MINTAGE: 5,373,235,677

Key to Collecting: Common in all grades including gem Mint State. Sharp strikes can be easily found.

1981-S

PROOF MINTAGE: 4,063,083

Enlarged 1.5x
(actual size 19 mm)

MARKET VALUES • 1981-S, Filled S, Proof

PF-65RD	PF-67RD	PF-67Cam	PF-68DCam
$3	$10	$11	$15

MARKET VALUES • 1981-S, Clear S, Proof

PF-65RD	PF-67RD	PF-67Cam	PF-68DCam
$15	$28	$38	$55

Proofs With "Filled S": Variety with punched S filled in at the center, making it appear as a blob. Deep cameo contrast. The Filled S was made by the Clear S punch, now eroded, of the 1979-S, and it is different in appearance from the 1979-S Filled S.

Proofs With "Clear S": Mintmark from a new S punch. Well defined at the center. In the distinct minority among Proofs of 1981-S (the Bureau of the Mint estimated 599,000 coins), and thus of considerable value. Deep cameo contrast is the rule. Mintmark size differences in 1981 are known also for the Susan B. Anthony Proof dollars, but not among other denominations.

THE YEAR 1982

In America: The economy did not show much improvement under Reagan. The unemployment rate stood at 9.7 percent, and for the average citizen inflation still outpaced gains in real income. On the movie screen, *E.T.—The Extra-Terrestrial* was a hit. The compact disc (CD) was introduced and in time replaced phonograph records as well as recorded tapes. The first permanent artificial heart was implanted. Genetic engineering was a controversial subject in the news.

In Numismatics: A commemorative half dollar observing the 250th anniversary of George Washington's birth was offered by the Bureau of the Mint. It was the first issue since 1954 and was welcomed by the numismatic community. This set in place an extensive commemorative program that extends to the present day.

The ANA had 41,462 members, including 846 clubs—a new record. ANACS reported that it had received 95,008 coins in the most recent fiscal year, equal to about 365 submissions per working day—also a record. ANA doubled its headquarters space, adding a second story to the building. The Young Numismatist Program, captained by Florence Schook, embraced hundreds of enthusiastic youngsters, many of whom attended the annual Summer Seminar in Colorado Springs. The ANA was riding high and handsomely.

News About Lincoln Cents: Never a part of the investment segment of the market, Lincoln cents continued to be very popular, although problems of erratic grading and the dipping and cleaning of coins continued for collectors seeking bargains in retail advertisements.

The Bureau of the Mint converted cent production from brass (often incorrectly called *bronze*) to copper-coated zinc, a move that made the production of cents more profitable, in the face of the high market price of copper. Released early in the year, the new coins contained 99.2 percent zinc and 0.8 percent copper as a coating. The new coins weighed about 25 percent less than the brass versions. All Proofs were struck in brass this year. The copper-coated zinc cents were soon found to be prone to discoloration and, less often, flaking or bubbling.

Mintmarkless cents struck at San Francisco and West Point cannot be differentiated from Philadelphia issues.

A new obverse hub, known as the Small Date, was introduced this year, having slightly lower relief and the sharpened lettering. What is now known as the Large Date variety is, as David W. Lange points out, the same as the *Small Date* of 1974. Confused?

An easy way to differentiate them is that on the Large Date the tops of 98 are above the tops of 1 and 2; while on the Small Date the tops of the numerals are even.

Further, this from the Wexler-Flynn text, *The Authoritative Reference on Lincoln Cents:*

> *1982 Large Date:* Larger digits, mushy letters. LIBERTY distinct, well defined letters. Larger bust, close to rim. IN GOD closer to rim, mushy. WE TRUST closer to rim, mushy.

> *1982 Small Date:* Date has smaller, sharper digits. Smaller bust. IN GOD farther from rim, much sharper letters. WE TRUST farther from rim, much sharper letters.

David W. Lange commented:

> The coin hobby enjoyed a real windfall when the U. S. Mint decided to make a major revision to the cent's obverse master hub midway through 1982. The new hub is most easily recognized by its much smaller date, and these Small Date cents were first struck September 3. Ultimately, a total of seven different combinations of date size, mint and composition were created for the circulating cent coinage in 1982, only a 1982-D Small Date brass cent being omitted. When one adds the 1982-S Large Date brass Proof cent to this mix, the result is a most memorable year for collectors.[56]

1982, Brass

Circulation Mintage: 10,712,525,000
(includes both metals)

Enlarged 1.5x
(actual size 19 mm)

1982, Brass, Large Date

Key to Collecting: Common in all grades including gem Mint State. Slightly more common than the Small Date. Sharp strikes can be easily found.

1982, Brass, Small Date

Key to Collecting: Common in all grades including gem Mint State. Slightly less common than the Large Date, but still exceedingly plentiful. Full Details coins abound.

1982-D, Brass

Circulation Mintage: 6,012,979,368
(includes both metals)

1982-D, Brass, Large Date

Key to Collecting: Common in all grades including gem Mint State. All brass 1982-D cents are Large Dates. These were coined until October 21. Sharp strikes can be easily found.

1982-S, Brass

Proof Mintage: 3,857,479

Market Values • 1982-S, Proof

PF-65RD	PF-67RD	PF-67Cam	PF-68DCam
$2.50	$10	$11	$15

Brass, Large Date, Proofs: Made with deep cameo contrast. Common. All Proof cents this year are in brass and of the Large Date style. It is said (Breen 1988, Lange 1995) that some Small Date Proofs were made, but destroyed.

1982, Copper-Plated Zinc

Circulation Mintage:
(included in brass figure above)

Enlarged 1.5x
(actual size 19 mm)

1982, Copper-Plated Zinc, Large Date

Key to Collecting: Common in all grades including gem Mint State. Discolored coins of this and other copper-plated zinc issues can be bypassed—there are enough nice ones to be found. Sharp coins are the rule.

1982, Copper-Plated Zinc, Small Date

Key to Collecting: Common in all grades including gem Mint State. Sharp strikes can be easily found.

1982-D, Copper-Plated Zinc

Circulation Mintage:
(included in brass figure above)

1982-D, Copper-Plated Zinc, Large Date

Key to Collecting: Common in all grades including gem Mint State. Some are discolored; ignore these. Sharp strikes are common.

1982-D, Copper-Plated Zinc, Small Date

Key to Collecting: Common in all grades including gem Mint State. Ignore unattractive coins. Sharp strikes can be easily found.

The Year 1983

In America: The economy was still fraught with difficulties, and unemployment stood at 9.6 percent. In approval polls in January President Reagan ranked at just 35 percent, a sorry showing. Motorola began testing cellular phone service. A new illegal drug, "crack" cocaine, was developed in the Bahamas and soon was widely sold in the United States.

In Numismatics: Coins certified by ANACS became increasingly popular. By year's end the investment part of the coin market was gaining strength, with gold coins in particular being in demand. Morgan silver dollars were also in the limelight. The annual "Financial Assets Report" by Salomon Brothers, Wall Street financiers, revealed that for 1983, rare U.S. coins showed an annual compound return of 25.7 percent, placing them first among all "hard asset" investments for the preceding decade. Their list of involved coins, furnished by Stack's years earlier, was mainly composed of scarce and rare issues in higher grades.

News About Lincoln Cents: Lincoln cents continued to be popular with collectors, but relatively few made them a long-term specialty. Copper-coated zinc continued as standard; discolored and irregular surfaces (e.g., tiny blisters or bubbles caused by the metals not bonding properly) were annoying to numismatists.

1983

CIRCULATION MINTAGE: 7,752,355,000

Enlarged 1.5x
(actual size 19 mm)

Key to Collecting: Common in all grades including gem Mint State. Avoid discolored coins and those with surface bubbling or problems. Sharp strikes can be easily found. Some, from dies finished too vigorously, have the FG initials weak or missing, and others lack the bottom of the E in CENT (making it look like an F). These are more curious than valuable. Mintmarkless coins struck at San Francisco and West Point cannot be differentiated from Philadelphia issues. Several struck in solid brass (pre-1982 composition) have been reported.

1983, Doubled Die Reverse: Doubling is strong on all peripheral letters. A detail of the motto is illustrated here. First reported in the summer of 1983, doubled-die coins were later found, according to Walter

Breen, in limited numbers in the Lewistown, Pennsylvania, area (with others in northern Florida, per Sol Taylor). All are seen with extensive die-finishing lines (i.e., microscopic raised lines) on the obverse, and this should not affect the certified grade.

1983 Brass-Plated Cent: See information about planchets in chapter nine. Values in the past have ranged from $25 to $35 for choice gem Uncirculated examples.

1983-D

CIRCULATION MINTAGE: 6,467,199,428

Key to Collecting: Common in all grades including gem Mint State. Avoid discolored coins and those with surface bubbling or problems. Sharp strikes are aplenty.

1983-S

PROOF MINTAGE: 3,279,126

MARKET VALUES • 1983-S, Proof

PF-65RD	PF-67RD	PF-67Cam	PF-68DCam
$3	$10	$11	$15

Proofs: Made with deep cameo contrast. "Quite subject to discoloration," observes David W. Lange, who comments that a fiberboard insert in the Proof set packaging, used beginning this year, may make the problem worse. "Only time will tell whether these coins can survive." Removing these and any other Proofs from such holders should solve the potential problem.

THE YEAR 1984

In America: The Bell system of regional telephone companies was dismantled, by federal decree, and various component companies began plans to compete individually. The economy showed improvement, as did President Reagan's ratings and the unemployment rate (7.5 percent). In the November election Reagan demolished Democratic contender Walter Mondale. On NBC the *Cosby Show*, soon becoming the most popular TV program, was launched. The Macintosh computer was introduced by Apple and featured a user-friendly system of icons, in contrast to the typed-in coding employed by IBM personal computers.

In Numismatics: The Bureau of the Mint changed its name to the United States Mint. Four coining facilities were in use: Philadelphia and Denver for most production, plus San Francisco and West Point for collector strikes and certain other issues.

News About Lincoln Cents: The relief of Lincoln's shoulder was lowered this year, thus reducing the problem of weakness in this area, which had characterized the series since its inception in 1909. After this time the annoying (to connoisseurs) minute planchet marks on Lincoln's shoulder were minimized.

1984

CIRCULATION MINTAGE: 8,151,079,000

Key to Collecting: Common in all grades including gem Mint State. Avoid discolored coins and those with surface bubbling or problems. Sharp strikes can be easily found. As is the case for 1983, mintmarkless coins struck at San Francisco cannot be differentiated from Philadelphia issues.

1984, Doubled Ear: This variety can be discerned under low magnification and shows part of an extra earlobe below and slightly left of Lincoln's ear, the result of doubling when the working die was made. Around 1,100 have been certified as MS-65RD or higher, suggesting perhaps that the total mintage was only in the low tens of thousands. This variety is listed in *A Guide Book of United States Coins*, increasing sharply the demand for and awareness of it.

1984-D

CIRCULATION MINTAGE: 5,569,238,906

Enlarged 1.5x
(actual size 19 mm)

Key to Collecting: Readily found in all grades including gem Mint State. Avoid discolored coins and those with surface bubbling or problems. Sharp strikes are common.

1984-S

PROOF MINTAGE: 3,065,110

MARKET VALUES • 1984-S, Proof

PF-65RD	PF-67RD	PF-67Cam	PF-68DCam
$4	$10	$11	$15

Proofs: Made with deep cameo contrast. Common.

THE YEAR 1985

In America: In his second term President Reagan's popularity increased even further, although some suggested he delegated too much responsibility. AIDS was an epidemic, and awareness of it was heightened by the death of film star Rock Hudson. Coca-Cola introduced "New Coke," which proved to have little sales effervescence.

In Numismatics: The coin market took on a largely positive tone in 1985. At *Coin World* long-time editor Margo Russell retired and was succeeded by Beth Deisher, who also proved to be long-time. By now sources of news and market information included that publication as well as *Numismatic News, COINage, Coins* magazine, the *Coin Dealer Newsletter*, and various electronic trading forums, among others. *A Guide Book of United States Coins* remained the standard annual reference on pricing.

News About Lincoln Cents: Beginning this year, the S mintmark was added to the master die to make Proofs. This eliminated positional differences in mintmarks. (This policy was extended to circulation-strike master dies in 1990.)

1985

CIRCULATION MINTAGE: 5,648,489,887

Key to Collecting: Common in all grades including gem Mint State. Most are very attractive. Sharp strikes are plentiful. Mintmarkless coins struck at West Point cannot be differentiated from Philadelphia issues.

1985-D

CIRCULATION MINTAGE: 5,287,339,926

Key to Collecting: Plentiful in all grades including gem Mint State. Most are very pleasing in appearance. A larger D mintmark was used this year. Sharp strikes are common.

1985-D Brass-Plated Cent: These are "light colored" cents, inadvertently made with about 90 percent copper and 10 percent zinc coating (due to zinc contamination of the copper plating bath for planchets) instead of 100 percent copper. The 1985-D is the most-often encountered of this anomalous variety. See information about planchets in chapter nine. Values in the past have ranged from $15 to $25 for choice gem Uncirculated examples.

1985-S

PROOF MINTAGE: 3,362,821

Enlarged 1.5x
(actual size 19 mm)

MARKET VALUES • 1985-S, Proof

PF-65RD	PF-67RD	PF-67Cam	PF-68DCam
$5	$11	$12	$15

Proofs: Made with deep cameo contrast. Common. A larger S mintmark was introduced this year. This was incorporated into the master die, rather than punched separately.

THE YEAR 1986

In America: On January 28 the *Challenger* space shuttle exploded after lift-off. Oprah Winfrey debuted on national TV. The Fox network was created, joining the big three of ABC, CBS, and NBC. The unemployment rate was 7.0 percent. Median household income was $24,897. Poor oversight of savings and loan institutions, coupled with unfortunate lending practices of banks, created an era of financial turmoil that would lead to the collapse of hundreds of banks across America.

In Numismatics: The Professional Coin Grading Service (PCGS), conceived by David Hall and formed with several dealer associates, began operations. The relatively new (but not unprecedented) procedure was to receive coins and grade them for a fee, with a single grade (not split, as ANACS used) to be marked on a sealed plastic holder. PCGS grew like wildfire and within a year was the sensation of the rare coin market. Other grading services were formed and issued plastic holders ("slabs"), including, the following year, the Numismatic Guaranty Company of America (NGC).

In summer 1986 the ANA board added numbers to its grading system: in the Mint State category, these included all digits from MS-60 and MS-61 continuously to MS-70. The U.S. Mint launched its gold and silver bullion "Eagle" coin program, which went on to great market success. *Coin World* published circulation figures for leading periodicals in the hobby: It had 80,394 subscribers, *Coins* magazine had 29,994, *COINage* had 60,367, *The Numismatist* had 33,072, and *Numismatic News* had 35,923. The market was strong at year's end.

News About Lincoln Cents: A minor reverse hub modification was made.

1986

CIRCULATION MINTAGE: 4,491,395,493

Key to Collecting: Common in all grades including gem Mint State. Most are very attractive. Sharp strikes are plentiful.

1986-D

CIRCULATION MINTAGE: 4,442,866,698

Key to Collecting: Readily available in all grades including gem Mint State. Excellent eye appeal is the rule. Coins with Full Details are plentiful.

1986-S

PROOF MINTAGE: 3,010,497

Enlarged 1.5x
(actual size 19 mm)

MARKET VALUES • 1986-S, Proof

PF-65RD	PF-67RD	PF-67Cam	PF-68DCam
$7	$11	$12	$15

Proofs: Made with deep cameo contrast. Common.

THE YEAR 1987

In America: Rotary Clubs were forced to admit women, per a Supreme Court ruling. *Platoon* took the "Best Picture" Oscar. The use of home computers was spreading, with Apple, Osborne, and other brands selling rapidly. An Apple Macintosh with a black-and-white printer (capable of printing two sheets per minute) cost on the long side of $5,000.

In Numismatics: PCGS-graded coins continued to increase in popularity. Numismatic Guaranty Corporation of America (later renamed the Numismatic Guaranty Company) was launched and soon became a strong competitor. Coin dealing became increasingly corporate and less personal.

1987

CIRCULATION MINTAGE: 4,682,466,931

Key to Collecting: Common in all grades including gem Mint State. Most coins are very attractive. Sharply struck coins are common.

1987-D

CIRCULATION MINTAGE: 4,879,389,514

Enlarged 1.5x
(actual size 19 mm)

Key to Collecting: Easily found in all grades including gem Mint State. Nearly all are very attractive—this comment being true for nearly all cents of the era. Many have Full Details.

1987-S

PROOF MINTAGE: 4,227,728

MARKET VALUES • 1987-S, Proof

PF-65RD	PF-67RD	PF-67Cam	PF-68DCam
$5	$10	$11	$13

Proofs: Made with deep cameo contrast. Common.

THE YEAR 1988

In America: President Ronald Reagan had been well liked for several years by now, the economy was in fine shape, unemployment and interest rates were down, and many Americans enjoyed their life and surroundings. In the November presidential election George H.W. Bush handily beat Democratic challenger Michael Dukakis. James Hansen of NASA warned Congress of global warming, a hitherto-obscure subject.

In Numismatics: By 1988 there were thousands of certified coins available from NGC and PCGS, plus some lesser-known services as well. Now coins could truly be bought and sold as investment vehicles because, it was thought, the problem of one great unknown—the grade of a coin—had been neatly solved. It was a simple matter to trade in certified coins by simply looking at the grade and market price. Interest spawned more interest, and soon Wall Street firms got into the act. Merrill Lynch, for one, started a coin fund, and other brokerage houses became involved. Here, indeed, was a product that could be sold to investors, which would yield greater fees and commissions than those obtained from simply buying and selling common stocks. The advent of "Wall Street money" was widely publicized, excitement prevailed, and prices of so-called "investment quality" silver and gold coins rose sharply. (As to that particular quality, it was generally defined as MS-65, or Proof-65, or finer.)

News About Lincoln Cents: Fortunately, Lincoln cents were not caught up in the investment excitement, and market prices continued to be based on what *collectors* were willing to pay—the true long-term foundation for any market.

1988

CIRCULATION MINTAGE: 6,092,810,000

Key to Collecting: Plentiful in all grades including gem Mint State. Most are very attractive. Full Details coins are common.

1988-D

CIRCULATION MINTAGE: 5,253,740,443

Key to Collecting: Easy to find in all grades including gem Mint State. Most are very attractive. Full Details coins are common.

1988-S

PROOF MINTAGE: 3,262,948

Enlarged 1.5x
(actual size 19 mm)

MARKET VALUES • 1988-S, Proof

PF-65RD	PF-67RD	PF-67Cam	PF-68DCam
$9	$11	$12	$13

Proofs: Made with deep cameo contrast. Common.

THE YEAR 1989

In America: In Alaska the tanker *Exxon Valdez* ran aground and ruptured, spilling 11 million gallons of crude oil into the sea, causing great concern. In distant Switzerland at the CERN scientific research facility, the World Wide Web was developed by Tim Berners-Lee, an event seemingly of little importance except to allow scientists to share findings. The Berlin Wall fell. These two events in Europe changed America and the entire world.

In Numismatics: Prices of certain coins went up and up, as excited fortune-seekers desired only "investment grade" coins, generally defined as gold or silver coins in MS-65 (or Proof-65) grade or higher. Prices of commemoratives, Peace silver dollars, and other darlings continued to soar. "Wall Street money" hastened to grab profit potential. Collectors, out-priced, sat on the sidelines.

News About Lincoln Cents: These were excluded from the investment excitement. A leading investment writer said, "Sell all copper." Not much attention was paid to 1909-S V.D.B.; 1914-D; 1955, Doubled Die Obverse; or any other Lincoln cents.

1989

CIRCULATION MINTAGE: 7,261,535,000

Key to Collecting: Readily found in all grades including gem Mint State. Nice eye appeal is the rule, not the exception. Full Details coins are easily acquired.

1989-D

CIRCULATION MINTAGE: 5,345,467,111

Enlarged 1.5x
(actual size 19 mm)

Key to Collecting: Plentiful in all grades including gem Mint State. Most are very attractive. Full Details coins are abundant.

1989-S

PROOF MINTAGE: 3,220,194

MARKET VALUES • 1989-S, Proof

PF-65RD	PF-67RD	PF-67Cam	PF-68DCam
$9	$11	$12	$13

Proofs: Made with deep cameo contrast. Common.

THE YEAR 1990

In America: The Bush administration, riding on the coattails of Ronald Reagan's popularity, acquitted itself to the satisfaction of most citizens. Iraqi dictator Saddam Hussein invaded and occupied Kuwait, prompting Bush to launch the Gulf War, a one-sided showdown that drove the marauders back to their homeland. The conflict ended quickly (in 1991).

In Numismatics: By 1989 and early 1990 *collectors* were no longer significant buyers of "investment grade" coins (see 1998). They sat on the sidelines on these, since they had been priced far beyond what seasoned numismatists would pay. Instead, they concentrated on early copper coins, colonials, obsolete bank notes, Washington medals, and other traditional numismatic series. Finally, in early 1990 the investment market ran out of steam. Few new buyers appeared. Offered coins found no investment buyers, and at 1989 levels few collectors were even slightly interested. The market collapsed, and many commemoratives, Peace dollars, and other favorites eventually descended to *small fractions* of their 1989 prices. (At this time, several years later, collectors resumed buying.)

News About Lincoln Cents: Changes, lessening the relief slightly, were made to the obverse and reverse hubs. The V.D.B. initials on Lincoln's shoulder were made slightly larger and much more noticeable. Reverse details, including the Lincoln statue and foliage, were made sharper. Minor adjustments were made in letter spacing. Beginning this year mintmarks were placed on the master dies for circulation-strike coins, not punched separately into working dies. (This had been done with Proofs beginning in 1985.) Hence, mintmark position variations came to an end. Beginning this year any doubled obverse dies would have the mintmark doubled as well.

1990

CIRCULATION MINTAGE: 6,851,765,000

Enlarged 1.5x
(actual size 19 mm)

Key to Collecting: Abundant in all grades including gem Mint State. Most are very attractive. Sharp strikes, having more detail than previously due to the modified hubs (see The Year 1990, News About Lincoln Cents), can be easily found.

1990-D

CIRCULATION MINTAGE: 4,922,894,533

Key to Collecting: Common in all grades including gem Mint State. Most are very attractive. Full Details coins are common.

1990-S

PROOF MINTAGE (WITH S): 3,299,559

PROOF MINTAGE (WITHOUT S, ERROR): 100 to 150 or so (estimate)

MARKET VALUES • 1990-S, Proof

PF-65RD	PF-67RD	PF-67Cam	PF-68DCam
$5	$10	$11	$13

MARKET VALUES • 1990-S, NO S, PROOF ††

PF-65RD	PF-67RD	PF-67Cam	PF-68DCam
$3,000	$3,500	$3,750	$4,000

Proofs: Made with deep cameo contrast. Common.

1990 Proof, No S: This is a dramatic error, the omission of the S mintmark having escaped the notice of at least 14 people during the die preparation and coining processes, as Shane Anderson notes in *The Complete Lincoln Cent Encyclopedia*. Apparently, a mintmarkless circulation-strike die had been given a mirror finish. The Mint provided information that an estimated 3,700 were coined without the S, and all but 145 were shipped. Those 145 were destroyed. Later a Mint official stated that with no facts on hand, this was simply a guess, and it was not known how many had been shipped. In 1995 David W. Lange commented: "A figure in the range of 100–150 is probable, though many purchasers of 1990-S proof sets who are not in tune with hobby news may have such coins and not yet know it." In 1996 John Wexler and Kevin Flynn stated, "Currently there are about 250 known." Sam Lukes reports that a client "who has researched this rarity since its discovery claims 200 to 250 actually exist."[57]

THE YEAR 1991

In America: The economy continued to be strong. Unemployment was at 6.8 percent, and the median household income was $30,126. As the states formerly constituting the Soviet Union became independent and set up their own governments, the Cold War came to an end. In the home, electronic gadgets included an increasing number of tabletop computers.

In Numismatics: The market for "investment grade" gem silver and gold coins was almost dead, and prices of many issues such as Morgan and Peace silver dollars, commemoratives, pre-1917 Proofs, and other former darlings dropped, in some instances, to fractions of their 1989 values. New commemorative coins included the rather repetitive designs on the Mount Rushmore 50 cent, $1, and $5 coins.

1991

CIRCULATION MINTAGE: 5,165,940,000

Key to Collecting: Easy to find in all grades including gem Mint State. Most are very attractive. Because these and other coins are so *cheap*, you may have to visit a coin shop to buy them—their value is not sufficient to merit their listing in catalogs and advertisements. Full Details coins are abundant.

1991-D

CIRCULATION MINTAGE: 4,158,446,076

Enlarged 1.5x
(actual size 19 mm)

Key to Collecting: Plentiful in all grades including gem Mint State. Most are very pleasing to the eye. Full Details coins are common.

1991-S

CIRCULATION MINTAGE: 2,867,787

MARKET VALUES • 1991-S, Proof

PF-65RD	PF-67RD	PF-67Cam	PF-68DCam
$12	$13	$14	$16

Proofs: Made with deep cameo contrast. Common.

THE YEAR 1992

In America: In the November presidential election Democratic candidate Bill Clinton and his running mate Al Gore demolished the reelection hopes of incumbent George H.W. Bush. The unemployment rate rose to 7.5 percent. Browsing access to the World Wide Web, soon universally referred to as the Internet, was gained by those who had the proper equipment and learned how to use special code sequences.

In Numismatics: Collectors ruled the day with scarcely an investor in sight.

News About Lincoln Cents: The hubs were changed slightly this year, part of a continuing process to increase the sharpness of the coins made on high-speed presses.

A new reverse, used sparingly in 1992 but placed in general use in 1993, can be distinguished by the very close positioning of AM (AMERICA) and the greater distance of the engraver's initials FG from the building.

Wide AM: Bottoms of letters spaced apart. FG close to building with F almost touching.

Close AM: Bottoms of letters almost touch. FG distant from building.

1992

CIRCULATION MINTAGE: 4,648,905,000

Key to Collecting: The normal die with Wide AM (AMERICA) is common in all grades including gem Mint State. Most are very attractive. Full Details coins are common.

1992 With Close AM (AMERICA): The letters AM almost touch; FG is close to the building. Extremely rare.

1992-D

Circulation Mintage: 4,448,673,300

Enlarged 1.5x
(actual size 19 mm)

Key to Collecting: The normal die with Wide AM (AMERICA) is common in all grades including gem Mint State. Most are very pretty. Full Details coins are easily found.

1992-D With Close AM (AMERICA): The letters AM almost touch; FG is close to building (the style regularly used in 1993). These must have been struck very late in the year and are very rare, although with any of these "AM" varieties, doubtless more await identification—for at present they are not widely known, despite listings in *A Guide Book of United States Coins*. Still, by now it is estimated that no more than 10 or so have been found. Only a handful have reached the leading circulation services.

1992-S

Proof Mintage: 4,176,560

Market Values • 1992-S, Proof

PF-65RD	PF-67RD	PF-67Cam	PF-68DCam
$5	$10	$11	$12

Proofs: Made with deep cameo contrast. Common.

The Year 1993

In America: In New York City a bomb was set off underground in the World Trade Center. The North American Free Trade Agreement (NAFTA) went into effect, prompting many American firms to set up facilities in Mexico, where labor was much cheaper.

In Numismatics: The market for higher-grade gold and silver coins was recovering, but most pieces were still far below their recent highs.

1993

Circulation Mintage: 5,684,705,000

Enlarged 1.5x
(actual size 19 mm)

Key to Collecting: An abundant supply beckons in all grades, including gem Mint State with beautiful surfaces. Full Details coins are readily available.

1993-D

CIRCULATION MINTAGE: 6,426,650,571

Key to Collecting: Easy to find in all grades including gem Mint State. Most are very attractive. Full Details coins are plentiful.

1993-S

PROOF MINTAGE: 3,394,792

MARKET VALUES • 1993-S, Proof

PF-65RD	PF-67RD	PF-67Cam	PF-68DCam
$9	$10	$11	$12

Proofs: Made with deep cameo contrast. Common.

THE YEAR 1994

In America: The news focused on President Clinton's activities and the murder trial of football hero O.J. Simpson. It was a curious year in professional baseball, with a strike (no pun intended) disrupting the season and canceling the World Series. "I Will Always Love You" was named song of the year. On the small screen *Friends* and *ER* debuted.

In Numismatics: The market continued to be strong, with most expensive coins now encapsulated in certified holders as they crossed the auction block.

News About Lincoln Cents: The obverse hub was altered to sharply lower the relief of Lincoln's shoulder, giving it an unnatural appearance when examined carefully.

1994

CIRCULATION MINTAGE: 6,500,850,000

Key to Collecting: Easy to buy in all grades including gem Mint State. Most are very attractive. Full Details examples are easily found.

1994-D

CIRCULATION MINTAGE: 7,131,765,000

Key to Collecting: Abundant in all grades including gem Mint State. Most are very attractive. Full Details coins are plentiful.

1994-S

PROOF MINTAGE: 3,269,923

Enlarged 1.5x
(actual size 19 mm)

MARKET VALUES • 1994-S, Proof

PF-65RD	PF-67RD	PF-67Cam	PF-68DCam
$9	$11	$12	$13

Proofs: Made with deep cameo contrast. Common.

THE YEAR 1995

In America: A truck parked in front of the Murrah Federal Building in Oklahoma City exploded, destroying the building and killing many of its occupants, including children in a day care center. John Paul II visited the United States and drew admiring crowds. In Cleveland the Rock and Roll Hall of Fame opened and soon proved to be a popular attraction. The news of a cloned sheep in England created great interest in the United States and stirred debates as to whether such practices were ethical and if experimentation should be extended to humans. The federal budget proved insufficient, and at year's end the shutdown of certain government services loomed.

In Numismatics: The redesign of the $100 bill with special coding and security features launched what would eventually be a modification of all denominations. There were simply too many new commemorative coins being issued, often featuring designs of events, places, or people that many considered irrelevant. The U.S. Mint was solidly the largest "coin dealer" in the world.

1995

CIRCULATION MINTAGE: 6,411,440,000

Key to Collecting: Common in all grades including gem Mint State. Most have great eye appeal. Full Details coins are everywhere.

1995, Doubled Die Obverse: In 1995 there was a free-for-all in the coin hobby when it was discovered, early in the year, that some Lincoln cents were slightly doubled on the obverse—not significantly at the date, but noticeably at LIBERTY and at certain letters of IN GOD WE TRUST. The coin was featured on the first page of *USA Today*.

1995-D

CIRCULATION MINTAGE: 7,128,560,000

Enlarged 1.5x
(actual size 19 mm)

Key to Collecting: Common, with superb eye appeal, in all grades including gem Mint State. Full Details coins are plentiful.

1995-S

PROOF MINTAGE: 2,797,481

MARKET VALUES • 1995-S, Proof

PF-65RD	PF-67RD	PF-67Cam	PF-68DCam
$9	$11	$12	$13

Proofs: Made with deep cameo contrast. Common.

THE YEAR 1996

In America: In November Republican Robert Dole and running mate Jack Kemp were thought, by many, to be sure winners in the election, but President Clinton was voted in for a second term. An estimated 30 million Americans were tied into the Internet.

In Numismatics: The top *Coin World* story of the year, according to a staff survey, was the breaking of the $1 million barrier for a coin at auction—the Eliasberg Collection 1913 Liberty Head nickel at $1,485,000 (with the present writer as the auctioneer at the podium). Legislation was passed authorizing the release of statehood quarter dollars, at the rate of five different designs per year, beginning in 1999.

News About Lincoln Cents: More people became seriously interested in this specialty as books by David W. Lange and the team of John Wexler and Kevin Flynn gained distribution (see the selected bibliography). Sol Taylor's Lincoln Cent Collectors Club continued to draw members.

1996

CIRCULATION MINTAGE: 6,612,465,000

Enlarged 1.5x
(actual size 19 mm)

Key to Collecting: Easy to find in all grades including gem Mint State. Nearly all are very attractive. Full Details coins are common.

1996-D

CIRCULATION MINTAGE: 6,510,795,000

Key to Collecting: Common in all grades including gem Mint State. Most are very attractive. Full Details coins are plentiful.

1996-S

PROOF MINTAGE: 2,525,265

MARKET VALUES • 1996-S, Proof

PF-65RD	PF-67RD	PF-67Cam	PF-68DCam
$4.50	$9	$10	$12

Proofs: Made with deep cameo contrast. Common.

THE YEAR 1997

In America: The Clinton administration enjoyed good times. The unemployment rate fell to 4.9 percent. Director James Cameron's *Titanic* film became one of the most popular movies of all time.

In Numismatics: New commemoratives, including unusual special sets combining such coins with Proofs and other special strikings, were made. Platinum bullion coins, up to $100 face value (not relevant to the actual value of one ounce), were first sold—these being the first pieces ever struck in this metal for American collectors and investors. The market for all coins was strong.

News About Lincoln Cents: "Lincoln to Get a Face Lift for 1997," by Paul Gilkes, *Coin World*, November 11, 1996, included this:

> Refinements are in store for 1997 to three of the coin denominations used for circulation and in numismatic collector sets. Lincoln's getting a facelift and spruced-up wardrobe. . . . George E. Hunter, the Mint's assistant director for process and quality control, said major strengthening of details has been done on the plaster models for the 1997 obverses of both the Lincoln cent and Kennedy half dollar to improve the overall looks and the reverse of the Washington quarter for striking improvements. . . . Lincoln's facial details and his coat will be strengthened, "Which will be a noticeable improvement," Hunter said. "The modifications are being made to the plaster models—one of the early stages of die manufacturing—to improve the aesthetic looks of the nation's longest-enduring and most-produced coin design." "Not everybody will notice the differences, Hunter said. "Some people wouldn't know if we changed the designs [completely]. The savvy collector will see a little more sharpened and strengthened details." . . . The cent can average 600,000 or more strikes per die. While design enhancements were undertaken, die production capabilities at all stages are also being revamped.

1997

CIRCULATION MINTAGE: 4,622,800,000

Key to Collecting: Plentiful in all grades including gem Mint State. Most are very attractive. Full Details coins are easy to find.

1997 Brass-Plated Cent: These "light colored" cents were inadvertently made with about 90 percent copper and 10 percent zinc coating (instead of 100 percent copper) due to zinc contamination of the copper plating bath for planchets. See information about planchets in chapter nine. Values in the past have ranged from $25 to $35 for choice gem Uncirculated examples.

1997-D

CIRCULATION MINTAGE: 4,576,555,000

Enlarged 1.5x
(actual size 19 mm)

Key to Collecting: Common in just about any grade desired. Most are very attractive. Full Details coins are plentiful.

1997-D Brass-Plated Cent: These "light colored" cents were inadvertently made with about 90 percent copper and 10 percent zinc coating (instead of 100 percent copper) due to zinc contamination of the copper plating bath for planchets. See information about planchets in chapter nine. Values in the past have ranged from $25 to $35 for choice gem Uncirculated examples.

1997-S

PROOF MINTAGE: 2,796,678

MARKET VALUES • 1997-S, Proof

PF-65RD	PF-67RD	PF-67Cam	PF-68DCam
$10	$12	$13	$14

Proofs: Made with deep cameo contrast. Common.

THE YEAR 1998

In America: *Harry Potter and the Sorcerer's Stone* reached stores and launched a publishing sensation, lifting the sales of other books as well. The best-educated and perhaps the most intelligent president of all time, Clinton, became a polarizing figure amid TV coverage of his liaison with a White House intern.

In Numismatics: "Trophy rarities" captured headlines, as did news about the forthcoming (in 1999) state quarters and (in 2000) Sacagawea dollars. The market continued to be very active. The Internet became increasingly important.

1998

CIRCULATION MINTAGE: 5,032,155,000

Key to Collecting: Easy to find in all grades including gem Mint State, with nice eye appeal. Full Details coins are plentiful.

1998 With Wide AM (AMERICA): The letters AM have significant space between them; FG is distant from the building. These are scarce. They were described by Charles D. Daughtrey in *Looking Through Lincoln Cents* and listed in *A Guide Book of United States Coins*.

1998 Brass-Plated Cent: These "light colored" cents were inadvertently made with about 90 percent copper and 10 percent zinc coating (instead of 100 percent copper) due to zinc contamination of the copper plating bath for planchets. See information about planchets in chapter nine. Values in the past have ranged from $15 to $25 for choice gem Uncirculated examples.

1998-D

CIRCULATION MINTAGE: 5,225,353,500

Enlarged 1.5x
(actual size 19 mm)

Key to Collecting: Abundant in all grades including gem Mint State. Most are very attractive. Full Details coins are common.

1998-S

PROOF MINTAGE: 2,086,507

MARKET VALUES • 1998-S, Proof

PF-65RD	PF-67RD	PF-67Cam	PF-68DCam
$9	$10	$11	$12

Proofs: The regular Proof die with Wide AM (AMERICA) was made with deep cameo contrast and is common.

1998-S Proof With Close AM (AMERICA): The letters AM almost touch; FG is close to the building (the style regularly used on circulation strikes this year). First publicized by Ken Potter in *Numismatic News*, May 3, 2005.

THE YEAR 1999

In America: Two teenage students carried weapons into Columbine High School in Littleton, Colorado, and killed 12 students, a teacher, and themselves. Clinton faced an impeachment trial on charges of perjury and obstruction of justice, but the U.S. Senate acquitted him. More than 75 million Americans were connected to the Internet. Cellular (cell) phones and laptop computers were by now a part of the American scene.

In Numismatics: The statehood quarters were launched, with that of Delaware being the first out of the starting gate. Collector and public interest soared to high levels. The Mint estimated that 130,000,000 or more people were coin collectors, mainly collecting statehood quarters.

News About Lincoln Cents: The hair on Lincoln was slightly sharpened this year.

1999

CIRCULATION MINTAGE: 5,237,600,000

Enlarged 1.5x
(actual size 19 mm)

Key to Collecting: Plentiful in all grades including gem Mint State. Most are very attractive. Full Details coins are easy to find.

1999 With Wide AM (AMERICA): The letters AM have significant space between them; FG is distant from the building. These are rare. They were described by Charles D. Daughtry in *Looking Through Lincoln Cents* and listed in *A Guide Book of United States Coins*.

1999-D

CIRCULATION MINTAGE: 6,360,065,000

Key to Collecting: Common in all grades including gem Mint State, with pleasing surfaces. Full Details coins are plentiful.

1999-S

PROOF MINTAGE: 3,347,966

MARKET VALUES • 1999-S, Proof

PF-65RD	PF-67RD	PF-67Cam	PF-68DCam
$6	$9	$10	$12

Proofs: The regular Proof die with Wide AM (AMERICA) was made with deep cameo contrast and is common.

1999-S Proof With Close AM (AMERICA): The letters AM almost touch; FG is close to the building (the style regularly used on circulation strikes this year). This variety was first publicized by Ken Potter in *Numismatic News*, April 12, 2005.

THE YEAR 2000

In America: Shades of 1929! Amateur investors were important in the stock market, parlaying savings, inheritances, and bonuses into fortunes by day trading—sometimes at desks gladly provided to them by many brokerage houses. Dot-com companies, these being existing or planned ventures with Internet businesses as their models, were the darlings. Then in March the bubble burst, and many such companies collapsed. The economy continued to be excellent, showing admirable control of the budget and an unemployment rate of just 4 percent. In November George W. Bush (George H.W. Bush's son) ran for president against Al Gore. The latter gained more popular votes, but problems in ballot counting in Florida intervened, and after much controversy Bush was declared the winner.

In Numismatics: Statehood quarters continued to make the news, including a weird error combining the obverse of a state quarter with the reverse of the new Sacagawea dollar. The Sacagawea dollars were launched with much fanfare—with affable Mint Director Jay Johnson earning an "A" for showmanship and enthusiasm—but the public did not use them in commerce. The marketing of gold coins and ingots from the wreck of the SS *Central America* made headlines and generated excitement, augmented by Dwight Manley's large and impressive "Ship of Gold" exhibit, displayed at the ANA Convention in Philadelphia and elsewhere.

2000

CIRCULATION MINTAGE: 5,503,200,000

Key to Collecting: Strikes from the normal die with Close AM (AMERICA) are very plentiful at any desired grade level, including gem Mint State. Most are very beautiful. Full Details coins are common.

2000 With Wide AM (AMERICA): The letters AM have significant space between them; FG is distant from building. This variety is relatively common and is listed in *A Guide Book of United States Coins.*

2000-D

CIRCULATION MINTAGE: 8,774,220,000

Enlarged 1.5x
(actual size 19 mm)

Key to Collecting: Easy to find in all grades including gem Mint State, and usually attractive. Full Details coins are common.

2000-S

PROOF MINTAGE: 4,047,993

Proofs: Made with deep cameo contrast. Common.

MARKET VALUES • 2000-S, Proof

PF-65RD	PF-67RD	PF-67Cam	PF-68DCam
$4	$7	$8	$10

THE YEAR 2001

In America: On September 11 Islamic terrorists gained control of four large jetliners, rammed two of them into the twin towers of the World Trade Center in New York City and another into the Pentagon, and crashed the fourth into a Pennsylvania field as passengers wrestled to take over control from the hijackers. Almost 3,000 people were killed. Thus began the "war on terrorism," which has been the main focus of the U.S. government since that fateful day. On TV *Survivor* was especially popular. The most popular late night shows were hosted, as they had been for years, by David Letterman and Jay Leno.

In Numismatics: In *Coin World* on March 12 editor Beth Deisher estimated that there were about two million serious coin collectors in America, plus many millions who saved the popular statehood quarter dollars. The Internet had become a focal point for numismatics, and most leading dealers had their own websites, as did several groups and organizations. The auction site eBay was the dominant exchange forum, but there were many problems because little seemed to be done to prevent misrepresented and phony coins from being offered. There were few problems, however, with transactions by dealers who had solid credentials—for example, members of the Professional Numismatists Guild. The American Buffalo $1 commemorative was a hit. Sacagawea dollars piled up in Treasury vaults. (No one wanted them except numismatists.)

News About Lincoln Cents: The trading activity in Lincoln cents now incorporated Internet images, which gave buyers a view of the actual color of each coin, although without the possibility of ascertaining whether the color was original.

2001

CIRCULATION MINTAGE: 4,959,600,000

Enlarged 1.5x
(actual size 19 mm)

Key to Collecting: Common in all grades including gem Mint State. Most are very attractive. Full Details coins are common.

2001-D

CIRCULATION MINTAGE: 5,374,990,000

Key to Collecting: Easy to find in all grades including gem Mint State. Most are very attractive. Full Details coins are everywhere.

2001-S

PROOF MINTAGE: 3,184,606

MARKET VALUES • 2001-S, Proof

PF-65RD	PF-67RD	PF-67Cam	PF-68DCam
$4	$7	$8	$10

Proofs: Made with deep cameo contrast. Common.

THE YEAR 2002

In America: In corporate America scandals swirled around alleged criminal actions by officers of Arthur Andersen (one of the "big four" accounting firms), Enron, Tyco, ImClone, Worldcom, Global Crossing, Qwest, Adelphia, and others. The economy was strong, with rising prices, in the housing market in particular, fueled by the easy availability of mortgages to those who had marginal credit. WalMart was the nation's leading retailer—by far, as it had been in recent years.

In Numismatics: The Stack's/Sotheby's sale of a 1933 double eagle for $7.59 million shattered worldwide records.

News About Lincoln Cents: In the auction market "ultra-grade" certified coins, especially if graded by PCGS or NGC, raised eyebrows: Pieces that were common and also inexpensive in gem grades such as MS-65 and 66 sold for astronomical prices if they were close to or at MS-70, even though only a tiny fraction of the available coins had been submitted for grading.

2002

CIRCULATION MINTAGE: 3,260,800,000

Key to Collecting: Common in all grades including gem Mint State. Most are very attractive. Full Details coins are plentiful.

2002-D

CIRCULATION MINTAGE: 4,028,055,000

Key to Collecting: Easy to locate in all grades including gem Mint State, with great eye appeal. Full Details coins are available in coin stores everywhere.

2002-S

PROOF MINTAGE: 3,211,995

Enlarged 1.5x
(actual size 19 mm)

MARKET VALUES • 2002-S, Proof

PF-65RD	PF-67RD	PF-67Cam	PF-68DCam
$4	$7	$8	$10

Proofs: Made with deep cameo contrast. Common.

THE YEAR 2003

In America: On February 1 the space shuttle *Columbia* exploded over the Southwest, during re-entry to the earth's atmosphere from a space mission. Based on information provided by advisors, President Bush informed the public that Iraqi dictator Saddam Hussein possessed "weapons of mass destruction." An invasion of that country was launched. The war dragged into a prolonged encounter that divided America. The federal deficit reached unprecedented levels. Experienced economists worried that such programs as Social Security and Medicare would eventually run out of funding. The unemployment rate was 6.0 percent.

2003

CIRCULATION MINTAGE: 3,300,000,000

Key to Collecting: Plentiful in all grades including gem Mint State. Most are very attractive. Full Details coins are available in coin stores everywhere.

2003-D

CIRCULATION MINTAGE: 3,548,000,000

Enlarged 1.5x
(actual size 19 mm)

Key to Collecting: Easy to find in all grades including gem Mint State. Most are very attractive. Full Details coins are common.

2003-S

PROOF MINTAGE: 3,298,439

MARKET VALUES • 2003-S, Proof

PF-65RD	PF-67RD	PF-67Cam	PF-68DCam
$4	$7	$8	$10

Proofs: Made with deep cameo contrast. Common.

THE YEAR 2004

In America: The November election pitted incumbent George W. Bush against Massachusetts Senator John Kerry. Bush was the winner. Military spending and protection against potential terrorism defined the emphasis of the federal government. Stem cell research was hailed as a medical frontier with wonderful prospects, although research was slowed by political issues. The Boston Red Sox won the World Series—for the first time since 1918. The Internet search firm Google went public. Apple's iTunes program registered its 200 millionth download sale. *Shrek 2* and *Spider-Man 2* were box office winners.

In Numismatics: The ANS relocated from its long-time (since 1908) headquarters at 155th Street and Broadway, New York City, to 96 Fulton Street, downtown. The Harry W. Bass Jr. Library was dedicated in the new premises. The Mint announced that members of the Artistic Infusion Program (AIP) would be recognized by having their initials placed on any coins, such as statehood quarters, they might design. Many earlier artists were not so honored. Sales of paper money enjoyed rapid growth in the marketplace. In the auction room record prices were paid for ultra-grade coins, often dates and mintmarks considered common in such grades as 65 or 66 but proclaimed to be rare if certified 68, 69, or 70. Registry Set competition was intense.

2004

CIRCULATION MINTAGE: 3,379,600,000

Enlarged 1.5x
(actual size 19 mm)

Key to Collecting: Easy to find in all grades including gem Mint State, with beautiful surfaces. Full Details coins are plentiful.

2004-D

CIRCULATION MINTAGE: 3,456,400,000

Key to Collecting: Plentiful in all grades including gem Mint State. Most are very attractive. Full Details coins abound.

2004-S

PROOF MINTAGE: 2,965,422

MARKET VALUES • 2004-S, Proof

PF-65RD	PF-67RD	PF-67Cam	PF-68DCam
$4	$7	$8	$10

Proofs: Made with deep cameo contrast. Common.

THE YEAR 2005

In America: As the use of home computers and the Internet expanded, and in-home theaters and entertainment centers became more popular, citizens bought fewer tickets to films and sports events. Museum attendance was down. In late August hurricane Katrina raked New Orleans and did widespread damage along the Gulf Coast. By now China had become a leading manufacturer of consumer goods marketed in America.

In Numismatics: Newspapers carried stories of problems with forged and misrepresented coins being sold on the Internet, either directly or through online auctions—with little in the way of solutions in sight. Abuses were perpetrated by amateurs and clever crooks but not by established numismatic firms. In the regular auction room sales remained strong, especially for coins perceived as rare by virtue of having low certified population numbers. Rare became common, so to speak—and 14 coins changed hands for $1 million or more each.

News About Lincoln Cents: As in Aesop's fable, the tortoise Lincoln cent specialty continued on its merry way, while the hare "trophy coins" in other series captured headlines. High-grade modern cents with low population numbers continued to bring strong prices.

2005

CIRCULATION MINTAGE: 3,935,600,000

Enlarged 1.5x
(actual size 19 mm)

Key to Collecting: From 2005 onward circulation strikes are common in all grades including gem Mint State. Most are very attractive. Full Details coins are abundant.

2005-D

CIRCULATION MINTAGE: 3,764,450,500

2005-S

PROOF MINTAGE: 3,273,000

MARKET VALUES • 2005-S, Proof

PF-65RD	PF-67RD	PF-67Cam	PF-68DCam
$4	$7	$8	$10

Proofs: Made with deep cameo contrast. Common.

THE YEAR 2006

In America: By 2006 the war in Iraq had cost more than 2,000 lives of American soldiers and far more of innocent Iraqi citizens. President Bush and many members of the Republican-controlled Congress were strongly criticized. Housing prices, which had been rising for years, experienced a chill, and many foreclosures were made—the prelude to an even worse scenario the next year.

In Numismatics: The market remained dynamic overall, although in late summer a shortage, among dealers, of ready cash threatened to start a market downturn, which more than just a few observers thought was overdue.

News About Lincoln Cents: Hearings were held in Congress as to whether the cent should be abolished, in view of such coins costing more than face value to produce. No action was taken, and high mintages continued.

2006

CIRCULATION MINTAGE: 4,280,000,000

Enlarged 1.5x
(actual size 19 mm)

2006-D

CIRCULATION MINTAGE: 3,944,000,000

2006-S

PROOF MINTAGE: 2,923,105

MARKET VALUES • 2006-S, Proof

PF-65RD	PF-67RD	PF-67Cam	PF-68DCam
$4	$7	$8	$10

Proofs: Made with deep cameo contrast. Common.

THE YEAR 2007

In America: A poll published by *The Economist* ranked the United States down at No. 97 in a list of the most peaceful countries (Norway was first). By June candidates of the Republican and Democratic parties were campaigning heavily for the November 2008 presidential election, more than a year away. The Iraq war, still in progress, was the prime topic of discussion and debate. In July the Dow-Jones Industrial Average crossed 14,000 for the first time. High interest rates and a falling real estate market threw many properties into default on sub-prime mortgages.

In Numismatics: The overall market weakened when the passion for "trophy coins" eased, although there were many exceptions in the auction room. With higher interest rates and slower sales, many dealers were short of funds. Interest in "collector coins," these being key issues in popular series in grades from Good to lower Mint State, enjoyed a strong market. Outside of the higher-grade coins of the silver and gold federal series, there was great strength in tokens, medals, and paper money. Realization of the John J. Ford Jr. Collection, which consisted nearly entirely of these (and not regular coins), crossed the $50 million mark at Stack's, making it the most valuable collection ever sold. The Internet continued to be dynamic, taking market share from conventions, coin stores, and mail-order catalog listings.

News About Lincoln Cents: Despite talk that the cents should be discontinued because they cost more than face value to produce, they remained a mainstay in everyday commerce and retailing.

2007

CIRCULATION MINTAGE: 3,762,400,000

2007-D

CIRCULATION MINTAGE: 3,638,800,000

2007-S

PROOF MINTAGE: 2,577,166

Enlarged 1.5x
(actual size 19 mm)

MARKET VALUES • 2007-S, Proof

PF-65RD	PF-67RD	PF-67Cam	PF-68DCam
$4	$7	$8	$10

Proofs: Made with deep cameo contrast. Common.

THE YEAR 2008

In America: The Afghanistan and Iraq wars continued. The economy entered a recession, prices fell, unemployment rose, and wild lending practices for mortgages contributed to many citizens owing more on their houses than they were worth. The stock market fell. The Federal Reserve cut its rediscount rate to banks to 2.25 percent. In December the Dow-Jones Industrial Average dropped 680 points. Bernard Madoff, praised as one of America's most successful financial advisors, was charged with massive fraud extending over a period of many years. Barack Obama won the presidential election on November 4, becoming the first African-American president of the United States. At the time the unemployment rate was 6.1 percent, the inflation rate was 4.9 percent, and the federal budget had been running at a deficit through the entire previous administration.

In Numismatics: The doctoring of coins was a popular subject for debate. Countless Morgan dollars in particular now had rainbow and other colorful toning, far more than had ever been seen in the market before. "Gradeflation" was endemic, and across the board the leading certification services often bumped MS-63 to MS-64, MS-64 to MS-65, and so on. This was a win-win situation for the owners of the coins, who came to believe their coins were worth more, and for the grading services that collected more fees.

In March the ANA appointed well-known Ohio dealer Larry Shepherd to be the new executive director. "His short term priority is to stabilize the organization," wrote David Harper, editor of *Numismatic News*.[58] The passion for otherwise very common coins bringing high prices was the subject of this comment by *Coin World* market analyst Mark Ferguson:

Coins graded as perfect Mint State and Proof 70 lack dealer buyback support, and the supply grows as more are graded as such, which could lead to a correction in market values for particular coins that have advanced to levels beyond ridiculousness, according to many seasoned collectors and dealers.[59]

2008

CIRCULATION MINTAGE: 2,558,800,000

Key to Collecting: This issue is common in gem Mint State.

2008-D

CIRCULATION MINTAGE: 2,849,600,000

Enlarged 1.5x
(actual size 19 mm)

Key to Collecting: This issue is common in gem Mint State.

2008-S

PROOF MINTAGE: 2,169,561

MARKET VALUES • 2008-S, Proof

PF-65RD	PF-67RD	PF-67Cam	PF-68DCam
$4	$7	$8	$10

Key to Collecting: These Proofs were made with deep-cameo contrast. This issue is common.

THE YEAR 2009

In America: Most financial institutions and securities businesses experienced losses, and some failed. Problems continued with mortgages. High interest rates on credit cards attracted federal scrutiny, but not much was done about the problem. In October the unemployment rate was 10 percent, the highest since 1983. In January U.S. Airways Flight 1549, out of LaGuardia Airport in New York City, lost power in both engines after a bird strike. The pilot glided the plane down to the Hudson River and all 155 passengers and crew were rescued: "the miracle on the Hudson." Citizens shooting innocent people with handguns made news headlines on a regular basis this year and in the era. Serious gun controls were few and far between.

In Numismatics: Going into the new year the Federal Reserve placed orders for just 3 billion coins for 2009, down from 10.1 billion in 2008. The Mint established a hiring freeze, and employment during the year dropped 10 percent. The 110th Congress considered 129 bills relating to coins and medals and passed 17 of them. There were too many commemoratives, many collectors said. The new Proof MMIX $20 gold coins, which were sold in quantities, were a favorite at the ANA convention. Executive Director Larry Shepherd proudly reported that the ANA budget did not show a deficit despite the economic downturn. Cliff Mishler, a long-time executive with Krause Publications, now retired and a popular author, was sworn in as the president of the ANA. In the marketplace prices dropped on a number of coins that were "conditionally rare"—common enough as MS-65 or 66, but with few certified MS-68 or higher.

THE BICENTENNIAL REVERSES INTRODUCED

2009, BIRTH AND EARLY CHILDHOOD, COPPER-COATED ZINC

CIRCULATION MINTAGE: 284,400,000

Key to Collecting: This issue is common in gem Mint State. Most examples are brilliant, well struck, and of very high quality, grading far above MS-65. Some of the various 2009 types in this composition have water spot–like stains and can be avoided.

Notes: The American economy was in a recession. What might have been a nationally dynamic release of the new Lincoln cents was delayed because banks were sufficiently stocked with old cents and did not need any new ones. About this time, banks around the country slowed down and in many instances stopped ordering Presidential dollars, Sacagawea dollars, and other coins for their customers. On February 23 Paul Gilkes reported in *Coin World*:

> The Feb. 12 nationwide release of the first of four Lincoln cents to be issued in 2009 may be delayed because Federal Reserve Banks and coin terminals are saturated with cents. Orders for new coins are not being placed because of the state of the U.S. economy, according to published reports, but unconfirmed by U.S. Mint officials . . . As of Feb. 6, U.S. Mint officials were reported to be considering offering Denver and Philadelphia Mint circulation strikes in rolls at the Mint's Web site, but there was no indication whether customers would be offered an option similar to its Direct Ship program . . . in order to get the coins in circulation. Larue High School in Hodgenville, Ky., may be the only place Feb. 12 that collectors can definitely and immediately obtain the first Lincoln cent, which shows a log cabin representative of Abraham Lincoln's birthplace . . .

Due to the slow economy and reduced needs for cents, the mintage for 2009 was projected to reach record lows for recent years. "If production of the remaining three Lincoln cents for 2009 stays at the level of the first coin, the total of 2.5 billion or so cents would be less than half the number of cents produced in 2008 and the lowest combined circulation-cent total in some 40 years," Paul Gilkes proposed in an article in *Coin World*, April 27, 2009.

2009, BIRTH AND EARLY CHILDHOOD, COPPER, SATIN FINISH

CIRCULATION MINTAGE: 784,614

Enlarged 1.5x
(actual size 19 mm)

MARKET VALUES • 2009, Birth and Early Childhood, Copper, Satin Finish

MS-68RD	MS-69RD
$15	$45

Notes: Paul Gilkes reported on the Mint's preparations to strike coins in the copper alloy originally used for Lincoln cents in *Coin World*, March 9, 2009:

> The U.S. Mint has placed orders for coin strip to make planchets to strike 2009 Lincoln cents for coin sets in the same alloy used in the first Lincoln bronze cents, introduced into circulation in 1909. The composition of the original planchets from 1909, each weighing 3.1 grams, is 95% copper, 5% tin and zinc. U.S. Mint spokesman Michael White said Feb. 20 that cents from 1909 were sampled and the tin level set at 2% for the new planchets . . . White said Feb. 18 that the coinage strip for the cents to be made for inclusion in the numismatic cents was ordered from Olin Brass, located in East Alton, Ill., one of two Mint vendors that supplies the U.S. Mint with coinage strip for copper-nickel 5-cent coins; copper-nickel clad dimes, quarter dollars, and half dollars; and manganese-brass clad Presidential dollars and Native American dollar coins. The cent strip will be shipped to Jarden Zinc Products in Greeneville, Tenn., where blanks will first be punched from the coinage strip and then processed into 'ready-to-strike' planchets with upset, or raised rims. Mint officials have not disclosed whether production has commenced on either the Proof or Uncirculated Mint set versions of the cent in the 1909 composition . . .

2009-D, BIRTH AND EARLY CHILDHOOD, COPPER-COATED ZINC

CIRCULATION MINTAGE: 350,400,000

Key to Collecting: This issue is common in gem Mint State. Some of the various 2009 types in this composition have water spot–like stains and can be avoided.

2009-D, BIRTH AND EARLY CHILDHOOD, COPPER, SATIN FINISH

CIRCULATION MINTAGE: 784,614

MARKET VALUES • 2009-D, Birth and Early Childhood, Copper, Satin Finish

MS-68RD	MS-69RD
$17	$95

Key to Collecting: All of these cents were sold at a premium to collectors. Nearly all examples are brilliant, sharply struck, and grade MS-69 or 70.

2009-S, BIRTH AND EARLY CHILDHOOD, COPPER

PROOF MINTAGE: 2,995,615

MARKET VALUES • 2009-S, Birth and Early Childhood, Copper, Proof

PF-65RD	PF-67RD	PF-67Cam	PF-68DCam
$4	$7	$8	$10

Key to Collecting: These Proofs were made with deep-cameo contrast. Most examples are brilliant and grade PF-69 or 70.

2009, Formative Years, Copper-Coated Zinc

Circulation Mintage: 376,000,000

Key to Collecting: This issue is common in gem Mint State. Some of the various 2009 types in this composition have water spot–like stains and can be avoided.

Notes: Paul Gilkes reported on the launch of this design in *Coin World*, June 1, 2009:

> Threatening weather failed to dampen the enthusiasm of the thousands of collectors and other members of the public who traveled to Lincoln State Park in Lincoln City, Ind., for a May 14 event launching the second 2009 Lincoln cent. Participants were afforded opportunities to acquire rolls of the second of four circulating commemorative Lincoln cents to be issued in 2009 marking Lincoln's 200th birthday. The second design reflects his formative years as a youth and young man in Indiana . . . After a nearly hour-long ceremony May 14 staged by the U.S. Mint at the park's 1,500-seat Lincoln Amphitheatre, representatives from Freedom National Bank in nearby Dale, Ind., began exchanging 50-coin rolls containing cents struck at the Philadelphia Mint for cash, for a minimum of two rolls, up to a maximum of six rolls (temporarily reduced to four, at the request of U.S. Mint officials, but then the six-roll maximum was reinstated just before the exchange began), during their first pass through the line.

2009, Formative Years, Doubled Die Reverse: The *Cherrypickers' Guide to Rare Die Varieties of United States Coins* notes: "Numerous doubled-die reverses appear on Lincoln cents of the Formative Years design. These are localized on the left hand, most often in what appears to be an extra index finger or thumb. The circulation-strike doubled die reverses listed here all exhibit either a strong or very strong spread." (Also see 2009-S, Formative Years, Copper, Proof on page 275).

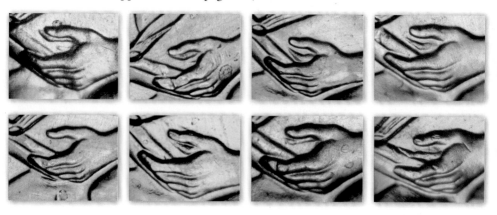

2009, Formative Years, Copper, Satin Finish

Circulation Mintage: 784,614

Market Values • 2009, Formative Years, Copper, Satin Finish

MS-68RD	MS-69RD
$15	$45

Key to Collecting: All of these cents were sold at a premium to collectors. Nearly all examples are brilliant, sharply struck, and grade MS-69 or 70.

2009-D, FORMATIVE YEARS, COPPER-COATED ZINC

CIRCULATION MINTAGE: 363,600,000

Enlarged 1.5x
(actual size 19 mm)

Key to Collecting: This issue is common in gem Mint State. Some of the various 2009 types in this composition have water spot–like stains and can be avoided.

2009-D, FORMATIVE YEARS, COPPER, SATIN FINISH

CIRCULATION MINTAGE: 784,614

MARKET VALUES • 2009-D, Formative Years, Copper, Satin Finish

MS-68RD	MS-69RD
$15	$250

Key to Collecting: All of these cents were sold at a premium to collectors. Nearly all examples are brilliant, sharply struck, and grade MS-69 or 70.

2009-S, FORMATIVE YEARS, COPPER

PROOF MINTAGE: 2,995,615

MARKET VALUES • 2009-S, Formative Years, Copper, Proof

PF-65RD	PF-67RD	PF-67Cam	PF-68DCam
$4	$7	$8	$10

Key to Collecting: These Proofs were made with deep-cameo contrast. This issue is common. Most examples are brilliant and grade PF-69 or 70.

2009-S, Doubled Die Reverse: The Fivaz-Stanton number for this variety is FS-01-2009S-801. This is the most popular doubled-die reverse for the Formative Years Proof. See 2009, Formative Years, Copper-Coated Zinc, on page 274 for more doubled dies of this design.

2009, PROFESSIONAL LIFE, COPPER-COATED ZINC

CIRCULATION MINTAGE: 316,000,000

Key to Collecting: This issue is common in gem Mint State. Some of the various 2009 types in this composition have water spot–like stains and can be avoided.

Notes: Paul Gilkes reported on the launch of this design in *Coin World*, August 31, 2009:

> Die-hard collectors, dealers and others converged on the Old State Capitol in Springfield, Ill., for the opportunity to exchange cash Aug. 13 for rolls of the 2009, Lincoln, Professional Life, cent. The cent depicts on its reverse a standing portrait of Lincoln as though delivering a speech, with the Old State Capitol in the background over his left shoulder . . .

2009, Professional Life, Copper, Satin Finish

Enlarged 1.5x
(actual size 19 mm)

Circulation Mintage: 784,614

Market Values • 2009, Professional Life, Copper, Satin Finish

MS-68RD	MS-69RD
$15	$45

Key to Collecting: All of these cents were sold at a premium to collectors. Nearly all examples are brilliant, sharply struck, and grade MS-69 or 70.

2009-D, Professional Life, Copper-Coated Zinc

Circulation Mintage: 336,000,000

Key to Collecting: This issue is common in gem Mint State. Some of the various 2009 types in this composition have water spot–like stains and can be avoided.

2009-D, Professional Life, Copper, Satin Finish

Circulation Mintage: 784,614

Market Values • 2009-D, Professional Life, Copper, Satin Finish

MS-68RD	MS-69RD
$15	$210

Key to Collecting: All of these cents were sold at a premium to collectors. Nearly all examples are brilliant, sharply struck, and grade MS-69 or 70.

2009-S, Professional Life, Copper

Proof Mintage: 2,995,615

Market Values • 2009-S, Professional Life, Copper, Proof

PF-65RD	PF-67RD	PF-67Cam	PF-68DCam
$4	$7	$8	$10

Key to Collecting: These Proofs were made with deep-cameo contrast. This issue is common. Most are brilliant and grade Proof-69 or 70.

2009, Presidency, Copper-Coated Zinc

Circulation Mintage: 129,600,000

Key to Collecting: This issue is common in gem Mint State. Some of the various 2009 types in this composition have water spot–like stains and can be avoided.

Notes: *Numismatic News* reported on December 1, 2009:

> The weather did not cooperate with the Nov. 12 launch of the fourth and final Lincoln cent design ceremony on the lawn of the U.S. Capitol Building at the Ulysses S. Grant Memorial in Washington, D.C., but some 250 people eagerly awaited the opportunity to trade folding money for Uncirculated rolls of the new coins. Heading up the list of dignitaries that braved the rain from the remnants of Hurricane Ida was Mint Director Ed. Moy. He was joined by Donald R. Kennon, chief historian of the U.S. Capitol Historical Society and Eileen R. Mackevich, executive director of the Abraham Lincoln Bicentennial Commission . . .

2009, PRESIDENCY, COPPER, SATIN FINISH

Enlarged 1.5x
(actual size 19 mm)

CIRCULATION MINTAGE: 784,614

MARKET VALUES • 2009, Presidency, Copper, Satin Finish

MS-68RD	MS-69RD
$15	$45

Key to Collecting: All of these cents were sold at a premium to collectors. Nearly all examples are brilliant, sharply struck, and grade MS-69 or 70.

2009-D, PRESIDENCY, COPPER-COATED ZINC

CIRCULATION MINTAGE: 198,000,000

Key to Collecting: This issue is common in gem Mint State. Some of the various 2009 types in this composition have water spot–like stains and can be avoided.

2009-D, PRESIDENCY, COPPER, SATIN FINISH

CIRCULATION MINTAGE: 784,614

MARKET VALUES • 2009-D, Presidency, Copper, Satin Finish

MS-68RD	MS-69RD
$15	$200

Key to Collecting: All of these cents were sold at a premium to collectors. Nearly all examples are brilliant, sharply struck, and grade MS-69 or 70.

2009-S, PRESIDENCY, COPPER

PROOF MINTAGE: 2,995,615

MARKET VALUES • 2009-S, Presidency, Copper, Proof

PF-65RD	PF-67RD	PF-67Cam	PF-68DCam
$4	$7	$8	$10

Key to Collecting: These Proofs were made with deep-cameo contrast. This issue is common. Most are brilliant and grade Proof-69 or 70.

THE YEAR 2010

In America: Middle East wars continued with no end in sight for America. America's military budget was multiples of that of either China or Russia, and domestically more people were in jail per capita than in any other leading Western country. Most crimes involved drugs, a modern-day reiteration of Prohibition. In March British Petroleum's Deepwater Horizon oil-drilling platform exploded, spilling large quantities of oil into the Gulf of Mexico. WikiLeaks published without authorization more than 400,000 documents and diplomatic cables relating to government military and security affairs. The Supreme Court lifted restrictions on political expenditures by corporations, unions, and certain others. This ruling would reshape the political landscape in its entirety. In 2010 world sales of gold were estimated at $150 billion. With 8,134 tons, the United States had the largest holding. The Tea Party political movement, which gained attention during the 2009 political season, held its first convention in 2010. Collectibles of nearly all kinds enjoyed a strong market, ranging from coins to automobiles to art. Action on eBay and other activity on the Internet were largely responsible.

In Numismatics: Bright-red copper coins that change color after being certified were the subject of new restrictions: "Since environmental factors can create changes in the color of copper beyond our control, we will not be guaranteeing the color of copper coins graded or sold after Jan. 1, 2010," PCGS announced.

THE SHIELD REVERSE TYPE INTRODUCED

2010

CIRCULATION MINTAGE: 1,963,630,000

Key to Collecting: This issue is common in gem Mint State. PCGS has certified many as having a Satin Finish.

2010-D

CIRCULATION MINTAGE: 2,047,200,000

Key to Collecting: Despite sometimes being labeled "Satin Finish," this is a regular issue. It is common in gem Mint State. PCGS has certified certain coins of this era as Satin Finish, although only the 2009 coins were sold using that designation.

2010-S

PROOF MINTAGE: 1,689,216

Enlarged 1.5x
(actual size 19 mm)

MARKET VALUES • 2010-S, Proof

PF-65RD	PF-67RD	PF-67Cam	PF-68DCam
$4	$7	$8	$10

Key to Collecting: These Proofs were made with deep-cameo contrast. Nearly all examples are well struck, brilliant, and in grades of PF-69 and 70.

THE YEAR 2011

In America: Youth unemployment became very high in America and other Western countries. Wall Street was still suffering from the dot-com bubble and the questionable nature of many mortgage and other financial deals. Osama bin Laden, head of the Al Qaeda terrorist organization and mastermind of the 2001 destruction of the World Trade Center, was killed by U.S. forces. In Tucson a deranged man shot U.S. Representative Gabrielle Giffords and 20 others. As part of budget constraints the government cut funding for National Public Radio (NPR). Organizations devoted to art, literature, music, education, and science suffered with reduced budgets. Much infrastructure was in need of upgrading, including bridges, roads, and rail systems.

In Numismatics: The rising price of copper and nickel, a concern for many years, prompted the Mint to experiment with other metals during this era.

2011

Enlarged 1.5x
(actual size 19 mm)

CIRCULATION MINTAGE: 2,402,400,000

Key to Collecting: This issue is common in gem Mint State.

2011-D

CIRCULATION MINTAGE: 2,536,140,000

Key to Collecting: This issue is common in gem Mint State.

2011-S

PROOF MINTAGE: 1,673,010

MARKET VALUES • 2011-S, Proof

PF-65RD	PF-67RD	PF-67Cam	PF-68DCam
$5	$7	$8	$10

Key to Collecting: These Proofs were made with deep-cameo contrast. Nearly all examples are well struck, brilliant, and in grades of PF-69 and 70. For any and all of these later-era Proofs, most survived in the condition as issued.

THE YEAR 2012

In America: The advent of fracking alleviated American dependence on foreign oil. Solar energy was being increasingly tapped, with government incentives helping. NASA's *Curiosity* rover landed on Mars. It carried a circulated 1909 V.D.B. Lincoln cent, the surface color of which was used to calibrate an optical device. *The Scream*, a painting by Edvard Munch, crossed the auction block at $120 million—a new record for art at auction. San Francisco set a $10-per-hour minimum wage, the highest in the country, precipitating calls for McDonalds (in particular) and other nationwide business to raise wages. For-profit prisons and hospitals drew criticism for exploiting the poor and the sick. In Florida unarmed Trayvon Martin, a 17-year-old African-American boy, was fatally shot while walking home through his neighborhood by a member of the neighborhood watch, energizing a nationwide debate on crime and the policing of Black bodies. In Newtown, Connecticut, a crazed young man went into an elementary school and shot and killed 27 people, including 20 children aged 6 and 7. Tropical storm Sandy ravaged the East Coast and caused storm surge damage that closed down parts of lower Manhattan. President Barack Obama won a return bid to the White House.

In Numismatics: The release of America the Beautiful quarters honoring national parks and historical places continued on a regular basis at the rate of five issues per year, as did the sale to collectors of three-ounce silver pieces with the same designs. Deputy Mint Director Richard A. Peterson announced a reorganization of the mid- and upper levels of the U.S. Mint administration to increase efficiency and for more effective marketing. The Mint reviewed 123 applications for the Artistic Infusion Program, whereby up to 20 artists and sculptors would be selected to aid in the preparation of coin and medal designs.

2012

CIRCULATION MINTAGE: 3,132,000,000

Key to Collecting: This issue is common in gem Mint State.

Enlarged 1.5x
(actual size 19 mm)

2012-D

CIRCULATION MINTAGE: 2,883,200,000

Key to Collecting: This issue is common in gem Mint State.

2012-S

PROOF MINTAGE: 1,239,148

MARKET VALUES • 2012-S, Proof

PF-65RD	PF-67RD	PF-67Cam	PF-68DCam
$5	$7	$8	$10

Key to Collecting: These Proofs were made with deep-cameo contrast. Nearly all examples are well struck, brilliant, and in grades of PF-69 and 70.

THE YEAR 2013

In America: The Affordable Care Act, dubbed "Obamacare," launched. At the Boston Marathon two Chechnya-born brothers set off bombs made with pressure cookers to kill three and wound 264 people. An eight-story factory in Bangladesh collapsed, killing 1,129 and injuring more than twice that number. This prompted American importers to inspect foreign factories that supplied clothing and other goods. Edward Snowden disclosed massive espionage that the American government had been conducting against unsuspecting citizens and others. On June 21 the U.S. Department of Justice charged Snowden on two counts of violating the Espionage Act of 1917, as well as theft of U.S. government or foreign government property. He sought asylum in Moscow, Russia. 3D printing made the news. The economy showed signs of recovery, and by November the Dow-Jones Industrial Average closed at 16,000 for the first time in history.

In Numismatics: A new design for the $100 note was released and created much excitement. Kim Kiick, a long-time employee of the American Numismatic Association, was named executive director. Counterfeit coins and precious-metal ingots, many originating in China, continued to be a challenge in the marketplace, resulting in increased use of the leading certification services.

2013

CIRCULATION MINTAGE: 3,750,400,000

Key to Collecting: This issue is common in gem Mint State.

2013-D

CIRCULATION MINTAGE: 3,319,600,000

Key to Collecting: This issue is common in gem Mint State.

2013-S

PROOF MINTAGE: 1,274,505

Enlarged 1.5x
(actual size 19 mm)

MARKET VALUES • 2013-S, Proof

PF-65RD	PF-67RD	PF-67Cam	PF-68DCam
$5	$7	$8	$10

Key to Collecting: These Proofs were made with deep-cameo contrast. Nearly all examples are well struck, brilliant, and in grades of PF-69 and 70.

THE YEAR 2014

In America: In December President Obama announced the resumption of normal relations with Cuba, which had been deemed a terrorist country since 1961. In Africa the Ebola virus spread and many American medical professionals went to help. Russia annexed the independent country of Crimea, which also endangered the Ukraine. A terrorist group once known as al-Qaeda in Iraq rebranded itself as the Islamic State of Iraq and the Levant (often shortened to ISIL or ISIS), in an attempt to legitimize itself as a governing body. In reality the group, responsible for war crimes and genocide in Iraq and Syria, is a fringe group with no claim to statehood and only the most threadbare claim to Islam—a religion whose tenets the group regularly violates, committing violent acts forbidden in the Qur'an and killing thousands of Muslims in addition to members of religious and ethnic minorities in the region. Personal drones equipped with cameras became popular with the public, while the military continued to use deadly remote-controlled drone aircraft. In Hollywood *12 Years a Slave* earned the Academy Award for Best Picture. Oil prices fell by nearly 50 percent as a flood of crude oil, extracted from shale by the fracking process, made America self-sufficient and no longer reliant on foreign countries.

In Numismatics: The U.S. Mint struck 1964–2014-dated Kennedy half dollars in gold to observe the 50th anniversary of the design. Speculation in modern Mint coins certified in grades such as MS-69 and MS-70 was controversial, especially coins labeled "early strike" and similar, which typically sold for no extra premium in the aftermarket. The Mint struck domed National Baseball Hall of Fame commemorative coins for sale to collectors. These were rounded on the obverse, showing a baseball, and recessed on the reverse, showing a baseball glove, in denominations of 50 cents, $1, and $5.

2014

CIRCULATION MINTAGE: 3,990,800,000

Key to Collecting: This issue is common in gem Mint State.

2014-D

CIRCULATION MINTAGE: 4,155,600,000

Key to Collecting: This issue is common in gem Mint State.

2014-S

PROOF MINTAGE: 1,190,369

Enlarged 1.5x
(actual size 19 mm)

MARKET VALUES • 2014-S, Proof

PF-65RD	PF-67RD	PF-67Cam	PF-68DCam
$5	$8	$8	$10

Key to Collecting: These Proofs were made with deep-cameo contrast. Nearly all examples are well struck, brilliant, and in grades of PF-69 and 70.

THE YEAR 2015

In America: Weather dominated headlines early in the year with record snowfall and cold east of the Mississippi and unprecedented drought on the West Coast. The shooting of unarmed African-Americans by police swelled into a major national concern. In June a young white man killed nine worshipers in a historic Black church in Charleston, South Carolina. The killer's fondness for the Confederate States flag led to a reappraisal of its use of on public buildings in the South and on merchandise in general. ISIS was involved in global terrorism, including an attack in Paris in November. This raised great alarm across the United States. The economy enjoyed a rebound that had been in process for several years. In December the Federal Reserve raised the discount rate 0.25 percent to 0.50 percent, the first such raise since the business recession of the late 2000s. In February, the New England Patriots became the second team in NFL history to win three Super Bowl championships within four years. Thoroughbred American Pharoah (whose name was an inadvertent misspelling) was the first horse in 37 years to win the Triple Crown. At one time in late summer 16 Republicans and five Democrats were running for their parties' respective presidential nominations. New York real-estate magnate Donald Trump became the darling of the media when he entered as a Republican candidate, often making inflammatory and controversial remarks.

In Numismatics: The U.S. Mint issued "reverse Proof" versions of certain coins for the collector market. Sales of silver Eagles were especially strong due to the relatively low price of that metal. Rhett Jeppson was named principal deputy director of the Mint. The American Numismatic Association World's Fair of Money was held in Rosemont, Illinois, for the third consecutive year. The Smithsonian Institution opened its "Value of Money" exhibit showcasing selections from the National Numismatic Collection.

2015

CIRCULATION MINTAGE: 4,691,300,000

Key to Collecting: This issue is common in gem Mint State.

Enlarged 1.5x
(actual size 19 mm)

2015-D

CIRCULATION MINTAGE: 4,674,000,000

Key to Collecting: This issue is common in gem Mint State.

2015-S

PROOF MINTAGE: 1,099,182

MARKET VALUES • 2015-S, Proof

PF-65RD	PF-67RD	PF-67Cam	PF-68DCam
$5	$8	$8	$10

Key to Collecting: These Proofs were made with deep-cameo contrast. Nearly all examples are well struck, brilliant, and in grades of PF-69 and 70.

THE YEAR 2016

In America: Mosquito-borne Zika virus outbreaks in Central and South America caused alarm in the United States. The Panama Papers were released, exposing offshore tax shelters used by prominent American celebrities and politicians. ISIS continued brutal attacks internationally, including a bombing July 3 in Baghdad, which killed more than 250 holiday shoppers preparing meals for the Muslim holy month of Ramadan. In

America ISIS inspired a string of attacks by "self-radicalized" individuals, including lone-gunman Omar Mateen, who killed 49 and wounded 53 in an attack on Pulse night-club in Orlando, Florida. The Pulse shooting was the deadliest terror attack in America since September 11, the worst-ever shooting by a single gunman, and the deadliest-ever attack against LGBTQ people in the United States. Elsewhere, federal and state governments debated whether religion was a valid reason for denying LGBTQ individuals access to public accommodations. In June Great Britain voted to leave the European Union. In July massive protests shut down highways in American cities following the police shootings of Alton Sterling and Philando Castille.

In Numismatics: The U.S. Mint released 2016-dated gold strikings of the 1916 Mercury dime, Standing Liberty quarter, and Liberty Walking half dollar designs, replicating the originals, but with tiny lettering on the reverse stating they are in gold and giving the weight in ounces. The Presidential "golden dollar" program came to a temporary end, as all eligible deceased presidents had been honored. The American Numismatic Association World's Fair of Money was held in Anaheim, California, in August.

2016

CIRCULATION MINTAGE: 4,698,000,000

Key to Collecting: This issue is common in gem Mint State.

2016-D

CIRCULATION MINTAGE: 4,420,400,000

Key to Collecting: This issue is common in gem Mint State.

2016-S

PROOF MINTAGE: 978,457

Enlarged 1.5x
(actual size 19 mm)

MARKET VALUES • 2016-S, Proof

PF-65RD	PF-67RD	PF-67Cam	PF-68DCam
$5	$8	$8	$10

Key to Collecting: These Proofs were made with deep-cameo contrast. Nearly all examples are well struck, brilliant, and in grades of PF-69 and 70.

THE YEAR 2017

In America: The start of 2017 marked the beginning of President Donald Trump's first year in office. It also saw the rise of controversial phrases like "alternative facts" and "fake news" in the media after both were used liberally by the president and others within his administration. Doubts of the legitimacy of his victory and rumors of Russian interference swarmed among political pundits. Hundreds of thousands of protestors descended on Washington for the Women's March. Advocating for women's rights, reproductive rights, and other human-rights reform policies, they held the largest single-day demonstration in U.S. recorded history. In April NASA astronaut Peggy Whitson broke the record for longest cumulative time spent in space by any NASA astronaut. The appointment of conservative justice Neil Gorsuch to the Supreme Court was confirmed; he filled the vacancy left by the death of Justice Antonin Scalia in 2016. Despite a memorable mishap in name announcement, *Moonlight*, a film centered around the life of a young Black gay male, won Best Picture at the 2017 Academy Awards. This came two years after the hashtag #OscarsSoWhite—which critiqued the lack of diversity within award nominations—went viral. The Academy also made a commitment to diversify its membership by inviting more entertainers and creators of color, and people with various gender identities and sexual orientations. In August white nationalists and those who identified as part of other historically prejudiced and racist groups led a rally in Charlottesville, Virginia, through the University of Virginia's campus. Violence ensued when many of the protesters clashed with counter-protesters. Later a man connected to the protesters drove his car head-on into a crowd of counter-protestors, killing one and injuring 19. Record-breaking hurricanes Harvey, Irma, and Maria rocked Texas, Florida, and Puerto Rico and some small Caribbean islands, respectively, causing massive amounts of death, damage, and displacement. Puerto Rico was left without power for months. In late August crowds came together across the U.S. to witness the awe-inspiring passing of a total solar eclipse. (The next one is slated to occur in the year 2024.) The #MeToo movement began when several high-profile women revealed the sexual harassment and abuse they had suffered from powerful Hollywood men, most notably film producer Harvey Weinstein. In December Republicans passed the largest federal tax-cut package since the Reagan era, and the world celebrated with Australia as it became the 25th country to recognize and support marriage equality.

In Numismatics: The U.S. Mint released into circulation the first one-cent coins to bear the Philadelphia "P" mintmark. A temporary one-year type, the 2017-P Lincoln cent coins were struck to celebrate the 225th anniversary of coinage at the U.S. Mint. Cents resumed being struck without the P mintmark in 2018, per tradition. Also released in recognition of the anniversary was the $100 American Liberty gold coin featuring an all-new design of Lady Liberty as an African-American woman. While not universally well received, the design marked a significant change in status quo, as the Mint has planned a series of more modern representations of Lady Liberty to be forthcoming in following years. In August it was announced that Barry Stuppler was selected as the new president of the Professional Numismatists Guild (PNG) for the 2017–2019 term. The first silver piece minted by the U.S. government in 1783, recently identified by numismatist David McCarthy, was on display at the American Numismatic Association's 2017 World's Fair of Money. The third edition of *Mega Red*—the Expanded Deluxe Edition of *A Guide Book of United States Coins*—featured a 314-page focus on Shield, Liberty Head, Buffalo, and Jefferson nickels, covering 545 varieties. The Numismatic Literary Guild awarded its "Book of the Year" prize to *1792: Birth of a Nation's Coinage*, by Pete Smith, Joel Orosz, and Leonard Augsburger.

2017-P

CIRCULATION MINTAGE: 4,361,220,000

Key to Collecting: This issue is common in gem Mint State.

2017-D

CIRCULATION MINTAGE: 4,272,800,000

Key to Collecting: This issue is common in gem Mint State.

2017-S

PROOF MINTAGE: 979,475

Enlarged 1.5x
(actual size 19 mm)

MARKET VALUES • 2017-S, PROOF

PF-65RD	PF-67RD	PF-67Cam	PF-68DCam
$5	$8	$8	$10

Key to Collecting: These Proofs were made with deep-cameo contrast. Nearly all examples are well struck, brilliant, and in grades of PF-69 and 70.

THE YEAR 2018

In America: The 2018 Winter Olympics in Pyeongchang, South Korea, saw the United States finish with a total of 23 medals, 9 of which were gold, 8 silver, and 6 bronze. In February the highly anticipated film *Black Panther* premiered to box-office–shattering records. It grossed over 1 billion dollars worldwide, becoming the third-highest-grossing film in the United States, surpassing *Titanic*. It was the first mega-blockbuster film to be directed by a Black director with a predominantly Black cast. Its impact was deemed so culturally significant that the Smithsonian Institution's National Museum of African American History and Culture acquired several items from the film for their collection. Later that month an armed student walked into Marjory Stoneman Douglas High School in Parkland, Florida, and killed 17 people, most of whom were students. This incident sparked the March for Our Lives movement, which sought to push reform of gun-control laws and institute more stringent regulations. The National Rifle Association of America was the movement's primary opponent. In April Americans discussed the swearing-in of Miguel Díaz-Canel as the president of Cuba, which marked the first time since 1959 that Cuba had not been led by a Castro brother. In May an American actress married into the British royal family. After a high-profile engagement and much anticipation, Prince Harry, Duke of Sussex, and Meghan Markle were wed at St. George's Chapel, Windsor Castle, making Markle the first person of African descent to become an official member of the British royal family. The 2018 United States–North Korea summit took place in June in Singapore. A historic event, the summit was the first meeting between a U.S. president and a leader of North Korea after decades-long tensions between the two countries. Supreme Court justice Anthony Kennedy announced his retirement, giving President Trump a second opportunity to appoint a member to the nation's highest court. The 2018 FIFA World Cup began in mid-July to uproarious global excitement, and for the first time in 32 years the American men's team failed to qualify, after a devastating loss to Trinidad and Tobago in October 2017. The event took place in Russia; in 2026, the United States, Canada, and Mexico will host the 23rd World Cup in 2026 as part of their North American "United" bid. The majority of games will take place in the United States, while Canada and Mexico will host ten matches each. It will be the first tournament to be hosted by three nations.

In Numismatics: In March David J. Ryder was confirmed as the new director of the United States Mint. The Citizens Coinage Advisory Committee met in Washington to discuss and review designs for the final years of the America the Beautiful Quarters® program. In Colorado Springs in June, on the campus of Colorado College, the American Numismatic Association held its 50th Summer Seminar, a two-week educational event with classes in coin grading, photography, numismatic writing and publishing, hobonickel carving, paper-money collecting, and other numismatic topics, as well as an auction to benefit the ANA Young Numismatist program, plus many opportunities for hobby camaraderie. In August the ANA held its annual World's Fair of Money in Philadelphia. The ANA experienced a noticeable increase in membership, likely due to the increased number of programs offered. The fourth edition of the massive 1,504-page *Mega Red* included a 294-page feature on 222 years of U.S. dimes, 1796 to 2018, covering 845 varieties, plus more than two dozen appendices, many of which featured dime-related topics.

2018

CIRCULATION MINTAGE: 4,066,800,000

Key to Collecting: This issue is common in gem Mint State.

2018-D

CIRCULATION MINTAGE: 3,736,400,000

Key to Collecting: This issue is common in gem Mint State.

2018-S

PROOF MINTAGE: 901,072 estimated.

Enlarged 1.5x
(actual size 19 mm)

MARKET VALUES • 2018-S, PROOF

PF-65RD	PF-67RD	PF-67Cam	PF-68DCam
$5	$8	$8	$10

Key to Collecting: These Proofs were made with deep-cameo contrast. Nearly all examples are well struck, brilliant, and in grades of PF-69 and 70.

THE YEAR 2019

In America: After the 2018 midterm elections, in January the Democratic Party took leadership of the House of Representatives, while the Republican Party increased its majority in the Senate. The New England Patriots won the Super Bowl in February, tying with the Pittsburgh Steelers for the most Super Bowl wins and giving quarterback Tom Brady his sixth NFL world championship. All eyes turned to the 2020 presidential elections, as 20 Democratic politicians announced their candidacies, the largest field in American history, and began campaigning. The two-year investigation by Robert Mueller into whether the Trump campaign helped Russia interfere in the 2016 presidential election concluded with the release of the Mueller report on March 22. *Avengers: Endgame* became the second highest-grossing film of all time. The wreck of the *Clotilda*, the last know slave ship to transport African slaves across the Atlantic to the United States, was found in the Mobile River in Alabama on May 22. The U.S. women's soccer team won its fourth World Cup. Following a rash of shootings, anti-gun rallies were held in more than 100 cities across all 50 states. On September 24, the U.S. House announced a formal impeachment inquiry against President Donald Trump. A new military branch, the U.S. Space Force, was established on December 20.

In Numismatics: The U.S. Mint switched from a .900-fine composition to .999-fine silver to mint its collectible silver coins, to entice new collectors and precious-metal investors. This change affected silver Proof Roosevelt dimes, Washington quarters, and Kennedy half dollars, as well as commemorative silver dollars. While .900 silver had been a standard since the 1830s, .999-fine silver coins have been used for American Silver Eagles since their launch in 1986.

America the Beautiful quarters featuring a W mintmark for the West Point Mint were minted for circulation, the first time that W-mintmarked coins were distributed into everyday commerce. Each of the five designs released in 2019 had a limited mintage of just two million coins.

The Chicago Coin Club marked its 100th anniversary with a special *Red Book*—a limited edition of only 250 copies with a customized hardcover.

Joseph Menna became the U.S. Mint's chief engraver in February 2019, the 14th person to hold that role. Menna initially joined the Mint in 2005 as its first full-time digitally skilled artist.

One of the most popular recent commemorative coin programs debuted: a clad half dollar, a silver dollar, and a $5 gold piece marking the 50th anniversary of the Apollo 11 moon landing.

In the American Innovation dollars program, launched the previous year with a single introductory coin, four new dollars were minted in 2019. They celebrated Delaware (Annie Jump Cannon's classification of the stars), Pennsylvania (the polio vaccine), New Jersey (the light bulb), and Georgia (the Trustee's Garden).

2019-P

CIRCULATION MINTAGE: 3,542,800,000
Key to Collecting: Gem Mint State is the norm for this issue.

2019-D

CIRCULATION MINTAGE: 3,497,600,000
Key to Collecting: Seek perfection and don't be satisfied with a coin in less than gem Mint State.

2019-S

PROOF MINTAGE: 1,061,558 estimated.

MARKET VALUES • 2019-S, Proof

PF-65RD	PF-67RD	PF-67Cam	PF-68DCam
$5	$8	$8	$10

Key to Collecting: Nearly all 2019-S Proofs grade PF-69 or PF-70. Most are well struck and brilliant, made in deep-cameo contrast. The mintage figure is not yet finally audited.

2019-W

CIRCULATION MINTAGE: 346,117 estimated.
Key to Collecting: These special coins were included as a premium in the U.S. Mint 2019 Uncirculated Coin Set. Quality is high, with gem Mint State being the norm.

2019-W, PROOF

PROOF MINTAGE: 600,423 estimated.

MARKET VALUES • 2019-W, Proof

PF-65RD	PF-67RD	PF-67Cam	PF-68DCam
$10	$15	$18	$20

Key to Collecting: The West Point Mint Proofs were included as a premium in the Mint's 2019 Proof sets.

2019-W, REVERSE PROOF

PROOF MINTAGE: 412,508 estimated.

Enlarged 1.5x
(actual size 19 mm)

MARKET VALUES • 2019-W, Reverse Proof

PF-65RD	PF-67RD	PF-67Cam	PF-68DCam
$10	$15	$18	$20

Key to Collecting: These coins, in their unusual Reverse Proof format, were included as a premium in the 2019 U.S. Mint Silver Proof Set.

THE YEAR 2020

In America: The COVID-19 pandemic was the defining event of 2020 across the globe. Its effects reached every facet of life, from stay-at-home orders and travel restrictions to school closures and supply-chain shortages. The first COVID-19 case reached the United States in January, and the first death occurred by the end of February. President Trump's impeachment trial began on January 16 and concluded on February 5, with the president acquitted of both charges. In February, the Kansas City Chiefs won the Super Bowl and *Parasite* became the first non-English-language film to win Best Picture at the Academy Awards. Around the country, protests sprang up in response to pandemic lockdown measures and against racial injustice and police brutality. In September, California set a new record for land area destroyed by wildfires, and the 2020 hurricane season also set a record with ten storms making landfall. The Los Angeles Dodgers won their first World Series in 32 years. Former vice president Joe Biden won the presidential election on November 3, 2020. As the nation continued to suffer from record-breaking numbers of daily COVID-19 cases and thousands of deaths, Congress passed a $2.3 trillion pandemic relief and omnibus spending bill in December. In the final weeks of the year the first two COVID-19 vaccines were approved for emergency use.

In Numismatics: As with the rest of the country, the U.S. Mint felt the impacts of the COVID-19 pandemic. Interrupted operations, supply-chain shortages, and increased demand created a challenging situation. The West Point Mint had to pause operations twice because employees tested positive for COVID, while the San Francisco Mint closed for more than a month due to executive orders in California.

A national coin shortage in the spring eased later in the year.

Like other businesses and organizations, the Citizens Coinage Advisory Committee began to meet by phone and online, instead of at Mint headquarters in Washington, D.C.

The Philippine Collectors Forum issued a special edition of the *Red Book* this year, honoring the 1920–2020 centennial of the opening of the Mint of the Philippine Islands, in Manila. There were 250 of these books printed, but several were destroyed in shipping. That left only 212 available to purchase. These quickly sold at $25 apiece, raising money for the PCF's educational programs. Today they sell for closer to $100, or more.

Congress authorized the Mint to reactivate its Presidential dollars program to mint a coin honoring George H.W. Bush, who had died in 2018, and a First Spouse gold coin remembering his wife, Barbara, who passed several months earlier.

2020-P

CIRCULATION MINTAGE: 3,560,800,000 estimated.
Key to Collecting: Most of the billions of Philadelphia-minted cents for 2020 are in brilliant gem Mint State.

2020-D

CIRCULATION MINTAGE: 4,035,600,000 estimated.
Key to Collecting: A beautiful gem specimen will be easy to find for your collection.

2020-S

PROOF MINTAGE: 824,332 estimated.

Enlarged 1.5x
(actual size 19 mm)

MARKET VALUES • 2020-S, Proof

PF-65RD	PF-67RD	PF-67Cam	PF-68DCam
$5	$8	$8	$10

Key to Collecting: Proofs of 2020 were made with deep-cameo contrast. Nearly all are well struck, with brilliant surfaces, and would grade at least PF-69, if not PF-70.

THE YEAR 2021

In America: On the first day of the new year, the United States surpassed 20 million COVID-19 cases. Newly approved vaccines became more accessible and reduced the severity and contagiousness of the disease. On January 6, supporters of President Donald Trump stormed the U.S. Capitol during the congressional certification of the 2020 election results. Members of Congress and Vice President Mike Pence evacuated the building but returned later that night to formally certify Joe Biden as the next president. Trump was impeached for a second time, for his actions on January 6 and for attempting to influence certain states' election results. He was not convicted. President Biden began to reverse many of his predecessor's executive orders. Juneteenth became a federal holiday, commemorating the end of slavery in the United States. In August, the U.S. withdrew its troops from Afghanistan after 20 years of war in the country. The hasty withdrawal led to the collapse of the Afghan government and a takeover by the Taliban, causing widespread poverty and loss of rights like women's education.

In Numismatics: The U.S. Mint launched new American Silver Eagle and American Gold Eagle reverse designs this year, for the first time since the coins were minted in 1986. Along with the new designs, the 2021 Type II coins included new security features, such as notched edges.

Numismatics picked up its pace as economic stimulus money and stay-at-home orders encouraged more collectors into the market. A new record was set for the most valuable coin ever sold at auction when Sotheby's offered the only privately owned 1933 Saint-Gaudens double eagle, which hammered for $18,872,250.

Kennedy half dollars, which hadn't been issued for circulation since 2001, stimulated collector curiosity when the coins began appearing more frequently in commerce and the Mint recorded higher-than-normal mintages for 2021-P and 2021-D Kennedy halves. The Federal Reserve ordered the coins for circulation, causing many to wonder if this was a response to the nationwide coin shortages or if there was some other reason. The Mint struck a cumulative 14.4 billion coins of various denominations for circulation, in response to the shortage.

The *Red Book* was in its 75th year in 2021, having evolved from a simple listing of two or three different conditions of coins to a detailed catalog with pricing in nearly a dozen grades. The first edition had included prices for about 3,400 different coins; the 75th had nearly 8,000, with some 32,000 retail valuations. To mark the diamond anniversary, the hardcover version featured special silver-foil lettering and an emblem on the back cover. At the annual American Numismatic Association convention, Whitman Publishing released Kenneth Bressett's *A Penny Saved: R.S. Yeoman and His Remarkable Red Book*, a combined history of the *Red Book*, biography of its creator (Richard S. Yeo, known professionally as R.S. Yeoman), and memoirs of Bressett himself.

In 2023 it would be announced that the 2021 American Liberty high-relief gold coin won "Best Gold Coin" in the annual Coin of the Year (COTY) international competition.

2021-P

CIRCULATION MINTAGE: 3,925,820,000 estimated.
Key to Collecting: Mint State coins, up to and including gem Mint State examples, are the norm.

2021-D

CIRCULATION MINTAGE: 3,982,800,000 estimated.
Key to Collecting: Brilliant gem Mint State coins are easy to locate for this issue.

2021-S

PROOF MINTAGE: 792,612 estimated.

Enlarged 1.5x
(actual size 19 mm)

Market Values • 2021-S, Proof

PF-65RD	PF-67RD	PF-67Cam	PF-68DCam
$5	$8	$8	$10

Key to Collecting: Given the high quality of the San Francisco Mint's Proof coinage, it would be unusual to find a 2021-S Lincoln cent that graded less than PF-69.

THE YEAR 2022

In America: The COVID-19 pandemic continued with the Omicron variant, which was generally more contagious but less severe than earlier variants. Restrictions on businesses and vaccine and mask mandates continued to be lifted throughout the year. The University of Georgia won its first National Championship in college football since 1980. The fallout from the January 6, 2021, breach of the U.S. Capitol continued, with rioters being arrested and put on trial. Russia invaded Ukraine in February; the U.S. stock market temporarily fell and oil prices rose, starting a trend of high gas prices that would last for months. President Joe Biden announced sanctions on Russia and military assistance to Ukraine. Ketanji Brown Jackson became the first Black woman on the Supreme Court when she was sworn in at the end of June. After the Supreme Court voted 6-3 in June to overturn Roe v. Wade, which had protected abortion access, several states with conservative political leaders quickly moved to pass restrictive limits or total bans on abortions. The last payphone in New York City was transferred to a museum in May. COVID-19 testing restrictions on international travel were lifted in June, and vaccines were approved by the CDC for infants and children under the age of 5. In response to mass shootings in Uvalde and other locations around the country, thousands of people protested on the National Mall and Congress passed new bipartisan gun regulations. Inflation rose to a record 9.1 percent in July. The Federal Reserve hiked interest rates several times in an attempt to slow inflation. In August, the FBI executed a search warrant on Mar-a-Lago, former President Donald Trump's Florida home, to find classified documents that had been illegally removed from the White House. Inflation and gas prices began to ease in August. The death of British monarch Queen Elizabeth II led to public mourning around the world. In October, Elon Musk took control of Twitter. In November, an anticipated "red wave" at the polling booth turned into a trickle, with Democrats maintaining control of the Senate and Republicans making only small gains in the House.

In Numismatics: The United States Mint marked its 230th anniversary in 2022, as it continued to mint billions of coins. The monumental new American Women Quarters series released its first five designs, with the program scheduled to continue through 2025.

Ventris Gibson was confirmed as the 40th director of the U.S. Mint in June. In July, the Philadelphia and Denver Mints reopened for public tours for the first time since the beginning of the COVID pandemic. Dr. Lawrence S. Brown Jr., a Vietnam veteran and Clinical Associate Professor of Medicine and Healthcare Policy and Research (Weill Medical College, Cornell University), was appointed chairman of the Citizens Coinage Advisory Committee.

In August, President Joe Biden signed the Harriet Tubman Bicentennial Commemorative Coin Act into law, to place abolitionist Harriet Tubman on three commemorative coins in 2024. This was a change from the Obama administration, which had planned to revise the $20 Federal Reserve Note to feature Tubman.

The Mint cancelled plans to produce 2022 Morgan and Peace dollar coins due to a silver shortage, but later in the year announced that production of the coins in Uncirculated and Proof formats would resume at the Philadelphia and San Francisco Mints in 2023.

In October, the Certified Acceptance Corp. announced plans to create CAC Grading Services, which would launch the following year.

The Bureau of Engraving and Printing announced a tentative production schedule for redesigned Federal Reserve Notes. Each will include raised tactile features to make it easier to distinguish the notes by touch. The BEP planned to release the redesigned $10 note in 2026, followed by the $50, $20, $5, and $100 notes, in that order, at various times between 2026 and 2038.

The eighth edition of *Mega Red* featured expanded sections on the "odd-denomination" coins of American numismatics: two-cent pieces; silver trimes and copper-nickel three-cent pieces; half dimes; twenty-cent pieces; and gold $1, $3, and $4 coins.

In Whitman Publishing's popular Bowers Series of numismatic references, volume 27 debuted in December—*A Guide Book of American Silver Eagles*, the latest book by author Joshua McMorrow-Hernandez.

2022-P

CIRCULATION MINTAGE: 2,492,200,000 estimated.
Key to Collecting: Gem Mint State coins are commonplace and easy to find.

2022-D

CIRCULATION MINTAGE: 2,428,000,000 estimated.
Key to Collecting: Denver's issue for 2022 is common in gem Mint State.

2022-S

PROOF MINTAGE: Final mintage not yet audited.

Enlarged 1.5x
(actual size 19 mm)

MARKET VALUES • 2022-S, Proof

PF-65RD	PF-67RD	PF-67Cam	PF-68DCam
$5	$8	$8	$10

Key to Collecting: Proofs of 2022 were made with deep-cameo contrast. Nearly all are well struck, with brilliant surfaces, and would grade at least PF-69, if not PF-70.

THE YEAR 2023

In America: The Republican Party officially took leadership of the House of Representatives in 2023, with California representative Kevin McCarthy negotiating deals to assume the Speaker role. The war in Ukraine continued with Russia facing increasing setbacks and losses, and Ukraine's allies finally providing much-needed tanks and, from the United States, long-range missiles. President Joe Biden made a surprise trip to Kyiv in February to stand with President Volodymyr Zelenskyy. The United States' solar-power capacity, which had increased 45 percent in 2022, was on track to increase again in 2023, with America projected to have as much solar-power capacity by itself in 2025 as existed in the entire world in 2022. The year started with inflation continuing to drop, and unemployment low. President Biden announced that COVID's emergency designation would be lifted on May 11. Mysterious high-altitude balloons drifted into U.S. airspace early in the year, leading to anxiety, military action, and international diplomatic discussions. Tech giants such as Salesforce, Meta, Twitter, Google, and Amazon cut thousands of jobs to correct the overhiring of recent years. Artificial Intelligence, or AI, brought pop-culture fascination and also some concern as technology was harnessed to create art and texts with surprisingly human-appearing output. In February the family of ailing Jimmy Carter announced that the 98-year-old former president would discontinue medical intervention and receive hospice care at home.

In Numismatics: The Citizens Coinage Advisory Committee met virtually to review candidate designs for the Harlem Hellfighters Congressional Gold Medal. The committee, which advises the secretary of the Treasury on coin and medal designs and themes, convened in Washington to discuss American Women quarter designs for 2024 and other upcoming programs.

For 2023, for the first time in nearly two generations, Congress authorized no new coins in the U.S. commemorative-coin program. However, *circulating* commemoratives continued to be minted, with quarter dollars issued to honor Bessie Coleman, Jovita Idar, Edith Kanaka'ole, Eleanor Roosevelt, and Maria Tallchief. The U.S. Mint announced a first-time-ever collaboration with the British Royal Mint: a gold coin and silver medal scheduled for release in 2024. The "Liberty and Britannia" works are jointly created by U.S. chief engraver Joseph Menna and Gordon Summers, chief engraver of the British Royal Mint.

2023-P

CIRCULATION MINTAGE: Final mintage not yet audited.
Key to Collecting: This issue is common in gem Mint State.

2023-D

CIRCULATION MINTAGE: Final mintage not yet audited.
Key to Collecting: This issue is common in gem Mint State.

2023-S

PROOF MINTAGE: Final mintage not yet audited.

Enlarged 1.5x
(actual size 19 mm)

MARKET VALUES • 2023-S, Proof

PF-65RD	PF-67RD	PF-67Cam	PF-68DCam
$5	$8	$8	$10

Key to Collecting: The San Francisco Mint is known for the high quality of its Proof coinage; for collectors, this translates into an abundance of beautiful PF-69 and PF-70 Lincoln cents to choose from.

LINCOLN CENT MINT ERRORS

by Fred Weinberg

This appendix was created by well-known mint error coin dealer and specialist Fred Weinberg, who for many years has gathered information about error coins of all kinds.

INTRODUCTION

As with all modern coins, mechanical errors occur on Lincoln cents. The most common mechanical error types are blank planchets and small off-centers. Double-struck cents with two dates visible are highly prized, and cents struck on planchets intended for dimes are even more important. Cents struck over previously struck dimes, with the dime design still visible, are the *crème de la crème* of cent errors.

This listing covers about 85 percent of the error types found on Lincoln cents. Each coin is different, so these are only general categories. An error with exceptional characteristics can be worth more. Generally, earlier dates are worth more—often much more. A double-struck 1910-S cent, with two dates visible, would be worth many multiples of a similarly double-struck 1992-D cent, for example. An error on a scarce variety always commands a strong premium.

Prices listed are for average coins, in Mint State, with no damage, scratches, or distracting features.

Among Lincoln cents, there are other error types, such as laminated or flaked planchets, edge clips, etc. These are worth a small premium to interested collectors—in most cases from a dollar or so up to $5 to $10 per coin—unless such an error has an exceptional characteristic.

Off-metal (copper alloy) strikes of the 1943 cent (normally in zinc-coated steel) are discussed in chapter 11.

VALUES OF REPRESENTATIVE LINCOLN CENT ERRORS

Blank Planchets: The blank disks of metal that are eventually struck by the cent dies, accidentally released into circulation without being struck.

Type 1: With no upset rim: $3.

Type 2: With upset or raised rim: $2.

Off-Center Strikes: Caused by a planchet being off center in the coining press when it is struck by the cent dies.

Wheat Reverse: Minor off center: $20, Major off center without date: $35, Major off center with date showing: $50+.

Memorial Reverse: Minor off-center: $5, Major off center without date: $10, Major off center with date showing: $15+.

Double Strikes: Immediately after being struck, the coin is struck again instead of being ejected to a bin of finished coins. Coins that have two or three additional strikes, each clearly defined, are rare and worth much more than the prices given below.

Wheat Reverse: Second strike 20 percent or more off center: $150+, second strike 80 percent or more off center: $100+.

Memorial Reverse: Second strike 20 percent or more off center: $40+, second strike 80 percent or more off center: $20+.

Indented Strikes: Another planchet was lying over the top of the original planchet when the cent was struck, leaving a circular indent.

Wheat Reverse: 10 percent to 20 percent indent: $50+, 30 percent to 80 percent indent: $75+.

Memorial Reverse: 10 percent to 20 percent indent: $20+, 30 percent to 80 percent indent: $35+.

Brockage Strikes: A previously struck coin was on top of this planchet when struck, leaving an incused indent with design.

Wheat Reverse: 10 percent to 20 percent brockage: $65+, 30 percent to 80 percent brockage: $100+.

Memorial Reverse: 10 percent to 20 percent brockage: $25+, 30 percent to 80 percent brockage: $40+.

Off-Metal Strikes: Lincoln Cents struck on blank planchets intended for Roosevelt dimes.

Wheat Reverse: On silver dime planchet: $1,400+.

Memorial Reverse: On silver dime planchet: $700+, on clad dime planchet $350.

Double Denominations: Cents struck on *previously struck* Roosevelt dimes, with much of the dime design remaining.

Wheat reverse: On silver dime: $3,000+.

Memorial reverse: On silver dime: $2,000+, on clad dime: $650.

PATTERN CENTS

The following pattern cents are take from *United States Pattern Coins*, tenth edition, by J. Hewitt Judd, M.D., edited by Q. David Bowers. More patterns, stretching back to the birth of our nation's coinage, can be found there.

J-1930: 1909 Cent, V.D.B. Reverse

Struck from regular dies. Reverse type not known. Presumably with V.D.B. May be a mint error.

J-1930

J-2080 and J-2081: 1942 Cent

Trial piece struck from regular dies.

J-2080

J-2051 to J-2069: 1942 Cent

Private issues struck from special Mint dies. Struck in a variety of materials. Not all exist in coined form today.

Obverse: Female head facing right, from the Colombian two-centavo coin. LIBERTY to the left, JUSTICE to the right. Date 1942 at the bottom border.

Reverse: Open wreath enclosing UNITED STATES MINT.

J-2051

J-2151 and J-2152: 1974 Cent

Struck from regular dies. Seven different alloys of aluminum were tested.

J-2151

J-2155: 1975 Cent

Trial piece struck from regular dies.

J-2155

ALTERNATIVE BICENTENNIAL DESIGNS

The Commission of Fine Arts and Citizens Coinage Advisory Committee reviewed several potential designs for the 2009 Lincoln cent. One design was sought for each of four aspects of Lincoln's life: (1) his birth and early childhood in Kentucky; (2) his formative years in Indiana; (3) his professional life in Illinois; and (4) his presidency. Proposed designs for these aspects are shown here, with numbers 1 through 4 indicating the corresponding aspects of Lincoln's life. (See chapters 4 and 11 for details on the winning designs.)

3

4

THE CCAC AND PROPOSED 2010 "UNION" DESIGNS

On April 28, 2009, the Citizens Coinage Advisory Committee met at U.S. Mint headquarters on Ninth Street in Washington, D.C., to review coinage designs including more than a dozen candidates for the reverse of the 2010 Lincoln cent.

The CCAC is a public body that advises the secretary of the Treasury on themes and design proposals for circulating, commemorative, and bullion coinage; Congressional Gold Medals; and national and other medals. In attendance at its April 2009 meeting were Chairman Mitch Sanders and members John K. Alexander, Doreen Bolger, Michael Brown (via telephone), Roger W. Burdette, Arthur Houghton, Gary Marks, Richard Meier, and Donald Scarinci.

Kaarina Budow, design manager of the United States Mint, presented the portfolio of 17 designs. She explained that Public Law 109-145 required the secretary of the Treasury, starting in 2010, to mint and issue one-cent coins in recognition of President Abraham Lincoln's preservation of the United States as a single and unified country. The cent's obverse would continue to feature Victor David Brenner's profile portrait of Lincoln.

During an initial round of discussion several committee members expressed disappointment regarding the proposed designs, considering them to be antiquated, cluttered, or insufficiently symbolic of Lincoln's preservation of the Union. Following this discussion, the committee narrowed the field to six designs: 1, 2, 13, 15, 16, and 17. After a second round of discussion, each committee member rated these designs by assigning points to them—either zero, one, two, or three points. With nine members present and voting, the maximum possible point total for any design was 27.

Design 13, showing a Union shield, received broad support from the committee, with nearly all members assigning it two or three points. In total it received 19 points. The committee minutes would later reflect that "members generally appreciated the clear composition of the shield," and judged it to be "a highly appropriate symbol."

The committee's recommendation letter to Treasury Secretary Timothy F. Geithner, May 5, 2009, expanded on its thinking. "Committee members considered the shield to be a classic symbol from the Civil War era, and appropriately emblematic of Lincoln's preservation of the Union. Design LP-13 was preferred over other shield-based designs due to its focus on a single design element, which members felt would promote clarity on a small coin."

Regarding other motifs within the portfolio: "Designs featuring the United States Capitol were generally considered to have only a tenuous relationship to the coin's theme, and attracted little support," wrote Chairman Sanders. "Of the Capitol designs, LP-02 was preferred due to its visual simplicity. However, this design received considerably less support than the committee's first choice, LP-13, and was also ranked behind the committee's second choice, LP-17, which features a naturalistic eagle."

Design 13 was the CCAC's recommendation to Treasury Secretary Timothy Geithner. It was ranked highest with a vote of 19 points.

The committee's second choice, design 17, featured an eagle with outstretched wings. It earned 10 points.

Designs 2 (the East front of the United States Capitol, focusing on the dome) and 15 (an eagle carrying a Union shield) each received 7 points.

Design 1 (the East front of the United States Capitol) earned 4 points.

Design 16 (an eagle in flight, with a banner in its beak reading "One Country One Destiny") received 3 points.

Design 3 (the West front of the United States Capitol)

Design 4 (the East front of the United States Capitol, with 13 stars)

Design 5 (an aerial view of the West front of the United States Capitol)

Design 6 (the West front of the United States Capitol)

Design 7 (the West front of the United States Capitol)

Design 8 (the East front of the United States Capitol, with a waving flag)

Design 9 (an American flag, waving)

Design 10 (a modern, graphical interpretation of the United States flag)

Design 11 (*Statue of Freedom*, located atop the Capitol Dome, with a United States flag)

Design 12 (a Union shield with quill pen and saber)

Design 14 (a Union shield with a laurel wreath, representing peace)

DESIGNER LYNDALL BASS

Lyndall Bass, the New Mexico artist who designed the Union shield motif, joined the Mint's Artistic Infusion Program (AIP) in February 2007 as an associate designer. The AIP was established in 2003. The Mint had used non-staff artists before then, but it created the AIP to develop and train a pool of talented outside artists qualified and ready to work with its full-time in-house sculptor-engravers. When a new coin or medal design is called for, AIP artists can be invited to submit proposals for consideration alongside those of Mint staff. Once a design is chosen, its final modeling—the translation from drawing to sculpture—is done by a Mint artist.

"Hollyhock Fireworks," oil on canvas, by Lyndall Bass.

The AIP was set up with student designers (enrolled in undergraduate or graduate-level visual-arts programs), associate designers (professional artists new to the program), and master designers (proven as valuable AIP artists for at least two years).

By 2007, when Bass joined the program, AIP artists had submitted successful designs for high-profile series such as the Westward Journey nickels, State quarters, Presidential dollars, First Spouse gold coins, American Platinum Eagles, and various commemorative coins and medals.

Bass is an American realist artist and teacher who creates primarily still lifes, floral tableaux, and symbolist figure paintings. On her art and inspirations, Bass states, "I was born in 1952 and have been stuck in the Renaissance ever since. Truth is, there is not much I'm really

Bass's "Magnificent Peonies," oil on canvas.

attracted to in 'Modern Art'" and "only Surrealism has caught my attention beyond Realism and my early love of Leonardo Da Vinci, Andrew Wyeth and Mary Cassatt." Bass lives and works in Santa Fe, New Mexico. She studied at Indiana University, earning there a bachelor's degree in Fine Art and a master's in education; at the Pennsylvania Academy of Fine Arts; at the Philadelphia College of Art; and at the Corcoran School of Art in Washington, D.C.

SCULPTOR JOSEPH MENNA

The Mint artist who sculpted Bass's Union Shield design was Joseph Menna, who joined the Mint's staff in 2005 following 18 years of classical training and professional experience. His skills are in traditional and digital sculpture and drawing. Menna is recognized as having helped bring the U.S. Mint into the digital design and production era. In 2013 his Mount Rushmore National Memorial quarter dollar design won a coveted "Coin of the Year" award for circulating legal tender.

In a Mint interview in December 2014, he said, "I was lucky to be the first digital artist at the Mint and so have had the opportunity to introduce a lot of new techniques and technology to how we make coins. It has been an honor and a privilege, and I only see us continuing to grow in that direction as we move forward in our mission."

Joseph Menna at the Philadelphia Mint in 2013.

A SNAPSHOT OF THE LINCOLN CENT MARKET IN 1946

The first print run of *A Guide Book of United States Coins* debuted in November 1946. Its initial 9,000 copies sold out so quickly that another 9,000 were printed in February 1947. By 1959 coin collectors were buying more than 100,000 copies annually. The 1965 (18th) edition, published in 1964, reached a peak of 1,200,000 copies. By then the "Red Book" was the most popular annual price guide in the hobby—a distinction it holds to this day.

These pages from the first edition of the *Red Book* offer an interesting snapshot of the retail market for Lincoln cents, including those of the retired second San Francisco Mint building, affectionately known as "The Granite Lady."

SMALL CENTS
Lincoln Head Type
1909 to Date

Victor D. Brenner designed this cent which was issued to commemorate the hundredth anniversary of Lincoln's birth. The designer's initials VDB appear on a limited quantity of cents of 1909. The San Francisco mint produced the smallest issue before the initials were removed, creating the scarcest and most sought-after Lincoln Head Cent. The initials were restored, in 1918, to the obverse side as illustrated below. This type cent was the first to have the motto "In God We Trust."

	Fine	Unc.	Proof
1909 V D B.	$ .05	$ .20	$ 6.00
1909 S, V D B.	8.00	15.00	

Same as the preceding type, but VDB omitted from the reverse.

	Fine	Unc.	Proof		Fine	Unc.	Proof
1909	$.05	$ .25	$3.00	1917S	$ .20	$2.50	
1909S	.75	3.75					
1910	.05	.65	3.00				
1910S	.25	1.25					
1911	.05	.60	3.00				
1911D	.35	2.50		**Designer's**			
1911S	.35	3.50		**Initials Restored**			
1912	.05	.60	3.00				
1912D	.50	5.50					
1912S	.35	3.50					
1913	.10	.60	3.00				
1913D	.40	6.00		1918	.05	.50	
1913S	.30	5.50		1918D	.20	3.75	
1914	.15	2.50	6.00	1918S	.20	4.50	
1914D	3.50	10.00		1919	.05	.50	
1914S	.35	5.50		1919D	.20	1.50	
1915	.15	3.00	7.00	1919S	.10	1.50	
1915D	.25	1.65		1920	.05	.40	
1915S	.30	3.50		1920D	.20	2.25	
1916	.05	.50	8.00	1920S	.20	4.00	
1916D	.20	2.00		1921	.15	1.25	
1916S	.20	3.00		1921S	.25	8.50	
1917	.05	.50		1922D	.35	2.50	
1917D	.20	2.50		1923	.05	.50	

[82]

In the 1947 *Guide Book of United States Coins* mintages were listed in the back of the book instead of alongside their coin listings in the main charts. Numismatics is a continuously changing hobby. Ongoing research can change the way collectors understand coins. For example, when the 1947 *Red Book* was written (in 1946), numismatists did not even include the 1922-D Weak D or the 1922-D "Plain" no D mintmark varieties. Die varieties at the time were not the hot collecting genre they are today: these varieties, along with the 1944-D, D Over S, which are included in today's *Red Book*, were yet to be popularized in the late 1940s.

SMALL CENTS

	Fine	Unc.	Proof
1923S	$ .20	$9.00	
1924	.05	1.50	
1924D	.50	8.00	
1924S	.35	6.50	
1925	.05	.50	
1925D	.10	2.25	
1925S	.20	5.50	
1926	.05	.50	
1926D	.20	1.75	
1926S	.25	6.50	
1927	.05	.40	
1927D	.20	2.25	
1927S	.25	5.00	
1928	.05	.50	
1928D	.10	2.25	
1928S	.15	3.25	
1929	.05	.30	
1929D	.05	.90	
1929S	.05	.30	
1930	.05	.15	
1930D	.05	.75	
1930S	.05	.30	
1931	.05	.90	
1931D	.15	3.00	
1931S	.50	1.35	
1932	.05	.60	
1932D	.05	.75	
1933	.15	.65	
1933D	.15	.45	
1934		.15	
1934D		.25	
1935		.10	
1935D		.15	
1935S		.15	
1936		.10	8.50
1936D		.15	
1936S		.15	
1937		.10	4.25
1937D		.15	
1937S		.15	
1938		.10	2.50
1938D		.15	
1938S		.15	
1939		.10	1.50
1939D		.12	
1939S		.12	
1940		.10	1.50
1940D		.10	
1940S		.10	
1941		.10	1.25
1941D		.10	
1941S		.10	
1942		.10	1.00
1942D		.10	
1942S		.20	

WARTIME STEEL CENTS

1943

Owing to a shortage of copper during the critical war year 1943 the Treasury Department resorted to the use of zinc coated steel for our cents. The experiment was short-lived however. The steel cent so closely resembled our dime that much confusion resulted when making change.

	Fine	Unc.	Proof
1943		$ .10	
1943D		.10	
1943S		.10	

"SHELL CASE" COPPER CENTS

A solution to the problem of procuring metal supplies for our cents was found when discarded shell cases were turned over for salvage to the Treasury Department in 1944. Although the color of the new cent is a little paler than the bronze cent of normal times, the coin has withstood all tests and has proved satisfactory in every respect. The "Shell Case" copper cent has answered the call for more and more small change and has gained the first-year distinction of being circulated in larger quantities than any other denomination of United States coin in a single year. The amazing total was 2,148,738,000 pieces, or over twenty-one million dollars in value.

	Fine	Unc.	Proof
1944		$ .05	
1944D		.05	
1944S		.05	
1945		.05	
1945D		.05	
1945S		.05	
1946		.05	
1946D		.05	
1946S		.05	
1947		.05	
1947D		.05	
1947S		.05	

[83]

HOW TO GET A NEW LINCOLN CENT DIE VARIETY INTO THE *RED BOOK*

A version of this article by Whitman publisher Dennis Tucker first appeared in the Journal of the Barber Coin Collectors' Society.

In the *Journal of the Barber Coin Collectors' Society*, member Bob Duzan shared his first-hand observations of some interesting Barber dime varieties ("A Variety Challenge," volume 26, no. 2). In his article he asked, "What should be the criteria for listing a coin variety in the 'Red Book' or other coin publications?"

It's a very good question, and one we think about quite a bit at Whitman Publishing. Having worked on 14 editions of *A Guide Book of United States Coins* (the "Red Book") and counting, I know that sometimes collectors and dealers can be very bullish on getting a favorite coin listed, in an attempt to increase popular interest (perhaps hoping to watch the value of their holdings climb higher, or simply as a way to share their enthusiasm for the coin). I explain to them that the *Red Book reports* on the market and collector trends; it doesn't seek to spearhead popular interest in any particular die variety or other coin. If the *Red Book's* editors (Senior Editor Jeff Garrett, Research Editor Q. David Bowers, and Editor Emeritus Kenneth Bressett) observe strong, broad interest within the hobby community for a variety, it has a much better chance of being included in the book.

"Strong, broad interest" can be measured many ways. If we see a number of letters to the editors of the hobby newspapers . . . or receive letters and emails ourselves . . . and hear people talking about the variety at coin shows, club meetings, and online . . . and read articles and possibly even books being written by collectors, dealers, and other numismatists . . . and observe the growth of a healthy and vibrant secondary market, with buy-sell-and-trade prices actively published and discussed . . . all of these things point toward a robust and popular interest in a particular die variety.

Do the editors and publisher of the *Red Book* have a vested interest in drumming up popular interest in any given variety? No. But we do want to report on well-developed trends that show signs of long-term "here to stay" activity within the hobby community.

As Bob Duzan pointed out in his article, the regular-edition *Red Book* includes two Barber dime varieties in its listings. For Barber quarters, the *Red Book* lists only regular issues (circulation strikes and Proofs) by date and mintmark. And for Barber half dollars, we include a single die variety.

Adding a new die variety to the *Red Book* is somewhat akin to Abraham Lincoln's description of his own learning style: "My mind is like a piece of steel—very hard to scratch anything on it, and almost impossible after you get it there to rub it out." This is traditionally how the editors of the *Red Book* have approached new irregular listings (overdates, doubled dies, repunched mintmarks, and the like): with a high level of scrutiny, knowing that once a coin is deemed significant enough to be listed, the hobby community expects it to *stay* listed.

The *Red Book* is meant as a reference guide. It's not comprehensive or encyclopedic, but it strives to provide as much valuable information as possible to as many readers as possible. Editor Emeritus Kenneth Bressett and I have had many conversations about his editorial philosophy, honed and sharpened since he first started working with hobby legend R.S. Yeoman in the late 1950s. "The *Red Book* has to be somewhat selective," Ken says, "and perhaps even a bit arbitrary, in deciding which minor varieties are listed in the book. The reasons for this are twofold: First, it must remain true to the title *Guide Book*, and not attempt to be an encyclopedic listing of every known variety. And secondly, minor variations are generally excluded from separate listing unless there is a wide variation in value, or a conspicuous collector demand for the item."

From 2009 to 2014, in the larger-format *Professional Edition Red Book*, we took a more relaxed approach. Where the regular-edition *Red Book* seeks to be an overview *guide* to U.S. coins, the *Professional Edition* went above and beyond the basic date-and-mintmark and major variety listings. It wasn't as meaty as the *Cherrypickers' Guide to Rare Die Varieties*, of course, but it included more die varieties than the regular-edition *Red Book* for many coin types.

We stopped publishing the *Professional Edition* after the sixth edition (2014) in order to focus on an even bigger new book: *A Guide Book of United States Coins, Deluxe Edition*. The first edition came out in March 2015, and it soon became popularly known as *Mega Red*. This 1,504-page volume carries forward the *Professional Edition*'s focus on including more die varieties.

Here's how the regular-edition *Red Book* and the current edition of *Mega Red* compare, using as a case study the circulating coins designed by U.S. Mint Chief Engraver Charles E. Barber:

NUMBER OF DIE VARIETIES, BY COIN TYPE
(DESIGNS BY CHARLES E. BARBER)

	Regular-Edition Red Book	MEGA RED
Liberty Head nickel	0	2
Barber dime	3	5
Barber quarter	0	0*
Barber half dollar	1	3

* But see below, under "Barber Quarters."

Liberty Head Nickels. The regular-edition *Red Book* lists only the standard dates and mintmarks among circulation strikes and Proofs. This includes both Variety 1 (Without CENTS) and Variety 2 (With CENTS) of the 1883 coin, which are not die varieties in the traditionally accepted sense, but rather a Mint-authorized design change. It also lists the 1913 Liberty Head nickels—not regular Mint issues, as they were never placed into circulation, but historically studied alongside their regular-issue kin.

Mega Red lists two Liberty Head nickel die varieties: the 1899 Repunched Date (FS-05-1899-301, illustrated with close-ups of both an Early Die State and a Late Die State), and the 1900 Doubled-Die Reverse (FS-05-1900-801).

Barber Dimes. The regular-edition *Red Book* includes line-item listings for the 1893 So-Called 3 Over 2, and the 1905-O Micro O. It also includes a chart note about the 1893-S with a boldly doubled mintmark being valued slightly higher than the normal coin. I count these as three die-variety listings, even though only two of them have line items in the charts.

In addition to those varieties, *Mega Red* includes listings and illustrations for the 1897 Repunched Date (FS-10-1897-301) and the 1912-S Doubled-Die Obverse (FS-10-1912S-101). It also shows comparative images of the Normal O and the Micro O mintmarks in the 1905-O issue.

Barber Quarters. The regular-edition *Red Book* focuses solely on normal dates and mintmarks for the Barber quarter series, listing no die varieties.

Mega Red currently has no line-item listings for Barber quarter die varieties, but it does illustrate the two kinds of 1892 reverse (Variety 1, with the eagle's wing covering only half of the E in UNITED; and Variety 2, where the wing covers most of the E). It also describes the two varieties in a narrative chart note, and delineates their relative scarcity.

Barber Half Dollars. In the regular-edition *Red Book*, the 1892-O Micro O is the sole die-variety listing.

In *Mega Red* additional listings include the 1909-S Inverted Mintmark (FS-50-1909S-501) and the 1911-S Repunched Mintmark (FS-50-1911S-501). These are illustrated with close-up photographs, as are the 1892-O Normal and Micro O mintmarks.

LINCOLN TOKENS AND MEDALS

This appendix was drawn from the expertise and collection of Fred Reed.

Alfred Satterlee's privately printed pamphlet *An Arrangement of Medals and Tokens, Struck in Honor of the Presidents of the United States* was the first publication to quantify and catalog the proliferation of numismatic tributes to Honest Abe, but since that 1862 treatise, Lincoln's popularity as a subject for tokens and medals has remained strong. The following are some interesting pieces from Lincoln's life and death.

Philadelphia diesinker Robert Lovett created this campaign token (King-48) in 1860, including language from the Republican platform. Its concentric reverse design has only 32 stars, though there were 33 states at the time.

Charles Lang of Knox & Lang, Worcester, Massachusetts, cut this portrait based on the same Hesler photographic model Lovett used.

This particular example of Salathiel Ellis and Joseph Willson's 1862 Lincoln Indian Peace medal design (Julian IP-38) is struck in fine gold. Silver examples, both large and small size, were presented to Native American allies of the United States. Julian lists this medal in gold, but a check of his appendix fails to disclose a nineteenth-century striking of this medal in gold at the U.S. Mint. It is believed this example was probably struck to order for a twentieth-century collector.

(a)   (b)

Whereas most campaign tokens for 1860 were quarter-sized (24.3 mm) or larger, 19-millimeter cent-sized medalets such as (a) dominated the 1864 campaign. Northern diesinkers had spent the past two years cranking out cent-sized tokens (b) to replace government cents, which were hoarded by the public.

Not all 1864 Lincoln campaign tokens were small size. This 31-millimeter militaristic, silvered-brass issue (O-80) had a low-relief, anonymous, and amateur Lincoln profile, but it was nearly the size of a half dollar.

New York medalist George H. Lovett created a fine likeness for this memorial medal (King-257) to commemorate "The Martyr President."

This is a non-Mint striking using Anthony Paquet's 19 mm Lincoln profile die to strike over a U.S. $5 gold piece, with a diameter of 21.6 mm.

This small (25.5 mm) commemorative medal (King-275) links George Washington and his "most worthy successor" Abraham Lincoln in a very direct manner. Lincoln's profile portrait sports Washington's colonial peruke. Several varieties of this small medal are known, including some with the obverse die cancelled before striking with a wedge-shaped occlusion behind Lincoln's head that reads "Treas. / Dept. / 1869."

NOTES

1. Today it is more popular to state the diameter as 19.1 mm, obscuring the "useful" diameter originally intended. The copper cents of 1857 and earlier measured about 29 mm.

2. Roger W. Burdette, communication to the author, June 29, 2007. Burdette reviewed National Archives and other material for his 2007 book, *Renaissance of American Coinage 1909–1915*.

3. Certain information is adapted from the author's booklet on American presidents written in 2007 in connection with the new presidential dollar coins.

4. Roger W. Burdette, correspondence, July 1, 2007, drawing upon Mint correspondence 1907–1912 and a letter to the Mint director, February 4, 1913.

5. Excerpts used here were reprinted in the *Boston Daily Globe*, May 2, 1909.

6. Interview with the author in Owego, New York, August 1960. By that time Ziemer was a well-known dealer in antiques. His numismatic interest was still strong, with a specialty in gold coins.

7. Courtesy of Roger W. Burdette. The full text of this letter and other correspondence appears in *Renaissance of American Coinage 1909–1915*.

8. *The Numismatist*, January 1918.

9. *Numismatic Scrapbook Magazine*, September 1943.

10. *Annual Report from the Director of the Mint*, 1944.

11. David W. Lange to the author, July 2007.

12. David W. Lange to the author, July 2007. From "The Transitional Cents of 1982," Lange, *The Numismatist*, February 2004.

13. Slightly edited.

14. Certain of the minting and other information is similar to that used in early *Official Red Book* titles, here adapted for application to Lincoln cents.

15. Information from David W. Lange, July 9, 2007.

16. Mint records contain little information about press adjustments, the use of variant-weight planchets, and the like. The information given here is assumptive in part, and in part based upon conversations with Mint press operators and Engraving Department staff. Research is ongoing.

17. Suggestion by Roger W. Burdette, July 1, 2007.

18. Silver dollars were an exception and in 1921 and 1922 were coined in large quantities due to special legislation. Such coins were not needed in commerce.

19. Where they went at the time remains a minor mystery, for when collectors began desiring such coins in the late twentieth century, quite a few popped up in the marketplace.

20. Letter to the author, July 5, 2007.

21. Letter to the author, July 5, 2007.

22. David W. Lange to the author, July 2007. From "The Transitional Cents of 1982," Lange, *The Numismatist*, February 2004.

23. David W. Lange, "Mint keeps some coins secret," *Coin World*, November 23, 1992.

24. In a letter to the author (August 7, 2007) Ken Potter advises that two die pairs are now known.

25. The wording of these notes is from the *Official ANA Grading Standards for U.S. Coins*, 6th edition, and may differ slightly from the present text.

26. Communication to the author, July 12, 2007.

27. *Coin World*, "Collectors' Clearinghouse," February 19, 1986. Also, Ken Potter, communications to the author, January 2007, including providing correspondence from Jerry Yellin, chief, Assay Division, U.S. Mint.

28. Reprinted courtesy of *The Numismatist*, official publication of the American Numismatic Association, www.money.org.

29. Letter to the author, July 5, 2007.

30. Roger W. Burdette, letter to the author, July 10, 2007.

31. Actually, the *Guide Book* does not describe color, but notes that coins toned brown are worth less than these Mint State figures, and those that are brilliant are worth more.

32. Letter to the author, July 5, 2007.

33. Original mintage and distribution not known. Modern estimates range from 400 to 1,194.

34. In *Coin World*, March 24, 1997, Kevin Flynn suggested that the number of Matte Proof 1909 V.D.B. cents actually struck was 1,194; the number of 1909 Lincoln cent Matte Proofs struck was 2,352; the number of 1910 Matte Proofs struck was 4,093; and the number of 1911 Matte Proofs struck was 2,411. These differ from the *Guide Book of United States Coins* figures for these particular dates.

35. Letter to the author, July 5, 2007.

36. Letter to the author, August 24, 1996.

37. Author's discussion with Pukall about Matte Proofs and Proof remainders in the 1950s.

38. The SLCC is operated by Sol Taylor, Ph.D., the author of *The Standard Guide to the Lincoln Cent*.

39. In a letter to the author, July 9, 2007, Roger W. Burdette suggests this is a "questionable coin."

40. *Encyclopedia*, 1988, p. 228.

41. Sam Lukes, letter, July 23, 2007.

42. Sam Lukes, letter, July 23, 2007.

43. *Chicago Herald* and *Chicago Examiner*, December 19, year not stated, as quoted in *The Numismatist*, October 1931.

44. *Encyclopedia*, 1988, p. 230.

45. Sent to the author, July 2007. Also used in Lange's "USA Coin Album" column in *The Numismatist*, April 2005.

46. Note to the author, July 17, 2007.

47. For a fee, Walter Breen was always willing to examine such coins at a convention, or by mail, and if one "looked good" he would issue a letter of authenticity. He also did this for many "Proof" coins, in various series. Many of these "calls" were later discredited.

48. In the course of studying prices, economics, and prevailing attitudes in the numismatic marketplace from the late 1930s through the early 1950s, in the 1960s I interviewed Abe Kosoff, Abner Kreisberg, Arthur M. Kagin, and others in depth.

49. *Numismatic Scrapbook Magazine*, May 1949.

50. Roger W. Burdette, letter to the author, July 9, 2007.

51. Sam Lukes was the seller (letter to the author, July 5, 2007).

52. *Swiatek Numismatic Report* received September 1998.

53. *Note:* A variety once called 1960-D Large Date, D over Horizontal, D, has been disproved as such and is now considered simply a triple-punched D.

54. David W. Lange to the author, July 2007. Earlier included in "The Transitional Cents of 1974," Lange, *The Numismatist*, April 2003.

55. For details on PVC and related holders, including their scientific and chemical aspects, as well as their effects on coins, and for methods of at least partially restoring PVC-damaged coins, see "Observations on Primitive Money," by E.B. Banning and L.A. Pavlish, *The Numismatist*, October 1980.

56. David W. Lange to the author, July 2007. From "The Transitional Cents of 1982," Lange, *The Numismatist*, February 2004.

57. Letter to the author, July 5, 2007.

58. Issue of March 25, 2008.

59. Issue of June 30, 2008.

Selected Bibliography

Anderson, Shane M. *The Complete Lincoln Cent Encyclopedia*. Iola, WI: Krause Publications, 1996.

Annual Report of the Director of the Mint, various years 1909 to date. Also related Treasury Department, House of Representatives, and Senate documents and reports.

Breen, Walter. *Walter Breen's Encyclopedia of U.S. and Colonial Proof Coins, 1792–1977*. Albertson, New York: FCI Press, 1977.

———. *Walter Breen's Complete Encyclopedia of U.S. and Colonial Coins*. New York: Doubleday, Inc., 1988.

Bressett, Kenneth E. (editor). *A Guide Book of United States Coins*, various editions, 1947 to date. Earlier editions edited by Richard S. Yeoman. Racine, WI, Atlanta, GA, and Pelham, AL: Whitman Publishing, LLC, 2007.

Bressett, Kenneth E., ed., and Q. David Bowers. *The Official American Numismatic Association Grading Standards for United States Coins*. 6th edition. Atlanta, GA: Whitman Publishing, LLC, 2005.

Burdette, Roger W. *Renaissance of American Coinage 1909–1915*. Great Falls, VA: Seneca Mill Press, 2007.

Coin World, Various issues 1961 to date. Sidney, OH: Amos Press and other entities.

Daughtrey, Charles D. *Looking Through Lincoln Cents: Chronology of a Series*. 2nd edition. Irvine, CA: Zyrus Press, 2005.

Fivaz, Bill, and J.T. Stanton. *The Cherrypicker's Guide to Rare Die Varieties*. 4th edition, Volume II. Atlanta, GA: Whitman Publishing LLC, 2006.

Lange, David W. *The Complete Guide to Lincoln Cents*. Wolfeboro, NH: Bowers and Merena Galleries, Inc., 1996.

Manley, Stephen G. *The Lincoln Cent*. Muscatine, IA: Liberty Press, 1981.

Numismatic Guaranty Corporation of America Census Report, various issues. Parsippany, NJ, later Sarasota, FL: Numismatic Guaranty Company of America, various issues.

PCGS Population Report. Newport Beach, CA. Professional Coin Grading Service, Various issues.

Raymond, Wayte. *Standard Catalogue of United States Coins and Paper Money* (titles vary). Scott Stamp & Coin Co. (and others): New York, 1934 to 1957 editions.

Taxay, Don. *U.S. Mint and Coinage*. New York: Arco Publishing, 1966.

Taylor, Sol. *The Standard Guide to the Lincoln Cents*, Fourth Edition. Anaheim, CA: KNI Publishers, 1999.

Tomaska, Rick Jerry, *Cameo and Brilliant Proof Coinage of the 1950 to 1970 Era*. Encinitas, CA: R&I Publications, 1991.

Vermeule, Cornelius. *Numismatic Art in America: Aesthetics of the United States Coinage*. Cambridge, MA: The Belknap Press of Harvard University Press, 1971.

Wexler, John and Kevin Flynn. *The Authoritative Reference on Lincoln Cents*. Rancocas, NJ: KCK Press, 1996.

ABOUT THE AUTHOR

Q. David Bowers, co-founder of Stack's Bowers Galleries, has been in the rare-coin business since he was a teenager in 1953. He also serves as numismatic director and as a writer for Whitman Publishing, LLC. The author is a recipient of the Pennsylvania State University College of Business Administration's Alumni Achievement Award (1976); he has served as president of the American Numismatic Association (1983–1985) and of the Professional Numismatists Guild (1977–1979); he is a recipient of the highest honor bestowed by the ANA (the Farran Zerbe Award); he was the first ANA member to be named Numismatist of the Year (1995); in 2005 he was given the Lifetime Achievement Award; and he has been inducted into the ANA Numismatic Hall of Fame, today being one of just 12 living recipients with that distinction. Bowers has received the highest honor of the Professional Numismatists Guild (the Founders' Award) and more "Book of the Year Award" and "Best Columnist" honors of the Numismatic Literary Guild than any other writer. In July 1999, in a poll published in *COINage*, "Numismatists of the Century," by Ed Reiter, Bowers was recognized in this list of just 18 names, including only six living people. In 2000 he was the first annual recipient of the Burnett Anderson Memorial Award for writing. In 2006 he was the honoree at the annual American Numismatic Society Gala held at the Waldorf-Astoria, New York City. He is the author of more than 50 books, hundreds of auction and other catalogs, and several thousand articles including columns in *Coin World* (now the longest-running by any author in numismatic history), *Paper Money*, and, in past years, *The Numismatist*. His prime enjoyments in numismatics are knowing "coin people," from newcomers to old-timers, and studying the endless lore, technical aspects, and history of coins, tokens, medals, and paper money.

CREDITS AND ACKNOWLEDGEMENTS

The author expresses appreciation to the following, including peers and specialists in Lincoln cents, for help in the ways indicated:

Stewart Blay provided images of certain coins from his collection. **Wynn Bowers** read the manuscript and made suggestions. **Roger W. Burdette** shared information located in the National Archives and helped in other ways. Of particular importance were copies of Treasury and other correspondence. **Randy Campbell** of ANACS provided suggestions and reviewed the text. **John Dannreuther** reviewed the manuscript and made valuable suggestions. **Charles Daughtrey** shared his thoughts in the foreword for the 1st edition. **Beth Deisher**, editor of *Coin World*, provided certain information relating to numismatic history. **BJ Dunn**, superintendent, Saint-Gaudens National Historical Site, Cornish, New Hampshire, provided access to work by the sculptor, including items pertaining to Lincoln. **Dave Enders** of www.davescollectiblecoins.com shared photographs. **Bill Fivaz** corresponded concerning die varieties and helped in other ways. **Kevin Flynn** furnished a copy of and gave permission to use information in his study (with John Wexler), *The Authoritative Reference on Lincoln Cents*, furnished photographs, and provided information about Victor D. Brenner and the Lincoln cent from the National Archives. **Katherine Fuller** supplied contemporary newspaper accounts and other information from historical archives. The late **Frank Gasparro**, chief engraver at the Mint and a fine personal friend, shared recollections of his work, including the Lincoln Memorial reverse of 1959, and always greeted the author on his visits to the Mint. **Lee Gast** submitted photographs. **Paul Gilkes** corresponded about the so-called "1959-D Wheat reverse" cents and other varieties. **David Hall**, founder of PCGS, gave permission to utilize data in the *Rare Coin Market Report* and helped in other ways. **Paul Houck** provided images of selected cents from the Stewart Blay collection as featured on coingallery.com. **Joel Iskowitz** shared his insights in the foreword for the 2nd edition. **D. Wayne Johnson** furnished images and information concerning a Brenner bust of Lincoln. **David W. Lange**, NGC, gave permission to use information in his study, *The Complete Guide to Lincoln Cents*, an encyclopedic compilation of useful data. In addition, he furnished files of commentaries and articles on cents created since the 1995 publication of his book and helped flesh out many descriptions. Lange also shared his recollections in this edition's foreword. **Sam Lukes** corresponded about Lincoln cents for many years and reviewed the manuscript. **Garland McKelvey** supplied a letter regarding the new 1959 cents. **Christine Metcalfe** reviewed the manuscript and made valuable suggestions. **Patty Moore** reviewed the manuscript and made valuable suggestions. **Ken Potter** corresponded concerning varieties and other aspects. **Bob Shippee** reviewed the manuscript and made valuable suggestions. **David Sundman**, Littleton Coin Company, provided photographs, including for grading-set coins, provided a commentary about buying Lincoln cents, and helped in other ways. **Frank Van Valen** reviewed the manuscript and made valuable suggestions. **Fred Weinberg** provided information and coins for illustration for the appendix.

Roberta A. French was the main research associate for the project, gathered information, compiled statistics, and helped in many other ways. **Susan Novak,** the author's administrative assistant, helped with correspondence and coordination with various contributors, and was valuable in many other ways. **Lawrence Stack** and the staff of Stack's Rare Coins reviewed and finalized pricing data compiled from multiple sources.

Photographs of basic date and mintmark issues are mainly by **Douglas Plasencia**, with others furnished by the author. **Bill Fivaz** and **J.T. Stanton** provided photographs of many die varieties. **Lee Gast, Mark Goodman,** and **Rob Miller** shared photographs.

INDEX